The Dynamics between Entrepreneurship, Environment and Education

EUROPEAN RESEARCH IN ENTREPRENEURSHIP

Series Editors: Alain Fayolle, *Professor of Entrepreneurship, EM Lyon and CERAG, France and Visiting Professor at Solvay Business School, Belgium and* Paula Kyrö, *Professor of Entrepreneurship Education, Helsinki School of Economics, Finland*

This important series is designed to highlight the unique characteristics and rich variety of European research in entrepreneurship. It provides powerful lenses to help identify and understand the importance of European cultural roots within the international entrepreneurship landscape.

The first volume of this book series, under the collective supervision of the European Entrepreneurship Summer Universities group (ESU Network), was published in 2005 by Edward Elgar Publishing with the title: *Entrepreneurship Research in Europe: Outcomes and Perspectives* and was edited by Alain Fayolle, Paula Kyrö and Jan Ulijn.

The Dynamics between Entrepreneurship, Environment and Education

Edited by

Alain Fayolle

Professor of Entrepreneurship, EM Lyon and CERAG Laboratory, France, and Visiting Professor, Solvay Business School, Belgium

Paula Kyrö

Professor of Entrepreneurship Education, Helsinki School of Economics, Finland

EUROPEAN RESEARCH IN ENTREPRENEURSHIP

Edward Elgar

Cheltenham, UK • Northampton, MA, USA

Published by
Edward Elgar Publishing Limited
The Lypiatts
15 Lansdown Road
Cheltenham
Glos GL50 2JA
UK

Edward Elgar Publishing, Inc.
William Pratt House
9 Dewey Court
Northampton
Massachusetts 01060
USA

A catalogue record for this book
is available from the British Library

Library of Congress Control Number: 2008932876

ISBN 978 1 84720 571 1

Printed and bound in Great Britain by MPG Books Ltd, Bodmin, Cornwall

Contents

Figures

Tables

Contributors

Odd Jarl Borch, Professor, Bodø Graduate School of Business and Nordland Research Institute, Norway

Felipe Rafael Cáceres Carrasco, Titular Professor of Applied Economics, University of Seville, Spain

Joaquín Guzmán Cuevas, Professor of Applied Economics, Department of Applied Economics I, University of Seville, Spain

Tobias Dalhammar, Department of Culture and Society, Malmö University, Sweden

Mahamadou Biga Diambeidou, PhD Researcher in Entrepreneurship, Louvain School of Management, Université catholique de Louvain, Belgium

Alain Fayolle, Professor of Entrepreneurship, EM Lyon, France

Damien François, Université catholique de Louvain, Department of Mathematical Engineering, Machine Learning Group, Belgium

Benoît Gailly, Professor of Innovation, Center for Research in Change and Innovation Strategies (CRECIS), Louvain School of Management, Université catholique de Louvain, Belgium

Jorunn Grande, Associate Professor, Nord-Trøndelag University College, Norway

Alena Hanzelková, PhD Director for academic matters and quality, Brno International Business School (BIBS, a.s.), Czech Republic

Ulla Hytti, Research Manager, D.Sc. (Bus. Adm. & Econ.), Adjunct Professor, TSE Entre, Turku School of Economics, Finland

Indrek Jakobson, MBA, PhD student, Tallinn University of Technology, Estonia

Juha Kansikas, Head of Master's Degree Programme in Entrepreneurship in Family Business, Jyväskylä School of Business and Economics, Finland

Robert Krauss, Manager, Mechanical & Electronic Technologies, Invest in Germany GmbH, Germany

Jan Krejci, PhD student of Brno University of Technology, Major Finance, Czech Republic

Paula Kyrö, Professor of Entrepreneurship Education, Helsinki School of Economics, Finland

Francisco Liñán, Assistant Professor, University of Seville, Spain

Hanns Menzel, TU Eindhoven, Department of Technology Management, Organisation Science and Marketing Group, the Netherlands

Einar Rasmussen, Bodø Graduate School of Business, Norway

Jaana Seikkula-Leino, Adjunct Professor, University of Turku, Finland

Villy Søgaard, Associate Professor, Danish Institute of Rural Research and Development (IFUL), Denmark

Roger Sørheim, Professor, Trondheim Business School and Bodø Graduate School of Business, Norway

Pilar Tejada, PhD student, Department of Applied Economics I, Faculty of Economics and Business Sciences, University of Seville, Spain

Jan Ulijn, Professor, Department of Organisation Science and Marketing, School of Industrial Engineering, Eindhoven University of Technology and Open University, the Netherlands

Urve Venesaar, Associate Professor and Vice-Dean for Research at the School of Economics and Business Administration, Tallinn University of Technology, Estonia

Michel Verleysen, Professor, Université catholique de Louvain, DICE – Machine Learning Group, Belgium

Mathieu Weggeman, Professor, Department of Organisation Science and Marketing, School of Industrial Engineering, Eindhoven University of Technology, the Netherlands

Vincent Wertz, Professor, Department of Mathematical Engineering, Université catholique de Louvain, Belgium

Foreword

Entrepreneurship as a research field emerged out of the changes and dynamics that we could identify in society during the 1970s and 1980s. Early research within the field was strongly rooted in the development of society at that time. Since then, entrepreneurship research has matured, and has become less sensitive to changes in society – the research has 'travelled away' from the strong societal orientation that we could find in the early days of entrepreneurship research. Instead it has become more inward-looking and more narrowly focused on theoretical research issues. As a consequence, we can question ourselves whether entrepreneurship research still focuses on the important questions in society – questions that have an impact on wealth creation in society.

This journey away from the strong societal orientation is occurring at the same time as the world, and not least the European scene, is changing more than ever. The diversity of entrepreneurial activities and innovativeness within European countries is pronounced, and this is an important issue that demands a better understanding of the relationship between entrepreneurship and society. Against this background, the theme for this book, edited by Alain Fayolle and Paula Kyrö, on the dynamics between entrepreneurship, environment and education is very timely – entrepreneurship research needs to be rooted in the changes that occur in society, and this book provides an excellent example of research topics that highlights the relationship between society and entrepreneurship research.

Entrepreneurship is a relatively new field of research, not more than 20–25 years old – or little more than half an academic career – that during the last decade has gained extensive interest beyond the usual areas of management studies (see Landström, 2005). As in many other fields of research in social sciences, entrepreneurship research has its roots in the development of and changes in society. In this case we can go back to the 1970s and 1980s, decades during which we experienced huge structural changes in society worldwide, an emerging development of the knowledge economy, and far-reaching political changes emphasizing stronger market-oriented ideologies. As a consequence new areas of interest emerged in society such as entrepreneurship, innovation, industrial dynamics, and job creation. It was in this context that the interest in entrepreneurship research grew, especially among researchers in the US, and we can identify a couple of pioneer researchers on entrepreneurship – researchers that could show that the future differs from the past, not least in terms of the importance of entrepreneurship – and a great number of scholars from different disciplines rushed into this new and promising field of research. The interest in entrepreneurship research was strongly linked to the development and dynamics of society, and the research conducted was deeply rooted in the changes that occurred in the society during the 1970s and 1980s.

Since the beginning of the 1990s we can find an enormous growth of entrepreneurship research. This expansion can be measured in various ways – with respect to the number of researchers, the number of published articles, number of conferences and journals opening up for entrepreneurship contributions – and the expansion is obvious, irrespective of the measurement employed. The research was still rooted in society and the expanding knowledge economy of the 1990s, resulting from rapid technological advances and the globalization of world trade. The quick changes, the complexity and uncertainty in society constituted a hotbed for entrepreneurship. In many countries, especially in Europe, entrepreneurship became a vehicle to solve regional and national problems and to stimulate entrepreneurship. The changes and interest in entrepreneurship taking place in society gave rise to new research questions, and many new topics emerged in entrepreneurship research. As a consequence the research in entrepreneurship became highly fragmented with many parallel 'conversations' in research.

But . . . the field of entrepreneurship research has matured, and I will argue that its maturity has made entrepreneurship researchers less sensitive to changes in society – the field of entrepreneurship research started to 'travel away' from the important questions in society, and the strong societal orientation that we found in entrepreneurship research since its beginning. As I see it, at present, the field seems to be caught between the efforts to overcome the drawbacks of newness and the need to achieve maturity. Research topics have stabilized, focusing on some core questions of interest within entrepreneurship research, and research has been more specialized, with groups of researchers being focused more narrowly on particular theoretical research issues, which also indicates that there are stronger theory-driven approaches within the field (Cornelius et al., 2006). Thus, the field has attained the characteristics of a more 'normal science approach' (Aldrich and Baker, 1997) with weaker links to and less sensitivity to changes in society. This development of the field counteracts its original openness towards stimuli from and interaction with important changes in society, and there is a risk that entrepreneurship researchers are no longer focusing their attention on important questions that have an impact on wealth creation in society.

With this background in mind I find this book refreshing. The editors, Alain Fayolle and Paula Kyrö, have recognized the need for creating an interface between entrepreneurship research and the dynamics of society, not least in the European context. In this book the significance of the relationship between entrepreneurship and society is clearly shown: the first part shows the dynamics between entrepreneurship and society in a more general sense; the second part continues the discussion on the relationship between entrepreneurship and society by looking on it from an education perspective; and finally, the third part of the book focuses on the ability and capability of different kinds of ventures to compete in different contexts. The authors of the chapters offer a broad variety of topics and approaches that significantly contribute to the understanding of changes in society, and the diversity of the contexts in which entrepreneurship occurs.

I am convinced that the book will inspire a dialogue, not only among researchers, but also between research and policy-makers in order that the changes and dynamics of society be better understood.

Hans Landström
Lund University, Sweden

REFERENCES

Aldrich, H.E. and T. Baker (1997), 'Blinded by the cites. Has there been progress in entrepreneurship research?' in D.L. Sexton and R.W. Smilor (eds), *Entrepreneurship 2000*, Chicago, IL: Upstart, pp. 377–400.

Cornelius, B., H. Landström and O. Persson (2006), 'Entrepreneurship studies: the dynamic research front of a developing social science', *Entrepreneurship Theory and Practice*, May, pp. 375–97.

Landström, H. (2005), *Pioneers in Entrepreneurship and Small Business Research*, New York: Springer.

Preface

This second book in the series 'European Research in Entrepreneurship' highlights the unique characteristics and rich variety of European research in the field of entrepreneurship, environment and education. Its three parts, with 14 chapters and 28 authors from 21 European universities and research institutions presenting findings from 13 countries enable a perception of the importance of European cultural roots within the international entrepreneurship landscape. The first volume of this book series, under the collective supervision of the European Entrepreneurship Summer Universities group (ESU Network www.esu.fi), was published in 2005 under the title: *Entrepreneurship Research in Europe: Outcomes and Perspectives*. Encouraging comments on it inspired us to continue this discourse and to go deeper into its different dimensions. The current landscape of the research introduced in this book exemplifies the expanding European dialogue between entrepreneurship, environment and education. We hope it delineates the shape, dimensions and horizon of the multidisciplinary landscape for others to learn from and explore further.

We also want the book to provide university students, teachers, researchers and policy-makers with new insights through which to understand the contextual dimensions and the broadening aspects of the current state-of-the-art in European research into the dynamics between entrepreneurship, environment and education.

To paint such a landscape always requires a sustained and intense commitment from different contributors. In our process the first step took place in 2005 with the start of the preparations for the third ESU meeting in Finland. A total of 63 participants from 15 countries presented their research for evaluation, obtained feedback and improved the first versions of their papers. Initial choices from these revised papers were then made by the ESU scientific publishing committee. The authors of the chapters selected were then supported by the excellent international reviewers who altruistically invested time and effort in helping the authors to improve the quality of their contributions. Also, during this process, the publisher was always willing to support our ideas. We would like to extend warm thanks to all these people for their help, intelligent involvement and capacity in this publishing process and hope its outcome will result in a better understanding of and engagement in the complex European landscape of entrepreneurship research.

Finally, as we approach the first step towards our next ESU meeting in Norway (August 2008), we have in mind a great number of ideas, thoughts and dreams about a third book in the series. We hope that, like its predecessors, such a book will be a great opportunity for young and older researchers in entrepreneurship to share and communicate original and fruitful research findings with a unique European flavour.

Alain Fayolle and Paula Kyrö

1. Introduction: broadening the scope and dynamics of entrepreneurship research in Europe

Paula Kyrö and Alain Fayolle

This book continues the discourse on the dynamics of entrepreneurship research set in motion in the first book in this series, *European Research in Entrepreneurship* (Fayolle et al., 2005). At that time our aim was to identify and elaborate the emergence of a European position in the entrepreneurship debate and to see what kind of a profile the European research might have. The positive response to that book indicated that European research does indeed have its specifics, which merit further research.

In our introduction, 'The entrepreneurship debate in Europe: a matter of history and culture', we anticipated that the dialogue between Europe and, for example, Asia will intensify in the future, challenging European research and efforts to enhance its entrepreneurial and innovative culture. This challenge is a reality today. For example the Chinese government has now taken a strategic decision to develop an innovation-based country by 2020 by integrating entrepreneurship into its education, developmental activities and research (Wang Xingsun, 2007). There is also a lot to do to catch up with the USA in this respect. Only the new EU member states, Latvia, Lithuania and Poland score better than the USA in the desirability of self-employment (European Commission, 2007). Inside Europe the assessment of the Total Entrepreneurial Activity (TEA) Index signals that the countries ranked high in innovativeness still have entrepreneurial activity below the European average, for example France, Finland and Estonia. These striking differences and contradictions in entrepreneurial activities, readiness and innovativeness within European countries and the proactive attitude and activities of European competitors impose a demand for a better understanding of the complex dynamics between entrepreneurship, environment and education. The spirit and pervasive theme of this book follow this new emerging and complex understanding of entrepreneurship and take advantage of the opportunities it offers to revitalize the ideas of the European historical roots of entrepreneurship. Each chapter investigates some aspect of the relationship between entrepreneurship and environment, and thus enhances this complex dialogue.

In this landscape our book will outline the different aspects of this dynamics exemplifying the expanding European dialogue between entrepreneurship, environment and education. Its 14 chapters, including the introduction and the conclusion, represent different disciplines, nationalities and approaches. Altogether they bring us findings from 13 countries, and 28 researchers from 21 universities and research institutions. By bringing these together we hope to define the shape, dimensions and horizon of the multidisciplinary landscape for others to learn from and explore further.

The first part of the book illustrates how the dynamics between entrepreneurship and environment has expanded and diversified, the second part further explores the dynamics between entrepreneurship and education, and the third part elaborates how this simultaneously culture-specific but globally oriented approach, changes the activities and developmental needs of the firms. Thus the book offers a perspective through which to understand the importance of European cultural roots within the international entrepreneurship research. It introduces both comparative chapters and chapters with specific cultural contexts to investigate what kind of aspects we might share in Europe and what aspects are culture-specific.

In this introduction we try to describe how entrepreneurship research has spread in a variety of directions as interactions with environment, educational systems and organizations. As anticipated in our last book, it has gained a more extended cultural and networking view in its efforts to contribute to renewing society. This has come a long way from the specificities of an individual entrepreneur and the basic functions of the small firm, opening up a new and complex landscape for researchers. This landscape is briefly developed in each section of our introduction, before the presentation of the chapters themselves from all these three different but interrelated spheres.

DIALOGUE BETWEEN ENTREPRENEURSHIP AND ENVIRONMENT

The dialogue between entrepreneurship and environment has been expanded and broadened both in policy documents and research. It is among the key factors in the EU innovation strategy, which emphasizes the importance of the creation of an entrepreneurial culture by fostering the right mindset, entrepreneurship skills and awareness of its career opportunity as an essential part of European competitiveness (Commission of the

European Communities, 2006). This broad cultural approach has also been reinforced in entrepreneurship research. It brings together multidisciplinary research, for example, from economics, sociology, management, marketing, strategy, education and geography, and links organizational, regional and national cultures to systems, structures and networks. It also includes public spheres of entrepreneurship research and provides new concepts for understanding their dynamics and interrelationships (Bjerke and Dalhammar, 2006). Besides the interplay between economics, businesses, firms and regional and national prosperity, entrepreneurship research has attached itself to broader concepts such as active citizenship, education systems, curriculum development and democracy.

This complexity has not been received without criticism. Some researchers feel that expanding entrepreneurship research to so many aspects, structures and processes of society dissolves its borders and blurs its identity. On the other hand there are others who ask how cultural changes and research of its dynamics are possible by isolating phenomena out of context and the dynamics that mould these contexts. These contradictory opinions are ingredients in the current research and mould the conceptualization of entrepreneurship. For example, Dalhammar argues here for the expanded approach and introduces us to a new concept of public entrepreneurship, which is not restricted to the economic sphere. As he defines it, 'The term "public" emphasizes public space, that is, the space that concerns all citizens and that is neither private nor official' (Dalhammar, this volume, p. 47)

Part I of the book, 'The dynamics between entrepreneurship and environment' contains four chapters. These four chapters together colour the landscape of interrelationships between environment and entrepreneurship, its structures, systems and processes that attract European scholars today. They all seek to expand the concepts and dimensions of research to complex processes, and combine company, local and national activities with the global problems we face today.

Chapter 2, 'New elements for the analysis of entrepreneurial structure', written by Cuevas and Carrasco of the University of Seville, analyses the quality perspective on entrepreneurial structure. Their interest comprehends the whole economic system in which the entrepreneurial activity is located. Thus they develop further the general ideas of Schumpeter on entrepreneurial innovation. The authors argue that their new concept of functional dependency within the scope of 'New Economic Geography' is quite close to the 'value chain' approach. Their findings from 400 enterprises in Andalusia in southern Spain open further two main research fields. On the one hand, it is possible to develop a comparative analysis among regions in order to identify the profile of those entrepreneurial clusters that contribute most/least to economic growth. On the other hand, their new concept may be useful in analysis of the role of SMEs in global value chains for different activity sectors. This chapter describes how the firms' and regions' growth is not only dependent on quantity but essentially on quality issues embedded in the structures of an economic system. These features are not only region-specific but reflect shared aspects of global value chains.

In Chapter 3, 'Micro–macro paradoxes of entrepreneurship', Søgaard of Denmark suggests that a strong micro focus in entrepreneurship research leads us to neglect macro-level explanations for entrepreneurship and to abstract it from the wider systems effects of stimulating or hampering entrepreneurship. Søgaard points out that the macro perspective is not an aggregation of micros but a far more complex social process. More specifically, he investigates this problem by analysing from the 2004 articles on Entrepreneurship and Regional Development to what extent entrepreneurship research does (or does not) address relevant 'systems effects' of entrepreneurial activity. The author concludes that a tendency to ignore the wider social implications of entrepreneurial activities should be taken seriously by any researcher wanting to see entrepreneurship as a fully-fledged member of the social sciences. To go further in that direction, he suggests, requires a commitment to understanding for the sake of understanding and more or less remembering the ideals of the classical Humboldt University.

Going further in that direction, in Chapter 4, 'New initiatives to revitalize society: public entrepreneurship in the south of Sweden', Dalhammar of the University of Malmö investigates public entrepreneurship that conceptualizes activities mainly belonging to society and not restricted to the economic sphere. This public entrepreneurship relates to the growing theoretical school of social entrepreneurship. The term 'public' emphasizes public space that concerns all citizens and that is neither private nor official. Together with Bjerke the author suggests that public entrepreneurship can be conceptualized by a social mission of creating something that others can use or benefit from. In this field social change theory can bring into entrepreneurship research an approach where change is seen as a structured process in which it may be possible to identify a specific direction or tendency. It can also lead us to investigate the changes that affect norms, values, behaviour, cultural meanings, and social relationships (Scott and Marshall, 2005).

As his case studies Dalhammar uses examples of new initiatives that deal with unemployment for marginalized people in urban areas, Job Emergency in Malmö and Business Pool in Landskrona. The results indicate how such initiatives can contribute to social change. These examples, which are in a specific cultural context containing at the same time commonalities and differences, provide ideas about how to increase the collaborative responsibility of dealing with huge immigration problems all over the world. As the author argues, public entrepreneurship is crucial as a means of revitalizing a city or a region, and even whole societies. In this context public entrepreneurship is a new concept that reflects the society of today and the society of tomorrow, helping us to critically study and evaluate public entrepreneurship initiatives and analyse their role in creating social value and contributing to social change.

Chapter 5 in Part I, 'Developing characteristics of an intrapreneurship-supportive culture' draws our attention to the intersection of national, professional and corporate culture. The research group of Menzel, Krauss, Ulijn and Weggeman from the Department of Technology Management in the Technological University of Eindhoven in the Netherlands identifies the conditions required in order to make intrapreneurship occur in the large established firms and other organizations. Using Hofstede's (2001) theory and terminology about national cultures, they develop a six-dimensional description of a culture conducive to intrapreneurship. Aggregating 329 quotations from 97 publications they identify 24 culturally-bound factors that provide Hofstede's dimensions with a new open system dimension. By this addition they believe it is possible to make a distinction between intrapreneurship-supportive and non-supportive cultures and thus improve the innovativeness and competitiveness of large firms and organizations. This chapter indicates how complex and multidimensional the cultural processes are and how professional and corporate cultures are intertwined in the processes enhancing entrepreneurial behaviours and practices.

DIALOGUE BETWEEN ENTREPRENEURSHIP AND EDUCATION

A new emerging discourse in entrepreneurship education addresses its attention to education systems, curriculum development and pedagogy. This branch of research regards learning entrepreneurial and enterprising readiness as a lifelong process which assumes multidisciplinary research and expertise throughout the educational system (Kyrö and Carrier, 2005). These points of departure provide a new direction and still unexplored landscape for entrepreneurship research. Education is both society's medium for adopting its ideas of a good life, and a process of preparation for the students of the future (Bowen, 1981). The European Commission Report in 2002 recommended acknowledging the importance of entrepreneurship teaching in the national curriculum as well as in the curricula for each level of the educational system as one of the key qualitative indicators for entrepreneurship education (European Commission, 2002). However, little is actually known in entrepreneurship research about the complex interrelationships between education systems, curriculum development and pedagogy.

In research this challenges us to combine expertise both from education and business-related disciplines, and to cross the borders of different educational levels. Perhaps the lack of such research is due to the fact that education and economics in Europe are historically regarded as two different spheres, and comprehensive and university-level education especially have emphasized the ideal of the civilized human being as a contradiction to the market actor. Still today entrepreneurship education in most cases is regarded as business education and many countries even today focus mainly on adult education, as Hytti's and Seikkula-Leino's chapters in this book demonstrate. To overcome these problems and contradictions we have to be able to open up the conceptual dialogue between these two spheres and consider their cultural differences. We also need to differentiate the dominating Anglo-American discourse from the continental European discourse to understand the impact of these differences and to benefit from their advantages (cf. Kyrö, 2006).

As Seikkula-Leino argues in Chapter 9, the curriculum is the most important document in the education system. It expresses the wishes and needs of a society and shows how to adopt these wishes in practice. It indicates what relevant skills should be achieved through education and what kind of education programmes should be provided (Bobbitt, 2004, p. 11). Thus changing the curriculum is about making changes in societies. Therefore values as well as ideological and political objectives drive these changes. The current policy proposal to integrate entrepreneurship education into the curricula of all EU member states represents such an ideological and political objective. The curriculum legitimates the idea of the 'right' knowledge and proceeding, being thus a powerful document that creates the basis for educational movements. A curriculum reform also expresses social pressures, such as developing equality and adjusting education to meet the needs of labour development (Flouris and Pasias, 2003). A curriculum also defines subject matter, pedagogical development and assessment, thus guiding what and how to teach and learn (cf. Flouris and Pasias, 2003).

The differences in developing entrepreneurship by mainstreaming it throughout curricula at all levels of education show considerable variation among European countries. For example Austria, Denmark, Finland, Iceland, Luxemburg, Norway, Spain and Sweden have already included entrepreneurship education throughout their curricula (European Commission, 2002; 2004). Hytti's comparative study in this book indicates how differently policy-makers understand the content and pedagogy of entrepreneurship education in different countries. It also explains how this understanding leads to different curricular decisions with direct bearing on practice. However, it might also represent cultural differences or confusion or lack of consensus about how entrepreneurial and enterprising education should be integrated into curricula and education systems.

Part II of the book, 'The dynamics between entrepreneurship and education', continues the discussion on the interrelationships of society and entrepreneurship, now from an education perspective. It explores the dimensions of integrating entrepreneurship into governmental support and education systems. Thus it draws our attention to the various aspects of education, their similarities and differences, thereby also imparting some ideas on how to be more successful in these processes.

Chapter 6, 'University entrepreneurship and government support schemes', starts this discussion by positioning spin-off processes to the larger international and national settings and structures. The authors, Rasmussen, Borch and Sørheim of the Bodø Graduate School of Business, argue for the need to reform the commercialization of research, both by changes in the academic system and in the instruments for research funding and by setting up separate structures to support such activities. They claim that due to the complexity of entrepreneurial activity in academic settings there is a need for tailor-made instruments which should also be adapted to the national agendas. However, they claim that few studies have investigated how these government schemes are designed and implemented. Their findings from a comparative study of government programmes in Canada, Finland, Ireland, Norway, Scotland and Sweden pave the way for conclusions regarding the kind of rationale behind the differences in the support schemes between these countries and the different ways of structuring the support programmes at government, university and project levels. This interplay sets the scene for the processes that provide innovations in education systems and further for the programmes and abilities needed to enhance them.

In Chapter 7, 'Enterprise education in different cultural settings and at different school levels', Hytti continues the educational discourse by claiming that as enterprise education does not take place in a vacuum, the entrepreneurial culture and environment of a given region, country or a particular school needs to be taken into consideration when planning the enterprise education programme. She suggests that since European countries have different entrepreneurial cultures, these differences should also be reflected in the enterprise education programmes and curricular structure. The comparative analyses of the differences in enterprise education programmes run in five European countries, Austria, Finland, Ireland,

Norway and UK identify these differences in the national approaches and the content of the programmes. In some countries especially the focus is solely on business abilities and there seems to be a lack of programmes at an earlier stage (kindergarten, primary schools), while only few programmes focus on building awareness and on supporting entrepreneurial behaviour. The author suggests that the bridges between entrepreneurship and education (pedagogy) should be stronger in order to make enterprise education as much about the process as about the subject. If the focus is only on developing the skills of potential and future entrepreneurs, these programmes will only cater for the needs of a small minority.

Chapter 8, 'Assessment and promotion of entrepreneurial initiative and attitudes towards entrepreneurship: the case of Estonia' by Venesaar and Jakobson, aptly exemplifies the situation in a country that only recently laid down new guidelines for entrepreneurship development and education from 2007 to 2013. This government's understanding of entrepreneurship follows the broad approach and highlights cultural and educational aspects. The authors report a situation of initiative and attitudes just before this programme was launched. Their first survey contains a sample of 1000 Estonians aged 16 to 64 and the second survey of 443 bachelor's and master's students. These findings give all of us some interesting ideas about the factors behind the high scores of Estonia, the similarities and differences between entrepreneurs and potential entrepreneurs, students and non-students. As Hytti suggests, they also lay the foundations for developing country-specific government actions and education.

Chapter 9 continues this discourse with the case of Finland, where enterprise education has a strong non-business focus compared to other countries in Hytti's study. Under the title 'Advancing entrepreneurship education in Finnish basic education: the prospects for developing local curricula', Seikkula-Leino introduces a partnership model based on curriculum theories. She suggests that using a partnership model in curriculum reform might help to better understand the complex dynamics between different partners involved. She further investigates through this model how the National Core Curriculum for Basic Education established in 2004 has succeeded locally. According to this, all municipalities are required to offer entrepreneurship education, at least after 2006. The survey of teachers, principals, curriculum coordinators, directors of education and cultural services departments, trades ombudsmen and representatives of local entrepreneurs (N 478) was conducted in spring 2005. Despite the numerous difficulties listed by respondents, one third of those in teaching were going to implement more entrepreneurship education in their future daily work. Despite this result, partners know relatively little or nothing about entrepreneurship education and the partnership model has not been as successful as expected. It seems that the curriculum that is taught and the curriculum that is learned can only develop if it is a vivid document that is able to be changed and shared by all partners involved in the process.

DIALOGUE BETWEEN ENTREPRENEURSHIP AND ORGANIZATION

Many businesses are faced by the growing competitive intensity of a complex and changing environment, and while their very existence depends on strongly established structures, they cannot remain in a precarious status quo. In order to survive, innovation is a key factor. Corporate entrepreneurship or intrapreneurship is precisely one business tactic adopted by these companies to bring new elements into their system without creating chaos. It consists in encouraging the emergence of new activities that bring about growth. These can take the form of internal ventures; organizations created or 'started up' within an already existing business frame.

Reproducing entrepreneurial attitudes and behaviours within existing companies and institutions therefore appears, at least theoretically, as an effective antidote to inertia and lack of innovation within these organizations (Stevenson and Jarillo, 1990; Fayolle and Basso, forthcoming). In practice, however, the difficulties experienced by the organizations that have tried to develop these behaviours and attitudes reveal another aspect of the phenomenon: the existence of contradictions and paradoxes linked to the combination of conflicting perspectives that result in counter-productive tensions. Current research in the field of corporate entrepreneurship study, among other topics, underlines the influence of key variables, such as culture for instance (see Chapter 5), on the firm's entrepreneurial behaviours. Moreover, the researcher is more and more trying to open the black box of organization in which appear the counter-productive contradictions and paradoxes between a traditional bureaucratic behaviour and a more entrepreneurial one.

In Part III of the book, 'The dynamics between entrepreneurship and small businesses', each of the four chapters investigates the landscape of small firm competitiveness from different perspectives. They contemplate the broadening horizon of small firms and organizations requiring methodological and theoretical renewal, ability and capability to adapt to and compete in the global landscape and find ideas for sustaining competitiveness in the future.

In Chapter 10, 'An empirical taxonomy of start-up firms' growth trajectories', the Belgian research group of Diambeidou, François, Gailly, Verleysen and Wertz seeks to develop a methodological solution for investigating the dynamic approach to new firm growth processes. They analyse the initial growth trajectories of 741 Belgian firms using their new applied mathematical method. Their results question the relevance of uniform quantitative approaches to studying growth processes and suggest that new firm growth is neither a continuous nor idiosyncratic process. It can be adequately described through a limited number of typical growth trajectories that can be identified in a systematic way.

In Chapter 11, 'Linking entrepreneurial orientation and dynamic capabilities: research issues and alternative models', Grande suggests that the interface between entrepreneurial orientation and dynamic capabilities offers an arena to small firms to increase their sustaining competitiveness. He develops different alternative models for analysing this interrelationship. This kind of theoretical development that brings entrepreneurial practices to the organizational context in small firms is still rare; even organizational entrepreneurship as a concept starts to be familiar to all of us. The contribution it can make to the future discourse at the interface of strategic management, learning organization and entrepreneurship is based on its ability to increase our understanding of the dynamic processes of entrepreneurial organizations, especially how to develop entrepreneurial practices.

Chapter 12, 'The impact of global value chains on Andalusian tourism SMEs', by the Spanish researchers Tejada and Liñán describes how the landscape of small firms in the tourism industry has changed, forcing them to adapt to the globalization process. They further argue that the competitiveness of small firms in tourism, as one of the most internationalized sectors in the world economy, is dependent on their integration into the global tourism value chain. By analysing this dynamics in seven hotels and travel agencies in the region of Andalusia the authors anticipate that these global value chains will offer an opportunity for competitiveness of small firms in the future.

Chapter 13, 'Family business responsible ownership: challenging the next generation's abilities', written by Kansikas, Krejci and Hanzelková concludes the book by bringing us ideas about how the next generation of responsible ownership could be developed. This kind of ideological discussion is very much needed to promote research in this field. It reminds us that, after all, to approach entrepreneurship as a dynamics between environment and education is impossible unless we are ready to reveal those values we believe can help the next generation to survive and enhance democracy and equality in the global landscape where the challenges are more complex than perhaps ever before.

CONCLUDING COMMENTS

All these chapters reflect how the European landscape of entrepreneurship research is now more complex than ever. Together they represent an overview of the current state of entrepreneurship research in Europe and, we hope, also reflect the future directions of research in this field. Even if it is rooted in Europe it views and positions itself in the global context. It also appears to gather around two dimensions; on the one hand it rather contextualizes than isolates research settings and on the other hand, more than before, it views entrepreneurship as a dynamic learning and developmental process, whatever context it takes place in. These developments point out the need for comparative research settings and methodological advance to gain access to the dynamic processes of these settings, examples of which are also introduced in this book. The third branch of research, still in its nascent phase, focuses on the ideological dialogue of entrepreneurship and expands its scope from business to society. This direction actually returns to the historical roots of entrepreneurship in Europe, which originates from the ideas of the Enlightenment. These roots draw on the ideal of democracy and equal opportunity in Europe, providing educational systems for enhancing these ideals. Whether any of these three research orientations will be more powerful than others in understanding the dynamics of entrepreneurship in the future or whether this complexity will even expand is the question that inspires us to continue this European dialogue. Perhaps this complexity is actually characteristic of the European view on entrepreneurship research and thus might even strengthen in the future. We hope the reader will find these questions as inspiring as they are to us and thus feels encouraged to continue the dialogue.

REFERENCES

Bjerke, B. and T. Dalhammar (2006), 'Public entrepreneurship – Definitely different', paper presented at the UIC Research Symposium, Chicago, 2–4 August 2006.

Bobbitt, F. (2004), 'Scientific method in curriculum making', in D.J. Flinders and S.J. Thornton (eds), *The Curriculum Studies Reader*, second edn, New York: Routledge Falmer, pp. 9–16.

Bowen, J. (1981), *A History of Western Education, Vol. 3: The Modern West, Europe and the New World*, London: Methuen & Co. Ltd.

Commission of the European Communities (2006), 'Communication from the Commission to the Council, the European Parliament, the European Economic and Social Committee and the Committee of the Regions. Putting knowledge into practice', Com (2006) 502 final, Brussels.

European Commission (2002), 'Final report of the expert group "Best Procedure" project on education and training for entrepreneurship, Enterprise Directorate General.

European Commission (2004), 'Final report of the expert group "Education for Enterpreneurship" making progress in promoting entrepreneurial attitudes and skills through primary and secondary education', Enterprise Directorate General.

European Commission (2007), 'Entrepreneurship survey of the EU (25 member states), United States, Iceland and Norway', Analytical Report, April 2007, Flash Eurobarometer No. 192.

Fayolle, A. and O. Basso (forthcoming), 'Entrepreneurial spirit and corporate entrepreneurship in large companies', *International Journal of Entrepreneurship and Small Business*.

Fayolle, A., J. Uljin and P. Kyrö (eds) (2005), *Entrepreneurship Research in Europe: Perspectives and Outcomes*, Cheltenham, UK and Northampton, MA, USA: Edward Elgar.

Flouris, G. and G. Pasias (2003), 'A critical appraisal of curriculum reform in Greece (1980–2002), trends, challenges, and perspectives', *European Education*, **35**(3), 73–90.

Grilo, I. and R. Thurik (2006), 'Entrepreneurship in the old and new Europe', *SCALES-paper N200516*, Zoetermeeter, January, 2006.

Hofstede, G.H. (2001), *Culture's Consequences: Comparing Values, Behaviors, Institutions and Organizations across Nations*, London: Sage Publications.

Kyrö, P. (2006) 'The continental and Anglo-american approaches to entrepreneurship education: differences and bridges', in A. Fayolle and H. Klandt (eds), *International Entrepreneurship Education, Issues and Newness*, Cheltenham, UK and Northampton, MA, USA: Edward Elgar, pp. 93–111.

Kyrö, P. and C. Carrier (eds) (2005), 'Entrepreneurial learning in universities: bridges across borders', in *The Dynamics of Learning Entreprenurship in a Cross-Cultural University Context*, Entreprenurship Education Series 2/2005, University of Tampere, Faculty of Education, Research Centre for Vocational and Professional Education: Saarijärven Offset, pp. 14–43.

Scott, J. and Marshall, G. (2005), *A Dictionary of Sociology*, Oxford: Oxford University Press, *Oxford Reference Online*, Oxford University Press, Malmo högskola, 16 November 2007, available at: http://www.oxfordreference.com/views/ENTRY.html?subview=Main&entry=t88.e242.

Stevenson, H.H. and J. Jarillo (1990), 'A paradigm of entrepreneurship: entrepreneurial management', *Strategic Management Journal*, 11, pp. 17–27.

Wang Xingsun (2007), 'Entrepreneurship education in Chinese universities. The challenges and opportunities', Shanghai Association of Promoting Employment of College Graduates (SAPECG), paper presented in the 2007 International Entrepreneurship Educators Conference, 10–12 September, University of Cambridge.

PART I

The Dynamics between Entrepreneurship and Environment

2. New elements for the analysis of entrepreneurial structure

Joaquín Guzmán Cuevas and Felipe Rafael Cáceres Carrasco

INTRODUCTION

In spite of the diversity of definitions of entrepreneurship within the traditional specialized literature, usually there is a clear distinction between the field that refers to the entrepreneur's action (entrepreneurial function) and the field that refers to the result or consequence of that action (enterprise). For example, the recent definition proposed by P. Thornton and K. Flynn states that: 'we define entrepreneurship as both the discovery and exploitation of entrepreneurial opportunities and the creation of new organization, which occur as a context-dependent social and economic process' (Thornton and Flynn, 2003). In the wide field of entrepreneurship one can distinguish, therefore, two aspects for analysis:

a) the entrepreneur;
b) the enterprise.

In this second field of entrepreneurship, it is possible to distinguish three approaches or levels of analysis. First, there is the 'micro' approach, whose prevalent interest of analysis is the individual one. The theories developed at this level frequently have the maximization of the firm owner's profit as their main objective. For instance, there are well-known theories such as the risk-uncertainty theory or the different psychological theories focusing on the optimization of an entrepreneur's behaviour which are based on this approach.

Secondly, beyond individual interest, the 'meso' approach has the firm's interest as its main focus. Logically, this study or field of research is wider than the first one and includes, among others, the transaction cost theory, the network theory, the spin-off process and, in general, every theoretical branch belonging to management.

Finally, in the 'macro' approach, the fundamental interest of analysis is not only that of the individual and that of the enterprise, but also the interest of the whole economic system in which the entrepreneurial activity is located. In recent years, some researchers have considered the relationship between entrepreneurship and economic growth an interesting issue to study. Four topics in particular have been the interest of numerous researchers. The first focuses on the creation of enterprises and includes contributions that consider a positive relationship between the number of enterprises in an economy and the rate of economic growth. (Wennekers and Thurik, 1999; Kent, 1982; Dubini, 1989; Storey, 1994; Acs and Armington, 2004). The second topic pays attention to cultural, historical and institutional variables as determinants of entrepreneurship and economic growth in a specific context or territory (McMillan and Woodruff, 2002; Yu, 1998; Baumol, 1990, Grabher, 1993; Courlet and Soulage, 1995; Garofoli, 1994). Another way in which entrepreneurship has been linked to economic growth is competition (Feldman and Audretsch, 1999; Nickell, 1996; Wennekers and Thurik, 1999). It considers that rivalry among enterprises increases with the number of firms (Porter, 1985) and reinforces the innovation process and the learning experience of organizations (Molero, 2001). The fourth is perhaps the topic which has received the most attention by researchers. After the important contribution by Schumpeter (1934, 1942 [1996]), a large group of researchers has pointed out a positive relationship between entrepreneurial innovation and economic growth (Fagerberg, 1988; Vespargen, 1992; Nadiri, 1993; Aghion and Howit, 1992; Grosman and Helpman, 1991). Moreover, the endogenous growth theory has introduced innovation as an essential factor to explain the increase of income (Romer, 1994). As a result, innovation has been considered as a principal function of enterprises in economic growth (Acs, 1992; Carree and Thurik, 2003; Audretsch and Thurik, 2004; Grabher, 1993; Holcombe, 1998; Courlet and Soulage, 1995; Garofoli, 1994).

Obviously, the relationship of the 'macro' approach with the two previous approaches is quite strong, but the main concern in this aggregate level may be represented, for example, through the following question: what should the entrepreneurial activity be like in order to maximize the economic growth of a territory? This approach is framed by what could be called quality of entrepreneurial structure.

ENTREPRENEURIAL STRUCTURE: A QUALITY PERSPECTIVE

In the field of entrepreneurship, few researchers have paid attention to the relationship between the characteristics of enterprises and economic growth.

Some interesting contributions concerning this issue focus on the characteristics of enterprises, but rarely connect them with economic growth. For example, the following classification can be established (Cotec, 1996):

- Parochial SMEs: oriented to the local market;
- Individualistic and global SMEs: compete in international market but are not associated to other firms;
- SMEs that manufacture components: make standard products;
- High technology SMEs;
- SMEs in clusters of production.

This classification, which shows different characteristics of firms that probably affect economic growth in different ways, raises several questions, for example: is it possible to quantify the contribution of every type of enterprise to the GDP? Why does the typology vary among territories? What is the role of entrepreneurship in the formation of typologies?

The shortage of background knowledge on the 'macro' approach to entrepreneurship is not surprising. The traditional theories on economic growth (Solow, 1956), including the most advanced models on endogenous growth (Romer, 1994), do not specifically consider entrepreneurship in relation to the variables that explain the process of economic growth. In this sense, despite the modern endogenous models, taking into account the general ideas of Schumpeter on entrepreneurial innovation, incorporating the technological process and the progress of knowledge, the entrepreneur's role is not specified in the implementation of new technology in the productive mechanism. Implicitly, one assumes that any innovation created in a research centre is automatically incorporated into the production process. Nevertheless, it is necessary to take into account, in order for this process to take place, that there must always be an enterprise to incorporate these innovations, and that this circumstance does not always occur, especially in the underdeveloped countries or regions. Furthermore, other contributions, as much in the microeconomic as in the macroeconomic approach, establish the importance of the capacity of innovation of enterprises for the territory's economic growth, but there are still many unknown aspects of the capacity of firms to innovate. For example: how should this capacity be measured?

The Schumpeterian ideas, and the economic models that consider the innovation in a territory, offer an interesting contribution for the analysis of connection between the entrepreneurial structure and economic growth. Thus, considering the role of the Schumpeterian entrepreneur, it is possible to classify the different qualitative categories of the entrepreneurial structure, according to the stronger or weaker entrepreneurial innovation dynamic. In this sense, it is possible, for instance, to distinguish (O'Kean, 1991):

1. Excellent entrepreneurial structure;
2. Imitator structure;
3. Routine structure; and
4. Empty structure.

Logically, it is predictable that an 'excellent' entrepreneurial structure, with a high degree of its own innovation, exerts great influence on the market and, therefore, will give rise to a high level of economic growth.

Nevertheless, aside from the innovation factor, within every entrepreneurial structure there are other characteristics that influence the economic process to a higher or lower degree (Guzmán and Santos, 2001). This is the case, for instance, in firm size, level of training of the personnel, the cooperation level among firms, the quality certificates of goods and services production, and so on. These are quite simple variables and easily observable, but there may be other ones which might help to explain the strengths and/or weaknesses of the entrepreneurial structure belonging to a territorial economy whether at a local, provincial, regional or national level. Specifically, we will concentrate on two less 'visible' variables:

1. Productive dependence;
2. Functional dependence.

Productive Dependence

In literature about entrepreneurship it is difficult to find references to this concept, because it has rarely been used to characterize the entrepreneurial structure. Nevertheless, productive dependence is, in our opinion, an important characteristic of enterprises to take into account, because it shows the vulnerability of firms. Then, from a 'macro' view, it could be a factor that affects sustainable development of economies.

Productive dependence refers to the level of concentration of firms in relation to the number of suppliers, on the one hand, and in relation to the number of clients, on the other. A higher productive dependence index with respect to purchasing means that a high proportion of input came from a small number of suppliers. Thus, a maximum value means that 100 per cent of purchasing is concentrated on only one supplier. On the side of sales, a maximum value of productive dependence means that 100 per cent of sales are concentrated on only one client. This is the case, for example, for a small firm working under a subcontract for another big company.

The productive dependence in a firm, whether with respect to sales or to purchasing, is an indication of the degree of risk and vulnerability of such a firm. Obviously if there is a high proportion of enterprises with a high degree of productive dependence in an economy, it would represent a negative aspect in the qualitative profile of the entrepreneurial structure.

Functional Dependence

This is a new concept. It is based on the level of concentration of purchases and sales with respect to their territorial origin and destination. Within the wide scope known as 'New Economic Geography' (Krugman, 1991), what is here called 'functional dependence' is quite close to the 'value chain' approach (Porter, 1985; Gereffi, 1994) of the 'value stream' (Womack and Jones, 1996) or even, in the French tradition, the concept of 'filière'. Nevertheless, there is an essential difference with respect to this analytical approach, because the so-called 'functional dependence' does not try to value either the governance relationships among firms or the links among productive sectors. It is possible to find other background information on this concept in contributions by Hirschman (1961) and, more recently, in national and regional programmes to encourage the level of enterprise interlinkages, in order to increase local sales (UNCTAD, 2001; Izushi, 1999).

From a territorial point of view, the economic literature has only pointed out a few hypotheses that have come to represent a higher degree in the relationship among SMEs to suppliers and to clients belonging to any territorial field – in comparison to big companies (Garofoli, 1994; Florio, 1996). However, it is possible that SMEs, within underdeveloped regions, are specialized in the functions of distribution or seeking out of the market ('market-maker' for the 'product-maker' firms, which are located in the advanced economies, Guzmán and Santos, 2006). For that reason, the functional dependence tries to evaluate the relationship between the inputs from an external market and the outputs bound for the internal market.

Based on empirical information for each enterprise of the purchasing and sales flows belonging to local, provincial, regional, national and international markets, it is possible to quantify the relationship between the territorial origin of inputs with respect to the territorial destination of outputs. Thus, a maximum value of the functional dependence index of a specific enterprise means that 100 per cent of its purchasing comes from the foreign market and 100 per cent of its sales go to the local market. By contrast, a minimum value of the functional dependence index means that the firm acquires 100 per cent of its inputs in the local market while 100 per cent of its outputs go to the international market.

THE FUNCTIONAL AND PRODUCTIVE DEPENDENCE IN THE EMPIRICAL ANALYSIS: RESULTS

In order to evaluate the importance of functional and productive dependence in the entrepreneurial structure of a territory, an empirical analysis has been developed using a database that has been created from a sample of 400 enterprises of different sizes and from different sectors, located in the province of Seville, within the Andalusian region in southern Spain. The information was obtained from personal interviews with entrepreneurs or those who developed the entrepreneurial functions in the firms polled.

The final objective of this inquiry is to test empirically if the new concepts, so-called 'productive dependence' and 'functional dependence', are key qualitative characteristics for evaluation of the entrepreneurial structure. The results obtained can perhaps contribute to macroeconomic evaluation of the entrepreneurial structure's quality in any territory or economy with new elements.

In order to achieve the objectives of this empirical study, a factor analysis has been developed from the 400 elements of the representative sample. Once the factor scores were obtained, the firms were classified into homogeneous clusters. These results reinforce the results of the factor analysis. They show the characteristics of the enterprises with different degrees of productive and functional dependence.

The factor analysis is developed based on a set of 15 variables which represent different characteristics of the quality of the entrepreneurial structure in the province of Seville. In Table 2.1 the variables and their maximum and minimum values are listed. The Functional Dependence Index (FDI) has been calculated by weighing (W_i) the responses given by the interviewees to ten questions about the percentage of both the sales (S_i) and purchasing (P_j) made by those enterprises in the local market, the rest of the provincial market, the rest of the regional market, the rest of the national market and foreign markets. The Functional Dependence Index increases when the level of concentration of purchases goes up or the border of input markets (local, regional, national, foreign countries) becomes more distant, and decreases when the level of concentration of sales goes up or the limits of output markets become closer.

$$\mathrm{FDI} = \Sigma\, S_i \cdot \mathrm{W}_i + \Sigma\, P_j \cdot W_i$$

The Purchasing Productive Dependence Index (PPDI) has been calculated by weighing (W_i) the responses to four questions of the questionnaire about the percentage of purchases that the polled enterprises usually make from the

Table 2.1 Variables in the analysis

Variable	Definition	Range
V1	Functional dependence index	−4 to 4
V2	Purchasing productive dependence index	0.2 to 1
V3	Sales productive dependence index	0.2 to 1
V4	Size (number of employees)	1 to 5000
V5	Employment growth (%)	−∞ to ∞
V6	Sales growth (%)	−∞ to ∞
V7	Formal agreement of cooperation with other enterprises*	0 – 1
V8	Informal agreement of cooperation with other enterprises*	0 –1
V9	R&D activity*	0 – 1
V10	Innovation index	0 – 4
V11	Possession of quality certificate*	0 – 1
V12	Actions for quality*	0 – 1
V13	Annual planning*	0 – 1
V14	University degree-holding managers (% of total workers)	0% to 100%
V15	University degree-holding employees (% of total workers)	0% to 100%

Note: * 0: no; 1: yes.

primary, the two primary, the five primary and the ten primary suppliers, and then adding them. The Sales Productive Dependence Index (SPDI) has been calculated in a similar way (W_j) but considering the percentage of sales.

$$\text{PPDI} = \Sigma W_i;\ \text{SPDI} = \Sigma W_j$$

Prior to the factor analysis, the suitability sample has been checked through the Kaiser–Meyer–Olkin Test, which achieved a value of 0.808 and Barlet's Sphericity Test which shows a significance level of 0.000. The factor analysis has been developed using the principal components method and the varimax rotation has been applied. Four factors with self-value higher than 1 have been identified. Table 2.2 shows the rotated component matrix and the variance that explains each of the four factors. Altogether, these four identified factors embrace more than 54 per cent of the original variable's variance.

The first factor explains more than 22 per cent of the total variance and is associated with eight variables which achieve a value higher than 0.5: V4, V7, V9, V10, V11, V12 and V13. These variables represent the size of the firms, the existence of formal agreement of cooperation with other enterprises, the R&D activity and innovation, the development of actions for quality and the possession of a certificate of quality, and the annual planning of actions. All these variables are strongly related to the activities

Table 2.2 Rotated component matrix[1]

	Component			
	1	2	3	4
V1	0.0043	0.228	−0.148	**0.746**
V2	−0.0746	−0.199	0.0027	**0.703**
V3	0.248	−0.317	0.195	−0.320
V4	**0.505**	0.037	−0.181	−0.278
V5	−0.109	**0.873**	−0.0171	0.0243
V6	−0.147	**0.862**	−0.0888	−0.0324
V7	**0.611**	−0.207	−0.0236	−0.214
V8	−0.191	0.0902	**0.530**	0.0304
V9	**0.691**	−0.243	0.0135	−0.273
V10	**0.668**	−0.324	0.0810	−0.172
V11	**0.733**	0.0296	0.0446	0.0887
V12	**0.683**	−0.082	0.190	0.0457
V13	**0.617**	−0.0588	0.244	0.125
V14	0.383	0.152	**0.657**	−0.151
V15	0.293	0.219	**0.739**	−0.101
%Variance explained	22.033	13.316	9.759	9.606
Cumulative variance explained	22.033	35.349	45.109	54.715

Notes:
Extraction method: Principal Component Analysis.
Rotation method: Varimax with Kaiser normalization.
1. Rotation converged in 6 iterations.

oriented towards improving the firms (Guzmán and Santos, 2001), that is, they are related to the entrepreneur's willingness to increase his or her enterprise's competitiveness. For this reason, this first factor may be called 'Action promoting competitiveness'.

The second factor explains more than 13 per cent of the total variance and it is strongly associated with the variables V5 and V6, which represent the employment and the sales growth of the firms, respectively. Therefore it will be named 'Growth'.

The third factor explains almost 10 per cent of the total variance and is basically associated with two variables related to 'Training': V14 (university degree-holding managers) and V15 (university degree-holding employees), although it is also related to a lesser extent to another variable, the informal agreement of cooperation.

The fourth factor explains more than 9 per cent of the total variance and it is very interesting in this analysis because it is strongly associated with the

Table 2.3 Cluster analysis

	Final clusters	
	1	2
Competitiveness factor	−0.33738	1.46199
Growth factor	0.16793	−0.72772
Training factor	−0.03263	0.14138
Dependence factor	0.12993	−0.56305
Number of cases in each cluster	325	75

variables V1 and V2, which represent the functional dependence and the purchasing productive dependence of firms in the sample. The identification of this fourth factor, which will be called 'Dependence', means that, in addition to other well-studied characteristics of the firms, such as innovation, collaboration, planning, actions to improve the quality of products, growth of sales and employment and the training degree of managers and the rest of personnel, it is also important to take into account the elements related to the dependence among firms in order to evaluate the profile of the entrepreneurial structure of a given territory.

The cluster analysis seems to reinforce the results of factor analysis. As was pointed out before, the clusters have been created based on the scoring of factors obtained from the factor analysis for each of the four identified factors. The cluster analysis is created through the K-mean for two groups, because after several tests, it was evident that the results obtained were the most appropriate for the purpose of this research. Table 2.3 displays the centre of the final clusters and the number of cases for each cluster. This result shows that:

- In cluster 1 there are 325 enterprises – more than 80 per cent of the sample – that have lower levels of action promoting competitiveness (factor 1) and training (factor 3) with respect to the enterprises in cluster 2, but, at the same time, the firms in the first cluster have more growth in terms of employment and sales, than the firms in cluster 1. How can this contrast be explained? Perhaps the response to this question lies in the theory of enterprise growth. According to this theory, the high level of 'growth' (factor 2) in the majority group is due to the smaller size of the firms. The Variance Analysis shows differences between the sizes of the two enterprise clusters, at 0.0000 level of statistical significance. The mean size is 340 employees in cluster 1 and only five employees in cluster 2.

- Cluster 2 is formed by only 75 enterprises – less than 20 per cent of the sample – which are characterized, in contrast to the larger group of 325 enterprises, by high levels of actions promoting competitiveness (factor 1), and extensive training of the managers and employees (factor 3). Therefore one may affirm that this minor quantitative group is shaped by the 'best' enterprises because they have the most innovation, have paid the most attention to the quality of their products or services, make the most formal agreements of cooperation, make the most planning actions, and have the most qualified personnel. Furthermore, the enterprises of cluster 2 show the lowest level of functional dependence and purchasing productive dependence. That is, on the one hand, the enterprises acquire a big part of their input from their territorial location (Province of Seville and the Andalusian region), and their sales are directed, in high proportion, toward the external territorial market. Therefore their contribution to endogenous economic growth is high with respect to the group of enterprises with the highest level of functional dependence. On the other hand, they are firms that buy their input from many different suppliers, and have a low level of vulnerability with respect to enterprises with a higher degree of purchasing productive dependence.

CONCLUSIONS

According to the previously theoretical approaches and based on the particular findings obtained by the empirical analysis, it is possible to point out some relevant aspects for future analysis of entrepreneurship from the perspective of the relationship between the entrepreneurial structure and the economic growth of a territory.

a. In the analysis of entrepreneurial structure of a territory, in addition to several well-known characteristics of enterprises, such as the size of firms, the activity sectors, the degree of innovation, the collaboration agreements, the training personnel, and so on there are others linked to inter-entrepreneurial dependence that acquire a special importance in the evaluation of entrepreneurship.
b. The new concepts 'productive dependence' and 'functional dependence' constitute structural elements which may acquire particular importance in an effort to improve the knowledge of the relationship between the characteristics of enterprises and the economic growth of a territory. The productive and functional dependence degree may

act favourably or unfavourably on the economic growth-development process, in a structural and permanent way.

c. At least two main research fields will be open in the future as a consequence of the use of these new analytical concepts. On one hand, it is possible to develop comparison analysis between regions in order to identify the profile of those entrepreneurial clusters which contribute to economic growth to the greatest/least extent. In the end, this first research line attempts to analyse –and to measure – the relationship between productive and functional dependences with economic growth. On the other hand, both new concepts may be useful in analysis of the role of SMEs in global value chains for different activity sectors.
d. From an economic policy perspective, these new concepts may represent a discriminating factor in order to improve institutional or public support for SMEs within a framework of regional economic development.

REFERENCES

Acs, Z.J. (1992), 'Small business economics: a global perspective', *Challenge*, **35** (November/December), pp. 38–44.

Acs, Z.J. and C. Armington (2004), 'Employment growth and entrepreneurial activity in cities', *Regional Studies*, **38**, pp. 911–27.

Aghion, P. and P. Howitt (1992), 'A model of growth through creative destruction', *Econometrica*, **60**, pp. 323–51.

Audretsch, D.B. (1995), *Innovation and Industry Evolution*, Cambridge, MA: MIT Press.

Audretsch, D. and R. Thurik (2004), 'A model of the entrepreneurial economy', *International Journal of Entrepreneurship Education*, **2**(2), 143–66.

Baumol, W.J. (1990), 'Entrepreneurship: productive, unproductive and destructive', *Journal of Political Economy*, **98**(3), 893–921.

Carree, M. and R. Thurik (2003), 'The impact of entrepreneurship on economic growth', in D.B. Audretsch and Z.J. Acs (eds), *Handbook of Entrepreneurship Research*, Boston: Kluwer Academic Publishers, pp. 437–71.

Cotec (1996), *Empresa e Innovación en Extremadura*, Madrid: Fundación COTEC para la Innovación Tecnológica.

Courlet, C. and B. Soulage (1995), 'Dinámicas industriales y territorio', in A. Vázqez Barquero and G. Garofoli (eds), *Desarrollo Económico Local en Europa*, Madrid: Colegio de Economistas.

Dubini, P. (1989), 'The influence of motivation and environment on business start-ups: some hints for public policies', *Journal of Business Venturing*, **4**(1), 11–26.

Fagerberg, J. (1988), 'International competitiveness', *Economics Journal*, no. 98, pp. 335–74.

Feldman, M.P. and D.B. Audretsch (1999), 'Innovation in cities: science-based diversity, specialization and localized monopoly', *European Economic Review*, **43**, pp. 409–29.

Florio, M. (1996), 'Large firms, entrepreneurship and regional development policy: growth poles in the Mezzogiorno over 40 years', *Entrepreneurship and Regional Development*, **8**, pp. 263–95.
Garofoli, G. (1994), 'Economic development, organization of production and territory', in G. Garofoli and A. Vazquez Barquero (eds), *Organization of Production and Territory: Local Models of Development*, Pavia: Universitá degli studi de Pavia.
Gereffi, G. (1994), 'The organization of buyer-driven global commodity chains: how US retailers shape overseas production networks', in G. Gereffi and M. Kornzeniewicz (eds), *Commodity Chains and Global Capitalism*, London: Praeger.
Grabher, G. (1993), 'Rediscovering the social in the economic of interim relation', in G. Grabher (ed.), *The Embedded Firm. On Socioeconomics of Industrial Networks*, London: Routledge.
Grosman, G.M. and E. Helpman (1991), *Innovation and Growth in the Global Economy*, Cambridge: MIT Press.
Guzmán, J. and J. Santos (2001), 'The booster function and the entrepreneurial quality: an application to the province of Seville', *Entrepreneurship and Regional Development*, **13**, pp. 221–28.
Guzmán, J. and J. Santos (2006), *Realidad Empresarial y Desarrollo Económico en la Provincia de Sevilla*, Seville: Consejo Andaluz de Relaciones Laborales, Junta de Andalucía.
Hirchsman, A.O. (1961), *La Estrategia del Desarrollo Económico*, Mexico: Fondo de Cultura Económica.
Holcombe, Randall G. (1998), 'Entrepreneurship and economic growth', *The Quarterly Journal of Austrian Economics*, **1**(2), 45–62.
Izushi, H. (1999), 'Can a development agency foster cooperation among local firms? The case of Welsh Development Agency's supplier association programme', *Regional Studies*, **33**(8), 739–50.
Kent, C.A. (1982), 'Entrepreneurship in economic development', chapter 12 in C.A. Kent, D.L. Sexton and K.H. Vesper (eds), *Encyclopaedia of Entrepreneurship*, Englewood Cliffs, New York: Prentice-Hall, pp. 237–56.
Krugman, P. (1991), 'Increasing returns and economic geography', *Journal of Political Economy*, **99**(3), 483–99.
McMillan, J. and C. Woodruff (2002), 'The central role of entrepreneurs in transition economies', *Journal of Economic Perspectives*, **16**(3), 153–272.
Molero, J. (2001), *Innovación Tecnológica y Competitividad en Europa*, Madrid: Editorial Síntesis.
Nadiri, I.N. (1993), 'Innovations and technological spillovers', *NBER Working Paper 4423*, Cambridge: National Bureau of Economic Research.
Nickell, S.J. (1996), 'Competition and corporate performance', *Journal of Political Economy*, **104**, pp. 724–46.
O'Kean, J. (1991), *Empresario y Entorno Económico*, Bilbao: Deusto.
Porter, M. (1985), *Competitive Advantage: Creating and Sustaining Superior Performance*, New York: The Free Press.
Romer, P.M. (1994), 'The origins of endogenous growth', *Journal of Political Economy*, **8** (1), 3–22.
Schumpeter, J.A. (1934), *The Theory of Economic Development*, Cambridge, MA: Harvard University Press (originally published in 1912).
Schumpeter, J.A. (1942 [1996]), *Capitalism, Socialism and Democracy*, New York: Harper and Row.

Solow, R.J. (1956), 'A contribution to the theory of economic growth', *Quarterly Journal of Economics*, **70**(1), 65–94.
Storey, D.J. (1994), 'Employment', chapter 6 in D.J. Storey, *Understanding the Small Business Sector*, London: Routledge, pp. 160–203.
Thornton, P. and K. Flynn (2003), 'Entrepreneurship, networks and geographies', in Z. Acs and D. Audretsch (eds), *The International Handbook of Entrepreneurship*, Boston/Dordrecht: Kluwer Academic Publishers.
UNCTAD (2001), 'Objetivo: fomentar las vinculaciones de integración hacia atrás', *Informe sobre las Inversiones en el Mundo 2001*, New York: United Nations.
Vespargen, B. (1992), 'Endogenous innovation in neo-clasical growth models: a survey', *Journal of Macroeconomics*, **14**, pp. 631–62.
Wennekers, S. and R. Thurik (1999), 'Linking entrepreneurship and economic growth', *Small Business Economics*, **13**(1), 27–56.
Womack, J. and D. Jones (1996), *Lean Thinking: Banish Waste and Create Wealth in Your Corporation*, New York: Simon Schuster.
Yu, T.F. (1998), 'Adaptative entrepreneurship and the economic development of Hong Kong', *World Development*, **26**.

3. Micro–macro paradoxes of entrepreneurship

Villy Søgaard

> Classical economics optimizes what already exists, as does mainstream economic theory to this day, including the Keynesians, the Friedmanites, and the Supply-siders. It focuses on getting the most out of existing resources and aims at establishing equilibrium. It cannot handle the entrepreneur but consigns him to the shadowy realm of 'external forces', together with climate and weather, government and politics, pestilence and war, but also technology. The traditional economist, regardless of school or 'ism', does not deny, of course, that these external forces exist or that they matter. But they are not part of his world, nor accounted for in his model, his equations, or his predictions.
> (Peter Drucker, 1985 [1994], p. 24)

INTRODUCTION

Over the past decades, entrepreneurship research has grown tremendously. Increasing numbers of journals, chairs, researchers, conferences, and so on are devoted to the field of entrepreneurship. Some researchers, such as Cornelius, Landström and Persson (2006), have empirically examined the 'maturing' of this field of research, that is, the process through which it comes to resemble other mature disciplines with an increasingly internal orientation of researchers citing one another, a stabilization of key topics, an increased level of specialization among researchers, and the emergence of a research community led by core researchers (Cornelius et al., 2006, p. 2).

No doubt this process reflects, at least in part, the growing insight and wisdom that comes with age and experience, but – as every teenage rebel knows – maturing and ageing can also lead to entrenched positions, to adult complacency and perhaps even resignation, as more and more windows of opportunity begin to close behind us. The maturing and stabilization of a research area is a *social* process, conditioning researchers to address some issues rather than others. For an excellent, historical overview, implicitly questioning the 'maturing hypothesis', the reader is referred to Fayolle et al. (2005). According to these authors, 'expectations for the future involve developing methods for studying . . . the interaction between individual and collective human processes' (ibid., p. 11).

One reason why this interaction has been neglected may be found in the 'Oedipal' aggressions of entrepreneurship research vis-à-vis neoclassical economics. As Peter Drucker so eloquently stated in the introductory quotation, entrepreneurship does not fit well into mainstream economic theory. In particular, the underlying assumptions of the textbook model of perfect competition (perfect information, rational choice, given preferences and technology, and so on) seem to rule out entrepreneurship altogether: if every market opportunity were already being fully exploited; if best practice technologies were readily available to every potential producer; if resources were already being allocated perfectly throughout the economy, there would be no room for improvement, no room for innovation, and little space for the entrepreneur (Baretto, 1989), except to secure the succession of generations.

It is hardly surprising, therefore, that scholars of entrepreneurship have been inclined to dismiss wholesale the lessons of received neoclassical orthodoxy. However, what economics has to offer is a *systems perspective*: economists of nearly all persuasions agree that the whole is more than the sum of its parts. The perfectly valid critique of the negligible role of entrepreneurship in mainstream economics does not permit us to sacrifice this fundamental insight. From an economic policy perspective it is not, as a rule, safe to assume that 'what is good for General Motors, is good for the United States'. Indeed what is good for the individual firm may in some cases be bad for society as a whole – or vice versa.

It seems obvious to draw a parallel to the aid-effectiveness literature and its so-called micro–macro paradox. According to a meta analysis undertaken by Doucouliagos and Paldam (2005), 'studies summarizing project evaluations typically find that about half of all projects succeed, while the other half fails, but hardly any harms development. Thus, by aggregation the macro evidence should show that aid increases growth'. It does not, however. The question is: what comes between micro and macro effects in the context of aid and economic development? And what about the macro effects of entrepreneurial activity? The much celebrated Schumpeterian concept of creative destruction should make it clear that the growth of the entrepreneurial firm need *not* contribute to the growth of the economy in any simple and additive way. Yet, how exactly does the fate of the firm influence that of the economic system of which it is part?

The present chapter is written on the assumption that, from a policy perspective, the sharp intellectual division between mainstream economics and entrepreneurship research constitutes a problem. Policy-makers are faced with a choice between a mainstream approach in which entrepreneurs hardly exist (or in which entrepreneurship is supposed to look after itself) and a body of entrepreneurship research characterized by a strong micro focus, both in terms of neglecting macro-level explanations for entrepreneurship and in terms of abstracting from the wider systems effects of stimulating or hampering entrepreneurship.

The primary aim of this chapter is to consider one side of this dual micro–macro problem – the extent to which entrepreneurship research does (or does not) address relevant 'systems effects' of entrepreneurial activity. The other side of the coin, the superficial treatment of entrepreneurship within mainstream economics, will be discussed only in passing.

It should be stressed that this does *not* amount to a claim that all entrepreneurship research should be conducted from a systems approach (see, for example, Arbnor and Bjerke, 1997). Other approaches may be useful, or even superior, when it comes to understanding the logic of entrepreneurial decision-making, entrepreneurs' use of ICT, or their interaction with venture capitalists. The fallacy of composition is not permissible to any approach, however. Each participant in a bicycle race can win by being fast enough, but no methodological school of thought allows its followers to conclude that all participants could win the same race if only they were all fast enough.

If a new enterprise outperforms an existing one, the number of people employed by the new enterprise is likely to overestimate the net employment effect of the new venture. In fact, the net employment effect could be negative, at least in the short run. Conversely, multiplier mechanisms may induce many more jobs than those within the walls of the company itself. It follows that aggregate employment effects of entrepreneurship cannot be found by simply adding the number of jobs within newly established enterprises. In order to integrate micro and macro perspectives one must take account of relevant systems effects.

In the following section the nature of such effects is set out. First, however, the social forces shaping the emerging research discourse are considered. The third section asks whether there is a 'micro–macro problem' in entrepreneurship research and considers the nature of this problem. The fourth section goes on to discuss possible reasons for this problem. A distinction is made between theoretical, methodological, ideological (or discursive) and institutional explanations.

WHAT SYSTEMS EFFECTS?

Many stakeholders have an interest in doing – or funding – research on entrepreneurship, and there are several motivations for doing so. Researchers, of course, have come from many different disciplinary backgrounds, which has undoubtedly hampered the development of entrepreneurship research into an integrated academic field. A great deal of research has been empirically oriented, focusing on such varied issues as the psychology of the entrepreneur, motivations for setting up a business, access to venture capital, and so on. Some of this research appears to be genuinely 'disinterested', that is, it does not flow directly from the desire to know how best to attain specific goals apart from gaining insight into specific aspects of entrepreneurship. Like all other forms of research, entrepreneurship research must be funded, however, which induces researchers to appeal to the incentives of external stakeholders.

Their incentives may be broadly divided into private and public motivations for taking an interest in this area of research. Some external stakeholders, such as seed or venture capitalists, business angels or (existing or would-be) entrepreneurs obviously have an interest in studies relating specific management practices, growth strategies or characteristics of firms or entrepreneurs to the survival or commercial success of the new enterprise. Unsurprisingly, a great deal of research has been aimed at shedding some light on these issues.

Political actors often take a strong interest in stimulating economic growth and renewal and frequently see entrepreneurship as a vehicle for doing so. For example, in an address to the British American Chamber of Commerce, Peter Mandelson, former Secretary of State for Trade and Industry, expressed the view that 'we need more entrepreneurs in the British economy; they are the real agents of economic change because enterprise is the bedrock of a modern economy. . . . Government must make this process as easy, accessible and effective as possible' (Mandelson, 1998).

Similarly, reports from the European Commission (for example, 2003) have repeatedly stressed the need for more entrepreneurship as a prerequisite for realizing the so-called Lisbon objectives of turning the European economy into the most competitive economy in the world by 2010 (see, for example, Communication from the Commission to the Council and The European Parliament on Implementation of the Risk Capital Action Plan (RCAP), COM(2001) 605 Final, p. 14). In general, a number of micro–macro issues have to be analysed to support public policy conclusions, however.

Is More Always Better?

Entrepreneurial skills, like other skills, are unevenly distributed, and some undoubtedly contribute more as employees than they might do as self-employed. This raises the question: who, and how many, should be encouraged to (or discouraged from) becoming entrepreneurs? The diminishing returns hypothesis is supported by empirical evidence. In a recent contribution, Carree et al. (2002) developed a statistical model to analyse the relationship between economic growth and business ownership, drawing on data for 23 OECD countries during the period 1976–1996. They found some evidence to support their claim that there is an equilibrium level of business ownership and a penalty for deviating – positively or negatively – from this optimum level. Also, their research suggests that the optimum level of business ownership varies with economic development.

Employment Effects

Entrepreneurial ventures may generate export revenues and create local, national or even international markets for their services and other inputs, thereby boosting local demand and employment. Or they may flourish and grow entirely at the expense of incumbent firms, adding nothing but another dose of uncertainty and 'creative destruction' to the business environment. Thus, as mentioned above, employment within entrepreneurial firms is highly unlikely to be an appropriate measure of the additional net employment generated by entrepreneurial activity. The activity within these firms affects, positively or negatively, the employment of many other firms – suppliers, competitors, and so on.

Alternatives to – and Opportunity Costs of – Entrepreneurship

Finally, entrepreneurship is but one of several sources of economic growth along with education, technical change and innovation, export growth, and a host of other factors. It is not clear *ex ante* which of these factors can do most to stimulate the economy, but the economic policy-maker, endowed with scarce resources, ought to be interested in knowing. The entrepreneur may decide to start up his or her own venture despite their lack of marketing knowledge, management skills, technical know-how and capital for fear that existing companies should steal their idea. In this situation, reducing the transaction costs involved in selling a new product or process idea to an existing firm might be more efficient in terms of generating growth than inducing the entrepreneur to go it alone. What sort of arrangements could be put in place to ensure that the business idea of the entrepreneur (or 'extrapreneur') is exploited in the best possible way? Where do we get the most of existing resources?

Risk and Uncertainty

Obviously, a macro assessment of the risk and uncertainty associated with entrepreneurial activity may differ substantially from the micro assessment of the individual entrepreneur. Whilst the significance of uncertainty avoidance has been addressed, for example, in a study undertaken by Wennekers, Thurik, Stel and Noorderhaven (Wennekers et al., 2003), contributions specifically addressing the micro–macro paradox at this point seem rare.

The chapter seeks to provide a general picture of how such key micro–macro problems have been addressed within the field of entrepreneurship research so far and discusses the possible need for a redirection of research against this background. It is, however, beyond the scope of the chapter to get deeply into substantive arguments concerning each of these 'paradoxes'.

Whilst studies based on the private motivations for doing entrepreneurship research may not have to take account of systems effects, the validity of studies based on public motivations hinge crucially on their taking account of such effects. Otherwise, entrepreneurship research may end up making false conclusions implicitly by aggregation. This tendency is clearly present in many studies on the role of small firms as 'job engines'. Since the pioneering work of Birch (1979), who found that no less than two-thirds of new (net) jobs in the US between 1969 and 1976 were created in small firms with less than 20 employees, many similar studies have been carried out in other countries. Although the validity of this research has been challenged on methodological grounds (cf., for example, Davis et al., 1996), this critique has been focused largely on statistical problems of little practical significance (Davidsson et al., 1998). The ways in which job creation by small firms might affect job creation elsewhere appear to have been largely neglected.

MICRO–MACRO PROBLEMS IN ENTREPRENEURSHIP RESEARCH

Since this chapter is concerned with entrepreneurship research, we shall focus mainly on one side of the dual micro–macro problem – the extent to which entrepreneurship research, based on public research motivations, takes account of systems effects. This chapter was inspired, of course, by a subjective impression that studies often fail to do so. Subjective impressions are fallible, however, and a more systematic approach seems called for to settle the issue. Figure 3.1 presents a crude framework for classifying this type of study.

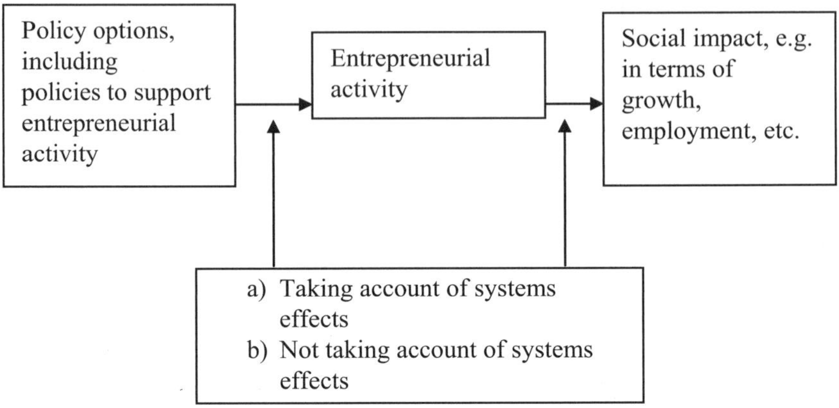

Figure 3.1 *Problem framework for studies that should take account of systems effects*

Based on the model of Figure 3.1 it is possible to distinguish between the following types of entrepreneurship research:

1. Research that does not expressly address the perspectives suggested in the model of Figure 3.1 – for example, research on entrepreneurs' use of ICT, of the succession of generations, of personal networks, and so on.
2. Research addressing policy impact on entrepreneurial activity.
3. Research addressing the socioeconomic impact of entrepreneurial activity.
4. Research into the socioeconomic impact of policies to influence entrepreneurial activity (vis-à-vis other policies).

Each type of research may then be graduated according to the way in which it takes account of systems effects.

By way of illustration, Table 3.1 presents a classification of articles from all issues of *Entrepreneurship and Regional Development* in 2004. This journal was chosen because its title explicitly links micro–macro (or at least micro–meso) issues, and the year 2004 was chosen for practical reasons (electronic access to PDF versions of all articles). It would obviously be desirable to include more journals over a longer period of time. A similar study, covering 337 articles published in leading entrepreneurship journals in 1999–2000 (Kyrö and Kansikas, 2005), suggests that macro-level research is equally rare in other leading journals.

About one in four articles (seven in 27) were more or less explicitly linking policy options and social impact. The remaining 20 articles were on

Table 3.1 Classification of articles from 2004 issues of Entrepreneurship and Regional Development

	Policy impact on entrepreneurial activity	Socioeconomic impact of entrepreneurial activity	Socioeconomic impact of policies on entrepreneurial activity	Other types of research
		'Public motivations'		'Private motivations' + 'Pure research'
Systems effects analysed	–	–	–	
Systems effects discussed	2	3	1	20
Systems effects not considered	–	–	1	

such issues as networking, the adoption of ICT, entrepreneurship in specific contexts, conceptual issues, and so on – that is, on issues reflecting 'private motivations' and, in a very few cases, pure research motivations.

The classification of chapters is inevitably somewhat subjective, of course, and the sceptical reader is invited to consult Appendix 3A.1, which indicates just how each individual article has been classified.

From the overall distribution of articles it appears that what has been labelled 'private motivations' are more important than 'public motivations' in generating entrepreneurship research. The numbers within the 'public motivations' columns are too small to allow for any general conclusions. Moreover, the classification of some of the papers in this category is admittedly questionable. For example, the article by Rehn and Taalas from the May 2004 issue (pp. 235–50), which is categorized here as one of three articles on 'socio-economic impact of entrepreneurial activity', is a highly interesting article on the Soviet Union 'as a fundamentally entrepreneurial society'. Similarly, it could be argued that the article on the Shell *Live*Wire venture creation programme by Greene and Storey from the March issue (pp. 145–59) is not really about policy impact on entrepreneurial activity, although the analysis does appear policy-relevant. Finally, Pereira's article on 'State entrepreneurship and regional development: Singapore's industrial parks in Batam and Suzhou' is classified under 'socio-economic impact of policies on entrepreneurial activity'. This chapter touches upon systems effects, but they are not systematically analysed.

The article entitled 'Is small beautiful?' (Johansson, 2004) does not take into account systems effects. It describes the growth of Swedish IT firms between 1993 and 1998, based on data covering all firms in the entire industry. The article demonstrates quite clearly that small firms have grown much faster than larger firms during this period. However, it does not take account of the interaction between the growth in small and larger firms. That is why it has been classified under 'systems effects not considered'.

The relative scarcity of research on socioeconomic impact suggests that policy-makers wanting to assess the impact of their policies will have to resort to other research sources – or do without. Moreover, the lack of attention to systems effects within the 'public motivations' columns suggests that there is reluctance to deal with tensions between the two types of motivations.

There are counter examples, however, as shown by the work of Carree et al. (2002), mentioned above. Similar research has been carried out by Martínez in an analysis of entrepreneurship and regional growth in Spain (Martínez, 2005).

Yet, on the whole, the sample of articles appear to confirm Rehn's and Taalas' view that

> at the core scholars in entrepreneurship are *pro* rather than *contra*. As a result, the community of academics that studies it by and large accepts entrepreneurialism as a good thing. When it comes to the place of the studied phenomenon in society, the analysis has often been restricted to questions regarding how to foster and support entrepreneurship in different contexts. Usually this has been done in a way that implicitly assumes that entrepreneurialism is an exogenous variable, something that is introduced into a society and that there is a constant lack of. Rehn and Taalas (2004, p. 235)

EXPLANATIONS OF THE MICRO–MACRO PROBLEMS

What are the reasons for this bias towards the fallacy of composition within entrepreneurship research? We suggest four elements that should be considered:

1. *Theoretical explanations*. Opposition to mainstream economics.
2. *Methodological explanations*. Design difficulties associated with addressing the micro–macro problem.
3. *Ideological explanations*. Glorification of ownership. Entrepreneurial universities, etc. The fate of the Humboldt University.

4. *Institutional explanations.* Specialization of research preventing researchers from seeing innovation, intrapreneurship, entrepreneurship and so on as alternative levers of economic renewal.

Theoretical Explanations

First, as mentioned in the opening paragraph, mainstream economics has traditionally tended to rule out entrepreneurship altogether. Thus, the concept of entrepreneurship does not appear at all in the indices of such widely accepted textbooks as Hal Varian's *Intermediate Microeconomics* (1999), Jehle and Reny's *Advanced Microeconomic Theory* (2001), Pindyck and Rubinfeld's *Microeconomics* (1997), or Eaton et al.'s *Microeconomics* (2002). Implicitly, the entrepreneur is relegated to some 'primordial ooze' from which the economic system once emerged. In Robert Frank's *Microeconomics and Behavior* (1991), Case and Fair's *Principles of Microeconomics* (1994), and Paul Samuelson's classic *Economics* (1973), the concept of entrepreneurship is mentioned only in passing. Parkin, Powell and Matthews describe entrepreneurial ability as 'the factor of production that organizes the business, makes business decisions, innovates and bears the risk of running the business. These activities would not be undertaken without the expectation of a return. The expected return for supplying entrepreneurial ability is called *normal profit.*' (Parkin et al., 1997, p. 214).

Some economists have taken a much stronger interest in entrepreneurship, of course. In particular, the so-called Austrian school of economists has levelled a serious criticism against the neoclassical framework. This criticism is serious because it is targeted at the very core assumptions of the neoclassical model. Competition is seen as a dynamic process and not as a static structure, and the perfect rationality assumptions of microeconomic theory are dismissed in favour of bounded rationality/procedural rationality assumptions.

These fundamental premises undoubtedly constitute the two overriding reasons for the neglect of entrepreneurship in economic theory. William Baumol (1968, 1990) is one of the few economists to have looked seriously into the relationship between economics and entrepreneurship, which earned him the International Award for Entrepreneurship and Small Business Research in 2003. On that occasion Eliasson and Henrekson (2004, p. 3), reviewing his work, noted how his

> analysis of the entrepreneur . . . has been guided by two principles that he formulated very early in his career: 1) Make your assumptions confer with reality as much as you can . . . but not to the extent that you cannot say anything.

> Therefore, it becomes necessary, he argues, to economize on the introduction of realism into analysis. 2) If possible, try to stay within the framework of neoclassical analysis.

The tension between these two principles raises the question if it *is* possible to carry out entrepreneurship research within the framework of neoclassical analysis. Many researchers have found it difficult, and it is possible that the systems approach has been dismissed along with the neoclassical heritage.

Methodological Explanations

Secondly, the systematic empirical inclusion of systems effects is demanding. The so-called meta analysis by Doucouliagos and Paldam (2005), based on a number of aid effectiveness articles, is an instructive case in point. The article largely fails to demonstrate the effectiveness of development aid. This is not tantamount to demonstrating its ineffectiveness, however – a subtle, but very important point. Among other things, this is to do with methodological difficulties such as the following:

- Development aid normally makes up only a small percentage of the economies of receiving countries. For example, suppose various economic injections were randomly administered to 70 countries over, say, a 5-year period. In order to be able to measure the impact of such injections, one would have to be able to attribute almost 20 per cent of the (unexplained) differences in economic growth to these injections to obtain a statistically significant effect. In practice, this is quite an ambitious target.
- Medical experiments are randomized to meet the *ceteris paribus* clause. One does not want to measure the effectiveness of a drug by comparing the health of a healthy person who never takes the drug on account of his good health to that of an unhealthy person who does so on account of his poor health. In contrast, the statistical comparisons underlying the aid-effectiveness literature are sometimes done as if aid actually *were* administered at random, unrelated to the needs of the receiving countries. If aid is given to compensate natural disasters, war, or poor governance, and if it fails to compensate fully for such evils, aid and growth may well be negatively correlated, even if the aid provided is in fact effective.
- Medical experiments are usually confined to one drug at a time. Development aid is nearly always a mixture of many different 'drugs' – schools, irrigation systems, power stations – the effects of which may be short-term or protracted over several decades.

Very similar problems pertain to assessing the social impact of entrepreneurial activity. The methodological difficulties involved in sorting out whether 'entrepreneurial spirit' is a source or a consequence of exceptional growth are quite challenging. Interestingly, a comprehensive analysis by Teasdale and McVey (2001) concluded that the most likely explanations for this were to be found in macroeconomic conditions (such as interest, business confidence, and so on). This finding significantly modifies the 'independent variable' perspective of entrepreneurship. However, while there is certainly room for improvement, work such as that of Carree et al. (2002), or Martínez (2005) suggests that this type of analysis is possible.

Ideological Explanations

In the article by Cornelius et al. (2006) the growth and maturing of entrepreneurship research is seen as a process similar to the maturation of other disciplines. One should not overlook, however, that it is also a process unfolding in a specific historical context. We are currently witnessing what Etzkowitz and Leydesdorff (1997) referred to as The Second Academic Revolution. In many respects this 'revolution' is an understandable reaction to a range of pressures: the increasing number of students, the emerging knowledge society and the competitive pressures from globalization, to name just a few.

Reforming the university system is a demanding enterprise, however. While the ideal type Humboldt University was caught in a dilemma between independency and social relevancy, there has recently been a tendency – probably in reaction to the leftist tendencies of the 1970s – to equate social and commercial relevancy.

For example, in Denmark, Research Minister Helge Sander has undertaken to reform university research under the slogan 'from research to receipt':

> Government has a clear position on development and research. Research is not something that should be collecting dust on university shelves. The Government wants an active interaction between knowledge institutions and businesses. Business should be using research actively to ensure the transfer of knowledge 'from heads to hands', from 'research to receipt'. In general, it is important that research and education be much more tightly related to firms as well as private investors. Government is in full swing securing this interaction. The new university reform is an obvious case in point. We'll now get university boards with an external majority – and with business representatives. (Source: http://www.oem.dk/sw7999.asp, accessed 30 April 2006)

The above quotation is from an address delivered by the Minister at Danske Maritime's reception, 25 June 2003.

There is no denying, of course, that commercial application is an important vehicle for social relevancy. Yet, reconciling financial dependence and academic independence is no small challenge. There may be profitable markets for the scientific approval of all sorts of messages, ranging from creationism to the harmlessness of sugar, bubble gum or carbon dioxide. Institutional safeguards are required to ensure that commercial relevancy is not bought at the expense of credibility, and that other forms of social relevancy are also being catered to. In an important article Fujigaki and Leydesdorff (2000) describe how the logic of scientific validation differs from that of market (or political) validation.

Institutional Explanations

Finally, the specialization of research that comes with the maturation of the research field may prevent researchers from adopting a more holistic view enabling them to see innovation, intrapreneurship, entrepreneurship and so on as alternative processes of economic renewal. It deserves notice, for example, that none of the articles on policy influence in the sample of Table 3.1 addressed relevant alternatives to policies to support entrepreneurialism.

CONCLUSIONS AND PERSPECTIVES

This chapter set out to examine the extent to which entrepreneurship research addresses, or fails to address, relevant systems effects of entrepreneurial activity. Although the empirical basis for drawing this conclusion could be expanded, the evidence presented strongly suggests that there is a tendency to ignore the wider social implications of entrepreneurial activities. This problem should certainly be taken seriously by any subject wanting to see itself as a fully-fledged member of the social sciences.

As mentioned in the previous section, important design difficulties must be overcome to handle such problems empirically. The cited work by Carree and Thurik (2003) is suggestive, but other approaches may prove useful as well.

Without denying or minimizing the sometimes impressive achievements of entrepreneurial individuals, it is a good thing that entrepreneurship research has matured beyond the so-called 'great man hypothesis' and the unqualified glorification of ownership. This process of maturation will undoubtedly continue.

Maturity means innocence lost, however, and the process of maturation is taking place in the context of a Second Academic Revolution, threatening to undermine the ideals of the classical Humboldt University. Theoretical and empirical studies of the wider social impact of entrepreneurialism are required for entrepreneurship research to move beyond the perspectives of the individual entrepreneur or venture capitalist and inform policy-makers in a reasonably objective fashion. Such studies require a commitment to understanding for the sake of understanding, and they may be difficult to undertake in a research environment depending more and more on private funding.

Above all, entrepreneurship research should address systems effects more explicitly and consistently, both theoretically and empirically. It is conceivable that further *theoretical* developments will clarify the nature of such effects. One need not pursue a mainstream or neoclassical research agenda to appreciate that the whole is more than the sum of the parts.

REFERENCES

Arbnor, I. and B. Bjerke (1997), *Methodology for Creating Business Knowledge*, 2nd edn, Thousand Oaks, CA, London and New Delhi: Sage Publication.

Baretto, H.V. (1989), *The Entrepreneur in Microeconomic Theory: Disappearance and Explanation*, London: Routledge.

Baumol, W.J. (1968), 'Entrepreneurship in economic theory', *The American Economic Review*, May 1968, pp. 64–71.

Baumol, W.J. (1990), 'Entrepreneurship: productive, unproductive and destructive', *Journal of Political Economy*, **98**(5), 893–921.

Birch, David L. (1979), *The Job Generation Process*, Cambridge, MA: MIT Program on Neighborhood and Regional Change.

Carree, M. and R. Thurik (2003), 'The impact of entrepreneurship on growth', in Zoltan J. Acs and David B. Audretch (eds), *Handbook of Entrepreneurship Research*, Boston: Kluwer Academic Publishers, pp. 437–71.

Carree, M., A. von Stel, R. Thurik and S. Wennekers (2002), 'Economic development and business ownership: an analysis using data of 23 OECD countries in the Period 1976–1996', *Small Business Economics*, **19**, pp. 271–90.

Case, K.E. and R.C. Fair (1994), *Principles of Microeconomics*, 3rd edn, New Jersey: Prentice Hall.

Commission of the European Communities (2003), 'Green Paper. Entrepreneurship in Europe', available at: http://europa.eu.int/eur-lex/en/com/gpr/2003/com2003_0027en01.pdf (accessed 4 March 2007).

Cornelius, B., H. Landström and O. Persson (2006), *Entrepreneurship Research: Towards a Domain Approach to Knowledge*, paper presented at the 14th Nordic conference on Small Business Research, 11–13 May 2006, Stockholm.

Davidsson, P., L. Lindmark and C. Olsson (1998) 'The extent of overestimation of small firm job creation – an empirical examination of the regression bias', *Small Business Economics*, 11, pp. 87–100.

Davis, S.J., J. Haltiwanger and S. Schuh (1996), 'Small business and job creation: dissecting the myth and reassessing the facts', *Small Business Economics*, 8, pp. 297–315.

Doucouliagos, H. and M. Paldam (2005), *Aid effectiveness on growth – a meta study*, working paper, available at: http://www.Martin.Paldam.dk.
Drucker, P. (1985 [1994]), *Innovation and Entrepreneurship*, Oxford: Butterworth-Heinemann Ltd.
Eaton, B.C., D.F. Eaton and D.W. Allen (2002), *Microeconomics*, 5th edn, Toronto: Prentice Hall/Pearson.
Eliasson, G. and M. Henrekson (2004), 'William J. Baumol: an entrepreneurial economist on the economics of entrepreneurship', *Small Business Economics*, **23**(1), 1–7.
Etzkowitz, H. and L. Leydesdorff (eds) (1997), *Universities in the Global Knowledge Economy: A Triple Helix of University–Industry–Government Relations*, London: Cassell Academic Publishers.
Fayolle, A., P. Kyrö and J. Ulijn (2005), 'The entrepreneurship debate in Europe: a matter of history and culture?', in A. Fayolle, P. Kyrö and J. Ulijn (eds), *Entrepreneurship Research in Europe: Outcomes and Perspectives*, Cheltenham, UK and Northampton, MA, USA: Edward Elgar Publishing, pp. 1–31.
Frank, R.H. (1991), *Microeconomics and Behavior*, Singapore: McGraw-Hill.
Fujigaki, Y. and L. Leydesdorff (2000), 'Quality control and validation boundaries in a triple helix of university–industry–government: "Mode 2" and the future of university research', *Social Science Information*, **39**(4), 635–55.
Greene, F.J. and D.J. Storey (2004), 'An assessment of a venture creation programme: the case of Shell Live WIRE', *Entrepreneurship & Regional Development*, **16**(2), 145–59.
Jehle, G.A. and P.J. Reny (2001), *Advanced Microeconomic Theory*, 2nd edn, New York: Addison-Wesley.
Johansson, D. (2004), 'Is small beautiful? The case of the Swedish IT industry', *Entrepreneurship & Regional Development*, **16**(4), 271–87.
Kyrö, P. and J. Kansikas (2005), 'Current state of methodology in entrepreneurship research and some expectations for the future', in A. Fayolle, P. Kyrö and J. Ulijn (eds), *Entrepreneurship Research in Europe. Outcomes and Perspectives*, Cheltenham, UK and Northampton, MA, USA: Edward Elgar Publishing, pp. 121–49.
Mandelson, P. (1998), Speech at The British American Chamber of Commerce, New York, 13 October, 1998, available at: http://www.dti.gov.uk/ministers/archived/mandelson131098.html (accessed 22 March 2007)
Martínez, B.J.A. (2005), 'Equilibrium entrepreneurship rate, economic development and growth. Evidence from Spanish regions', *Entrepreneurship & Regional Development*, **17**(2), 145–61.
Parkin, M., M. Powell and K. Matthews (1997), *Economics*, 3rd edn, New York: Addison-Wesley.
Pereira, A.A. (2004), 'State entrepreneurship and regional development: Singapore's industrial parks in Batam and Suzhou', *Entrepreneurship & Regional Development*, **16**(2), 129–44.
Pindyck, R.S. and D.L. Rubinfeld (1997), *Microeconomics*, 4th edn, New Jersey: Prentice Hall.
Rehn, A. and S. Taalas (2004), 'Znakomstva I Svyazi' (Acquaintances and connections) – Blat, the Soviet Union, and mundane entrepreneurship', *Entrepreneurship & Regional Development*, **16**(3), 235–50.
Samuelson, P.A. (1973), *Economics*, 9th edn, Tokyo: McGraw-Hill.

Teasdale, P. and B. McVey (2001), *Scottish Economic Report 2001*, available at: http://www.scotland.gov.uk/Resource/Doc/158287/0042861.pdf.
Varian, H.R. (1999), *Intermediate Microeconomics – A Modern Approach*, 5th edn, London: Norton and Company.
Wennekers, S., R. Thurik, A. van Stel and N. Noorderhaven (2003), *Uncertainty Avoidance and the Rate of Business Ownership across 22 OECD Countries, 1976–2000*, Amsterdam: ERIM.

APPENDIX 3A.1 SAMPLE OF ARTICLES CLASSIFIED

Entrepreneurship and Regional Development 2004

Key to the classification of articles

	Policy impact on entrepreneurial activity	Socioeconomic impact of entrepreneurial activity	Socioeconomic impact of policies on entrepreneurial activity	Other types of research
Systems effects analysed	A	B	C	
Systems effects discussed	D	E	F	J
Systems effects not considered	G	H	I	

'In what sense "regional development?": entrepreneurship, underdevelopment and strong tradition in the periphery', by Paul Benneworth, *Entrepreneurship & Regional Development*, November 2004, **16**(6), 439–58. E

'Policies to promote new knowledge-intensive industrial agglomerations', by Colm O'Gorman and Mika Kautonen, *Entrepreneurship & Regional Development*, November 2004, **16**(6), 459–79. D

'Beyond portfolio entrepreneurship: multiple income sources in small firms', by Sara Carter, Stephen Tagg and Pavlos Dimitratos, *Entrepreneurship & Regional Development*, November 2004, **16**(6), 481–99. J

'Internationalization of private firms: environmental turbulence and organizational strategies and resources', by Paul Westhead, Mike Wright and Deniz Ucbasaran, *Entrepreneurship & Regional Development*, November 2004, **16**(6), 501–22. J

'Networks and linkages among firms and organizations in the Ottawa-region technology cluster', by Judith J. Madill, George H. Haines Jr. and Allan L. Riding, *Entrepreneurship & Regional Development*, September 2004, **16**(5), 351–68. J

'High technology localization and extra-regional networks', by John N.H. Britton, *Entrepreneurship & Regional Development*, September 2004, **16**(5), 369–90. J

'Entrepreneurs' networks and the success of start-ups', by Peter Witt, *Entrepreneurship & Regional Development*, September 2004, **16**(5), 391–412. J

'Creating space for play/invention – concepts of space and organizational entrepreneurship', by Daniel Hjorth, *Entrepreneurship & Regional Development*, September 2004, **16**(5), 413–32. J

'Networks, weak signals and technological innovations among SMEs in the land-based transportation equipment sector', by Pierre-André Julien, Eric Andriambeloson and Charles Ramangalahy, *Entrepreneurship & Regional Development*, July 2004, **16**(4), 251–69. J

'Is small beautiful? The case of the Swedish IT industry', by Dan Johansson, *Entrepreneurship & Regional Development*, July 2004, **16**(4), 271–87. I

'International entrepreneurship and the small business', by Denise Fletcher, *Entrepreneurship & Regional Development*, July 2004, **16**(4), 289–305. J

'Financial bootstrapping and venture development in the software industry', by Richard T. Harrison, Colin M. Mason and Paul Girling, *Entrepreneurship & Regional Development,* July 2004, **16**(4), 307–33. J

'Self-employment in the era of the new economic model in Latin America: a case study from Nicaragua', by Michael J. Pisani, José A. Paán, *Entrepreneurship & Regional Development*, July 2004, **16**(4), 335–50. J

'Reclaiming the space of entrepreneurship in society: geographical, discursive and social dimensions', by Chris Steyaert and Jerome Katz, *Entrepreneurship & Regional Development*, May 2004, **16**(3), 179–96. J

'A cross-national study of culture, organization and entrepreneurship in three neighbourhoods', by Lauretta Conklin Frederking, *Entrepreneurship & Regional Development*, May 2004, **16**(3), 197–215. J

'Depleted communities and community business entrepreneurship: revaluing space through place', by Harvey Johnstone and Doug Lionais, *Entrepreneurship & Regional Development*, May 2004, **16**(3), 217–33. E

' "Znakomstva I Svyazi" (Acquaintances and connections) – Blat, the Soviet Union, and mundane entrepreneurship', by Alf Rehn and Saara Taalas, *Entrepreneurship & Regional Development*, May 2004, **16**(3), 235–50. E (?)

'Networking, trust and embeddedness amongst SMEs in the Aberdeen oil complex', by Danny MacKinnon, Keith Chapman and Andrew Cumbers, *Entrepreneurship & Regional Development*, March 2004, **16**(2), 87–106. J

'Human capital, social capital, and innovation: a multi-country study', by Mourad Dakhli and Dirk De Clercq, *Entrepreneurship & Regional Development*, March 2004, **16**(2), 107–28. J

'State entrepreneurship and regional development: Singapore's industrial parks in Batam and Suzhou', by Alexius A. Pereira, *Entrepreneurship & Regional Development*, March 2004, **16**(2), 129–44. F

'An assessment of a venture creation programme: the case of Shell *Live*WIRE', by F.J. Greene and D.J. Storey, *Entrepreneurship & Regional Development*, March 2004, **16**(2), 145–59. D

'Strategic marketing practices and the performance of Chinese small and medium-sized enterprises (SMEs) in Taiwan', by Siu Wai-Sum, Andrew Wenchang Fang and Andrew Tingling Lin, *Entrepreneurship & Regional Development*, March 2004, **16**(2), 161–78. J

'Cities and cyberspace: new entrepreneurial strategies', by Marina Van Geenhuizen, *Entrepreneurship & Regional Development*, January 2004, **16**(1), 5–19. J

'Fibre tracks: explaining investment in fibre optic backbones', by Edward J. Malecki, *Entrepreneurship & Regional Development*, January 2004, **16**(1), 21–39. J

'Pizza over the Internet: e-commerce, the fragmentation of activity and the tyranny of the region', by Helen Couclelis, *Entrepreneurship & Regional Development*, January 2004, **16**(1), 41–54. J

'ICT policies for SMEs and regional disparities. The Spanish case', by Juan R. Cuadrado-Roura and Antonio Garcia-Tabuenca, *Entrepreneurship & Regional Development*, January 2004, **16**(1), 55–75. J

'Breeding places for ethnic entrepreneurs: a comparative marketing approach', by Enno Masurel, Peter Nijkamp and Gabriella Vindigni, *Entrepreneurship & Regional Development*, January 2004, **16**(1), 77–86. J

4. New initiatives to revitalize society: public entrepreneurship in the south of Sweden

Tobias Dalhammar

INTRODUCTION

This chapter deals with an important subfield in entrepreneurship research labelled public entrepreneurship. Related to the growing theoretical school of social entrepreneurship, public entrepreneurship conceptualizes an activity that mainly belongs to society and is not restricted to the economic sphere. The term 'public' emphasizes public space, that is, the space that concerns all citizens and that is neither private nor official. In their research, Hjorth and Bjerke (2006) use the original Latin meaning of the word 'publicus', which means something that concerns all citizens and that nobody can disclaim responsibility for. Examples of public issues are unemployment, residency, environment and education. Entrepreneurship is conceptualized as enterprise in a wider sense. That is, to create something that others can use or benefit from (Bjerke and Dalhammar, 2006).

In recent years, there has been a growing interest in initiatives with a social mission. By initiative, the meanings in the Concise Oxford English Dictionary (2006) are intended: 1. the ability to initiate or begin something, including the power or opportunity to act before others do; 2. a fresh strategy intended to resolve or improve something. Generally, public entrepreneurship initiatives aim to create social value and to contribute to social change. The Canadian Oxford Dictionary (2004) offers some clarity to the definition of social values: 'the principles or moral standards of a person or social group . . .; the generally accepted or personally held judgment of what is valuable or important in life.'[1] Regarding social change, theories on the topic cover many aspects and are complex. It is one of the central problems of sociology, where change is seen not as a mere succession of separate events (as depicted in some narrative histories) but as a structured process in which it may be possible to identify a specific direction or tendency. Social change theories now cover a broad range of phenomena, including short-term and long-term, large-scale and small-scale changes, from the level of global society to the level of the family. Further, sociologists are also interested in changes that affect norms, values, behaviour, cultural meanings and social relationships (Scott and Marshall, 2005).

Research has shown that an important factor for the success of a city or region is the practice of what we can refer to as 'collaborative advantage' (Henton et al., 1997; Dees et al., 2002). In successful cities/regions actors collaborate in order to strengthen their position in relation to other cities and regions. There are tight relationships between business, administration and non-profit organizations, and previous research has shown that heterogeneity and diversity foster entrepreneurship, leading it to become more effective (Johannisson, 1994; Aldrich, 1999). Driving forces at the core of these cities/regions are a number of people we could label 'public entrepreneurs'. Public entrepreneurs could come from any of the three sectors, but they often have a background in or links to the non-profit sector. Generally, they practise a leadership based on collaboration between all three sectors and they often act without formal authority or position. It is argued that public entrepreneurship is crucial as a means of (re-)vitalizing a city or a region, and even whole societies (Catford, 1998). However, there are voices stating that civil society with strong citizen engagement can only be restored at the community, not the national level (Sandel, 1996).

The focus of public entrepreneurship initiatives is generally employment or related activities that are meaningful to the people who constitute the target group of these initiatives. It is argued that unemployment among groups of citizens leads to marginalization and segregation and thereby increased social problems in certain neighbourhoods (Ekberg, 1999). For example, people with no income other than social allowance cannot choose where to live but are reduced to public housing apartments, which in general are located in the least attractive areas of urban cities. The consequence is concentration of these people and increased social problems (Ekberg and Rooth, 2000).

Two cities that experience such problems are Malmö and Landskrona in the south-western part of Scania ('Skåne' in Swedish), the most southern region in Sweden. This has led to 'ghettoization' in some neighbourhoods. This 'ghettoization' coincides with increased immigration to the cities since official policies for bringing these 'new' citizens to the labour market have failed. In this chapter I present two case studies – one from each city – which represent initiatives that aim to increase job opportunities for people who are outside the labour market. The findings from the cases show that these initiatives – which use new ways to try to solve social problems – can get results and provide new paths and models for dealing with complex public issues today and in the future. The two case studies do not make social change by themselves, but they are part of a larger movement of public entrepreneurship initiatives that together contribute to social change in urban cities like Malmö and Landskrona. Thus, although the results are specific for these contexts and environments, the issues are relevant both in a national and international perspective as well. Therefore, public entrepreneurship research generates learning and knowledge that are useful throughout the world.

Problem and Purpose

Three broad questions guide me in this research:

1. *How can societies act to create more self-support and commitment in meaningful activities among their inhabitants?*
   It is suggested that public entrepreneurship initiatives can help people utilize resources and competences not utilized today. This implies that new creative processes have a role to fill in the future development of cities like Malmö and Landskrona.
2. *What new knowledge is needed?*
   By this it follows that researchers have to study examples of public entrepreneurship, present what these concepts mean and how they can contribute to social change and in the longer run to the (re)vitalization of cities, regions and societies.
3. *How would it be possible to identify obstacles and remove them or turn them into opportunities?*
   Researchers need to communicate the knowledge generated (point 2 above) and present a sound critique that brings up both positive and negative sides of public entrepreneurship. Using these findings as a basis for discussion and dialogue, they could provide understanding and more public support for initiatives that contribute to social change and actually make a difference for citizens. No matter how innovative and potentially successful these initiatives are, they still need strong public support to be functional and reach success. This is evident not the least when it comes to grassroot initiatives that have a clear 'bottom up' approach.

The overarching question is if and how public entrepreneurship can create social value and contribute to social change regarding a public issue like unemployment. In a wider perspective these issues concern democracy: to participate as a citizen in the city/region and in society, since labour provides people with opportunities. For example, people get options to choose where to live.

By using case studies I want to grasp factors and aspects that provide understanding about what the reality for the practice of public entrepreneurship looks like: how do initiatives work with a social mission to create social value with respect to a public issue and thereby contribute to social change?

It should be stated here that I do not cover all aspects that the complex field of public entrepreneurship constitutes. Rather, this chapter aims to exemplify its potential by using two cases from two cities. An analysis and discussion concerning these cases provide insights on possible paths for future research.

Outline of the Chapter

The rest of the chapter is organized in the following way: in the next section I discuss the process that has led to the current situation of labour and residential segregation in Sweden, a process that to a great extent coincides with increased immigration to the country. Thereafter, I present theories on public entrepreneurship and their relation to the dominating subfield of social entrepreneurship.

Next, I discuss the methodology used for my case studies. I introduce them by presenting the situation in the cities of Malmö and Landskrona, and exemplify with two neighbourhoods in these cities mentioned above – Rosengård in Malmö and Öster in Landskrona – where aspects of high concentration of immigrants and labour and residential segregation are present. My two cases – Job Emergency in Malmö and Business Pool in Landskrona – are examples of public entrepreneurship, in this instance of new initiatives that deal with unemployment for marginalized people in urban areas. My analysis shows that the concept of public entrepreneurship adds learning and knowledge to research on practices that aim for social change. A deeper analysis brings up the role that actors such as public housing companies could play for public entrepreneurship initiatives and how they can contribute to social change. In a concluding discussion, researchers are urged to study new initiatives and processes that public entrepreneurship exemplifies in order to understand and learn how to address important social issues in society. I also make some suggestions on how public entrepreneurship initiatives ought to be studied to maximize learning experiences.

BACKGROUND TO THE DEVELOPMENT OF IMMIGRATION AND LABOUR AND RESIDENTIAL SEGREGATION IN SWEDEN

Many cities in Sweden today face problems related to labour and residential segregation. Two cities that experience and live with these issues are

Malmö and Landskrona in the very south-western part of Scania ('Skåne' in Swedish) – the most southern region in Sweden. These two cities have also received great numbers of immigrants, above all refugees, mainly during the past 20 years. Therefore, this is also a question that to a great extent concerns immigration. Since all people who have a legal right to stay in Sweden are entitled to support from the social welfare system, unemployment and thus social allowance dependency put costly strains on the economy. Besides, this situation results in personal pressure on these people. Further, the marginalization of people in certain areas of the cities means that resources and competences of these people – including immigrants and ethnic minorities – are lost.

The immigration to Sweden that took place before the mid-1970s was generally labour-driven, and these new citizens adjusted to Swedish society relatively easily. However, by then, there was little focus on integration. The consequence was that different cultures could exist together and mix successfully, but the immigrants were expected to assimilate themselves into Swedish society (Andersson et al., 2002). The development in Sweden in the 1980s and especially in the 1990s and onwards is one of increasing immigration, mainly of refugees, to this country (Ekberg and Rooth, 2000). This new immigration has shifted the structure of how people live and work, not the least in areas in Malmö (Cars and Hagetoft, 2000) and Landskrona (Andersson et al., 2002). The cities of Malmö and Landskrona are divided cities concerning issues like residency and employment and although they do not fit the description or definition of metropolises, they have residents that fit the description of 'ghetto poor'. Examples of districts in which these people live are Rosengård in Malmö and Öster in Landskrona, where there is high concentration of immigrants and where unemployment and social allowance dependency rates are high. This has been an ongoing development that has mainly taken place during the past 15–20 years and has accelerated from the mid-1990s.

At the same time as Rosengård in Malmö and Öster in Landskrona are defined neighbourhoods with distinct characteristics, their development cannot be treated separately from other processes that take place in their respective cities, in Swedish society and internationally. Their developments coincide with similar processes in other parts of the world and make these social problem issues important topics for most people on this planet, regardless of whether they are researchers, policy-makers or experiencing these problems personally. In recent years, researchers have become increasingly interested in studying these matters and presenting solutions and models to deal with them.

When dealing with labour and residential segregation, one has to conclude that many official policies initiated to deal with these issues have failed. Different programmes, despite great economic resources, have provided poor results (Ekberg and Rooth, 2000; Åslund, 2000). One of the basic and paramount reasons seems to be that these programmes do not engage the citizens that represent the target group. There appear to be huge physical and above all mental distances between policy-makers and citizens who experience these problems in their daily lives. Thus, there is a demand for other ways of facing and dealing with these social problems.

PUBLIC ENTREPRENEURSHIP AS PART OF THE SOLUTION

The generally accepted term for social initiatives targeting social issues like the ones discussed above is social entrepreneurship (Dees, 1998; Sullivan Mort et al., 2003; Peredo and McLean, 2006). Further, there are related terms like 'government' entrepreneurship (Osborne and Gaebler, 1993) ,'civic' entrepreneurship (Henton et al., 1997), 'community' entrepreneurship (De Leeuw, 1999; Dupuis and de Bruin, 2003), 'idealistic' entrepreneurship (Piore and Sabel, 1984) and 'mundane' entrepreneurship (Rehn and Taalas, 2004). Another closely connected term often used is social enterprise/social enterprising (Chell, 2007). All these theories constitute important subfields and widen the overall field of entrepreneurship. Recently, a new term has been elaborated on and conceptualized anew, namely public entrepreneurship. Below, I first go through the concept of social entrepreneurship and move on to public entrepreneurship in order to clarify their meaning and to prepare a later discussion about the relevance of studies in the field of public entrepreneurship.

Social Entrepreneurship

The academic field of entrepreneurship has – particularly during the past decade – been revitalized and challenged by one strong subfield, namely what in general is labelled 'social entrepreneurship'. The interests various actors in society have in social entrepreneurship mainly concern the hopes they have about this phenomenon. Dees (1998) states that we 'need social entrepreneurs to help us find new avenues toward social improvement as we enter the next century'. Sullivan Mort et al. (2003, p. 76) define social entrepreneurship as 'the entrepreneurship leading to the establishment of new social enterprises and the continued innovation in existing ones'. Further, Dees et al. (2001) state that social entrepreneurs strive for more innovative solutions that should lead to sustainable improvements and for increased openness to experimentation with various methods in the social sector. Other researchers discuss similar things. Peter Drucker claims that social entrepreneurs 'change the performance capacity of society' (Gendron, 1996, p. 37). Bornstein (1998, p. 36) characterizes social entrepreneurs as 'pathbreakers with a powerful new idea, who combine visionary and real-world problem-solving capacity, who have a strong ethical fiber, and who are "totally possessed" by their vision for change'. Thompson et al. (2000, p. 238) describe social entrepreneurs as 'people who realize where there is an opportunity to satisfy some unmet need that the welfare system will not or cannot meet, and who gather together the necessary resources (generally people, often volunteers, money and premises) and use these to "make a difference"'. Thus, it is suggested that social entrepreneurship has the ambition and potential to revitalize today's post-welfare societies that struggle with issues like unemployment and residential segregation previously discussed in the text.

Sullivan Mort et al. (2003) bring up one of the major problems with the field of social entrepreneurship: there are a number of current usages of the term. In fact, it shares this lack of clarity with the overall field of entrepreneurship. At the same time, this lack of clarity is one of the major advantages for the field of entrepreneurship in general and perhaps for the subfield of social entrepreneurship in particular. It creates free space for researchers and a dynamic that often is not present in other fields. And from time to time, researchers attempt to conceptualize what the field is all about, which forms bases for debates and future directions.

Dees (1998) conceptualizes social entrepreneurship by tracking the roots of the overall theory on entrepreneurship and combining it with the social dimension of the term. When reviewing the field of entrepreneurship he summarizes the French classics by using the eighteenth and nineteenth century philosopher/economist, Say, and moves on to the early twentieth century legend, Schumpeter. He also draws on two major modern contributors in the entrepreneurship field, Drucker and Stevenson, to find the meaning of 'social entrepreneurship'. Dees puts a strong focus on the individuals – the social entrepreneurs. In Dees's (1998) conceptualization, social entrepreneurs:

1. Act as change agents in the social sector;
2. Adopt a mission to create and sustain social value;
3. Recognize and relentlessly pursue new opportunities;
4. Engage in a process of continuous innovation, adaptation and learning;
5. Act boldly without being limited by resources currently in hand;
6. Exhibit a heightened sense of accountability to the constituencies served and for the outcomes created.

The conclusion from Dees's (1998) conceptualization is that social entrepreneurs are a rare breed of leaders with behaviours that are exceptional. By and large, Peredo and McLean (2006, p. 64) agree with these conceptualizations. In order to distinguish social entrepreneurship from other forms of entrepreneurship, they put strong emphasis on the aim to create social value. 'It is a commitment to providing social value that marks the divide between social and other forms of entrepreneur.' According to Johnson (2003, p. 2) one commonality emerges from almost every description of a social entrepreneur: 'the "problem-solving nature" . . . is prominent, and the corresponding emphasis on developing and implementing initiatives that produce measurable results in the form of changed social outcomes and/or impacts.'

Useful as they are, these paramount theories on social entrepreneurship to some extent fall short of understanding the practice of initiatives that aim to create social value and strive for social change. Another newly conceptualized term that covers the same field and that could move the topic forward is public entrepreneurship.

Public Entrepreneurship

As briefly described in the introduction to this chapter, public entrepreneurship refers to entrepreneurship that neither belongs to the private nor the official (although it can have relations to and include both private and official actors) and has dimensions outside business and administration (Hjorth and Bjerke, 2006; Bjerke et al., 2007). It should be stated that the concept of public entrepreneurship is confusing in English, since it commonly refers to entrepreneurship carried out in the so-called public or official sector ('offentliga sektorn' in Swedish). The generally accepted English term is social entrepreneurship, although other suggestions, such as 'government' entrepreneurship (Osborne and Gaebler, 1993) and 'civic' entrepreneurship (Henton et al., 1997) have been proposed (see above).

Public entrepreneurship conceptualizes entrepreneurship as enterprise or enterprising in a wider sense, that is to create something new that other people can use and benefit from (Bjerke and Dalhammar, 2006). This is not limited to a product or a service at a commercial market where producers serve other people as consumers, but could be education, venues and meeting places where citizens strive to create social value for themselves and other citizens (Spinosa et al., 1997; Dees, 1998; Peredo and McLean, 2006; Hjorth and Bjerke, 2006; Bjerke and Dalhammar, 2006; Chell, 2007; Bjerke et al., 2007). The concept of public entrepreneurship is guided by old Roman philosophical principles of *abundantia* (which means that there should be abundance and welfare for all citizens) and *aequitas* (equality between citizens). The original meaning of the term 'public' is used, as in the Latin word 'publicus', which means something that concerns all citizens and that nobody can disclaim responsibility for. However, it is up to each citizen to choose to do something about public issues in society (Hjorth and Bjerke, 2006; Bjerke et al., 2007). Thus, all citizens in a society that are able to do something have a responsibility to act to find solutions to public issues. Put differently, Sullivan Mort et al. (2003, p. 83) quote the Schwab Foundation (an organization that works practically with social entrepreneurship), and this organization expresses a belief that all people have social entrepreneurial virtues. They mention 'an unwavering belief in the innate capacity of all people to contribute meaningfully to economic and social development; a driving passion to make that happen; a practical but innovative stance to a social problem.'

This brings two important changes regarding people's role in society. The first is the move *from consumer to citizen*; the other is the move *from social to public*. Public entrepreneurs act as citizens and engage in public issues (that is, issues that are for all citizens and that nobody can disclaim responsibility for) in order to drive social change. In such processes they create *sociality*, which can be understood as collective investments in a common image of how a phenomenon in society should or should not be; where people are united by a striving for change and of sympathy and solidarity for each other (Hjorth and Bjerke, 2006). In other words: a common view on a phenomenon in society that is of public interest (= concerns all) and a commitment to create change in relation to that phenomenon. Examples of public issues are employment, residence, activities for young people, environment and education.

There are two reasons for developing theories on public entrepreneurship instead of using social entrepreneurship theories. First, the term 'public' has a clearer meaning than the term 'social'. More or less everything in social science has to do with society and relations in one way or another – thus are social – but not all things in society are public – that is, concern all citizens. Second, the ruling social entrepreneurship discourse is clearly influenced by business entrepreneurship (McLeod, 1997; Drayton, 2002; Sullivan Mort et al., 2003). This strong influence makes it harder to understand the driving forces to create social value that several researchers regard as crucial (Dees, 1998; Sullivan Mort et al., 2003; Bjerke and Dalhammar, 2006). In their studies of public entrepreneurship initiatives and processes in the south of Sweden, Bjerke et al. (2007) found that paramount social entrepreneurship theories fail to provide a deeper understanding for these initiatives and the processes they represent. It seemed as if the 'contagiousness' of business aspects on social entrepreneurship was preventing learning and knowledge generation from taking place. Other researchers have acknowledged this incorporation of business aspects in social entrepreneurship as well. 'By moving towards social entrepreneurship as a profession, however, and emphasising its business skills, there is a danger that its full complexity may be submerged and remain unrecognised' (Sullivan Mort et al., 2003, p. 81).

An imaginative example: an entrepreneur hardly chooses between starting an IT business and making $100 million, and helping unemployed tenants in public housing to get jobs (unless he can employ them all in his/her IT business, but it is neither likely that he could hire them all, nor that they would have the competences the entrepreneur needs!). The driving forces are different. However, there also are things that unite. One such factor is that all forms of entrepreneurship to a large extent deal with the issue of resource acquisition. Typically, entrepreneurship starts with a good idea but empty hands (Gartner, 1985; Alvarez and Busenitz, 2001).

Theories on public entrepreneurship add some dimensions to the conceptualizations on social entrepreneurship. These are:

1. The concept of public and what it means for the motive of public entrepreneurship;
2. The concept of sociality and what it means for the behavioural aspects of public entrepreneurship;
3. The concept of citizenship and what it means to the identity perspective of public entrepreneurship.

METHOD USED FOR THE CASE STUDIES OF PUBLIC ENTREPRENEURSHIP

I have conducted case studies in the two cities Malmö and Landskrona. Through academic connections I have established contacts with people who work at the public municipal housing companies in each town: MKB Fastighets AB in Malmö and AB Landskronahem in Landskrona. Both companies have taken an active role in improving the situation for many of their tenants. Thus, they have traditions in initiating and being involved in initiatives to create social value and to contribute to social change. Basically, there are economic interests, since the companies want to maintain the value of their properties, that is, their buildings. But the way they do this is not merely the traditional way through technical renovation and maintenance of the buildings. Instead, they focus on the tenants who live in the apartments. If the tenants do not appreciate and take care of their homes, this depreciates the value of the property in more ways than one: direct damage and destruction of the buildings, for example through vandalism; the clientele are people that other people do not find attractive to have as neighbours; the area gets a bad reputation, which means that people do not want to live there voluntarily, and so on. Therefore, they have adopted policies to invest in people, just as much as they invest in buildings.

In both MKB and Landskronahem, there have been people in the managerial bodies that have an interest in social work, and these people could be labelled public entrepreneurs in the sense that Henton et al. (1997) characterize them. In my research, I have had the opportunity to follow their everyday work over time. I have taken a closer look at two initiatives/cases that were introduced a couple of years ago and that have an influence on their target groups. Both initiatives deal with a high priority issue that addresses the focus of this chapter, namely new ways of creating job opportunities for marginalized people, including immigrants and ethnic minorities, in segregated urban areas. The first one is 'Job Emergency' ('Jobbakuten' in Swedish) in Malmö and the second 'Business Pool' ('Företagspoolen' in Swedish) in Landskrona. I have spoken to people in different positions involved in the initiatives and have looked at project documentation in order to understand how these initiatives can bring about social change (see Appendix 4A.1 for detailed information about data collection). There is value in conducting studies in both cities, since Malmö and Landskrona have different backgrounds and characteristics. Comparisons between the two cases can then help us to understand why certain enterprises may work better in some contexts than others.

Case studies are an appropriate qualitative method when the researcher wants to provide a 'dense' description of a phenomenon. It is mainly grounded in first-hand empirical data, which means that it is holistic (gives a fully covering picture) and provides a picture that is close to the real situation. This information is simple for the reader to understand, sheds light on different meanings and can generate 'silent' (or tacit) knowledge. Above all, however, case studies are valuable because they provide information based on which one can make an assessment. Such an assessment is the final result of an evaluation (Merriam, 1998). Therefore, case studies generally include description, interpretation, evaluation and assessment.

Wigren (2007) states that qualitative studies represent a spread of different qualitative techniques and approaches. She refers to Denzin and Lincoln (1994:2), who define qualitative research in the following way: 'Qualitative research is multimethod in focus, involving an interpretive, naturalistic approach to its subject matter. This means that qualitative researchers study things in their natural settings, attempting to make sense of, or interpret, phenomena in terms of the meaning people bring to them.' Thus, conducting qualitative studies means learning from experiences of the people and organizations involved. I mainly gathered data by talking to (rather than interviewing) people in different positions. I have had regular meetings and made follow-up calls with people involved in the initiatives to check the status of the initiatives. Through these people I also obtained different secondary sources of documentation, like protocols, which I used with caution. I have been careful not to accept any sources too lightly without checking them first and this means that I have compared them with other sources and checked with people who are able to verify them.

It is difficult to use the term 'successful' when talking about public entrepreneurship initiatives that aim to create social value and to contribute to social change. There are many qualitative but few quantitative factors, a matter that makes assessment difficult. Further, it is hard to measure exactly how a specific initiative has contributed to social change in a certain context and what time span should be used. However, public entrepreneurship deals with change and although many initiatives have vague visions and goals, most initiatives formulate some goals for what they want to change and what they want to achieve. This provides the opportunity to compare with goals set in advance. These goals may be more or less clear. Further, they may be more qualitative or more quantitative in character. Either way, one should be able to assess that an initiative has created social value and contributed to social change. Even though these changes are small and it is difficult to comment on their long-term effects, together with other initiatives they represent a direction or trend in cities like Malmö and Landskrona today.

CASES OF PUBLIC ENTREPRENEURSHIP IN MALMÖ AND LANDSKRONA

In this section I present my cases on public entrepreneurship initiatives in Malmö and Landskrona. I include an introduction to the cases in which I present the background for each city and the specific neighbourhoods of Rosengård in Malmö and Öster in Landskrona. These two districts are concrete contexts and environments where marginalization and unemployment take place.

An Introduction to Malmö and Rosengård

The residential and labour market segregation presented in the background section above, in many ways matches the process of a particular district in Malmö, namely Rosengård. Malmö is the third largest city in Sweden with a population of little more than 270 000 inhabitants. The Rosengård district has almost 8000 apartments in nine quarters. About 50 per cent of the apartments are owned by the public municipal housing company in Malmö (MKB Fastighets AB) and the rest by private landlords (Cars and Hagetoft, 2000). About 21 000 people live in the area and the majority of them have their roots in other countries in the world (Official statistics about Malmö).[2]

The infrastructure in areas like Rosengård is a strong heritage of the 'Million homes programme', whose aim was to build 1 million new apartments in Sweden in ten years (1965–1974). The result in Malmö – as in most Swedish cities – was large-scale housing city-quarters or suburbs. Many of them, like Rosengård, comprise high-rise buildings, a lack of focus on outdoor living facilities and no division of public, semi-public and private space. Between 1967 and 1974, close to 6000 new apartments were built in Rosengård, which meant that around 25 000 people were offered a place to live. According to Cars and Hagetoft (2000, p. 3), these new residents were filled with a 'pioneer spirit'. However, soon after its completion, a debate arose that was critical of construction projects like Rosengård. The critical voices stated that the project was focused on mere rationality, efficiency and profit, without caring about the people who should live there. Naturally, the neighbourhood and its residents took a beating in the debate, further nurtured by the fact that they were without real power to affect what was said. Besides, it became clear that services in the area, such as child care, were not adequate. This negative process was further nurtured when the economic recession appeared in the early 1970s. Malmö, an old manufacturing blue-collar worker town, faced worse problems than many other cities in Sweden, and many of the people who had just moved to Rosengård belonged to that category. Soon after that, empty flats started to appear in Rosengård. When the Rosengård project was finalized in the mid-1970s, many rootless people lived in the neighbourhood, and with the immigration waves that followed in the years to come, this situation worsened. One social project after another was initiated with little or no success. Cars and Hagetoft (2000) claim that they have failed because they are not anchored locally, which means that the residents cannot relate or commit to them.

Rosengård has fewer residents today than when the neighbourhood was completed in the mid-1970s, but since the 1990s the numbers have slowly increased. The average age is relatively low, and there is an overrepresentation of young people and children. This consistently high number of school and pre-school children also indicates that the population is not stabilizing. As previously noted, the number of immigrants is high. In the whole city of Malmö, about one out of four has an immigrant background. In Rosengård, the number of immigrants is 75 per cent, or three out of four. There are high proportions of refugees from Yugoslavia, Bosnia and Iraq in the neighbourhood. Typical for the neighbourhood is a high turnover in apartments. The municipal housing company – MKB Fastighets AB – has equal or lower vacancy levels in other areas in Malmö.

Official websites of the City of Malmö state that Malmö has a higher unemployment rate than average for Sweden (5.2 per cent as against 4.1 per cent).[3] In Rosengård, these numbers are much higher, although there are big differences within the neighbourhood. For the whole area of Rosengård, the number of people in employment is 37 per cent, but only 8 per cent were registered as unemployed.[4] This implies that many people seem to have abandoned hope of ever getting a job and/or have lost faith in official actors. Further, although it is difficult to study the activities in a shadow economy, there are likely to be hidden figures within a rather influential black economy. However, one should bear in mind that some studies tend to lean to the conclusion that the unemployed are less inclined to become involved in black market activities than people who are already in the labour market (see for example a report from the Swedish Tax Authority).[5] Further, about one quarter of the residents receive social allowance, and Cars and Hagetoft (2000) claim that the social allowance dependency is as high as 50 per cent. The average income is 14 per cent lower than for the city of Malmö as a whole. Disposable income has decreased for both men and women since the 1990s, and women have a lower income than men. It is important to make clear that there are differences within the Rosengård neighbourhood. In quarters with only rental flats, a majority of the households live on social allowances.

An Introduction to Landskrona and Öster

The distance between Landskrona and Malmö is only about 40 km (24.85 miles), but the cities differ in size and background. At the same time, there are similarities, mainly in the adjustment to a new economic reality with new conditions. A new economy has to replace the old, and this transition has affected both cities.

Landskrona – just like Malmö – is an old shipyard town. However, according to statistics at the official website of the municipality of Landskrona, since the town only has a population of about 40 000 people,[6] its dependency on this particular industry was greater. In the 1970s, around 40 per cent of the working population worked in the town's shipyard 'Landskronavarvet' (Andersson et al., 2002). Therefore, the shipyard crisis that followed in the late 1970s and early 1980s affected Landskrona deeply. In 1983, the decision to terminate the yard's business was taken, leaving several thousands of people unemployed. Although major government programmes were initiated to help these people find new jobs or start studying, there was a severe decline in the town, economically but also mentally and morally.

From 1985 to 2000, Landskrona had a refugee camp that annually received between 50 and 75 refugees. Between 1993 and 1995, following the war in former Yugoslavia, Landskrona received 2000 refugees, which corresponds to 5–10 per cent of the town's population. This put pressure on the town, and a treaty from 1994 between the municipality and the Swedish Immigration Agency states that Landskrona should aim to receive no more refugees for the years that followed. Despite this, over the last ten years about 100 refugees per year have arrived and settled in Landskrona. Landskrona today has an immigrant population of about 20–25 per cent, and according to a manifesto about integration in Landskrona accepted by the municipal council in 2001, the town is facing problems with labour and residential segregation, unemployment and high rates of social allowance dependency.[7] Major immigrant groups are (in declining numbers) people from former Yugoslavia (including Albanians), Danes, Bosnians (who now count as a separate group since Bosnia is now an independent country), Finns, Germans and Lebanese (Andersson et al., 2002). While Malmö has its segregated areas at the outskirts or in certain areas outside the city centre, Landskrona has its problem areas in the very centre of the town. Thus, Landskrona differs from most other Swedish cities in this respect, and instead it can be compared to the situation in many cities in the USA, where the middle- and upper-classes move to the suburbs and leave the less fortunate in declining city cores (Webster, 1995). One such area is Öster.

In 2001, Landskronahem acquired apartments in the Öster area, located close to the town centre. One reason was that Landskronahem wanted to offer more centrally located apartments to its tenants. Further, since the 1990s the situation at Öster had been a burden for the housing market in Landskrona, and since Landskronahem was the major housing company, it was strongly affected by this situation. By acquiring apartments in Öster, the company wanted to drive the development in the right direction. From the very beginning, Landskronahem was aware that the situation in Öster could not be solved by only using traditional methods for a housing company, that is, by renovating and maintaining the physical structure of the area and the buildings. In 2002, the company board decided to launch the Österprojektet for a period of three years, from 1 January 2003 to 31 December 2005.

The report that evaluated the Österprojektet[8] states that it covered a number of sub-projects. Sometimes these were part of the bigger overall project, sometimes they were collaborations across borders of different activities, sometimes they were generated from the overall project and sometimes just sponsored economically or morally by the overall project. What made the Österprojektet different were the many social and cultural sub-projects. Altogether, about 15 different subfields with projects and initiatives were somehow connected to the overall project. Examples are projects like Barnen i Centrum ('Children in the Centre'), Levande Centrum ('Living Centre'), as well as a concrete physical rebuilding of the Öster area, scientific projects, cultural projects and marketing projects.

The evaluation of Österprojektet was based on five criteria: (1) the quality in living, both concerning property management and investments and improvement measures in the living environment; (2) the development of Öster as a neighbourhood in Landskrona, focusing on social and economical business ratios; (3) the marketing effort carried out to promote a living at Öster; (4) the attractiveness of Öster as an alternative on the housing market in Landskrona; (5) an evaluation of the effort made at Öster. The overall evaluation shows that some internal goals have been reached while others have not been fulfilled. There are still things to improve, particularly concerning security, since tenants do not feel as safe in Öster as they do in other areas of Landskrona. However, in an overall perspective most factors have been improved during the three years the project lasted. As an example, the percentage of people dependent on social allowance has dropped from around 35–40 per cent in 2002 to around 25 per cent in 2004.

Immigration and Globalization: the Development in an International Perspective

Although cities like Malmö and Landskrona and the areas of Rosengård and Öster have unique and specific characteristics, they are also affected by outside forces. Immigration does not take place in a vacuum. Many other international processes affect where, what and how immigration takes place and the order and intensity of that process. For example, Cars and Hagetoft (2000, p. 4) conclude that Rosengård's problems 'were no longer isolated problems in one neighbourhood; they consisted of a complexity of symptoms that were a reflection of an entire society in crisis, with often unpredictable structural transformations and increasing marginalisation of substantial groups of the population'. Thus, the situation in Rosengård and Öster mirrors many characteristics of residential and labour market segregation, both in Sweden and internationally.

Sassen (1998) asserts that the USA as an 'immigration country' should acknowledge its responsibility for how immigrants live in the country. Derrida (2001) also makes this statement when he discusses the duty of the host and that the rights to residence for refugees – not just visitation – must be regulated. From the description of the historical process of, for example,

Rosengård, research states that official policies have greatly contributed to the situation and thus authorities should take a great deal of responsibility regarding helping people (Cars and Hagetoft, 2000). This help could include actual support for public entrepreneurship initiatives incorporating and engaging citizens themselves, like the ones presented below.

A Public Entrepreneurship Initiative in Malmö: Job Emergency

MKB has a tradition of initiating and/or engaging in different activities in Rosengård. MKB have initiated some of these projects themselves, but most are results of collaborations with other actors. MKB's role is then more of support whereby the company utilizes its position as a strong and influential actor. One concrete example is an alternative employment agency outside the official system in Malmö where people can go on a daily basis to find out about new temporary jobs. This is called 'Job Emergency' ('Jobbakuten' in Swedish, and started in 1998) (see www.jobbakuten.nu). MKB initiated the idea and hired a private consulting firm to run the organization. The reason for their interest in a venture like this is that it aims to provide jobs for its tenants. 'The background was that the tenants came to us and asked if we could help them find a job. We're no unemployment agency, but when the official unemployment agency shut down its office here in Rosengård we came up with the idea to start an alternative unemployment agency. That's what we've done', the 'project leader for social issues' at MKB and the driving person behind this initiative, explains.

Job Emergency matches people who want a job with companies that need to increase their workforce for a short or long period. Registration is free of charge and the service is also free for the companies that use it. The demands are that the employer pays wages according to contract and has proper insurance for the workforce. In practice, the initiative works in the following way: employers who want temporary workers contact Job Emergency and specify what skills they need. The people who work with the organization then try to match the qualifications with the people who want a job. People who look for jobs can sign up in a database, but they can also contact Job Emergency on a daily basis to find out about new jobs. This practice works as follows: a minibus labelled Job Emergency drives to different blocks in Rosengård according to a schedule set in advance. People who look for a job come to the bus and find out if there are any jobs available that match their qualifications and skills. According to the project leader at the private consulting firm:

> Typically, many jobs are service jobs in restaurants or cleaning firms so there are no high demands on the people that should do the job. But there are also

> craftsmen that need people to carry out different jobs and we have many qualified immigrants that can do jobs in carpentry, painting, water and electricity installation.

No official registration is done regarding these jobs, since the idea is to get people who are motivated to find a job and not the ones who want to register for another period of unemployment benefit or social allowance. The initiative has been successful in creating new jobs, whereof most are temporary in character. One person at MKB involved in the initiative says: 'These temporary jobs give these people references and if they do a good job, they have chances to get a permanent job. This is a means for the employers to test someone without taking big financial risks.'

Voices have been raised stating that this is nothing a public housing company should engage in. The newspapers have said things like 'MKB annoys the official unemployment agency'. 'But I think this is exactly what a public housing company should do', the project leader for social issues at MKB emphasizes. 'This is management of living, not just management of housing! For us it is a key issue to work for the tenants in the grey zones that lie between government, private and municipal activities.' The reasoning behind this thinking is that parents and children who are occupied in activities they regard as meaningful assist in creating stable and pleasant neighbourhoods with minimal damage. Also that employment is a recipe against segregation – and partly also against health problems.

The results have overall been positive. Just three years after the initiative started, Job Emergency's register has covered more than 100 businesses and more than 800 people who wanted a job. 'We know that many of these people never were enrolled in the official government unemployment agency's databases', the project leader at the private consulting firm says. His explanation for this fact is that many people – and particularly immigrants and ethnic minorities – are suspicious of official actors like the unemployment agency. The project leader for social issues at MKB states:

> There could be many reasons for this. One is that they come from countries where people generally are suspicious or afraid of government actors and they also identify us [MKB] as one. And they don't know what the unemployment agency stands for. Sometimes their knowledge about the Swedish society is very poor.

He continues by saying that the official unemployment agency has failed to reach these people and build trust with them. 'Despite nice words and big programs these people have got little help.'

The rolling bus also visited other districts in Malmö. Thus, Job Emergency spread outside Rosengård and incorporated several neighbourhoods in Malmö. In fact, the city of Malmö was so impressed by its results that in 2004 it started its own Job Emergency – including a minibus – which used the same concept. However, the initiative will be terminated at the end of 2007. 'Partly this has to do with the favourable labour market at the moment. And the initiative may have outplayed its role since even the city accepted and incorporated the idea', a person at MKB involved in the initiative says. Besides, he adds that people within the MKB organization claim that the costs generated by Job Emergency are greater than the benefits from the jobs created. 'But that's the downside of projects like this. If we can't count them as profitable within a short time period, people don't see the larger social values they produce.'

A Public Entrepreneurship Initiative in Landskrona: Business Pool

Just like MKB, Landskronahem has ambition to improve conditions for its tenants. One example is the above-mentioned Österprojektet, where Landskronahem was one of the main actors. This project included many other actors, including grassroots people who are able to work with the tenants directly using their natural venues. Another concrete example was initiated a couple of years ago. A group of public and private actors – including actors from Landskronahem – formed an informal network named 'Business Pool' ('Företagspoolen' in Swedish) which aims to increase employment among members of an immigrant community where unemployment is high.

The background was that out of about 150 adult members of the local basketball club BF Bosna Basket in Landskrona, only one had a job. These people were Bosnian immigrants who arrived in the early 1990s when the war broke out in former Yugoslavia. 'I spoke to people from the basketball club and I found this shocking when I heard about it!', remarked the contact person in the managerial body with the title 'project leader' at Landskronahem. He says that he finds the question of employment a key issue for making life better for the tenants. 'I felt I had to do something. I somehow "own" the question because many of these people are tenants that live in Landskronahem's apartments. And since I have connections I was in a position to help.' BF Bosna Basket was the owner of the initiative. The original actors included – besides the above-mentioned basketball club and Landskronahem – a local bank, a tenants' society, a local private company and two private landlords. This initiative was launched in 2002 in a context outside the professional agendas of these people and organizations, and was something they did not get paid to do, which means that they did not have much time to spend on this initiative. This also explains why the Business Pool is not that well-known among the wider public.

The aim is to form a basis for employment, and whenever a member of the network gets the information that there is a free job position somewhere, they turn to the immigrant community to see if there is anyone qualified. 'The financial support to the initiative is of course important, but we can also act as "door openers" for the adult immigrant population in Landskrona. With our help, they may integrate better in society and thereby get a job', the CEO for the tenant society says. For example, they can provide references which will aid job applications. Recently, one person who had earlier been employed by the local bank involved in the initiative secured a new position at that bank. His previous job was at the counter, but he had to resign after the bank was robbed. Unfortunately, memories from his past in the former Yugoslavia exacerbated the psychological reaction and shock following this experience. He had a gun pointed at him in the past, and the bank robbery brought back traumatic memories. However, the back-office job he was offered minimized the risk that he would have to face the same situation again. 'Of course I'm a bit nervous, but I'm thankful for this opportunity', he says.

The Business Pool was appreciated and from the original five initiators, between 10 and 20 big and small companies and institutions later became involved in the initiative. These actors have contacts with other companies and thus they have a good opportunity to scan the labour market for both formal and informal job opportunities. In 2004, when the basketball club wanted to do something about high rates of unemployment among young adults aged 18–25 – an initiative called 'Our Future' ('Vår Framtid' in Swedish) – they used the Business Pool as an important part of the basis for an application to the European Union.

Since the network started, around 50 per cent of the original 150 adults have got different kinds of jobs – both temporary and permanent – as a consequence of this project. 'It's not sufficient, but it's better than that only one person has a job. And this is done with small costs for the actors involved. The big investment is the personal commitment by the members of the network', the project leader at Landskronahem stated. Today, however, the initiative has been inactive for more than a year since the originator and former chairman of the basketball club has moved from Landskrona. The project leader at Landskronahem summarizes: 'Despite the actual and potential value of an initiative like this, to a large extent it is dependent on key people. If important people leave the initiative, the initiative can fade away.'

Unlike Job Emergency in Malmö, Business Pool never began in a limited geographical context. Instead, it was the immigrant group that was the focus. 'But all people are welcome', the project leader at Landskronahem assures. Thus, other people outside this group can also turn to the pool for help. 'We wouldn't support an initiative that discriminates people. The problem rather is that it is hard to reach certain groups – particularly immigrants – and we need to connect to leading people with influence on members of those groups', he adds. However, Landskrona is a much smaller town than Malmö and initiatives can more easily be distributed throughout the city. The people involved in Business Pool see no limitations but intend to enhance the network and the concept further. 'In the longer run, new initiatives and networks who use the same concept could embrace more immigrant communities. We may be able to create something new out of this', one representative from BF Bosna Basket states.

ANALYSIS OF THE CONTRIBUTIONS OF THE CASES

Both the Job Emergency and Business Pool initiatives are examples of entrepreneurship that has a social mission to create social value and contribute to social change. Relating them to theories on this topic, much of what the paramount field of social entrepreneurship covers is relevant in the light of the cases. However, in order to create a deeper understanding regarding the practices of these two initiatives, there is a need for public entrepreneurship theories as well. Briefly, I use the cases to go through the conceptualizations on social entrepreneurship deriving from Dees' (1998) six points and thereafter I move on to discuss the three additional points covered by Hjorth and Bjerke's (2006) conceptualizations on public entrepreneurship that I presented in the theoretical section.

Using Social Entrepreneurship Theories

Social mission, social value, acting as change agents in the social sector, measuring impact

Both initiatives have a clear focus on an important social problem. The people involved definitely have a social mission with these initiatives and they have also succeeded in creating social value and contributing to social change. They have also assured that they – at least to an acceptable extent – measure the impact these initiatives have on the situation for the target group.

Innovative

They also organize these initiatives in new and creative ways, particularly in those contexts and environments. In this way, the organizers are able to provide a springboard for the aims of these initiatives: that they are able to come up with new solutions to severe social problems we face today and will face tomorrow.

No resource constraints
The actors involved in the initiatives are not hindered by lack of resources. In fact, they rather find ways to minimize the use of resources. In comparison with the billions of euros the national government has spent on big support programmes – that to a large extent can be regarded as failures – these initiatives show that collaborative organizations can contribute to change using few resources. This emphasizes the potential effectiveness of small and informal new solutions in comparison to large and inflexible structures.

Bringing in Public Entrepreneurship Theories

No matter how relevant social entrepreneurship theories are, it is evident that if we really want to understand what the cases consist of and how they can contribute to social change we need to incorporate theories on public entrepreneurship as it is conceptualized by Hjorth and Bjerke (2006).

Public issue
The notion of the public extends beyond that of the social. It is clear that both Job Emergency and Business Pool have social missions, want to increase social value and contribute to social change. However, the actors have recognized that the public issue at hand – employment opportunities for marginalized citizens in segregated areas (including immigrants) – is precisely a public issue, that is that it concerns all citizens and nobody can disclaim responsibility for it. Still, this is something that the actors involved did not have to do, but they realized they were in a position to help and took responsibility.

Create sociality
It is obvious that the actors who formed the initiatives and the networks around them are committed to providing jobs when possible. They do not even use the initiatives to market themselves externally and they do not let their own interests take over. They deal with a public issue and try to gather others to foster a common view that says they can collaborate to do something and make a difference.

Act as citizens
The initiators involved act rather as citizens than as professionals. If they were to act as professionals, they probably would have done things differently and perhaps also different things. Now they act as citizens who help other citizens. This connects to the discussion about both the public issue and the sociality sections above. They neither have the need nor the

ambition to use this in their marketing, although it might be a good thing to use them as part of their goodwill in order to make these initiatives more visible.

Public Entrepreneurship an Important Concept for the Future

One should bear in mind that Job Emergency and Business Pool are relatively small initiatives in limited contexts. However, by using new solutions they were able to make a difference regarding public issues. The Job Emergency initiative wanted to help marginalized people without jobs. The actors involved in the Business Pool initiative engaged in the public issue of unemployment among members of an immigrant group. Although similar initiatives may exist elsewhere, when they were introduced Job Emergency and Business Pool were innovative in their specific contexts and environments. They were committed to improving employment for marginalized people in urban environments and acted to find new ways to deal with this situation in the particular contexts and environments, that is the cities of Malmö and Landskrona.

Further, one should remember that these initiatives to a certain degree are controversial. In the local debate, actors have wondered if public housing companies should engage in such matters and collaborations. This may be a reason why these initiatives start in a modest and rather secretive manner. However, one important matter with these initiatives is precisely that they are initiated in the first place. This shows that Malmö and Landskrona may be heading in the direction Henton et al. (1997) talk about: the collaborative advantage that makes cities and regions competitive in comparison to other cities and regions. Characteristic for such cities/regions is that actors from different sectors collaborate and that the collaborative networks are permeated by public entrepreneurship. Further, Henton et al. (1997) define a few key individuals – the public entrepreneurs that exemplify this spirit. In the cases presented in this text, the developing manager at MKB (Job Emergency) and the contact person/project leader at Landskronahem are the people who come closest to being labelled public entrepreneurs. Who the public entrepreneurs will be higher up in the hierarchy in the cities of Malmö and Landskrona, hopefully is a story that time will tell.

Public Housing Companies as Public Entrepreneurs

The cases show that public housing companies can play an important role in creating social value and contributing to social change and thus have a key role in public entrepreneurship initiatives. They have natural connections to citizens who need help and they are also able to build trustful relations with these citizens. The cases show that the tenants – that is the citizens – asked for help, and the people at the housing companies (and other actors involved) felt that they were in a position to help. Although the 'public' in public housing companies mainly equates with the term 'official', in these instances they take a public responsibility in the sense that Hjorth and Bjerke (2006) talk about: they engage in a public issue that concerns all citizens and try to do something about it. In Sweden today there are legal barriers to what public housing companies can do. However, if public (and private) housing companies had the opportunity to engage more in different initiatives, they could help to shape whole local neighbourhoods. It is perhaps far-fetched, but not unlikely that MKB could run local neighbourhood schools in a not-too-distant future. In the past, MKB provided facilities as replacement classrooms when a local school shut down. Thus, such ideas and local collaborations already exist. In an international perspective this may not seem to be a big deal, but in Sweden this is definitely an innovation. One could even speak about a revolution in comparison to the situation only 15–20 years ago.

What can we Learn from Public Entrepreneurship Studies?

The cases presented conclude that concrete initiatives as examples of public entrepreneurship show how we can utilize people's resources at the same time as they represent the kinds of flexible and functional supportive initiatives that cities like Malmö and Landskrona need. Here, it is important to note that public entrepreneurship means engagement and participation. Public entrepreneurship has nothing to do with charity. That is, public entrepreneurship initiatives engage people and make them create value themselves. Above all, 'bottom up' initiatives that engage and include citizens directly affected by them – like the two cases in this text – are needed in order to foster motivation, commitment and participation. These 'bottom up' initiatives have different logics and drivers than those that are simply 'top-down' implemented from above. This is particularly true if a number of actors with different backgrounds come together and collaborate. Thereby, just as the literature suggests, heterogeneity and diversity foster entrepreneurship to become more effective (Johannisson, 1994; Aldrich, 1999).

One of the main reasons for conducting research on public entrepreneurship should be to create knowledge based on learning about why public entrepreneurship creates change and makes a difference for citizens, that is, revitalizes cities/regions and societies. The research should also help us to understand how public entrepreneurship initiatives:

- Create sociality and collaboration;
- Create new spaces, both physical and mental;
- Make participative actors form functional collaborations.

There has been talk about the importance of sociality in this text, and sociality is conceptualized as mutual consensus concerning how a phenomenon in society ought to be. However, reality is seldom as simple as that a number of actors from different sectors come together and form functional collaborations around a public issue regarding which they have the same view. Rather, there are negotiations or conflicts where some actors demonstrate and exert power to get what they want. One has to remember that generally actors have their own reasons for participating in these collaborations. I do not discuss the question of power further, but recognize that it is of crucial importance for the success of public initiatives that the participating actors are able to realize that it is the public issue and nothing else that is in focus, that is that they create sociality around a certain phenomenon and leave their own special interests behind.

CONCLUDING DISCUSSION

At the beginning of this chapter, I concluded that there is a rising interest in new initiatives and processes that have social missions. This is nothing new as such. Entrepreneurship has been present throughout the history of mankind, albeit in different forms and sometimes with other labels. But just as with increasing globalization (movement of people, resources and so on), the order and intensity of such processes and initiatives have increased rapidly (and probably are still speeding up at an ever-increasing rate). It is not possible to grasp all parts of such complex processes: society is genuinely complex, to use a semantic paradox.

It is argued that what I refer to as public entrepreneurship is crucial as a means of (re-)vitalizing a city or a region, and even whole societies (Henton et al., 1997; Catford, 1998). But there are voices stating that civil society with strong citizen engagement can only be restored at the community, not the national, level (Sandel, 1996). Bringing in voices from the field of globalization and immigration, Kapur (1997) argues that in today's globalized world local initiatives unite people, even if they live at the very borders of this globalized world – mentally or physically – or do not participate fully in public life. This may be part of an answer: an enterprising spirit where people form collaborative initiatives to get their voices heard (Hymes, 1996) and simultaneously form alliances with other minorities (Asad, 2000) in order to increase their influence and power in today's society. Thereby, phrases and concepts like inclusion and integration can find a breeding ground to function in practice.

Finally, I want to calm sceptics who may think this looks like the emperor's new clothes. Public entrepreneurship is a new concept that reflects the society of today and the society of tomorrow, but it is yet to be studied closely by researchers. What are needed in order to challenge these new processes in society scientifically are thorough studies of public entrepreneurship initiatives and the processes that take place in relation to these initiatives. That is, to study and evaluate public entrepreneurship initiatives critically and analyse their role in creating social value and contributing to social change (if, how, why and where). We need to create learning and knowledge concerning what these public entrepreneurship initiatives mean to cities like Malmö and Landskrona. We also need to evaluate what aspects are context-specific and what aspects are more general in order to make clear what learning and knowledge can be transferred to other cities and regions and perhaps to higher levels, like the nation, the European Union or the so-called industrialized world. In a wider perspective, research on public entrepreneurship should cover what value public entrepreneurship initiatives may bring to cities, regions and societies today and in the future. I would like to see more local studies in different settings that show how public entrepreneurship initiatives affect these cities and/or regions. We would gain much knowledge from comparisons of cases that can help us understand commonalities and differences. Learning experiences from such studies can help us navigate through the challenges we face today and meet the challenges we will face tomorrow.

NOTES

1. http://www.oxfordreference.com/views/ENTRY.html?subview=Main&entry=t150.e75663.
2. http://www.malmo.se/stadsdelar/rosengard/ faktaomrosengard.4.33aee30d103b8f15916800046362.html.
3. http://www.malmo.se/download/18.fe3a2d310a090ba6c380005954/M-info+KLAR+mars+06+F%C3%A4rg.pdf.
4. http://www.malmo.se/download/18.d2883b106e53ae64c80001627/20.Roseng%C3%A5rd.pdf+2005.
5. http://www.skatteverket.se/download/18.18e1b10334ebe8bc8000111627/1521j.pdf.
6. http://www.landskrona.se/pages/cgi-bin/PUB_Latest_Version.exe?pageId=1434&allFrameset=1&r=1148903756934.
7. http://www.landskrona.se/pages/cgi-bin/PUB_View_File.exe?pageId=1393&objType= 4&versionId=1&objByName=Vi%20kan%20bättre.doc.
8. The text about the Österprojektet is mainly is mainly taken from an internal report that evaluates the Österprojecktet entitled 'Österprojektet I Landskrona: utvärdering av Börje Winker våren 2006' (Wikner, 2006).

REFERENCES

Aldrich, H.E. (1999), *Organizations Evolving*, Thousand Oaks, Sage Publications.

Alvarez, S. and L.B. Busenitz (2001), 'The entrepreneurship of resource-based theory', *Journal of Management*, **27**, 755–75.

Andersson, Å., J. Malmsten and A.S. Wigerfelt (2002), 'Delrapport II till Integrationsverket angående Landskrona kommuns arbete mot rasism och främlingsfientlighet inom ramen för pilotkommunprojektet', report to the Swedish Immigration Agency, available at: http://www.sverigemotrasism.nu/upload/docs/landskrona2.doc (accessed 29 May 2006).

Asad, T. (2000), 'Muslims and European identity', in E. Hallam and B.V. Street (eds), *Cultural Encounters*, London: Routledge, pp. 11–27.

Åslund, O. (2000), 'Health, immigration and settlement policies', Doctoral dissertation, *Economic Studies*, no. 53, Uppsala.

Baber, K. (2004), *The Canadian Oxford Dictionary*, Oxford University Press, *Oxford Reference Online*, Oxford University Press, Malmö högskola, 16 November 2007, available at: http://www.oxfordreference.com/views/ENTRY.html?subview=Main&entry=t150.e75663.

Bjerke, B. and T. Dalhammar (2006), 'Public entrepreneurship – definitely different', paper presented at the UIC Research Symposium, Chicago, 2–4 August 2006.

Bjerke, B., D. Hjorth, H. Larsson and C.-J. Asplund (2007), *Publikt entreprenörskap – det marginella görs centralta* (*Public Entrepreneurship – The Marginal is Being Made Central*), Folkbildningsföreningen, Malmö: Att bygga den glokala staden 1 (To build the global city 1), Holmbergs Malmö 2007.

Bornstein, David (1998), 'Changing the world on a shoestring', *The Atlantic Monthly*, **281**(1), 34–9.

Cars, G. and J. Hagetoft (2000), 'Evaluation of local socio-economic strategies in disadvantaged urban areas: case study report on Malmö-Rosengård', available at: http://www.elses.ils.nrw.de/down/malmoe.pdf, accessed 10 May 2006.

Catford, J. (1998), 'Social entrepreneurs are vital for health promotion – but they need supportive environments too', Editorial, *Health Promotion International*, **13**, 95–8.

Chell, E. (2007), 'Social enterprise and entrepreneurship: towards a convergent theory of the entrepreneurial process', *International Small Business Journal*, **25**(1), 5–26.

De Leeuw, E. (1999), 'Healthy cities: urban social entrepreneurship for health', *Health Promotion International*, **14**(3), 261–69.

Dees, J.G. (1998), '*The meaning of "social entrepreneurship"*', Stanford University: draft report for the Kauffman Center for Entrepreneurial Leadership, 6 pp, available at: http://www.fntc.info/files/documents/The%20meaning%20of%20Social%20Entreneurship.pdf.

Dees, J.G., J. Emerson and P. Economy (2001), *Enterprising Nonprofits. A Toolkit for Social Entrepreneurs*, New York: John Wiley.

Dees, J.G., J. Emerson and P. Economy (2002), *Strategic Tools for Social Entrepreneurs. Enhancing the Performance of Your Enterprising Nonprofit*, New York: John Wiley.

Denzin, N. and Y. Lincoln (1994), 'Introduction: entering the field of qualitative research', in N. Denzin and Y. Lincoln (eds), *Handbook of Qualitative Research*, Thousand Oaks: Sage Publications, pp. 1–17.

Derrida, J. (2001), 'On cosmopolitanism', Part 1 from J. Derrida, *On Cosmopolitanism and Forgiveness*, London: Routledge, pp. 3–24.

Drayton, W. (2002), 'The citizen sector: becoming as competitive and entrepreneurial as business', *California Management Journal*, **12**(1), 29–43.
Dupuis, A. and A. de Bruin (2003), 'Community entrepreneurship' in A. de Bruin and A. Dupuis (eds), *Entrepreneurship: New Perspectives in a Global Age*, Aldershot, UK: Ashgate Publishing, pp. 109–27.
Ekberg, J. (1999), 'Immigration and the public sector. Income effects for the native population in Sweden', *Journal of Population Economics*, **12**(3), 411–30.
Ekberg, J. and D.-O. Rooth (2000), 'Arbetsmarknadspolitik för invandrare', Rapport till Riksdagens revisorer, *Working Paper series* no. 6, School of Management and Economics, Växjö University.
Gartner, W.B. (1985), 'A conceptual framework for describing the phenomenon of new venture creation', *Academy of Management Review*, **10**(4), 696–706.
Gartner, W.B. (1990), 'What are we talking about when we talk about entrepreneurship?', *Journal of Business Venturing*, **5**(1), 15–28.
Gendron, George (1996), 'Flashes of genius: interview with Peter Drucker', *Inc.*, 16 May, **18**(7), 30–37.
Henton, D., J. Melville and K. Walesh (1997), *Grassroots Leaders for a New Economy: How Civic Entrepreneurs are Building Prosperous Communities*, San Francisco, USA: Jossey-Bass.
Hjorth, D. and B. Bjerke (2006), 'Public entrepreneurship: from social/consumer to public/citizen', in C. Steyaert and D. Hjorth (eds), *Entrepreneurship as Social Change*, Cheltenham, UK and Northampton, MA, USA: Edward Elgar.
Hymes, D. (1996), *Ethnography, Linguistics, Narrative Inequality: Toward an Understanding of Voice*, London: Taylor & Francis.
Internal report about Österprojektet, *Österprojektet i Landskrona: Utvärdering av Börje Wikner våren 2006*.
Jobbakuten's web page, source: www.jobbakuten.nu, accessed 5 May 2007.
Johannisson, B. (1994), *Entrepreneurial Networks. Some Conceptual and Methodological Notes*, Lund: Institutet för Ekonomisk Forskning.
Johnson, S. (2003), 'Young social entrepreneurs in Canada', Canadian Centre for Social Entrepreneurship, University of Alberta, available at, http://www.business.ualberta.ca/ccse/publications/default.htm, accessed 7 May 2007.
Kapur, G. (1997), 'Globalization and culture,' *Third Text*, **39**, 21–38.
McLeod, H. (1997), 'Cross over: the social entrepreneur', *Inc.*, Special Issue: State of Small, **19**(7), 100–104.
Merriam, S.B. (1998), *Fallstudien som Forskningsmetod*, Lund: Studentlitteratur.
Official websites of the City of Malmö, available at: http://www.malmo.se/download/18.fe3a2d310a090ba6c380005954/M-info+KLAR+mars+06+F%C3%A4rg.pdf (accessed 10 May 2006).
Official websites of the City of Malmö, available at: http://www.malmo.se/download/18.d2883b106e53ae64c80001627/20.Roseng%C3%A5rd.pdf+2005 (accessed 10 May 2006).
Official websites of the municipality of Landskrona, available at: http://www.landskrona.se/pages/cgi-bin/PUB_Latest_Version.exe?pageId=1434&allFrameset=1&r=1148903756934 (accessed 29 May 2006).
Osborne, D. and T. Gaebler (1993), *Reinventing Government*, New York: Penguin Books.
Peredo, A.M. and M. McLean (2006), 'Social entrepreneurship: a critical review of the concept', *Journal of World Business*, **41**, 56–65.

Piore, M.J. and C.F. Sabel (1984), *The Second Industrial Divide. Possibilities for Prosperity*, New York: Basic Books.

Rehn, A. and S. Taalas (2004), '(Acquaintances and connections) – Blat, the Soviet Union, and mundane entrepreneurship', *Entrepreneurship & Regional Development*, **16**, pp. 235–50.

Report at the website of the municipality of Landskrona (2001), 'Vi kan bättre! – Integrations- och mångfaldsprogram för Landskrona kommun', available at: http://www.landskrona.se/pages/cgi-bin/PUB_View_File.exe?pageId=1393&objType=4&versionId=1&objByName=Vi%20kan%20bättre.doc, (accessed 29 May 2006).

Report at the website of the Swedish tax authority, available at: http://www.skatteverket.se/download/18.18e1b10334ebe8bc8000111627/1521j.pdf (accessed 10 May 2006).

Sandel, M. (1996), *Democracy's Discontent: America in Search of a Public Philosophy*, Cambridge, MA: Belknap Press.

Sassen, S. (1998), 'America's immigration "problem"', in S. Sassen, *Globalization and its Discontents*, New York: The New Press, pp. 31–53.

Scott, J. and G. Marshall (2005), *A Dictionary of Sociology*, Oxford University Press; *Oxford Reference Online*, Oxford University Press, Malmo högskola, 16 November 2007, available at: http://www.oxfordreference.com/views/ENTRY.html?subview=Main&entry=t88.e242.

Soanes, C. and A. Stevenson (eds) (2006), *The Concise Oxford English Dictionary*, 11th edn revised, Oxford University Press, *Oxford Reference Online*, Oxford University Press, Malmo högskola, 16 November 2007, available at: http://www.oxfordreference.com/views/ENTRY.html?subview=Main&entry=t23.e28576.

Spinosa, C., F. Flores and H.L. Dreyfus (1997), *Disclosing New Worlds: Entrepreneurship, Democratic Action, and the Cultivation of Solidarity*, Cambridge, MA: MIT Press.

Sullivan Mort, G., J. Weerawardena and K. Carnegie (2003), 'Social entrepreuship: towards conceptualisation', *International Journal of Nonprofit and Voluntary Sector Marketing*, **8**(1), 76–88.

Thompson, J., G. Alvy and A. Lees, (2000), 'Social entrepreneurship – a new look at the people and the potential', *Management Decision*, **38**(5), 328–38.

Webster, F. (1995), 'Information and urban change: Manuel Castells', in F. Webster, *Theories of the Information Society*, London: Routledge, pp. 193–214.

Wigren, C. (2007), 'Assessing the quality of qualitative research in entrepreneurship', in H. Neergaard and J.P. Ulhøi (eds), *Handbook of Qualitative Research Methods in Entrepreneurship*, Cheltenham, UK and Northampton, MA, USA: Edward Elgar.

Wikner, Börje (2006), 'Österprojektet I Landskrona: utvärdering av Börje Wikner våren 2006', internal evaluation report about Österprojektet in Landskrona.

APPENDIX 4A.1 DOCUMENTATION OF MEETINGS, INTERVIEWS, PHONE CALLS AND OTHER CONTACTS

Job Emergency

Primary sources:

Meetings with the 'project leader for social issues' at MKB Fastighets AB; 5 meetings during the period 9 February 2006–24 May 2007.
Meeting with the project leader at the private consulting firm who ran Job Emergency 24 April 2006.
Meeting with operative personnel at MKB Fastighets 15 March 2007.
Phone conversations with the 'project leader for social issues' at MKB Fastighets AB. At least 10 conversations during the period 9 February 2006–24 May 2007.
Mail contacts. At least 10 mail contacts during the period 9 February 2006–24 May 2007.

Secondary sources:
Internal project documentation from MKB Fastighets AB and the private consulting firm.
Article about Job Emergency in the periodical *Bofast* March 2006.
Job Emergency's website, http://www.jobbakuten.nu.

Business Pool

Primary sources:

Meetings with the project leader from the managerial body at Landskronahem; 10 meetings during the period 9 February 2006–27 September 2007.
Meetings with representatives from BF Bosna Basket; 5 meetings during the period 5 May 2006–13 November 2007.
Phone conversations with the project leader from the managerial body at Landskronahem. At least 10 conversations during the period 9 February 2006–15 November 2007.
Mail contacts. At least 30 mail contacts during the period 9 February 2006–15 November 2007.

Secondary sources:
Internal project documentation from Landskronahem and BF Bosna Basket.
Article about Job Emergency at Landskrona Direkt 17 December 2002.
BF Bosna Basket's website, http://www.proteamonline.se/?Id=42.

5. Developing characteristics of an intrapreneurship-supportive culture

Hanns Menzel, Robert Krauss, Jan Ulijn and Mathieu Weggeman

INTRODUCTION

Intrapreneurship is nowadays a topic with a high attraction equally to many scholars and managers in companies of any size. It can be broadly defined as entrepreneurship within existing organizations, and there is broad consensus both in academia and business practice about the relevance and the need of bringing entrepreneurship into established companies. Already Schumpeter (1934), who stated that 'new enterprises are mostly founded by new men and the old businesses sink into insignificance', identified the need to instil the logic of entrepreneurship into the established businesses.

What Drucker (1985) stated some twenty years ago, that 'today's businesses, especially the large ones, simply will not survive in this period of rapid change and innovation unless they acquire entrepreneurial competence', still seems to hold true today. Besides existing small and medium sized companies (Aaltio, 2002; Carrier, 1994, 1997; Fayolle, 2003; Veenker et al., 2004), in particular big companies are turning towards intrapreneurship because they are not getting the continuing innovation, growth and value creation that they once had (Heinonen and Korvela, 2003; Mair, 2005; Pinchot, 1985; Pinchot and Pellman, 1999).

Moreover, intrapreneurship is especially important for R&D as a valuable source to develop radical innovation – that is the discovery and exploitation of completely new business opportunities that go beyond the existing mainstream business of the firm (Antoncic and Hisrich, 2003; Burgelman, 1983; Fayolle, 2003; Hornsby et al., 2002; Kelley et al., 2002; Klein, 2002; Klein and Specht, 2002; Lorange, 1999; Vanhaverbeke and Kirschbaum, 2005). Mature organizations can develop new business activities based on highly innovative technologies which they would miss without intrapreneurship.

Yet, especially large industrial companies have difficulty in accommodating intrapreneurship and managing radical innovations. Usually R&D

in these companies focuses on the short term and emphasizes incremental innovations that require the exploitation of existent resources and pathways rather than on radical innovations that demand the exploration of new and unknown paths. Furthermore, R&D engineers and scientists are often not at all entrepreneurial in their approaches. They focus too much on technical issues and lack an integrated approach. In order to facilitate intrapreneurship in R&D, both individual intrapreneurs and a supportive organizational setting must be present simultaneously.

In this respect, an emergent body of literature seeks to identify the conditions that are required in order to make intrapreneurship occur in organizations (Carrier, 1994). Several authors stress that entrepreneurial and innovating behaviours of both individuals and organizations depend on cultural factors (Anfuso, 1999; Carrier, 1994; Eesley and Longenecker, 2006; Fayolle et al., 2005; Miles and Covin, 2002; Morris et al., 1993; O'Connor and Ayers, 2005; Smith, 1998; Sommerlatte, 2001; Ulijn and Brown, 2004; Ulijn et al., 2001; Ulijn and Weggeman, 2001). Such a culture would build on all principles relating to the way an organization operates that will raise opportunities of creating profitable newness or difference in doing business. But what does this mean more concretely? What kind of organizational structures and resources should be available? What has to be provided by top management? And what are the requirements on the team and on the individual level?

Still, it is not fully clear how to define, build and measure such a culture that supports intrapreneurship in its entirety. A large body of both scholarly and practice-oriented literature deals with this topic, but a holistic approach towards modelling intrapreneurship-supportive culture still seems to be missing. Hence, this work aims to identify the relevant contributions in this domain. Based on an extensive literature review, intrapreneurship-supportive culture is conceptualized as an intersection of national, professional and corporate culture types. A framework is proposed that – once further developed and empirically tested – would serve as an instrument both to measure and to determine relevant levers to shape intrapreneurship-supportive culture.

Therefore, the first section explores the underlying concepts of intrapreneurship-supportive culture – namely national, professional, and organizational culture – and their interaction. Then, the second section presents the literature review by clustering and assigning retrieved factors and constituents to cultural dimensions. Leading on from this rich reservoir of knowledge, the third section describes and assesses the profile of an intrapreneurship-supportive culture. Finally, the fourth section discusses the results and gives recommendations about how to shape, implement and maintain an intrapreneurship-supportive culture on the organizational level.

BUILDING BLOCKS OF AN INTRAPRENEURSHIP-SUPPORTIVE CULTURE

An appreciation of the importance of culture and cultural differences is highly relevant for entrepreneurship and innovation. From an organization's point of view, innovation activities are basically built around interaction processes between individuals and the surrounding organization, including the interaction and transfer of people across national, professional and corporate cultural boundaries. The seminal research by Hofstede (1980) has inspired much of the cross-cultural research activity since 1980 and has been one of the dominant research paradigms in cross-cultural studies. Culture, as Hofstede suggests, is something like the 'software of the mind', the operating system that allows human individuals to share and make sense of experience (Hofstede and Hofstede, 2005). It refers to a set of shared norms, values, beliefs and attitudes held by the members of a group, such as a nation or organization (Hofstede and Hofstede, 2005).

Recognizing and understanding differences in cultural patterns provides individuals with a framework for interpreting the goals, motivations and behaviours of others. Intrapreneurship-supportive culture can be understood as a set of culture-bound patterns shared by a group of individuals. These patterns are shaped, changed or maintained through the interaction between individuals of the group or organization. These interaction processes are fed by each single individual's 'learned' cultural background. People are born in a national culture context, acquire a certain professional culture, in particular starting from the age of 18 or earlier depending on the educational level, and are then exposed to a corporate culture when entering a company to work with. As Ulijn and Weggeman (2001) point out, these three culture types are most relevant for an individual's education and working experience and can, therefore, be considered as constituents of intrapreneurship-supportive culture (as depicted in Figure 5.1).

The human behaviour in companies is obviously influenced by the national culture of the country in which the individuals and the companies are based. Since national culture is already 'programmed' into individuals' minds early in life, where the family and later school and friends are important cultural influences, behaviour tends to be on average more or less consistent with this national culture (Hofstede, 2001; Wennekers et al., 2002). With regards to the context of intrapreneurship, this finds support from earlier work suggesting that national culture has a significant impact on how entrepreneurship and innovation is achieved (Fayolle et al., 2005; Nakata and Sivakumar, 1996; Ulijn et al., 2004). Shane et al. (1995) and Shane (1997), for instance, pinpoint national culture as a leading principle

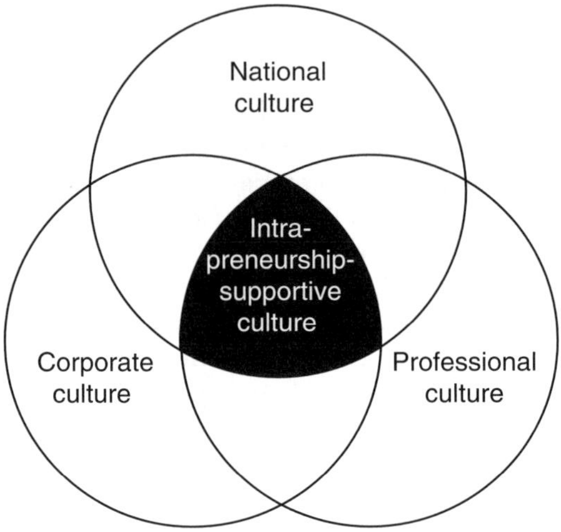

Figure 5.1 Intrapreneurship-supportive culture as the nexus of national, professional and corporate culture types

for innovative output and performance of organizations. Also Jones and Davis (2000) study the link between dimensions of national culture and innovative activities and the implications for locating global R&D operations. They conclude that national culture affects innovation and should be considered as a factor informing the location decision for innovative capabilities.

Not only does national culture play an important role for intrapreneurship, but so also does the influence of professional culture and its interaction with national culture. Professionals entering an organization bring in a large repertoire of cultural knowledge gained not only from the wider society but also from their professional training and previous work experience (Bloor and Dawson, 1994). Professional culture orientations find their roots during childhood and early years of education. A more important influence of professional culture is given later through the professional education or the studies one chooses. Certainly, both professional training on the job and university studies determine and stabilize one's professional orientation.

However, there are preliminary indications that there may be differences in professional cultures across national cultures, and to complicate matters even more, they may interact in unexpected ways (Ulijn and Weggeman, 2001). Ulijn et al. (2001) report a study that indicates that not only the professional background as such, but its interaction with national culture is decisive for this transition process. The study examines factors among German and Dutch engineers that account for a different transition from a technology towards a market orientation and the impact of national cultures. The study found that the technology versus market orientation of the Dutch engineer is not different from that of the German engineer. However, the transition from technology towards market orientation occurred earlier for the Dutch engineers than for the German ones. A plausible reason for this is that the strong feminine values of Dutch national and corporate culture (Hofstede, 1980) might lead to a customer orientation more easily than the more masculine German values keeping a strong internally driven technological base.

Besides national and professional culture, corporate culture is commonly understood to have a strong impact on innovation (Chandler et al., 2000; Peters and Waterman, 1982; Sherwood, 2002). This brings about the question why certain types of organizations are perceived to be more innovative than others, but also the question regarding what type of organizational culture this would refer to. And what organizational culture would be most appropriate to support intrapreneurship? For instance, Hofstede et al.'s (1990) typology includes dimensions of organizational culture that appear to be crucial for innovation, such as the open system, loose control or pragmatism. Ulijn and Weggeman (2001) stress that an innovation-supportive culture would prosper in an organization that is grounded on a combination of the clan/Anglo-Nordic and the guided missile/Germanic culture types. Thus, dimensions of corporate culture certainly influence intrapreneurship-supportive culture and, in turn, the innovative output and performance of a firm.

However, since the influence of corporate culture on individuals' personality occurs rather late in their careers, together with a tendency towards increased job rotation across both national and corporate culture borders, its impact on intrapreneurship-supportive culture might be weaker than is often assumed. Research indicates that even in companies that are known for their strong corporate culture, national culture remains of paramount importance in explaining its employees' business-related behaviour (Hofstede et al., 1990). National culture differences are reflected, for instance, in the way organizations solve problems in different countries, but also in the validity of management theories in the countries. Different national cultures have different preferred ways of structuring organizations and different patterns of employee motivation. For example, they limit the options for performance appraisal, management by objectives, strategic management and humanization of work. It is due to these individual-based influences that – especially large – organizations are unlikely to exhibit a homogeneous corporate culture across the entire organization.

Given this, intrapreneurship-supportive culture would be formed through the intersection of national, professional and corporate culture types. People are born in a national culture context, acquire a certain professional culture, and then they are exposed to the corporate culture of the organization they enter. Hence, an intrapreneurship-supportive culture seems to be very much rooted in the national and also professional culture imprints of the individuals. This is the picture that provides the basic understanding and framework to guide the development of a holistic conceptualization of intrapreneurship-supportive culture. The objective of the following section is, therefore, to collect – based on a literature investigation – evidence that helps to conceptualize intrapreneurship-supportive culture.

TOWARDS A DESCRIPTION OF AN INTRAPRENEURSHIP-SUPPORTIVE CULTURE

As outlined above, intrapreneurship-supportive culture would appear as an integration of national, professional and corporate cultures and refers explicitly to the intrapreneurship process: while national and professional cultures seem to be bound to the individual level, corporate culture is rather linked with the organizational level of intrapreneurship. To comprehensively describe the culture that supports intrapreneurship, an extensive literature study was conducted. Articles in scientific journals and books of the following research fields were taken into account: innovation, entre-/intrapreneurship, marketing, change management, national, professional and organizational/corporate cultures. The study has been conducted in two steps.

In the first step, constituents and factors that are deemed to be conducive to intrapreneurship have been identified in the literature. By means of an inductively conducted context analysis, the review of 97 publications resulted in an unstructured list of 329 quotations. It became apparent that, regarding the validity of the factors, roughly two categories of contributions exist. The first provides on the basis of anecdotal evidence and case studies qualitative descriptions of how an intrapreneurship- and innovation-friendly organizational climate can be implemented in (established) organizations; it was striking that this type of contribution is clearly practitioner-oriented with limited scientific rigour regarding conceptualizing, empirical testing and modelling. The other puts emphasis on the impact that national culture has on innovation output and performance of companies; here, the findings are mainly based on empirical testing and validation, but lack the link to applicable knowledge that would allow organizations to shape and implement an intrapreneurship- and innovation-supportive culture.

In the second step, all 329 quotations taken from the literature have been clustered and aggregated to 24 factors that seem to foster intrapreneurship. Based on that, Ulijn and Weggeman's (2001) conceptualization of innovation culture served as an auxiliary framework to assign these factors to the following six cultural dimensions: high vs. low power distance, high vs. low uncertainty avoidance, individualism vs. collectivism, masculinity vs. femininity, long-term vs. short-term orientation, and open vs. closed system orientation. While the first five dimensions are known from Hofstede's (1980) terminology of national culture, the sixth dimension, open vs. closed system orientation, was elaborated from Ulijn and Weggeman's (2001) dimension innovation drive and Hofstede and Bond's (1988) dimension, open vs. closed system. The result of this stepwise research process is presented in the following subsections. Each of the six dimensions of an intrapreneurship-supportive culture is described in detail by linking and summarizing the reasoning retrieved from the original publications.

High Versus Low Power Distance

Power is an integral part of innovation activities. It is needed to facilitate, orchestrate and shape innovation (Dougherty and Hardy, 1996; Kanter, 1983), and often organizations resist innovative ideas because of the allocation of power in organizations and inertia (Shane et al., 1995). This is because the way power is distributed and structured within the society or organization is a question of culture. Power distance indicates how individuals regard power differentials within the society or organizations (Hofstede, 1980).

In cultures scoring low on power distance, emphasis is put on egalitarian values, meaning that people prefer democratic leadership, cooperative strategies and striving for consensus. Authority is distributed equally, and power is a matter of facts rather than positions; people aim at democratic leadership, cooperation and consensus. In contrast, cultures with high scores of power distance accept and expect that power is not distributed equally within the society or an organization. They tend to adhere more rigidly to organizational hierarchies, prefer centralized decision-making, and they accept authoritarian leadership and obedience to superiors.

Innovation depends strongly on interaction, information sharing, and debates between people across disciplines and hierarchies (Anfuso, 1999; Ekvall, 1996; Nicholson, 1998; Rice, 2003). It is important that innovators and R&D teams adopt participative approaches and aim at widespread support for innovative projects before formal attention is paid by those in authority. This support enables the participants to convince the decision makers that innovation needs broad-based support in the organization

(Ahmet, 1998; Cooper and Kleinschmidt, 1995; Frishammar and Hörte, 2005; Hisrich, 1990; Kahn, 1996; Kanter, 1985; Kumpe and Bolwijn, 1994; Luchsinger and Bagby, 1987; Martins and Terblanche, 2003; McGinnis and Verney, 1987; Ottum and Moore, 1997; Pinchot, 1985; Rodriguez-Pomeda et al., 2003; Russell, 1999).

Innovation efforts will obviously fail when goals and directions are made only by a few people at the top and then forced top-down. They should be discussed, deliberated and changed, based on feedback from and communication between people at all levels: top-down, bottom-up, and all across functions and disciplines. Accordingly, the management and decision-making structure should be flat and decentralized, with multiple informal networks, to mobilize people, enable direct access resources, as well as to enhance entrepreneurial behaviour (Ahmet, 1998; Dougherty and Hardy, 1996; Eesley and Longenecker, 2006; Fry, 1987; Haskins and Williams, 1987; Howell and Higgins, 1990; Kanter, 1985; McGinnis and Verney, 1987; Nakata and Sivakumar, 1996; Rodriguez-Pomeda et al., 2003; Stevenson and Gumpert, 1985). Creating a true feeling of empowerment, that is delegating managers' power and responsibility towards the employees is vital in order to foster a culture of innovation (Fayolle, 1999; Higgins, 1995; Kanter, 2000; Kotter and Heskett, 1992; Kumpe and Bolwijn, 1994). In particular, the perception that management is supportive is central to a culture that facilitates innovation because management trust enables people to take risks without fear or undue penalty for failure (Ahmet, 1998; Bitzer, 1991; Chandler et al., 2000; Chisholm, 1987; Cooper and Kleinschmidt, 1995; Fry, 1987; Haskins and Williams, 1987; Hisrich, 1990; Kuratko and Montagno, 1989; Kuratko et al., 1990; Rule and Irwin, 1988; Süssmuth Dyckerhoff, 1995). This helps to signal trust, triggers active individual participation, and encourages personal responsibility for outcomes.

Organizational hierarchies, which to a certain extent are necessary in an organization, should not imply that there is too much power distance between higher ups and lower downs on the process and working level. In sum, the literature suggests that an intrapreneurship-supportive culture requires low power distance, building on flat hierarchies, decentralized power, and egalitarian values in order to foster communication and interaction in all directions, and to empower employees.

High Versus Low Uncertainty Avoidance

Uncertainty is implicitly inherent in innovation, and especially in radical innovation. The exploitation of new technologies faces huge uncertainties concerning the uses and potential future applications, but it also encourages exploration along a wide variety of alternative paths (Rosenberg,

1996). The way uncertainty is dealt with (that is, its avoidance or acceptance) has strong implications for the nature of the innovations pursued – exploration versus exploitation, high risk versus low risk, radical versus incremental. Uncertainty-avoiding individuals have a concern for security, and prefer established rules and formalization/planning of activities in order to reduce risk. In contrast, in an uncertainty-accepting culture, individuals are more flexible, rules are not necessary, and decision-making is pragmatic and situational.

The process of developing new ideas towards successful products is about discovery, exploration and pursuing new ways; it is a risk-intensive process that requires significant capital outlays and a long time-horizon where predictable resource needs and control over the environment are lacking. The literature suggests that (individual) willingness to accept risk and to face uncertainty is a fundamental element of an innovation-supporting culture (Ahmet, 1998; Bitzer, 1991; Brazeal, 1996; Chisholm, 1987; Czernich, 2004; Draeger-Ernst, 2003; Duncan et al., 1988; Eesley and Longenecker, 2006; Ekvall, 1996; Fayolle, 2003; Kuratko and Montagno, 1989; Kuratko et al., 1990; Martins and Terblanche, 2003; Mokyr, 1990; Pinchot, 1985; Rothwell and Wissema, 1986; Stevenson and Gumpert, 1985; Thornberry, 2001). This is especially relevant for top executives where control of uncertainty is a major issue (Quinn, 1979; Stevenson and Gumpert, 1985). Without top management's willingness to support highly risky R&D projects, large-scale innovation can not reach fruition.

Related with risk is failure. Not all new ideas lead to successful innovation; only a minor fraction of new ideas will finally yield sustainable profits (Rosenberg, 1996). In an intrapreneurship-supportive culture failures are regarded as opportunities and lessons to learn from, and not as occasions for punishment (Ahmet, 1998; Bitzer, 1991; Bretani and Kleinschmidt, 2004; Chisholm, 1987; Collins and Porras, 1994; Cooper and Kleinschmidt, 1995; Draeger-Ernst, 2003; Eesley and Longenecker, 2006; Frohman, 1998; Fry, 1987; Haskins and Williams, 1987; Higgins, 1995; Hisrich, 1990; Kuratko and Montagno, 1989; Kuratko et al., 1990; Nicholson, 1998; Pinchot, 1985; Russell and Russell, 1992; Russell, 1999; Sherwood, 2002; Smith, 1998; Süssmuth Dyckerhoff, 1995). The acceptance of failure is essential when it comes to promoting entrepreneurial behaviour within the organization. In this way, a culture of continuous learning is established. When an idea's final result is not successful, emphasis is placed on what was learned and people do not fear losing their job.

Taken together, there is strong agreement that an innovation-supporting culture builds on low uncertainty avoidance realized through individual risk-awareness, tolerance of failure, fewer rules and less formalization.

Individualism Versus Collectivism

Individualism (in contrast to collectivism) refers to the relationship that individuals have with the society that surrounds them, that is, whether people are rather concerned about themselves or about others (Hofstede, 1980). In individualistic cultures, ties between individuals are loose, and self-reliance, autonomy, independence and leadership are considered important. Individualistic people seek to differentiate themselves from others, emphasize personal outcomes over relationships, and value individual needs, interests and goals over those of the group (Triandis, 1995; Trompenaars and Hampden-Turner, 2001).

In contrast, collectivistic cultures are characterized by a tight social framework in which people distinguish between their own groups (so-called in-groups) and other groups. The in-group is built and maintained through harmonious relationships, rules of behaviour, membership and loyalty (Hofstede and Hofstede, 2005; Triandis, 1995). Collectivistic people value group interests, goals and outcomes over those of the individual and, as a result, they strive to minimize disruption. They rather pursue cooperative strategies, show more concern about attaining the other party's goals than about attaining their own goals, and are more willing to make sacrifices for their in-group (Lewicki et al., 1994; Triandis, 1995).

It is commonly understood that an intrapreneurship-supportive culture is grounded on policies and practices that provide degrees of individual freedom and autonomy to act in order to stimulate initiative and personal responsibility to pursue creative ideas (Ahmet, 1998; Draeger-Ernst, 2003; Eesley and Longenecker, 2006; Ekvall, 1996; Fayolle, 2003; Fry, 1987; Haskins and Williams, 1987; Kanter, 1985; Luchsinger and Bagby, 1987; Lumpkin and Dess, 1996; Martins and Terblanche, 2003; McGinnis and Verney, 1987; Morris et al., 1994; Nicholson, 1998; Peters and Waterman, 1982; Pinchot, 1985; Pinchot and Pellman, 1999; Rodriguez-Pomeda et al., 2003; Russell, 1999; Salomo et al., 2003a; Schmid, 1987; Ulijn and Weggeman, 2001). These individualism-reinforcing characteristics will stimulate people to think, be creative, take initiative, and to show responsibility, which is important for innovation.

However, it is questionable whether a purely individualistic culture will make innovation happen; it will also stimulate people to focus too strongly on their personal ambition, tasks and goals. This will create a sphere of high competition among the employees, which will eventually force people to keep their ideas for themselves instead of sharing them across different departments, groups or disciplines (Deloitte Touche Tohmatsu, 2005; Eesley and Longenecker, 2006; Ulijn and Weggeman, 2001). Innovation is an interrelated process that involves various cross-disciplinarily, iteratively and sequentially linked stages including idea generation, evaluation, development and implementation (Specht et al., 2002; Weule, 2002). No single individual has the skills, let alone the resources, to take an idea right through to implementation, and even small groups can find this very difficult (Sherwood, 2002). Combining ideas, exchanging information, and verifying each other's ideas seems to be crucial for innovation.

However, successful innovation evidently also requires collective forces. This means that an intrapreneurship-supportive culture fundamentally needs 'we' consciousness, group spirit, sense of belonging, loyalty, obligation to contribute, and strong cohesion between all members of the group or organization (Ekvall, 1996; Frohman, 1998; Kanter, 1985; Kumpe and Bolwijn, 1994; Nakata and Sivakumar, 1996; Robbins, 1998; Shane et al., 1995; Ulijn and Weggeman, 2001). As a consequence, employees need to commit themselves to the organization and greater goals that go beyond their self-interest (Ahmet, 1998; Kahn, 1996; Kanter, 1985; Kuratko and Montagno, 1989; Martins and Terblanche, 2003; McGinnis and Verney, 1987; Pinchot, 1985; Russell, 1999). Especially in today's complex, interdisciplinary innovation processes, in which work activities are increasingly based on collaboration and organized around groups rather than individuals, collaborative methods, such as networks, cross-boundary teams, supply chain partnerships and strategic alliances, are crucial in building a culture of innovation (Kanter, 2000; Ulijn and Weggeman, 2001). This is also supported by Schmeling (2001) who empirically finds that collectivism positively predicts helping behaviours and values.

We may conclude that in order to build an intrapreneurship-supportive culture, a combination of individualistic and collectivistic orientations is needed (Morris et al., 1993; Morris et al., 1994; Ulijn and Weggeman, 2001). It could be achieved in the way that Kanter (2000) suggests, that leaders should mobilize individual talent in the pursuit of collective goals to make employees responsible for their companies and empowered, but not bounded by their jobs.

Masculinity Versus Femininity

Masculinity versus femininity refers to the extent of clarity and distinctiveness of gender roles (Hofstede, 1980). In a masculine culture emphasis is on success and achievement: people live to work, they are goal oriented, show ambition and need to excel. On the other hand, in feminine cultures quality of life and a harmonious, playful atmosphere are important: people work to live, and put emphasis on interdependency and nurturance. Given the results of our literature review, it is rather difficult to provide a clear-cut proposition regarding whether an intrapreneurship-supportive culture should be driven by masculine or feminine orientations. There is only little (empirical) work dedicated to this question.

On the one hand, there are indications that femininity would be supportive of an intrapreneurship-supportive culture. To foster creativity, idea development and opportunity recognition, an intrapreneurship-supportive culture certainly needs to be based on a playful atmosphere, good relationships, communication, and exchange among the participants (Ekvall, 1996; Thwaites, 1992). Furthermore, the level of conflict should be low, and personal tension, prestige differences, or power and territory struggles and gossip should be avoided. Thus, high degrees of femininity through a focus on people and the establishment of warm, supportive climates affect the initiation stages of new product development positively (Nakata and Sivakumar, 1996). Indeed, as Ulijn et al. (2001) suggest, the high femininity values of the Netherlands and also Scandinavian countries appear to foster technical innovation in the initial stages of the innovation process.

On the other hand, femininity alone would not make innovation happen. Masculinity also has a positive effect on intrapreneurship-supportive culture, which is also built on purposefulness, clear goal-setting, and an orientation towards achieving these goals (Barczak and Wilemon, 1992; Bitzer, 1991; Chisholm, 1987; Collins and Porras, 1994; Draeger-Ernst, 2003; Eesley and Longenecker, 2006; Frohman, 1998; Luchsinger and Bagby, 1987; McGinnis and Verney, 1987; Nakata and Sivakumar, 1996; Pinchot and Pellman, 1999; Quinn, 1979; Rodriguez-Pomeda et al., 2003; Stevenson and Gumpert, 1985; Thamhain, 1990). Creativity and the discovery of a business opportunity is one step in innovation, but the other is pursuing the idea towards implementation and market. Addressing clearly identified customer needs and attempting to deliver the best possible solution to the customer has a lot of what can be described as being typically masculine. These objectives must be clear to all participants involved, because challenging goals stimulate and commit people to look beyond the feasible to the possible.

Goals should not only be formulated in terms of money or technical objectives, but control, motivation, and reward systems must be redesigned to support innovation and intrapreneurial goals (Ahmet, 1998; Anfuso, 1999; Bretani and Kleinschmidt, 2004; Chandler et al., 2000; Duncan et al., 1988; Fry, 1987; Haskins and Williams, 1987; Higgins, 1995; Hisrich, 1990; Kanter, 1985; Kuratko and Montagno, 1989; Kuratko et al., 1990; Luchsinger and Bagby, 1987; Martins and Terblanche, 2003; McGinnis and Verney, 1987; Nicholson, 1998; Pinchot, 1985; Rule and Irwin, 1988; Schmid, 1987; Sherwood, 2002; Süssmuth Dyckerhoff, 1995). On top of that, Quinn (1979) finds that successful major innovations require a certain admiration for the achiever. Interestingly, some highly innovative countries, such as France, Germany, Japan and the United States score high on the masculinity dimension. In general, the cultures of these countries put emphasis on achievement orientation and are among the major innovating nations worldwide, also because of their strength in engineering (Fayolle, 1999; Fayolle et al., 2005; Johnston, 1989; Nakata and Sivakumar, 1996; National Academy of Engineering, 2005; Shaw et al., 2003), which basically builds on solution- and target-driven, thus, very masculine approaches.

Given this, we may conclude that an intrapreneurship-supportive culture scores medium on the masculinity dimension based on a combination of both feminine and masculine cultural orientations. The former puts emphasis on people and relationships between people, whereas the latter is concerned with goal, result and task orientation.

Long-term Versus Short-term Orientation

Long-term versus short-term orientation has great implications for the pursuit of innovative activities. This dimension of culture refers to people's time horizons, attitude to tradition and change as well as preferences for static or dynamic environments (Hofstede and Bond, 1988). Long-term oriented cultures put emphasis on a dynamic, future-oriented mentality, including openness to the new, persistence and hard work. In contrast, short-term oriented cultures have a concern for rather static environments combined with a focus on the past and the present, on tradition and on keeping within well-known and well-accepted boundaries (Hofstede and Bond, 1988).

Basically, innovation is about change and future. Therefore, an intrapreneurship-supportive culture values longer time horizons (Bingham, 2003; Nakata and Sivakumar, 1996; Quinn, 1979; Ulijn and Weggeman, 2001), which is especially beneficial for major innovations that usually take a long time to develop, to absorb in the market, and to yield profit (Rosenberg, 1996). This includes a future orientation to long-term business objectives (Brazeal, 1996; Fry, 1987; Hisrich, 1990; Pinchot, 1985; Rothwell and Wissema, 1986), as well as a challenging vision and imagination of the future technological and market environment (Bitzer, 1991; Kanter, 1985; Pinchot, 1985; Schmid, 1987). A static perspective of technology and market would not be conducive in an environment where new, uncommon ideas and solutions, experimentation and iterative testing are demanded. It is important that people are flexible and quickly adapt to a changing environment (Ahmet, 1998; Cooper and Kleinschmidt, 1995; Draeger-Ernst, 2003; Haskins and Williams, 1987; Kanter, 1985; Martins and Terblanche, 2003; Özsomer et al., 1997; Pinchot, 1985; Rule and Irwin, 1988).

As we can see from the major part of the literature, it is suggested that an intrapreneurship-supportive culture builds on exploration, openness towards the new and unknown, long-term orientation, acceptance of change, and persistence in iterative and long work processes. However, as Kumpe and Bolwijn (1994) state, the right balance between renewal and stability must be kept, which is especially a task for R&D management, who need to keep a tight rope between the short-term demands of business unit leaders, while at the same time leaving enough room to work on long-term research. This is in line with Funke and Andonian (2005) who identify the need for a balanced capital structure that has a long time horizon combined with a short-term profit orientation. This allows for courageous and future-oriented management decisions and prevents the company from losing financial robustness. Given this, we may conclude that an intrapreneurship-supportive culture scores medium to high on the long-term orientation dimension.

Open Versus Closed System Orientation

As the literature investigation reveals, the six-dimensional framework used by Ulijn and Weggeman (2001) is not fully appropriate to cover intrapreneurship-supportive culture in its entirety. In order to distinguish intrapreneurship-supportive culture, the orientation of people to the inside and/or the outside must be taken into account, too.

The so-called system orientation basically refers to the degree to which the organization and its members monitor and respond to changes in the external environment, as well as the ability to be in exchange-relations with other communities and organizations (Chesbrough, 2003; Robbins, 1998). An open system puts emphasis on issues such as cooperation, networking, sharing of knowledge as well as search and curiosity across the boundaries of the firm. In contrast, a closed system orientated community would rely very much on their internal (re)sources and capabilities; exchange with external groups would be minimized or even avoided.

Indeed, the literature suggests that companies, and especially the large ones, need to overcome their natural tendency to focus inward and open up their system to the outside world. This means that initiating, handling and using a portfolio of inter-organizational relationships is highly important for innovation (Bingham, 2003; Chesbrough, 2003; Ritter and Gemünden, 2003; Tushman, 2004). The origin of innovation is the ability of individuals to discover new, innovative business opportunities (Kirzner, 1997; Klevorick et al., 1995) which are not necessarily to be found within the boundaries of the organization. In order to discover external sources and resources of innovation, members of organizations should continuously monitor and respond to changes in the external environment, such as customers, users, suppliers and venture partners (Chesbrough, 2003; Kanter,

2000; O'Connor and Ayers, 2005; Russell and Russell, 1992; von Hippel, 2005).

In particular, it is suggested that market orientation – a clear orientation towards the customer and the value added for the customer – is a crucial element of successful innovation (Bitzer, 1991; Draeger-Ernst, 2003; Eesley and Longenecker, 2006; Frishammar and Hörte, 2005; Fry, 1987; Haskins and Williams, 1987; Hisrich, 1990; Kohli and Jaworski, 1990; Martins and Terblanche, 2003; McGinnis and Verney, 1987; Pinchot, 1985; Rice, 2003; Rodriguez-Pomeda et al., 2003; Russell, 1999; Salomo et al., 2003b; Souder, 1981). Empirical evidence suggests that market or customer orientation is an antecedent component of innovativeness and, in consequence, to the firm's capacity to innovate, that is, to introduce new products successfully into the market (Atuahene-Gima, 1995; Hurley and Hult, 1998; Salomo et al., 2003b). The impact of this increases with the degree of product innovativeness (Salomo et al., 2003b). Market orientation is not only increasing the direct contact with the market/customer, but also facilitating physical proximity to research, production and marketing so that future users have a hand in research and development (Quinn, 1979).

Hence, an open organization is recommended for promoting innovativeness, but opening up the processes also involves specific risks. Without concurrent closure of processes to absorb these greater risks, greater openness produces not a further increase but a drop of innovativeness. More specifically, an intrapreneurship-supportive culture builds on the coexistence of internal and external factors of innovation along the whole value chain: funding of innovation, idea generation, sourcing and sharing of knowledge, joint development, marketing and distribution. This is what Chesbrough (2003) calls open innovation: it is neither a fully closed nor a fully open system, but the boundaries of the organization are permeable, both from the inside to the outside and the other way round. Thus, we may conclude that an intrapreneurship-supportive culture would score medium on the open system dimension to make best use of both internal and external factors and sources of innovation.

THE SIX DIMENSIONS OF AN INTRAPRENEURSHIP-SUPPORTIVE CULTURE

The result of the literature study is a six-dimensional profile building on 24 culturally-bound factors that seem to support the occurrence of intrapreneurship in the context of large, established organizations. It can be understood as a holistic description of an intrapreneurship-supportive culture as it was deductively developed based on an investigation of relevant literature.

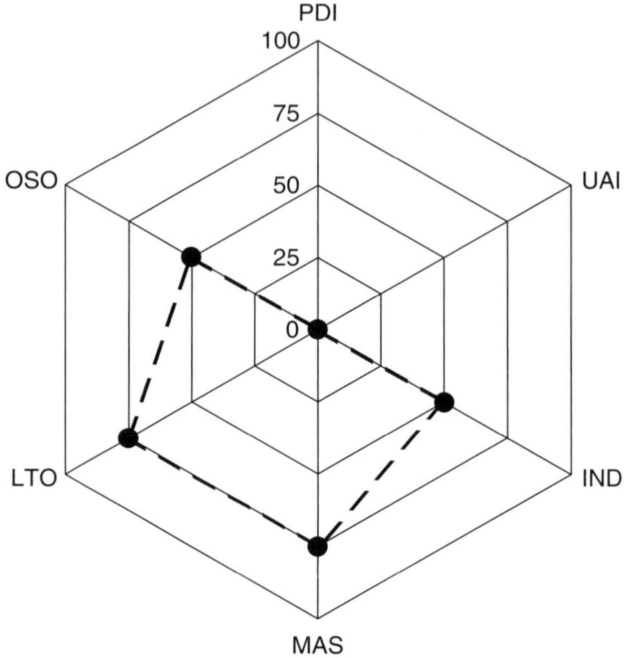

Figure 5.2 A deductively developed description of an intrapreneurship-supportive culture

As depicted in Figure 5.2, the radar plotting technique can be used to visualize the profile. Thereby, the score of each dimension was determined by qualitatively estimating the impact that each dimensions may have on intrapreneurship. A five-point scale was used to evaluate if the factors' impact appears to be very low (0 points) or very high (100 points).

Low power distance (PDI = 0 points) Despite organizational hierarchies that are given in large organizations, the power distance between the organizational and the individual level of intrapreneurship should be low. To avoid the intrapreneurship conflict emerging and remaining unsolved, intrapreneurs must be encouraged to openly deliberate their ideas and initiatives across all hierarchies. This requires management to be accessible and actively to establish direct links to the individual level. Hence, intrapreneurship-supportive culture clearly builds on flat hierarchies, decentralized power structures and egalitarian values.

Low uncertainty avoidance (UAI = 0 points) Intrapreneurship presupposes that the individual and the organizational level are simultaneously willing to accept and take risks. Evidently, the intrapreneur is the one who initiates the risk-intensive new venture process, but without top management's willingness to support highly risky R&D projects and new venture initiatives, large-scale innovation can not reach fruition. Moreover, intrapreneurship will only emerge if rules and formalization are reduced and people are fault-tolerant. In this way, continuous learning is established, encouraging employees to engage again and again in new intrapreneurial ventures.

Medium individualism (IND = 50 points) A balanced combination of individualistic and collectivistic orientations is essential for intrapreneurship. The intrapreneur, who certainly needs to be individualistic to some extent, must not forget the interests of the organization and its stakeholders. Pursuing entrepreneurial opportunities individually may be successful in the case of independent entrepreneurship but will probably fail when it comes to intrapreneurship. Both the intrapreneur and the management have to pursue cooperative strategies in order to achieve a greater, common goal.

Rather high masculinity (MAS = 75 points) Intrapreneurship-supportive culture seems to have both masculine and feminine elements, with an emphasis on the former. For radical innovation necessitating enormous R&D effort, the personality of the intrapreneur appears to feature typical masculine orientations, such as goals and achievement orientation, problem solving and implementation. Yet, he or she must not forget the larger organizational context where a good atmosphere and relationships between people need to be maintained, which may be particularly relevant for the early stages of the intrapreneurship process.

Rather long-term orientation (LTO = 75 points) Intrapreneurship requires a general openness to explore the new and unknown, long-term orientation and vision of the future, acceptance of change, and persistence in engaging in an iterative and long development process. Still, the organization must not disregard the fact that renewal and stability should be balanced, which is especially a task of R&D management that needs to keep a tight rope between the short-term demands of the daily business, while, at the same time, leaving enough room to work on long-term research.

Medium open system orientation (OSO = 50 points) The open organization is recommended for promoting intrapreneurship which, however, does not imply that the system be opened up entirely. It is neither a fully closed nor a fully open system, but the boundaries of the organization are permeable, both from the inside to the outside and the other way round to make best use of both internal and external factors and sources of innovation. Such an organizational setting provides a bigger variety of options to the intrapreneur than a closed system would do, affecting the entire intrapreneurship process from opportunity recognition and idea generation, sourcing and sharing of knowledge, joint development and funding to marketing and distributing the new product.

DISCUSSION AND CONCLUSION

The objective of this chapter was to conduct an extensive literature review in order to identify the state of the art of both research on and practical relevance of an intrapreneurship-supportive culture. By using Hofstede's (2001) theory and terminology about national cultures and Ulijn and Weggeman's (2001) conceptualization of innovation culture as auxiliary frameworks, the review of 97 publications resulted in a deductively developed six-dimensional description of an intrapreneurship-supportive-culture. Aggregated from 329 quotations, 24 culturally-bound factors could be identified and assigned to the five Hofstedian dimensions PDI, UAI, IND, MAS, and LTO, or to the newly established sixth dimension, OSO. Given the number and quality of sources studied, it can be assumed that a fairly complete picture of intrapreneurship-supportive culture could be drawn. Still, a critical reflection seems to be recommended.

Admittedly, this framework does not and can not claim to be complete, but – as the literature review shows – it certainly contains and builds on culture-bound constructs that are relevant for intrapreneurship-supportive culture. Still, deductively developed description needs to be validated empirically. Also, in order to measure intrapreneurship-supportive culture on the group or organizational level, we have to be clear about what innovation as a dependent variable does precisely mean. Thus, there is a need to correlate the framework to measures that reflect organizational inventiveness, innovativeness, performance, or the like.

This also includes what has been addressed earlier by Nakata and Sivakumar (1996), who suggest that an innovation culture would appear differently in the early and later stages of the innovation process. The early phases, often described as the fuzzy front end with a long distance to application, require creativity, higher degrees of freedom, divergent research, and exploration. In contrast, the later phases centre on exploitation, process efficiency and planning, convergent development, and implementation towards application. In contrast to this standpoint, Miron et al. (2004) find indications that an intrapreneurship-supportive culture would not be competing with a culture that promotes efficiency and quality, both characteristics of the later phases of exploitation and implementation. In any case, the focus of this contribution is on the early phases to promote intrapreneurship and the development of radical innovation.

Furthermore, questions of relevance and implications for practice must be addressed. We may ask, for instance, whether this kind of culture is relevant for the context of business economics. If so, does intrapreneurship-supportive culture exist in certain highly innovative organizations? And, if not, how can we trigger cultural change? Therefore, organizational members must become aware that sustainable innovation and intrapreneurship require a specific culture. Usually, processes of cultural change require that people recognize that 'survival of the community' is at stake (Trompenaars and Hampden-Turner, 2001). Thus, promoting an intrapreneurship-supportive culture must be done in such a way that people realize that a certain old way of doing things does not work any more.

Yet, sensitizing people is not enough to facilitate cultural change to the extent that it effectively changes the behaviour of people and other individual and organizational outcomes. The individual intention and willingness to change are prerequisites of change in behaviour. This is because culture is made by interaction of people, confirmed by others, conventionalized and passed on to others or newcomers to learn, and at the same time determines further interaction (Trompenaars and Hampden-Turner, 2001). Thus, given empirical validation of the conceptualization, concrete levers of action must be defined in order to effectively facilitate a change towards an intrapreneurship-supportive culture.

Based on this, several recommendations for further research can be derived. Given the literature-based approach, it is necessary to test and verify this description of an intrapreneurship-supportive culture empirically. Both longitudinal and multidimensional studies are recommended to relate intrapreneurship-supportive culture to organizational innovativeness and performance (Ulijn and Weggeman, 2001). Also, it might be interesting to compare our approach (based on culture) with other empirical studies on factors and determinants of innovation and intrapreneurship (independent from culture).

This would be in line with what has been suggested by Damanpour (1991), that new studies should consider different dimensions and variables, such as the individual, organizational and environmental level and include measurement of innovation using not only technical, but also organizational and administrative aspects. Next, given the various contributions which qualitatively describe intrapreneurship-supportive culture and give – often incomplete – advice of how to implement it, this topic certainly has high relevance for business practice. Thus, there is a need to produce practice-relevant outcomes and to make an effort in order to better understand how this concept of intrapreneurship-supportive culture can be linked to some concrete levers of action to effectively shape it on the company level.

REFERENCES

Aaltio, I. (2002), 'How to save entrepreneurship over time in a small business firm', paper presented at the 47th World Conference of the International Council for Small Business (ICSB), San Juan, Puerto Rico.

Ahmet, P.K. (1998), 'Culture and climate for innovation', *European Journal of Innovation Management*, **1**(1), 30–43.

Anfuso, D. (1999), 'Core values shape W.L. Gore's innovative culture', *Workforce*, **78**(3), 48–53.

Antoncic, B. and R.D. Hisrich (2003), 'Clarifying the intrapreneurship concept', *Journal of Small Business and Enterprise Development*, **10**(1), 7–24.

Atuahene-Gima, K. (1995), 'An exploratory analysis of the impact of market orientation on new product performance. A contingency approach', *Journal of Product Innovation Management*, **12**(4), 275–93.

Barczak, G. and D. Wilemon (1992), 'Successful new product team leaders', *Industrial Marketing Management*, **21**(1), 61–8.

Bingham, P. (2003), 'Pursuing innovation in a big organization', *Research Technology Management*, **46**(4), 52–8.

Bitzer, M.R. (1991), *Intrapreneurship – Unternehmertum in der Unternehmung*, Stuttgart: Schäffer.

Bloor, G. and P. Dawson (1994), 'Understanding professional culture in organizational context', *Organization Studies*, **15**(2), 275–95.

Brazeal, D.V. (1996), 'Managing an entrepreneurial organizational environment', *Journal of Business Research*, **35**(1), 55–67.

Bretani, U. and E. Kleinschmidt (2004), 'Corporate culture and commitment: impact on performance of international new product development programs', *Journal of Product Innovation Management*, **21**(5), 309–33.

Burgelman, R.A. (1983), 'Corporate entrepreneurship and strategic management: insight from a process study', *Management Science*, **29**(12), pp. 1349–65.

Carrier, C. (1994), 'Intrapreneurship in large firms and SMEs: a comparative study', *International Small Business Journal*, **12**(3), 54–69.

Carrier, C. (1997), 'Intrapreneurship in small businesses: an exploratory study', *Entrepreneurship: Theory & Practice*, **21**(1), 5–20.

Chandler, G.N., C. Keller and D.W. Lyon (2000), 'Unraveling the determinants and consequences of an innovation-supportive organizational culture', *Entrepreneurship Theory & Practice*, **25**(1), 59–76.

Chesbrough, H.W. (2003), *Open Innovation: The New Imperative for Creating and Profiting from Technology*, Boston: Harvard Business School Press.

Chisholm, T.A. (1987), 'Intrapreneurship and bureaucracy', *S.A.M. Advanced Management Journal*, **52**(3), 36–40.

Collins, J.C. and J.I. Porras (1994), *Built to Last: Successful Habits of Visionary Companies*, New York: HarperBusiness.

Cooper, R.G. and E.J. Kleinschmidt (1995), 'Benchmarking the firm's success factors in new product development', *Journal of Product Innovation Management*, **12**(5), 374–91.

Czernich, C.H. (2004), *When Ideas meet Organizations: The Survival of Entrepreneurial Ventures inside the Established Firm*, Stockholm: Stockholm School of Economics.

Damanpour, F. (1991), 'Organizational innovation: a meta-analysis of effects of determinants and moderators', *Academy of Management Journal*, **34**(3), 555–90.

Deloitte Touche Tohmatsu (2005), 'Fostering an innovative culture: sustaining competitive advantage', *Growth, The Executive Series for Dynamic Companies*, available at: http://www.growth-insights.com/articles/GES_FosteringInnovativeCulture.pdf (accessed 11 November 2007).
Dougherty, D. and C. Hardy (1996), 'Sustained product innovation in large, mature organizations: overcoming innovation-to-organization problems', *Academy of Management Journal*, **39**(5), 1120–53.
Draeger-Ernst, A. (2003), *Vitalisierendes Intrapreneurship: Gestaltungskonzept und Fallstudie*, Munich: Hampp.
Drucker, P.F. (1985), *Innovation and Entrepreneurship: Practice and Principles*, New York: Harper & Row.
Duncan, W.J., P.M. Ginter, A.C. Rucks and T.D. Jacobs (1988), 'Intrapreneurship and the reinvention of the corporation', *Business Horizons*, **31**(3), 16–21.
Eesley, D.T. and C.O. Longenecker (2006), 'Gateways to intrapreneurship', *Industrial Management*, **48**(1), 18–23.
Ekvall, G. (1996), 'Organizational climate for creativity and innovation', *European Journal of Work and Organizational Psychology*, **5**(1), 105–23.
Fayolle, A. (1999), *L'ingénieur Entrepreneur Français: Contribution à la Compréhension des Comportements de Création et Reprise d'entreprise des Ingénieurs Diplômés*, Paris: L'Harmattan.
Fayolle, A. (2003), 'Instiller l'esprit d'entreprendre dans les grandes entreprises et les organisations, *Gérer et Comprendre*, no. 72, 26–39.
Fayolle, A., J.M. Ulijn and J.-M. Degeorge (2005), 'The entrepreneurial and innovative orientation of French, German and Dutch engineers: The proposal of a european context based upon some empirical evidence from two studies', in A. Fayolle, P. Kyrö and J.M. Ulijn (eds), *Entrepreneurship Research in Europe: Outcomes and Perspectives*, Cheltenham, UK and Northampton, MA, USA: Edward Elgar, pp. 227–55.
Frishammar, J. and S.A. Hörte (2005), 'Managing external information in manufacturing firms: the impact on innovation performance', *Journal of Product Innovation Management*, **22**(3), 251–66.
Frohman, A.L. (1998), 'Building a culture for innovation', *Research Technology Management*, **41**(2), 9–12.
Fry, A. (1987), 'The post-it note: an intrapreneurial success', *S.A.M. Advanced Management Journal*, **52**(3), 4–9.
Funke, C. and A. Andonian (2005), *Hightech-Standort Europa akut gefährdet*, Munich: McKinsey&Company.
Haskins, G. and R. Williams (1987), *Intrapreneurship in Action: Successful European Company Practices*, London: The Economist Publications.
Heinonen, J. and K. Korvela (2003), 'How about measuring intrapreneurship?' paper presented at the 33rd Entrepreneurship, Innovation and Small Business Conference, 10–12 September, Milan, Italy.
Higgins, J.M. (1995), 'Innovate or evaporate', *The Futurist*, **29**(5), 42–8.
Hisrich, R.D. (1990), 'Entrepreneurship/intrapreneurship', *American Psychologist*, **45**(2), 209–22.
Hofstede, G.H. (1980), *Culture's Consequences: International Differences in Work Related Values*, Beverly Hills: Sage Publications.
Hofstede, G.H. (2001), *Culture's Consequences: Comparing Values, Behaviors, Institutions and Organizations across Nations*, London: Sage Publications.

Hofstede, G.H. and M.H. Bond (1988), 'The Confucius connection: from cultural roots to economic growth', *Organizational Dynamics*, **16**(4), 5–21.

Hofstede, G.H. and G.J. Hofstede (2005), *Cultures and Organizations: Software of the Mind*, New York: McGraw-Hill.

Hofstede, G.H., B. Neuijen, D.D.Ohayv and G. Sanders (1990), 'Measuring organizational cultures: A qualitative and quantitative study across twenty cases', *Administrative Science Quarterly*, **35**(2), 286–316.

Hornsby, J.S., D.F. Kuratko and S.A. Zahra (2002), 'Middle managers' perception of the internal environment for corporate entrepreneurship: assessing a measurement scale', *Journal of Business Venturing*, **17**(3), 253–73.

Howell, J.M. and C.A. Higgins (1990), 'Champions of technological innovation', *Administrative Science Quarterly*, **35**(2), 317–30.

Hurley, R.F. and G.T.M. Hult (1998), 'Innovation, market orientation, and organizational learning: an integration and empirical examination', *Journal of Marketing*, **62**(3), 42–54.

Johnston, D.L. (1989), 'Engineering contributions to the evolution of management practice', *IEEE Transactions on Engineering Management*, **36**(2), 105–13.

Jones, G.K. and H.J. Davis (2000), 'National culture and innovation: implications for locating global R&D operations', *Management International Review*, **40**(1), 11–39.

Kahn, K.B. (1996), 'Interdepartmental integration: a definition with implications for product development performance', *Journal of Product Innovation Management*, **13**(2), 89–166.

Kanter, R.M. (1983), *The Change Masters: Innovation for Productivity in the American Corporation*, New York: Simon and Schuster.

Kanter, R.M. (1985), 'Supporting innovation and venture development in established companies', *Journal of Business Venturing*, **1**(1), 47–60.

Kanter, R.M. (2000), 'A culture of innovation', *Executive Excellence*, **17**(8), 10–11.

Kelley, D., H.M. Neck, G.C. O'Connor and A. Paulson (2002), 'Developing radical innovation capabilities: opposing forces from the corporate entrepreneurship and organizational systems', in W.D. Bygrave (ed.), *Frontiers of Entrepreneurship Research 2002: Proceedings of the Twenty-second Annual Entrepreneurship Research Conference*, Babson Park: Babson College, Arthur M. Blank Center for Entrepreneurship.

Kirzner, I.M. (1997), 'Entrepreneurial discovery and the competitive market process: An Austrian approach', *Journal of Economic Literature*, **35**(1), 60–85.

Klein, H. (2002), *Internal Corporate Venturing: Die Überwindung von Innovationsbarrieren in DAX-100-Unternehmen*, Wiesbaden: Dt. Univ.-Verl.

Klein, H. and G. Specht (2002), 'Internal corporate venturing. An exploratory study on how large German corporations foster radical innovations', Working Paper No. 15, Darmstadt: Darmstadt University of Technology, Institute of Business Administration, Technology Management & Marketing.

Klevorick, A.K., R.C. Levin, R.R. Nelson and S.G. Winter (1995), 'On the sources and significance of interindustry differences in technological opportunities', *Research Policy*, **24**(2), 185–205.

Kohli, A.K. and B.J. Jaworski (1990), 'Market orientation: the construct, research propositions, and managerial implications', *Journal of Marketing*, **54**(2), 1–18.

Kotter, J. and J. Heskett (1992), *Corporate Culture and Performance*, Indianapolis: MacMillan.

Kumpe, T. and P.T. Bolwijn (1994), 'Toward the innovative firm – challenge for R&D management', *Research Technology Management*, **37**(1), 38–44.
Kuratko, D.F. and R.V. Montagno (1989), 'The intrapreneurial spirit', *Training & Development Journal*, **43**(10), 83–5.
Kuratko, D.F., R.V. Montagno and J.S. Hornsby (1990), 'Developing an intrapreneurial assessment instrument for an effective corporate entrepreneurial environment', *Strategic Management Journal*, **11**(Summer Special), 49.
Lewicki, R.J., J.A. Litterer, J.W. Minton and D.M. Saunders (1994), *Negotiation*, (2nd edn), Homewood, IL: Irwin.
Lorange, P. (1999), 'The internal entrepreneur as a driver of growth', *General Management Review*, **2**(1), 8–14.
Luchsinger, V. and D.R. Bagby (1987), 'Entrepreneurship and intrapreneurship: Behaviors, comparisons, and contrasts', *S.A.M. Advanced Management Journal*, **52**(3), 10–13.
Lumpkin, G.T. and G.G. Dess (1996), 'Clarifying the entrepreneurial orientation construct and linking it to performance', *Academy of Management Review*, **21**(1), pp. 135–72.
Mair, J. (2005), 'Entrepreneurial behavior in a large traditional firm: exploring key drivers', in T. Elfring (ed.), *Corporate Entrepreneurship and Venturing*, Vol. **10**, New York: Springer, pp. 49–72.
Martins, E.C. and F. Terblanche (2003), 'Building organisational culture that stimulates creativity and innovation', *European Journal of Innovation Management*, **6**(1), 64–74.
McGinnis, M.A. and T.P. Verney (1987), 'Innovation management and intrapreneurship', *SAM Advanced Management Journal*, **52**(3), 19–23.
Miles, M.P. and J.G. Covin (2002), 'Exploring the practice of corporate venturing: some common forms and their organizational implications', *Entrepreneurship: Theory & Practice*, **26**(3), 21–40.
Miron, E., M. Erez and E. Naveh (2004), 'Do personal characteristics and cultural values that promote innovation, quality, and efficiency compete or complement each other?', *Journal of Organizational Behavior*, **25**(2), 175–99.
Mokyr, J. (1990), *The Lever of Riches: Technological Creativity and Economic Progress*, Oxford: Oxford University Press.
Morris, M.H., R.A. Avila and J. Allen (1993), 'Individualism and the modern corporation: Implications for innovation and entrepreneurship', *Journal of Management*, **19**(3), 595–612.
Morris, M.H., D.L. Davis and J.W. Allen (1994), 'Fostering corporate entrepreneurship: cross-cultural comparisons of the importance of individualism versus collectivism', *Journal of International Business Studies*, **25**(1), 65–89.
Nakata, C. and K. Sivakumar (1996), 'National culture and new product development: an integrative view', *Journal of Marketing*, **60**(1), 61–72.
National Academy of Engineering (2005), *The Engineer of 2020: Visions of Engineering in the New Century* (7th edn), Washington: National Academies Press.
Nicholson, G.C. (1998), 'Keeping innovation alive', *Research Technology Management*, **41**(3), 34–40.
O'Connor, G.C. and A.D. Ayers (2005), 'Building a radical innovation competency', *Research Technology Management*, **48**(1), 23–31.
Ottum, B.D. and W.L. Moore (1997), 'The role of market information in new product success/failure', *Journal of Product Innovation Management*, **14**(4), 258–73.

Özsomer, A., R. Calantone and A. Di Benedetto (1997), 'What makes firms more innovative? A look at organizational and environmental factors', *Journal of Business & Industrial Marketing*, **12**(6), 400–416.
Peters, T.J. and R.H. Waterman (1982), *In Search of Excellence: Lessons from America's Best-run Companies*, New York: Harper & Row.
Pinchot, G. (1985), *Intrapreneuring: Why you do not Have to Leave the Corporation to Become an Entrepreneur*, (1st edn), New York: Harper & Row.
Pinchot, G. and R. Pellman (1999), *Intrapreneuring in Action: A Handbook for Business Innovation*, San Francisco: Berrett-Koehler Publ.
Quinn, J.B. (1979), 'Technological innovation, entrepreneurship, and strategy', *Sloan Management Review*, **20**(3), 19–30.
Rice, G. (2003), 'The challenge of creativity and culture: a framework for analysis with application to Arabian Gulf firms', *International Business Review*, **12**(4), 461–77.
Ritter, T. and H.G. Gemünden (2003), 'Network competence: its impact on innovation success and its antecedents', *Journal of Business Research*, **56**(9), 745–55.
Robbins, S.P. (1998), *Organizational Behavior: Concepts, Controversies, Applications*, (8th edn), Upper Saddle River: Prentice Hall.
Rodriguez-Pomeda, J., F. Casani-Fernandez de Navarrete, P. Morcillo-Orega and J.M. Rodriguez-Anton (2003), 'The figure of the intrapreneur in driving innovation and initiative for the firm's transformation', *International Journal of Entrepreneurship and Innovation Management*, **3**(4), 349–57.
Rosenberg, N. (1996), 'Uncertainty and technological change', in R. Landau, T. Taylor and G. Wright (eds), *The Mosaic of Economic Growth*, Stanford: Stanford University Press, pp. 335–447.
Rothwell, R. and H. Wissema (1986), 'Technology, culture, and public policy', *Technovation*, **4**(2), 91–115.
Rule, E.G. and D.W. Irwin (1988), 'Fostering intrapreneurship in the new competitive edge', *Journal of Business Strategy*, **9**(3), 44–7.
Russell, C.J. and R.D. Russell (1992), 'An examination of the effects of organizational norms, organizational structure, and environmental uncertainty on entrepreneurial strategy', *Journal of Management*, **18**(4), 639–56.
Russell, R.D. (1999), 'Developing a process model of intrapreneurial systems: a cognitive mapping approach', *Entrepreneurship: Theory & Practice*, **23**(3), 65–84.
Salomo, S., A. Krieger and H.G. Gemünden (2003a), 'Autonomie von Innovationsvorhaben', TU Berlin, Institut für Technologie und Management, Lehrstuhl für Innovations- und Technologiemanagement.
Salomo, S., F.Steinhoff and V. Trommsdorff (2003b), 'Customer orientation in innovation projects and new product development success – the moderating effect of product innovativeness', *International Journal of Technology Management*, **26**(5/6), 442–63.
Schmeling, E. (2001), 'Good citizens in a global economy. Individualism-collectivism and power distance as predictors of organizational citizenship behavior', unpublished dissertation, Universität Konstanz, Konstanz.
Schmid, M. (1987), 'Intrapreneurship: ein Konzept für innovatives Verhalten in bürokratischen Unternehmen', *Zeitschrift Führung + Organisation*, **56**(1), 20–26.
Schumpeter, J.A. (1934), *The Theory of Economic Development*, Cambridge: Harvard University Press.

Shane, S.A. (1997), 'Cultural differences in the championing of global innovation', in J.A. Katz (ed.), *The Human Side of Managing Technological Innovation: A Collection of Readings*. New York: Oxford University Press, pp. 296–303.

Shane, S.A., S. Venkataraman and I. MacMillan (1995), 'Cultural differences in innovation championing strategies', *Journal of Management*, **21**(5), 931–52.

Shaw, V., C.T. Shaw and M. Enke (2003), 'Conflict between engineers and marketers: The experience of German engineers', *Industrial Marketing Management*, **32**(6), 489–99.

Sherwood, D. (2002), *Creating an Innovative Culture*, Oxford: Capstone Publishing.

Smith, M. (1998), 'The development of an innovation culture', *Management Accounting: Magazine for Chartered Management Accountants*, **76**(2), 22–4.

Sommerlatte, T. (2001), 'Voraussetzungen für Innovationen in Unternehmen – das harmonisierende Zusammenspiel von Innovationsstrategie, Innovationsprozess und Innovationskultur', in M. Braun, A. Feige and T. Sommerlatte (eds), *Business-innovation: Quantensprünge statt 'Innovatiönchen'; ein Wegweiser zur zielgerichteten Geschäftserneuerung*, Frankfurt a.M.: FAZ-Institut für Management-, Markt- und Medieninformationen.

Souder, W.E. (1981), 'Encouraging entrepreneurship in the large corporations', *Research Management*, **24**(3), 18–22.

Specht, G., C. Beckmann and J. Amelingmeyer (2002), *F&e-Management: Kompetenz im Innovationsmanagement*, (2nd edn), Stuttgart: Schäffer-Poeschel.

Stevenson, H.H. and D.E. Gumpert (1985), 'The heart of entrepreneurship', *Harvard Business Review*, **63**(2), 85–94.

Süssmuth Dyckerhoff, C. (1995), *Intrapreneuring: Ein Ansatz zur Vitalisierung reifer Gross-Unternehmen*, Bern: Haupt.

Thamhain, H.J. (1990), 'Managing technologically innovative team efforts toward new product success', *Journal of Product Innovation Management*, **7**(1), 5–18.

Thornberry, N.E. (2001), 'Corporate entrepreneurship: Antidote or oxymoron?', *European Management Journal*, **19**(5), 526–33.

Thwaites, D. (1992), 'Organizational influences on the new product development process in financial services', *Journal of Product Innovation Management*, **9**(4), 303–13.

Triandis, H.C. (1995), *Individualism and Collectivism*, Oxford: Westview Press.

Trompenaars, F. and C. Hampden-Turner (2001), *Riding the Waves of Culture: Understanding Cultural Diversity in Business*, (2nd edn), London: Nicholas Brealey.

Tushman, M.L. (2004), 'From engineering management/R&D management, to the management of innovation, to exploiting and exploring over value nets: 50 years of research initiated by the IEEE-TEM', *IEEE Transactions on Engineering Management*, **51**(4), 409–11.

Ulijn, J.M. and T. Brown (2004), 'Innovation, entrepreneurship and culture, a matter of interaction between technology, progress and economic growth? An introduction', in T. Brown and J.M. Ulijn (eds), *Innovation, Entrepreneurship and Culture: The Interaction Between Technology, Progress and Economic Growth*, Cheltenham, UK and Northampton, MA, USA: Edward Elgar, pp. 1–38.

Ulijn, J.M. and M. Weggeman (2001), 'Towards an innovation culture: what are its national, corporate, marketing and engineering aspects, some experimental evidence', in S. Cartwright, C.L. Cooper and P.C. Early (eds), *The International Handbook of Organizational Culture and Climate,* Chichester: Wiley, pp. 487–517.

Ulijn, J.M., A.M.T. Lincke and F. Wynstra (2004), 'The effect of Dutch and German culture on negotiation strategy: an exploratory study to compare innovation and operations contexts', *International Negotiation*, **9**(2), 201–28.

Ulijn, J.M., A. Nagel and W.L. Tan (2001), 'The impact of national, corporate and professional cultures on innovation: German and Dutch firms compared'. *Journal of Enterprising Culture*, **9**(1), 21–51.

Vanhaverbeke, W. and R. Kirschbaum (2005), 'Building new competencies for new business creation based on breakthrough technological innovations', in R. Sanchez and A. Heene (eds), *A Focused Issue on Understanding Growth: Entrepreneurship, Innovation and Diversification*, Oxford: Elsevier Science, pp. 139–157.

Veenker, S., P.C. van der Sijde, W. During and A. Nijhof (2004), '*The perception of corporate entrepreneurship in Dutch organisations*', paper presented at the High-Technology Small Firms Conference, Enschede.

von Hippel, E. (2005), *Democratizing Innovation*, Cambridge: MIT Press.

Wennekers, S., L.M. Uhlaner and R. Thurik (2002), 'Entrepreneurship and its conditions: a macro perspective', *International Journal of Entrepreneurship Education*, **1**(1), 25–64.

Weule, H. (2002), *Integriertes Forschungs- und Entwicklungsmanagement: Grundlagen – strategien – Umsetzung*, Munich: Hanser.

PART II

The Dynamics between Entrepreneurship and Education

6. University entrepreneurship and government support schemes

Einar Rasmussen, Odd Jarl Borch and Roger Sørheim

INTRODUCTION

The formation of spin-off companies from research organizations is seen as one of the most effective ways of commercializing new knowledge and technology (Bray and Lee, 2000; Brett et al., 1991; Davenport et al., 2002; Rogers et al., 2001). It is found that university spin-offs often commercialize early-stage inventions where existing companies fail to commercialize or show no interest in the technology (Matkin, 1990; Thursby et al., 2001). Furthermore, several studies indicate that the formation of spin-off companies is a more successful route to commercialization of university inventions than licensing (Bray and Lee, 2000; Gregory and Sheahen, 1991; Rogers et al., 2001). Thus, the university spin-off firm may be seen as a distinct channel for technology transfer for some types of inventions.

National and regional authorities see a potential for economic growth and increased employment resulting from the resources that are invested in the universities (OECD, 2000), and universities are seen as engines of regional economic growth (Candell and Jaffe, 1999). In the US, the number of university patents, licenses, and equity ownerships has grown dramatically in the last 20 years, partly following the implementation of the Bayh-Dole Act in 1980 (Mowery et al., 2001). The great success in the US in bringing new research findings to the marketplace has inspired countries to undertake reforms aiming to increase the extent of commercialization of research, by changes both in the academic system and in the instruments for research funding (Benner and Sandstrom, 2000; Slaughter and Leslie, 1997), and through setting up separate structures to support such activities (Guston, 1999; Hellström and Jacob, 2003; Mian, 1997). Policies have been induced top-down from the government and its agencies, while other initiatives are emerging bottom-up from individuals and from inside the university (Goldfarb and Henrekson, 2002;

Rasmussen et al., 2006). Some initiatives are formal, while informal mechanisms are in many cases found to play an even more significant role (Franklin et al., 2001).

In this chapter a spin-off firm is defined as a new venture based on university research. Recent studies have recognized the heterogeneity of university spin-offs (Heirman and Clarysse, 2004; Mustar et al., 2006), and that policy measures need to be tailored to the specific contexts, entrepreneurs and resources required (Lockett et al., 2005; Wright et al., 2004). This study addresses the range of government programs to facilitate the creation of research-based university spin-off firms. Several studies have investigated university spin-off formation and the role of policy schemes (Lockett et al., 2005; Mustar, 1997; Rasmussen et al., 2006). However, few studies have investigated how government schemes are designed and implemented.

The objective of this chapter is twofold. First, we discuss the different types of support mechanisms that might be available to governments aiming to facilitate the creation of university spin-offs. Second, we analyze the challenges when designing government support programs. We elaborate on the different organizational mechanisms used to manage the implementation of the government support measures. As a point of departure we take the creation of a university spin-off and the entrepreneurial process. Birley (2002) asserts that entrepreneurial activity is more complex in academic settings than anywhere else, related both to technological and organizational challenges. Hence, there might be a need for tailor-made instruments to facilitate commercialization activities within universities. Moreover, we claim that there is a need to adapt these instruments to the national agendas, the university context, and the project characteristics.

The chapter is structured as follows. First, we elaborate on the complex process of research-based spin-off firm formation from universities, and the role of government support. We look in particular at the development phases from research idea to the launching of a new high-tech firm. Second, the findings from a study of government programs to support commercialization of research in Canada, Finland, Ireland, Norway, Scotland and Sweden are presented. We discuss the rationale behind the differences in the support schemes between these countries and the different ways of structuring the support programs at government, university and project levels. Finally, conclusions and implications for further research and policy implications are provided.

FRAME OF REFERENCE

The Spin-off Process and the University Context

Key topics in the process of new venture creation include the opportunity or business idea on which the new venture is based, the individuals or entrepreneurs involved in the start-up, and the organizational context in which the firm is initiated (Bruyat and Julien, 2001; Phan, 2004; Rasmussen, 2006; Stevenson and Jarillo, 1990). University spin-off firms are special due to some common characteristics. They are developed from an opportunity emerging within academic research. The academic inventors often play a key role in the development process, and the initial phases of development often take place within a university setting.

The university setting is complex due to multiple outputs, ambiguous goals, and stakeholders with differing interests (March and Olsen, 1976). Universities provide composite products within education and research. To achieve its objectives the university organization is characterized by a fragmented structure with loose couplings between different parts of the organization (Weick, 1976). Participation in the decision-making process is often fluid, and the number and role of actors involved, and the amount of effort they put in, are uncertain and changing (Cohen et al., 1972).

The complexity of university spin-off development is evident from the many stakeholders involved and their interwoven objectives. Diverse goals and outputs such as teaching, doing basic and applied research, societal utility, and a combination of non-profit and commercial activity add to this complexity (Lee, 1996; Navarro and Gallardo, 2003). The internal complexity is due to the highly specialized competence and autonomous work practice of the employees, the creative nature of work tasks, and the norms and structure of the science system (Merton, 1973; Stephan, 1996). The external complexity is evident from the many stakeholders such as students, funding agencies, industry, and other adopters of research results, combined with the changing operational contexts and expectations of universities (Shane, 2004). The academic culture appreciates publishing and open accessible research, while entrepreneurial activity may be a sensitive issue (Ndonzuau et al., 2002). For the spin-off activity, this may create challenges related to opportunity recognition, incentives for the researcher to exploit the opportunity, and access to university resources necessary for further commercialization.

The venturing scientists meet the potential for conflict with traditional academic values and tasks. The entrepreneurs initiating university spin-offs are embedded in a context where for instance environment support (Reitan, 1997), local group norms (Louis et al., 1989), and university culture

(Franklin et al., 2001) affect their behavior. The academics involved in setting up a spin-off company have little in common with the heroic and solitary Schumpeterian entrepreneur (Mustar, 1997). Based on their study of professorial entrepreneurship, Kenney and Goe (2004, p. 679) suggest that 'being embedded in an academic department and disciplines with cultures that are supportive of entrepreneurial activity can help counteract the disincentives created by a university environment that is not strongly supportive of these activities'. This indicates a complex structure where academics are part of different cultures within their scientific discipline, department, university and external environment. To gain the necessary resources, academic entrepreneurs are dependent on networks and integration between a wide variety of actors embedded in different sub-cultures (Mustar, 1997). For the academic wanting to pursue a commercial idea, this might imply breaking norms and creating emotional strain on the relation to the academic culture.

The Spin-off Process and the Entrepreneurial Characteristics

Interaction over a long period of time is often needed to transfer research-based knowledge to a commercial setting. University spin-off projects are characterized by a dynamic interaction of different individuals throughout the start-up process (Chiesa and Piccaluga, 2000; Clarysse and Moray, 2004; Roberts and Malone, 1996; Vanaelst et al., 2006). Arguably, a large share of research findings consists of tacit knowledge, making it important that the researcher(s) possessing this knowledge are involved in the commercialization process. Several studies point to the risk that advanced knowledge-based ideas may fade away if the idea is separated from the creator or researcher (Henrekson and Rosenberg, 2001; Stankiewicz, 1986). Jensen and Thursby (2001, p. 241) found that most licenses from US universities comprise technologies that 'are so embryonic that additional effort in development by the inventor is required for a reasonable chance of commercial success'.

For the spin-off venture, the dependency on the original inventor represents both an advantage and a possible future challenge. On the negative side, several studies show that lack of business experience and management skills is recognized as a potential barrier to success for venturing scientists (Radosevich, 1995; Samsom and Gurdon, 1993). Hence, an entrepreneurial team consisting of both the academic inventor and experienced entrepreneurs may be favorable, and this is also found to be common among university spin-offs (Birley, 2002). Also the use of entrepreneurs from outside the university, so-called surrogate entrepreneurs, is found to be a viable strategy for spin-off creation (Franklin et al., 2001; Radosevich, 1995).

The Spin-off Process and the Need for External Resource Acquisition

The complexity and the often long time horizon of the spin-off process makes it difficult to acquire the resources needed to develop the project, in particular the financial resources. It is often difficult to anticipate the commercial potential of university spin-off projects in the first stage, and it is generally difficult to obtain funding for further development of early stage, high-risk projects (Westhead and Storey, 1997; Wright et al., 2006). The business opportunities exploited by university spin-offs are often based on many years of research effort and have high knowledge content. New research findings often need large investments in further development before they can reach the marketplace as new products or services (Jensen and Thursby, 2001). These investments might not be induced without a proper protection of the intellectual property (IP), thus securing exclusivity of the rights to economic exploitation (Granstrand, 1999; Monotti and Ricketson, 2003). Patent scope has been found to increase the probability that university inventions are commercialized through a spin-off venture (Shane, 2001). For the spin-off venture, funding may be obtained through the entrepreneurs' and the university's internal funding, or through debt and equity finance (Wright et al., 2006). Due to the early stage nature and high knowledge content of the technologies, asymmetric information may lead to a high degree of market failure when it comes to the funding of university spin-offs.

The relation with the external context is crucial for spin-off development and for spin-off processes to meet challenges in obtaining market knowledge and commercial networks and resources. As noted by Rosenberg (1991), innovations are increasingly interdisciplinary, and close cooperation between a number of specialists is required to succeed. There might be a communication gap between academics, the investors, government representatives and industry due to differences in expertise, culture and language. In order to understand scientific reports and to communicate with academics there is a need for specialized competence, which might not be present in industrial companies or other adopters. Likewise, academics may have problems understanding industry's needs. Network activities with the university, customers, suppliers and the regional innovation network seem important for spin-off development (Pérez and Sánchez, 2003). For instance, Shane and Stuart (2002) found that founders of university spin-offs who had prior relations to venture capitalists are more likely to receive venture funding and less likely to fail. Another source of resources to develop the business concept is through strategic alliances (Carayannis et al., 2000). For the spin-off venture, the academic entrepreneurs have to create cooperating networks towards arenas within the business community where they have limited knowledge and experience.

The Role of Government Support

The characteristics of the university setting, the academic entrepreneur and project complexity make the structuring of government support a challenging task. The discussion above shows that the university setting leads to several pitfalls that may severely hamper the process of bringing a promising research idea through the commercialization process towards a new spin-off firm. For the university, contributing to this specific type of knowledge-intensive commercialization processes may therefore call for several new measures. Lerner (2002) emphasizes the special challenges of the bureaucracy meeting the markets, especially when dealing with professional investors and a broad set of stakeholders. Hence, it is important to find administrative mechanisms at university level that increase the market impulses and market interests of the new venture in an early stage, without hampering the other stakeholders' interests and the other university tasks. The government support system needs to find organizational solutions to govern the efforts channeled into the commercialization process to avoid endless 'garbage can' processes within the anarchic university organization (Cohen et al., 1972). At the same time, the governance regime must not induce a lot of red tape hampering the dynamism of the interests behind the spin-off.

The university serves as a stakeholder both as research provider and through IP ownership, and by representing the interests of society and the government. The government may have several stakes in this process both as policy-maker, owner, and provider of financial support. Hence, there may be different national agendas that have to be taken into consideration, in addition to the university context and the commercialization project characteristics. Some countries are striving to increase the number of spin-offs, while others are focusing on supporting the development of existing companies through publicly supported research. Several countries are looking for strong clusters that may influence the priority of the funding and the need for more centralized control. In some countries, the new public management ideas of decentralization and privatization may have a strong influence (Czarniawska and Genell, 2002).

The types of roles that public funding initiatives can play in promoting the commercialization of research may be divided in two main groups. First, initiatives can promote institutional changes with the long-term view to create structures and build competence for the commercialization of research. This approach might be seen as an attempt to correct systemic failure which inhibits the ability of universities and private actors to develop viable opportunities into spin-off firms. This can be done by inducing changes in the culture, attitudes and incentives; by networking and training; and by establishing organizational structures such as technology transfer offices (TTOs), incubators, and entrepreneurship centers within the universities to support the entrepreneurs (Klofsten and Jones-Evans, 2000; Rasmussen et al., 2006). Furthermore, initiatives could also be developed in boundary organizations (Hellström and Jacob, 2003) operating in the intersection between the university and the business sector, such as incubators, science parks, network organizations and consultants.

Here, government support programs can provide permanent basic funding for maintaining a relevant infrastructure for technology transfer. Examples are, for instance, when the TTOs or comparable actors are dependent on some government funds to secure their basic operation. This is a way for governments to support changes in the university sector helping the institutions to change and become more entrepreneurial universities (Clark, 1998).

The second group of government initiatives provides direct support to specific commercialization projects. The rationale for this approach is to mitigate market failure by stimulating the supply and demand side for research-based technologies. Examples of such support could be direct financial support (grants, loans, equity), direct 'soft' support (training, counseling, infrastructure), and efforts to stimulate private sector investments (networking, co-funding).

Furthermore, the government can take a role as an innovator by fueling experimentation, launching new initiatives, and disseminating knowledge about best practice. In this way the government schemes can assist both public and private actors to implement new insights, thus overcoming 'anticipatory myopia' (Salmenkaita and Salo, 2002). Commercialization is an area of high complexity and uncertainty, and experimentation is necessary to find solutions to the specific challenges of specific contexts. Government programs can take the initial risk and cost and create new and better routines and arrangements for the commercialization of research. The lessons learned from such investments may benefit several actors.

As a consequence, in the design of spin-off support tools the government has to find the right types of incentives and has to look into the organizational configuration of the support scheme at different levels. The government support schemes may vary regarding the range of control and coordination by national agencies, the organizational solutions at university level, and ways to organize at the project level. Hence, specific organizational design is needed for these types of ventures at different levels: the research idea and the entrepreneur at project level, the university structure at the organizational level, and the government with its national agencies working on behalf of the public interests at the regional and national levels.

METHODOLOGY

Sample

The empirical data used in this study cover government programs to support the commercialization of research in six countries: Canada, Finland, Ireland, Norway, Scotland and Sweden. The countries were selected for having comparable characteristics related to population size, economy, educational system, geography, living standards and industry structure. In addition, some of the countries have some specific characteristics such as long geographical distances and a business sector consisting mainly of SMEs. All the countries have a well developed university sector where the major source of funding for university research is basic funding and grants from the government. Furthermore, all countries have well developed national policy schemes for the commercialization of research (Lundström and Stevenson, 2005).

Data Collection and Analysis

Information was obtained from a literature review and interviews with well informed people in each country. A large number of policy reports in the form of statistical information, benchmarking studies, case studies and program evaluations provided extensive background information about the innovation policy and the government programs in each country. Further, we obtained updated brochures, descriptions and criteria about the specific programs. This information allowed us to define the key research questions and develop a model to guide further data collection. Next, we conducted semi-structured interviews with well informed people in each country; such as policy-makers, program managers, policy researchers, university administrators and program users. In total, we interviewed about 100 persons in 80 face-to-face and 20 telephone interviews. A case description about each country was written and has been verified by key people in all these countries except Ireland.

Some challenges related to the data collection should be noted. Few countries provide detailed national statistics on the number of spin-offs and other outputs from the commercialization of research. Exact comparisons of the various initiatives in the countries studied would be unreliable as the different areas of operation, other initiatives in place, and different contexts make each program unique. Therefore, it makes limited sense to compare the quantitative output from one program in one country with another program in another country because of different ways of measuring data, differences in industry structure, highly diverse composition of initiatives, and differences in scope. Also, the output numbers are not directly comparable due to the variation in the definitions used. Further, it is even more difficult to relate the output metrics to any specific programs or initiatives as the additionality is not clear-cut. That is, the output may have occurred even if the program did not exist. Most often, several initiatives are involved in supporting each commercialization project, and isolating the effects of single measures is a challenging task. In this study, we have emphasized the main characteristics of the different programs and the organizational solutions through in-depth discussions with officials on different levels. During these discussions, the specific characteristics of the commercialization process and the university setting have been targeted. The data have been analyzed inductively by a team of researchers in cooperation with practitioners.

FINDINGS

This section presents the range of government measures to commercialize research emanating from universities and research institutes in the six different countries.

Country Descriptions

Canada

Among the countries in this study, Canada has the longest track record of formal support for university spin-offs. This is more than 20 years in some of the leading research universities. Despite this rather long tradition, the government resources to support the commercialization of research are increasing and the number of programs at federal and provincial level is vast. One survey identified 178 initiatives having CAD3.2 billion expenditure a year (Gault and McDaniel, 2004). At the universities, the industrial liaison offices (ILOs) or TTOs play a central role as coordinators of the different funding sources. The Canadian universities have different approaches to IP ownership, but the quantitative results from their commercialization activities do not seem to be affected by IP policy (Clayman, 2004). As the commercialization and technology transfer infrastructure in Canada has matured, both government programs and university ILOs take a broader view on technology transfer than just patenting and licensing. For government agencies, the benefits for Canada and Canadians are central, while the universities increasingly view technology transfer as a strategic part of their activities. In total, the Canadian efforts to commercialize research have passed the pioneering period and have developed into a more operational phase where these activities are generally seen as an important part of research and innovation activity.

Finland

Policy studies often refer to Finland as a world class model having an innovation environment with high R&D investments, a high number of patents filed, a highly educated workforce, and a high share of high-technology based firms, just to mention a few indicators. The Finnish innovation support system consists of several actors responsible for a high number of policy measures. The major funding schemes have a strong collaborative approach and usually require university–industry collaboration. Hence, only a few rather young initiatives are targeted at the commercialization of research findings in the pre-start-up phase or in the stage before an industrial partner is involved. Although one of the strengths of the Finnish system is claimed to be the close networking between a number of different public innovation actors, the complicated system with many actors may confuse the users of the different initiatives. The culture for commercialization of research at the Finnish universities is not very strong. The collaboration with companies has worked well, but little is invested in competence in licensing and creating spin-offs. To build an infrastructure at Finnish universities has not been a priority until recently. According to our interviewees there is, however, a shift towards a more proactive attitude among university managers to increase the commercialization of research. The attitude is becoming increasingly more positive among university faculty, but many professors are still reluctant to mix business and academic activities.

Ireland

During the last years there have been increased efforts towards technology oriented R&D in Ireland. There has been a five-fold increase in research funding over the six-year period up to 2006. The new policy is very much based on cluster thinking, especially within ICT and biotechnology. This emphasis has consequences for the organization and the tools implemented at the university level, with increased emphasis on high potential research areas. Government support agencies are active at university level, supervising the commercialization process and providing coordinative links between universities and industry. The strong coordination efforts are followed up at university level. The integrated Research and Innovation Centres are coordinating R&D applications, applications for commercialization support, and supporting technology transfer. The main responsibility for the infrastructure is placed at the universities and the TTOs and innovation centers. At national level, Ireland has a support scheme for the education of spin-off entrepreneurs in the later phase of commercialization.

Norway

Commercialization of research has not been a core activity for Norwegian universities until recently, although significant public support for commercialization has been granted to boundary organizations in the university cities. Due to the low level of industry R&D expenditure, the Norwegian government considers it to be particularly important to foster the creation of new research-based firms. Legislative changes in 2003 and the subsequent establishment of TTOs at the major research universities have resulted in a higher emphasis on commercialization. The infrastructure and competence to support spin-offs is still under construction in Norway. The main government schemes for the commercialization of university research are taken care of by one program in the national research council. This program has been in operation since 1994, and is regarded as quite successful in terms of supporting the establishment of an infrastructure at the universities, the number of successful projects supported, and its flexible unbureaucratic operations. The program provides support to the regional science parks and the university TTOs, which are responsible for following up the spin-off projects. In addition, new schemes are launched according to perceived needs, such as proof-of-concept funding, a commercialization grant for academics, and networking activities.

Scotland

The basic rationale related to governmental support of commercialization of research from Scottish universities and research institutes is related to the fact that Scotland has a strong science base while their industry base is less developed. There is a belief that it is possible to strengthen the industry base by stimulating the commercialization of research from Scottish universities. There is a dedicated focus in supporting the industrialization of research within life science, energy and tech-media. In Scotland there is a strong recognition that stimulating entrepreneurship within universities and research institutions is very different from stimulating entrepreneurship in general. These projects and entrepreneurs are nurtured through separate programs in order to generate future high-growth companies. Both top-down and bottom-up approaches are used in order to form a more streamlined pipeline for commercialization projects from research institutions. However, Harrison and Don (2004) point out that even though much is already being done in terms of stimulating the exploitation of Scotland's science base, there is still scope for more effective coordination of these various schemes and for a more robust focus on the business development models appropriate for the creation of world class high-growth companies.

Sweden

Sweden has long traditions that focus on R&D and collaboration between university and industry. The R&D level in Sweden is the highest in the world, particularly due to the high level of research in industry. There are, however, few national programs for the commercialization of research from universities. Independent foundations in seven regions have addressed this issue since the mid-1990s. This is now reorganized from seven independent foundations into one company with seven subsidiary companies. Despite the lack of national innovation programs aimed at the university sector, there seems to be a history of a high activity level at many universities and colleges. At the university level the holding companies were established in the mid-1990s. To some extent the holding companies have taken the role to build commercial competence at the universities, but, with few economic resources, the holding companies have had a limited effect.

Country Characteristics Compared

The national objectives and main focus in the policy to commercialize university research differ between the six countries, as summarized in Table 6.1.

The main focus ranges from broad efforts to increase the number of industries and make the 'thousand flowers bloom' to a more selected focus on specific research areas. The support is both decentralized to the regional level, as in the Nordic countries, and centralized, as in Ireland and Scotland. Canada excels through a broad range of tools and a multi-level support structure. Regarding financial support, the countries with the most centralized schemes also have the broadest range of financial support tools covering all the steps in the development process. Canada has emphasized competence and training within the universities to be able to tackle the high complexity of the spin-off firm formation process. Finland has strongly emphasized industry partner solutions, not least due to the success of the mobile phone company Nokia. This may result in a high industry involvement in the design of government efforts. However, it may also increase the dependency on a few larger companies.

The countries in this study can be divided in three groups. Finland, together with Sweden, is in a particular situation as these countries are number one and two in the world when it comes to research spending as a share of gross domestic product (GDP). This is due to the high level of research in industry, which is also reflected in these countries'

Table 6.1 Characteristics of the government efforts to support commercialization of research

	Canada	Finland	Ireland	Norway	Scotland	Sweden
Main focus in commercialization	Create research-based new industry	University–industry collaboration	Excellence in selected areas	Create research-based new industry	Excellence in selected areas	University–industry collaboration
Main level of support operation	Multi-level	Regional	Central	Regional	Central, but support to University initiatives	Regional
Government control and evaluation	High focus, but varies between programs	Medium, regular program evaluations	Medium	Medium, keep statistics	High focus, some comprehensive plans	Mostly done at regional level
Focus on building infrastructure	High	Low, but increasing	Medium	High	Medium	High, from regional level
Early phase seed funding	Well developed	Many recent initiatives	Medium	Medium	High, good coordination	Medium, new regional initiatives
Focus on proof of concept funds	High, but varies between institutions	Industry partner usually needed	High	Medium, increasing	High	Low, some at regional level
Focus on commercialization project funds	High, from many sources	Industry partner usually needed	High, especially directly to selected projects	High	High, especially directly to selected projects	Regional level
Programs level training TTO level expertise	High	Low	Medium	Low, but regional initiative	Medium, also for academics	Low

commercialization policies. Thus, the focus is more on university–industry collaboration, rather than fostering new spin-off firms. Although this picture is nuanced and there is significant focus on spin-off creation, it seems fair to say that Sweden and Finland have a shorter history and fewer initiatives to support spin-off firm formation from universities.

The second group of countries consists of Canada and Norway, which have a low share of R&D spending in industry, in contrast to Sweden and Finland. Due to limited possibilities to commercialize university research in domestic industry, policy-makers in Canada and Norway have seen it as important to facilitate the creation of new spin-off firms. The third group, Ireland and Scotland, stands out with a much more focused effort to achieve excellence in research and commercialization in selected areas. This is also evident in the more centralized operation of government support schemes in these countries compared to the others in this study.

ANALYSIS

The countries in this study have implemented a broad range of measures to facilitate university spin-offs. The governments' responses to the challenges regarding commercialization of university research are summarized in Table 6.2.

One type of government measure is targeted at changing the institutional setting in order to make it better equipped to create and support spin-off projects. In this category we identified programs to change the attitudes and culture within universities to be more supportive to commercialization and spin-off activity, programs to build competence in commercialization and business development at universities, and programs to build an effective infrastructure in the form of commercialization support units and facilities such as TTOs and incubators.

Another type of program is addressing specific commercialization projects. In this category, different models of proof-of-concept funding were frequently used. Furthermore, many programs supported business development in early phases of the development of a spin-off firm. Furthermore, we also identified that government schemes may play the role of inducing improvements in the commercialization system and developing new initiatives. Thus, government schemes are acting as a facilitator for transferring best practice from other countries and institutions and acting as an innovator and risk-taker in developing new initiatives. In this section we will discuss these three types of schemes and different ways of organizing these government initiatives.

Table 6.2 Challenges to entrepreneurship in universities and government schemes

Characteristics of spin-off process	Challenge for commercialization of research results	Target area for government schemes
University role	Universities are institutions of education and basic research with multiple goals and stakeholders	Support organizational change within universities (infrastructure)
Cultural differences	Commercialization projects need to make a transition from academic to commercial culture	Support the entrepreneurial process with both infrastructure and project support
Interactive process	Different competencies and collaboration needed throughout the commercialization process	Support competence development and networking activities
Financial capital	Early-stage high-risk nature of projects	Financial support to projects in areas of market failure and incentives for private investors
External relations	Networks and communication crucial	Support networking activities

Programs to Change Culture and Build Infrastructure

How to get academics and universities more involved in the commercialization of research is a key issue among agencies and people working to promote commercialization. This relates both to increasing the entrepreneurial orientation of the university faculty and staff, and to reducing administrative barriers within the university.

The infrastructure may be organized in two different ways; in boundary organizations acting as mediators between the academic and the business community or as initiatives within the universities. In Norway and Finland commercialization activities are in some cases outsourced to separate commercialization units, while in countries like Canada, Ireland and Scotland, activities are organized within the universities with close links to the university administration. In Ireland, strong efforts are made to meet with the researchers at institutes and to present role model examples of entrepreneurs.

Science parks have become a natural part of the environment at most universities. Some of these play a role as administrators of government schemes to promote the commercialization of research results from the adjacent university. Examples of other types of infrastructure organized in boundary organizations are external advisors connected to science parks, network organizations, and specialized government agencies. It seems, however, to be difficult for this type of initiative to achieve close interaction with the university departments, and alignment with the other missions of a university might be a challenge.

Technology transfer is increasingly seen as a strategic tool for universities in order to increase their impact on society. Thus, the role of TTOs is currently evolving more towards being a part of university activities. This development was particularly visible in Canada, where the TTO infrastructure has been in operation for up to 20 years. We identified several examples where government support schemes contributed to the development of a professional TTO function within universities both by direct funding and through training programs for TTO personnel. There are also many examples of schemes that support the establishment and operation of on-campus incubators at the universities. Other activities that are set up to increase the commercial orientation of university scientists and to identify promising business ideas are seminars and training programs for scientists, business plan competitions, and other 'marketing' activities. Still, it is a challenge to reach all the researchers in the universities.

We found that the awareness and focus on commercialization varies a great deal, not only between countries but also between universities and research groups. Hence, the appropriate measures vary depending on the maturity of the commercialization topic at each institution and research group. Although there is no doubt that academics are increasingly becoming more positive towards the commercialization of research, few recipes or best practice to stimulate this change can be found. As efforts to change culture mainly have to be implemented at the institutional level, few government programs are aimed directly at researchers for such issues. This is often a more internal affair at universities, and perhaps not prioritized very much in all institutions. Thus, it seems clear that a commitment from the university management is crucial for the government initiatives to be effective.

It seems that the need for competence in the field of technology transfer is becoming more evident as the infrastructure becomes more established. This competence is not easily available and may be facilitated through the development of a portfolio of experienced consultants supporting the projects. In countries with a long track record, such as Canada and Scotland, the focus on training programs seems to be particularly strong. In Canada, for instance, there seems to be a general agreement that there is a lack of competent people in the research institutions to handle commercialization projects. Hence, several government schemes have focused their funds more on networks, partnerships and training programs (hands-on internships). There is a strong focus on developing talent and it is very often stated that technology transfer also includes the transfer of people. Specialized training programs for all those involved in the commercialization process may prove beneficial. This includes consultants, the researchers themselves, and the TTO staff.

Programs to Support Specific Commercialization Projects

Government programs may provide direct support to commercialization projects in several ways, from direct funding and physical infrastructure to 'soft' support in the form of mentoring, training and networking. The focus on 'soft' support is increasing and is related to an increased emphasis on skills and competence, not only financial and physical resources. We identified several training programs for academic entrepreneurs, and the government schemes often supported mentors and consultants who contributed with their experience and networks to the spin-off projects.

In most countries, it is acknowledged that there is a funding gap between the research-based inventions made within the universities and commercial concepts that are of interest to industry and private capital. The investors and industry often feel that the risks are too high to support the development of a research-based idea. The first phase of this funding gap is primarily addressed by grant-based programs, while programs in later stages usually require private co-funding and sometimes equity in the projects. It seems, however, that projects where no company or investor has shown interest will be cut off from programs requiring cost sharing.

Some countries have set up development grants or so-called proof-of-concept funds providing funds to verify the industrial applicability of the research-based invention. Often, a second round of funding is available if an investor or industrial partner is committed to the project. A reported challenge of such proof-of-concept grants is to make sure that the funding is used for commercialization activities, and not for further research.

Several programs are set up to stimulate private sector investment in spin-off projects. It seems generally difficult to get seed funds to invest in university technologies in early phases of development, but some funds have been set up with formal university ownership. More common, however, are attempts to connect with business angels and venture capital firms both through formal networks and networking arenas.

Inducing Improvements and Developing New Initiatives

To experiment with new initiatives is both risky and costly, but this is necessary in order to learn and to find new and better models that could be applied across many institutions. Hence, the responsibility for supporting new experiments might be at the national level, as the risk might be too high for single organizations or agencies at regional level. An experimental approach was especially visible in Canada, where new pilots were common in order to test the viability of concepts to see if they could be launched as a general initiative.

Another trend in several of the Canadian programs is that they fund networking between institutions or even require that a consortium is made to be eligible for receiving funds. The diversity of approaches and a willingness among some of the public actors to experiment with new initiatives also gives rise to some new and innovative instruments. Thus, they seem more eager to design new initiatives than to operate the existing infrastructure, such as funding the initial set-up of networks and TTOs which are supposed to be operated by the universities after the initial public support is spent. The aim of many government initiatives is to make themselves redundant and not to become a basic funder of infrastructure. In this way the government schemes are taking on the cost and initial risk of developing new initiatives, but assume that if the initiative becomes successful it will be able to acquire funding from other sources.

The Organization of Government Initiatives

Some countries, such as Canada and Finland have a number of autonomous actors who are initiating programs, while other countries, such as Ireland and Scotland have a more centrally coordinated system. Sweden relies heavily on regionally based initiatives, while in other countries the programs are governed centrally. The countries with a clear national ambition and cluster orientation, such as Ireland and Scotland, have more centralized organizations. These countries have specialized efforts towards a limited number of industries. Moreover, we also observe that this makes their universities even more focused on achieving research and commercialization excellence within a few main areas. With a more centralized organization the universities are followed closely; sometimes with government representatives on campus securing the interests and coordination between the commercialization units.

The degree of governmental intervention and how the different countries choose to organize these activities varies. Governments are actively encouraging universities to include commercialization as a part of their mission, rather than being a responsibility for actors outside the university. Some countries acknowledged that a wider range of structural changes than just providing funds through support programs was needed to change the culture at universities. One challenge may be that two different government levels are responsible for academic research (for example ministry of education) and for industry development (for example ministry of industry). For instance in Canada, Finland and Norway, it seems that the latter are much more occupied with promoting commercialization than the former, and some of the efforts might benefit from a better coordination between these levels.

In some of the government agencies, especially in Canada, there were worries that the universities had too narrow a focus on achieving quantitative output goals. Many of the TTOs in Canada, Scotland, Ireland and Finland have a broader mission, including writing applications and contact with industry partners. An interesting observation is that the revenue from some TTOs in Ireland and Scotland goes back to the university, and not the TTO. In this way the TTO does not get too focused on the financial measures. In addition, it is easier to gain legitimacy for the TTO and commercialization activity if the revenue from this activity is shown to the academics by means of direct funding for research.

The empirical findings from this study suggest that more specialized efforts are beneficial in order to create networks among scientific fields, between universities, and towards specific industries. Networking between regional actors at a national level is seen as important. One possible strategy to promote networking by government programs is through enforced networks. Here, the staff are employed directly at the government level, but are operating within the research institutions. Another strategy is to accept only consortia or networks as eligible applicants for commercialization infrastructure grants. We also see that government programs are supporting regional network organizations.

Often there are other general programs that provide significant add-on funding to the commercialization initiatives. Although this study considers programs specially targeted at research-based innovations, these projects frequently benefit from more general initiatives such as grants, loans and equity schemes for start-ups; incubators and training for entrepreneurs; and grants and tax deductions for R&D activity.

The results above show that the countries have put significant efforts into developing an innovation policy with influence on other areas like regional, industrial, education, and research policy. In the countries included in our study we find a varying degree of systematic analyses mapping the market imperfections and efforts towards finding the right level of the different types of support schemes. Typical gaps identified are lack of competent people, lack of internationalization, lack of funding for the early stages, lack of venture capital, and lack of culture and infrastructure within the universities. Some agencies spend considerable resources on benchmarking and evaluation studies in order to discover and highlight best practice from relevant sources.

CONCLUSIONS

This study has shown that due to the complexity of commercialization support schemes, there is considerable need for knowledge related to the design and implementation of government schemes for spin-off ventures. There is a need for a special focus on initiating new ideas and tools towards entrepreneurial culture and orientation (Chrisman et al., 1995; Kenney and Goe, 2004). As the spin-off ideas proceed through the commercialization process, new problems emerge and new tools are needed to meet imperfections such as lack of financial resources (Wright et al., 2006). There is also an active interplay between the support instruments and the university infrastructure for commercialization.

In parallel with the development of the support, there is a need to develop the organizational platform to handle spin-off creation within the universities. A well developed organizational platform may then change the need for government support as commercialization activities mature and better formal and informal infrastructures are developed.

The university context and tailor-made solutions are important. Hence, government initiatives with success in a country or institution with a long track record and a well developed infrastructure for commercialization may not be suited to a context where the activity and infrastructure is lacking. It might be that the complexity of the technology transfer field and the need for specialized competence will become clearer only after some degree of local experience (Rasmussen et al., 2006). This is in line with the academic entrepreneurship literature finding that university researchers lack commercialization experience and knowledge, especially in the early phase of development (Bird and Allen, 1989; Vohora et al., 2004).

An established external network and strategic alliances with people and companies that may take the idea further towards building a business platform are found crucial in prior studies (Bower, 2003; Davidsson and Klofsten, 2003; Grandi and Grimaldi, 2003). In some countries the foundation for this type of cooperation is lacking, meaning that the university and the entrepreneur have to take the idea the whole way towards establishing a new firm. In this study we found that countries with weak cooperation between industry and research institutions tend to establish more comprehensive programs to facilitate commercialization in the form of spin-off firms.

Countries with well-established links between industry and research institutes tend to pay less attention to direct spin-off support. In designated areas these countries seem to have industries with an absorptive capacity to capitalize on the basic and applied research undertaken at universities and research institutes. These countries also emphasize meeting places like science parks on the university campus. Hence, the introduction of more extensive efforts in order to commercialize research 'directly' from research institutions may not be successful because researchers oriented towards commercialization already use their capacity in research–industry collaboration.

New policies may focus on specific knowledge-intensive industries in the fields where the countries have or seek to develop an international competitive advantage. This may take the form of emphasis on specific industry clusters, influencing the innovation support system to prioritize much of the commercialization support towards the same areas. However, this may create challenges in other areas. The need for specialized competence within specific areas creates a need for sector-based initiatives. There has to be, in particular, a focus on the market imperfections in different areas and in different growth phases of the commercialization projects.

This study shows that countries with a clear national ambition and cluster orientation have more centralized funding agencies. The universities are monitored closely, sometimes with government representatives on campus, securing the interests and the coordination between commercialization units. The universities in these countries are also taking broader responsibility for the whole infrastructure and for coordinating the R&D activities. In countries with larger national R&D locomotives, there is less emphasis on spin-off activity and less centralized schemes. Some of the countries experiment with decentralized funding in several ways. However, here they face incentive challenges and conflicts of interest between different stakeholders. The independent commercialization units often become powerful compared with the researchers and the spin-off project. This may hamper the commercialization process as it proceeds into firm establishment and the seed-stage.

Policy Implications

Due to the complexity of the university spin-off process and the different history and characteristics of the national settings, interpretation of the implications from this study should be made with caution. In particular, it would be doubtful to compare statistics and quantitative outputs between the diverse settings, especially because there are few common definitions and the measurement methods are diverse. Still, several trends can be identified and important lessons can be learned from these cases.

It seems clear that commitment from the university is crucial in order to succeed with commercialization and research-based spin-off firm formation. Thus, for some initiatives to be effective there is a need to induce changes in the university organization. For instance, it would not be very relevant to introduce opportunities for proof-of-concept funding unless the universities were able to identify promising opportunities and were equipped to handle the projects funded by such grants.

There has to be a focus on experimenting with new initiatives (bottom-up). Also one has to be aware that technology transfer is a profession that needs specific competence and training. This also includes network capabilities. Increased focus on networking and specialization, sometimes imposed from the government level, is important. For the government, broad output metrics are needed to secure public interest and avoid agency problems.

A critical issue when addressing market failure through project support is the decision about what projects to support. In early phases, such as proof-of-concept, the decisions usually have to be based on some form of assessment or evaluation, as there are no markets for embryonic early-stage ideas. In later phases, programs may rely on private actors by requiring that private capital has been invested in order to be eligible for receiving public funds. Leaving the decision about what projects to support to the market might tend to favor projects in established rather than emerging industries.

Suggestions for Further Research

This study emphasizes the need for further in-depth studies of commercialization processes and how to organize public support. There is a need for more studies looking at how university programs can bring forward latent resources in the university or regional context, and not only considering the financial needs of the venture. Furthermore, research should focus on the organizational capabilities of the support programs that balance interests without hampering the dynamism of the projects and the entrepreneurial spirit of the researchers involved. In particular, there is a need to look more closely into the interplay between the financial support schemes and the administrative solutions chosen. It may be found that successful administrative solutions and entrepreneurial orientation in the university support staff may reduce the need for financial support.

There is a need for more comparative research between different universities, including in-depth studies following the commercialization process through its different stages. At national level, future studies should look more closely into the balance between targeting commercialization efforts towards established university–industry networks and established industry clusters versus a more open-ended, bottom-up approach facilitating more ideas and contributing to a more diverse entrepreneurial community.

REFERENCES

Benner, M. and U. Sandstrom (2000), 'Institutionalizing the triple helix: research funding and norms in the academic system'. *Research Policy*, **29**(2), 291–301.

Bird, B.J. and D.N.Allen (1989), 'Faculty entrepreneurship in research university environments', *Journal of Higher Education*, **60**(5), 583–96.

Birley, S. (2002), 'Universities, academics, and spinout companies: lessons from Imperial', *International Journal of Entrepreneurship Education,* **1**(1), 1–21.

Bower, D.J. (2003), 'Business model fashion and the academic spinout firm', *R&D Management*, **33**(2), 97–106.

Bray, M.J. and J.N. Lee (2000), 'University revenues from technology transfer: licensing fees vs. equity positions', *Journal of Business Venturing*, **15**(5–6), 385–92.

Brett, A., D.V. Gibson and R.W. Smilor (1991), *University Spin-Off Companies*, Lanham, MD, USA: Rowman & Littlefield Publishers.

Bruyat, C. and P.A. Julien (2001), 'Defining the field of research in entrepreneurship', *Journal of Business Venturing*, **16**(2), 165–80.

Candell, A. and A.B. Jaffe (1999), 'The regional economic impact of public research funding: a case study of Massachusetts', In L.M. Branscomb, F. Kodama and R. Florida (eds), *Industrializing Knowledge*, Cambridge, MA: MIT Press, pp. 510–30.

Carayannis, E.G., S.K. Kassicieh and R. Radosevich (2000), 'Strategic alliances as a source of early-stage seed capital in new technology-based firms', *Technovation*, **20**(11), 603–15.

Chiesa, V. and A. Piccaluga (2000), 'Exploitation and diffusion of public research: the case of academic spin-off companies in Italy', *R&D Management*, **30**(4), 329–39.

Chrisman, J.J., T. Hynes and S. Fraser (1995), 'Faculty entrepreneurship and economic development: the case of the University of Calgary', *Journal of Business Venturing*, **10**(4), 267–81.

Clark, B.R. (1998), *Creating Entrepreneurial Universities: Organizational Pathways of Transformation*, Oxford: Elsevier Science.

Clarysse, B. and N. Moray (2004), 'A process study of entrepreneurial team formation: the case of a research-based spin-off', *Journal of Business Venturing*, **19**(1), 55–79.

Clayman, B.P. (2004, '*Technology transfer at Canadian Universities: Fiscal Year 2002 Update*, Ottawa: Canada Foundation for Innovation.

Cohen, M.D., J.G. March and J.P. Olsen (1972), 'A garbage can model of organizational choice', *Administrative Science Quarterly*, **17**(1), 1–25.

Czarniawska, B. and K. Genell (2002), 'Gone shopping? Universities on their way to the market), '*Scandinavian Journal of Management*, **18**, 455–74.

Davenport, S., A. Carr and D. Bibby (2002), 'Leveraging talent: spin-off strategy at industrial research', *R&D Management*, **32**(3), 241–54.

Davidsson, P. and M. Klofsten (2003), 'The business platform: developing an instrument to gauge and to assist the development of young firms', *Journal of Small Business Management*, **41**(1), 1–26.

Franklin, S., M. Wright, and A. Lockett (2001), 'Academic and surrogate entrepreneurs in university spin-out companies', *Journal of Technology Transfer*, **26**, 127–41.

Gault, F. and S. McDaniel (2004), 'Summary: Joint Statistics Canada – University of Windsor Workshop on Intellectual Property Commercialization Indicators,

Windsor, Science, *Innovation and Electronic Information Division Working Papers* no. 6, p. 38.
Goldfarb, B. and M. Henrekson (2002), 'Bottom-up versus top-down policies towards the commercialization of university intellectual property', *Research Policy*, **32**(4), 639–58.
Grandi, A. and R. Grimaldi (2003), 'Exploring the networking characteristics of new venture founding teams', *Small Business Economics*, **21**(4), 329–41.
Granstrand, O. (1999), *The Economics and Management of Intellectual Property: Towards Intellectual Capitalism*, Cheltenham, UK and Northampton, MA, USA: Edward Elgar.
Gregory, W.D. and T.P. Sheahen (1991), 'Technology transfer by spin-off companies versus licensing. in A. Brett, D.V. Gibson and R.W. Smilor (eds), *University Spin-Off Companies*, Rowman & Littlefield Publishers, Lanham, MD, USA: pp. 133–52.
Guston, D.H. (1999), 'Stabilizing the boundary between US politics and science: the role of the office of technology transfer as a boundary organization', *Social Studies of Science*, **29**(1), 87–111.
Harrison, R. and G. Don (2004), 'The equity risk capital market in scotland: a benchmark analysis and report', Equitas, Centre for Entrepreneurship Research, University Of Edinburgh Management School, Edinburgh: Equitas.
Heirman, A. and B. Clarysse (2004), 'How and why do research-based start-ups differ at founding? a resource-based configurational perspective', *The Journal of Technology Transfer*, **29**(3–4), 247–68.
Hellström, T. and M. Jacob (2003), 'Boundary organizations in science: from discourse to construction'. *Science and Public Policy*, **30**(4), 235–8.
Henrekson, M. and N. Rosenberg (2001), 'Designing efficient institutions for science-based entrepreneurship: lessons from the US and Sweden'. *Journal of Technology Transfer*, **26**: 207–31.
Jensen, R. and M. Thursby (2001), 'proofs and prototypes for sale: the licensing of university inventions', *American Economic Review*, **91**(1), 240–59.
Kenney, M. and W.R. Goe (2004), 'The role of social embeddedness in professional entrepreneurship: a comparison of electrical engineering and computer science at UC Berkley and Stanford', *Research Policy*, **33**(5), 679–844.
Klofsten, M. and D. Jones- Evans (2000), 'Comparing academic entrepreneurship in Europe: the case of Sweden and Ireland', *Small Business Economics*, **14**(4), 299–309.
Lee, Y.S. (1996), ' "Technology transfer" and the research university: a search for the boundaries of university–industry collaboration', *Research Policy*, **25**(6), 843–63.
Lerner, J. (2002), 'When bureaucrats meet entrepreneurs: the design of effective "public venture capital" programmes', *Economic Journal*, **112**(477), F73–F84.
Lockett, A., D. Siegel, M. Wright and M.D. Ensley (2005), 'The creation of spin-off firms at public research institutions: managerial and policy implications', *Research Policy*, **34**(7), 981–93.
Louis, K.S., D. Blumenthal, M.E. Gluck and M.A. Stoto (1989), 'Entrepreneurs in academe: an exploration of behaviors among life scientists', *Administrative Science Quarterly*, **34**, 110–31.
Lundström, A. and L. Stevenson (2005), *Entrepreneurship Policy: Theory and Practice*, New York: Springer.
March, J.G. and J.P. Olsen (1976), *Ambiguity and Choice in Organizations*, Bergen: Universitetsforlaget.

Matkin, G.W. (1990), *Technology Transfer and the University*, Phoenix, AZ: Oryx Press.
Merton, R.K. (1973), *The Sociology of Science: Theoretical and Empirical Investigations*, Chicago: University Of Chicago Press.
Mian, S.A. (1997), 'Assessing and managing the university technology business incubator: an integrative framework', *Journal of Business Venturing*, **12**(4), 251–85.
Monotti, A. and S. Ricketson (2003), *Universities and Intellectual Property. Ownership and Exploitation*, New York: Oxford University Press.
Mowery, D.C., R.R. Nelson, B.N. Sampat and A.A. Ziedonis (2001), 'The growth of patenting and licensing by US universities: an assessment of the effects of the Bayh-Dole Act of 1980', *Research Policy*, **30**(1), 99–119.
Mustar, P. (1997), 'Spin-off enterprises. How French academics create high-tech companies: the conditions for success or failure', *Science and Public Policy*, **24**(1), 37–43.
Mustar, P., M. Renault, M.G. Colombo, E. Piva, M. Fontes, A. Lockett, M. Wright, B. Clarysse and N. Moray (2006), 'Conceptualizing the heterogeneity of research-based spin-offs: a multi dimensional taxonomy', *Research Policy*, **35**(2), 289–308.
Navarro, J.R. and F.O. Gallardo (2003), 'A model of strategic change: universities and dynamic capabilities', *Higher Education Policy*, **16**, 199–212.
Ndonzuau, F.N., F. Pirnay and B. Surlemont (2002), 'A stage model of academic spin-off creation' *Technovation,* **22**(5), 281–9.
OECD (2000), *Benchmarking Industry–Science Relationships*, Paris: OECD.
Pérez, M.P. and A.M. Sánchez (2003), 'The development of university spin-offs: early dynamics of technology transfer and networking', *Technovation*, **23**(10), 823–31.
Phan, P.H. (2004), 'Entrepreneurship theory: possibilities and future directions', *Journal of Business Venturing*, **19**(5), 617–20.
Radosevich, R. (1995), 'A model for entrepreneurial spin-offs from public technology sources', *International Journal of Technology Management*, **10**(7–8), 879–93.
Rasmussen, E. (2006), 'Facilitating university spin-off ventures – an entrepreneurship process perspective', Bodø, Norway. Bodø Graduate School of Business.
Rasmussen, E., Ø. Moen and M. Gulbrandsen (2006), 'Initiatives to promote commercialization of university knowledge', *Technovation*, **26**(4), 518–33.
Reitan, B. (1997), 'Fostering technical entrepreneurship in research communities: granting scholarships to would-be entrepreneurs', *Technovation*, **17**(6), 287–96.
Roberts, E.B. and D.E. Malone, (1996), 'Policies and structures for spinning off new companies from research and development organizations', *R&D Management*, **26**(1), 17–48.
Rogers, E.M., S. Takegami and J. Yin (2001), 'Lessons learned about technology transfer', *Technovation*, **21**(4), 253–61.
Rosenberg, N. (1991), 'Critical issues in science policy research', *Science and Public Policy*, **18**(6), 335–46.
Salmenkaita, J.-P. and A. Salo (2002), 'Rationales for government interventions in the commercialization of new technologies', *Technology Analysis & Strategic Management*, **14**(2), 183–200.
Samsom, K.J. and M.A. Gurdon (1993), 'University scientists as entrepreneurs – a special case of technology-transfer and high-tech venturing', *Technovation*, **13**(2), 63–71.

Shane, S. (2001), 'Technological opportunities and new firm creation', *Management Science*, **47**(2), 205–20.

Shane, S. (2004), *Academic Entrepreneurship: University Spinoffs and Wealth Creation*, Cheltenham, UK and Northampton, MA, USA: Edward Elgar.

Shane, S. and T. Stuart (2002), 'Organizational endowments and the performance of university start-ups', *Management Science*, **48**(1), 154–70.

Slaughter, S. and L.L. Leslie (1997), *Academic Capitalism: Politics, Policies, and the Entrepreneurial University*, Baltimore: Johns Hopkins University, Press.

Stankiewicz, R. (1986), *Academics and Entrepreneurs. Developing University–Industry Relations*, London: Frances Printer.

Stephan, P.E. (1996), 'The economics of science', *Journal of Economic Literature*, **34**(3), 1199–235.

Stevenson, H.H. and J.C. Jarillo (1990), 'A paradigm of entrepreneurship: entrepreneurial management', *Strategic Management Journal*, **11**, 17–27.

Thursby, J.G., R. Jensen and M.C. Thursby (2001), 'Objectives, characteristics and outcomes of university licensing: a survey of major US universities', *Journal of Technology Transfer*, **26**(1/2), 59–72.

Vanaelst, I., B. Clarysse, M. Wright, A. Lockett, N. Moray and R. S'jegers (2006), 'Entrepreneurial team development in academic spinouts: an examination of team heterogeneity', *Entrepreneurship Theory and Practice*, **30**(2), 249–71.

Vohora, A., M. Wright and A. Lockett (2004), 'Critical junctures in the development of university high-tech spinout companies', *Research Policy*, **33**(1), 147–75.

Weick, K.E. (1976), 'Educational organizations as loosely coupled systems' *Administrative Science Quarterly*, **21**, 1–19.

Westhead, P. and D. Storey (1997), 'Financial constraints on the growth of high technology small firms in the UK', *Applied Financial Economics*, **7**, 197–201.

Wright, M., S. Birley and S. Mosey (2004), 'Entrepreneurship and university technology transfer', *The Journal of Technology Transfer*, **29**(3/4), 235–46.

Wright, M., A. Lockett, B. Clarysse and M. Binks (2006), 'University spin-out companies and venture capital', *Research Policy*, **35**(4), 481–501.

7. Enterprise education in different cultural settings and at different school levels

Ulla Hytti

INTRODUCTION

Enterprise education and entrepreneurial studies have been strongly promoted and in some countries included by legislation in the national curricula. European countries have different entrepreneurial cultures, and differences should be reflected in the enterprise education programmes and curriculum structure. Terminology differs according to culture, and this makes transnational exchange of knowledge and research in the field difficult. In planning research in the area of enterprise education we encountered a lack of comparable material across Europe. The terms used in one culture do not carry the same meaning in other cultures, and this makes theory and programme development difficult.

Hence, any understanding and interpretation of entrepreneurship must reflect the social, cultural and historical environment in which the activity is embedded. In different times and places entrepreneurship has had different meaning, such as (external) entrepreneurship, which is about setting up and managing small businesses and/or growth-oriented, entrepreneurial ventures; intrapreneurship, which is understood as an entrepreneurial way of action within an organization; and enterprising behaviour, which deals with the behaviours, skills and attributes of any individual in all spheres of life (Kyrö, 1996). The differentiated understandings of entrepreneurship are linked to different sets of learning objectives in enterprise education which may be categorized under three headings: (1) learning to understand entrepreneurship; (2) learning to become entrepreneurial; and (3) learning to become an entrepreneur (see also Hytti et al., 2002; Hytti and O'Gorman, 2004).

As enterprise education does not take place in a vacuum, the entrepreneurial culture and environment of a given region, country or a particular school needs to be taken into consideration when planning the enterprise education programme. If there is a strong interest in entrepreneurship as a desirable career option, it makes sense to place the focus on providing programmes that support the activity. Vice versa, if the interest in entrepreneurship is low, it does not make sense to provide start-up courses but to focus on building awareness and on supporting entrepreneurial behaviour. Another major element that needs to be incorporated in the planning is the school level: the younger the students, the more the focus should be on supporting entrepreneurial behaviour, not on preparing the students for the world of business.

While it appears that at the European level all of these different approaches can be found, there are important differences in the national approaches. It seems that the programmes target school levels appropriately: the business focus on education is introduced only at vocational level (secondary schools, higher education). However, in certain countries there seems to be a lack of programmes at an earlier stage (kindergarten, primary schools), and only few programmes focus on building awareness and on supporting entrepreneurial behaviour. In some countries enterprise education is taken exclusively to mean training for persons who are interested in becoming self-employed. For example, in Austria and Norway there is a strong business focus on enterprise education, that is its role is understood as the capability to increase the number of start-ups. In Austria this is perhaps grounded in the role of Chambers of Commerce and the particular examinations required from entrepreneurs. In Norway, large firms have dominated the labour markets and fairly little attention has been paid to SMEs or entrepreneurship. Based on surveys, however, the entrepreneurial culture in Austria and Norway is quite weak – meaning that only a minority is interested in entrepreneurship as a career option. Hence, there might be a need to shift the focus. The situation is quite different in Finland, where enterprise education has a strong non-business focus; this reflects the entrepreneurship culture in the country quite well and is potentially able to strengthen it for the future. Therefore, enterprise education means more than education for those who are interested in becoming self-employed as it also encompasses education aimed at increasing the entrepreneurial behaviour of students and employees. In Ireland and the UK, there seems to be a mixed approach. Interestingly, the approach in these countries is based on differentiated policy development. In the UK, enterprise education has been explicitly present in education policy over the decades, while in Ireland the initiatives have been many but they are not related to any comprehensive enterprise education policy.

This research is grounded in a larger European research project that aimed at establishing a common frame-of-reference that would allow Europe-wide comparability in order to create new knowledge of enterprise education and facilitate transnational academic and pedagogic discussion and cooperation among theorists and practitioners in this field. This chapter reports the differences of enterprise education programmes run in five European countries (Austria, Finland, Ireland, Norway and the UK).

ENTERPRISE EDUCATION: DIFFERENT GOALS, METHODS AND OUTCOMES

Enterprise Education in Different Cultural Settings

The role and aims of enterprise education are connected to the meanings assigned to entrepreneurship. The history of entrepreneurship studies has relied on psychology and has aimed at profiling the 'Entrepreneur' (characteristics, demographics, and so on). In the field of management and business economics, these so-called trait studies were the key interest area until the 1990s (Brockhaus, 1982; Kovalainen, 1989). In such studies the personal characteristics of entrepreneurs were under investigation. These studies did not provide any conclusive results because the characteristics identified were largely similar to that of other groups, such as managers or creative people (Gartner, 1988; Gartner, 1989; Bird, 1989; Baron, 1998). From the point-of-view of enterprise education the identification of certain characteristics of entrepreneurs does not seem to be a promising approach – if such innate attributes given at birth were found to be exclusive to some people the role of enterprise education becomes redundant.

Recently it has been suggested that it is the process of entrepreneurship and not the individuals that should be in the focus of entrepreneurship research. Hence, entrepreneurship is about exploring, discovering and exploiting opportunities (Shane and Venkataraman, 2000). From this perspective entrepreneurship is more of an act of doing than a state of existence. In this vein, entrepreneurship is not reserved for certain people (business founders) but could be seen to be a process that can touch many people in different forms. From this perspective enterprise education has a distinctive role in aiming at developing the attitudes, competences and skills of the individuals to engage in the process of entrepreneurship. A framework for understanding the different forms of entrepreneurship (elaborated from Kyrö, 1996) is provided in Figure 7.1.

An important element in this framework is the entrepreneurial culture and environment of a given country, region or even a school. The planning of enterprise education programmes and models should reflect the entrepreneurial culture. If entrepreneurship is a widely accepted and desirable activity, it might be that the focus on the national or regional level is largely

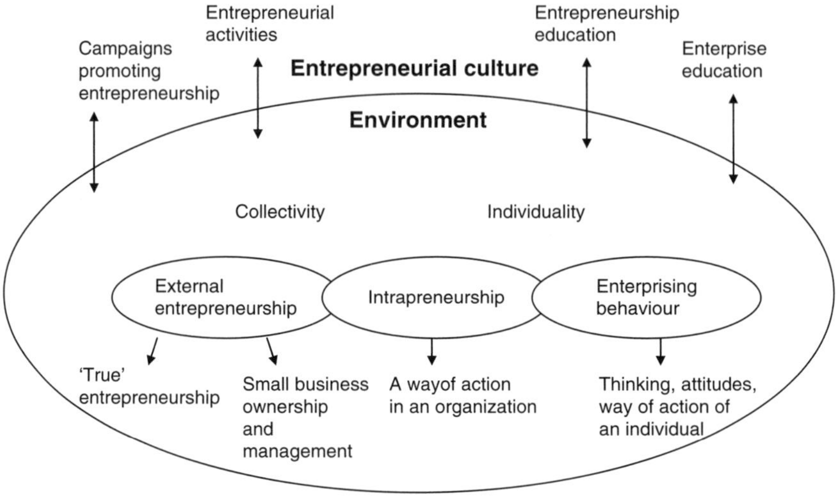

Source: Elaborated from Kyrö (1996).

Figure 7.1 Forms of entrepreneurship

on external entrepreneurship – providing the necessary skills in becoming and acting as an entrepreneur. However, if waged work remains the preferred option in a country or a region, and entrepreneurship is considered to be an option only for the few, selected individuals, this suggests that the main focus cannot be solely on promoting external entrepreneurship but should be placed on developing enterprising behaviour and intrapreneurial activity.

The European Commission tracks the preferences at the country level and the results from the most recent Flash Eurobarometer are presented in Figure 7.2 (European Commission, 2007). The question posed to the respondents is 'How desirable is it for you to become self-employed within the next five years?' and the figure represents the number of respondents that claim it is very desirable. The results demonstrate that there are important differences across the different countries. In some new member states (Latvia, Poland and Lithuania), about 50 per cent of the people consider self-employment as a desirable career option. The option is even more desirable than in the US which is mostly presented as *the* country when it comes to entrepreneurship. At the same time in some old member states only less than 20 per cent of the people consider self-employment as desirable. Almost half those in the old member states (EU-15) (49 per cent) have never thought about starting up a business. When compared to the US, this is almost double (27 per cent). However, the situation is again different in

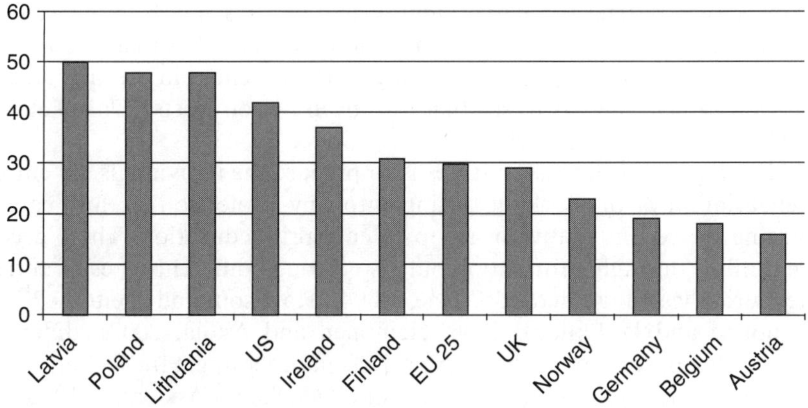

Figure 7.2 Desirability of self-employment (% of respondents) in selected European countries and the US (European Commission, 2007)

the new member states: there only 40 per cent have never thought about starting up a business.

The analysis of an entrepreneurial culture might also be interesting from a school's perspective: for example to examine the general attitudes and intentions of students in a particular school or university vis-à-vis an entrepreneurial career, which might serve as assessment of the platform for enterprise education (Schwarz and Grieshuber, 2000; Harju et al., 2004). Students interested in enterprise education may be interested in becoming entrepreneurs themselves or they may attend the course just to fulfil their curiosity (Hytti, 2001) or to increase their understanding of business (Heinonen et al., 2006).

Following this, it is suggested here that these cultural differences should be taken into consideration when planning the enterprise education curricula at the national level and also to some extent at the school level. If only a small minority of the students would prefer or even consider entrepreneurship as a career option, the programme needs to be different from the case where a significant number of the students share this idea. In the countries on the right-hand side of Figure 7.2 the focus on enterprise education should be more on awareness-raising, informing people that option exists and what it is in general about (Jack and Anderson, 1998; Chen et al., 1998). For this purpose there is a need to organize, for example, media campaigns or seminars and lectures in the open fora. Awareness-building can of course also be understood as the first ladder in also preparing people to pursue an entrepreneurial career at a later stage since an individual's propensity to pursue alternative employment paths is greatly influenced by knowledge of the existence of other options. This implies that in order to be able to make the choice of becoming an entrepreneur in the later stages of one's career, one has to see that this given option exists. (Oakey et al., 1998; Vesalainen et al., 1999).

Also important in these cultures is to prepare the individuals for entrepreneurial ways of working, fitting into any profession or any career forming the second status or group of enterprise education. These needs are fulfilled through information but also through different types of entrepreneurial learning methods (Rae, 2004; Harrison and Leitch, 2005; Heinonen and Poikkijoki, 2006; Heinonen and Akola, 2007), different types of team work, workshops or projects in order to get the feeling of an entrepreneurial process and to learn from it (Jack and Anderson, 1998).

In the countries representing the left-hand side, enterprise education seems to show more demand for programmes that actually prepare people to act as entrepreneurs and manage businesses (Jack and Anderson, 1999; Solomon et al., 2002). Those seriously interested and/or determined starters might be in need of experimenting and playing with the idea, trying entrepreneurship out in controlled circumstances, for example in a class setting by setting up mini-businesses or through workshops. This third group – including determined starters, nascent entrepreneurs and in some cases also start-up firms – are also in need of the basic skills and information directly linked to setting and running a small firm, acting as an entrepreneur.

Here a rather dichotomous divide is presented between the left and right-hand side countries in terms of the supply of enterprise education. However, in practice all the different aims need to be covered at the national level and this discussion is meant to suggest where the focus of enterprise education should be on a country level. This also implies that it might be difficult to transfer enterprise education programmes from one country to another if these cultural differences are not taken into consideration.

Enterprise Education Policies in the Different Countries

Next, the enterprise education policies and their development in the countries involved in this research will be briefly outlined.

Austria

Since the mid-1990s, policy-makers have intensified their efforts to increase the rate of business creations and to create a positive environment for entrepreneurship, for example by raising the awareness of the wider Austrian public regarding how new enterprises have a positive impact on employment, innovation and competitiveness. Since then, by implementing a series of measures, attempts have been made to facilitate and accelerate business creations and to create better conditions for young entrepreneurs. Also at this time enterprise education in schools was launched. The inclusion of the training firm concept in the curricula of the secondary schools and colleges as well as the creation of junior firms in other school types have led to an encouragement of entrepreneurship education in the upper secondary education sector (schools for students aged between 14 and 18/19). In contrast to the training firms, students in junior firms do not simulate the start-up and management of a company, but actually create and manage businesses. In addition, action has been taken in higher education by appointing new chairs in entrepreneurship and also increasing study programmes in teacher education. (Stampfl, 2002) Hence, in Austria the focus is largely on the business approach, and the understanding of enterprise education is reflected through the aim of promoting more start-ups.

Finland

Since the early 2000s enterprise education has been mentioned as a subject in its own right in the basics of the curriculum of the comprehensive school, and is currently included in the lower level and upper level basic education. In addition, all vocational examinations include basic entrepreneurial skills. The objective of enterprise education is, in general terms, the development of the entrepreneurial qualities of individuals in addition to providing them with entrepreneurship skills. Enterprise education includes everybody within the school system. Enterprise education aims at developing an intrapreneurial attitude, which is a combination of flexibility, initiative, risk-taking ability, self-direction and on the other hand cooperation skills and a strong motivation to achieve, knowledge of entrepreneurial activity, and knowledge of the requirements of entrepreneurial activity from the point of view of career orientation and further studies. The overall objective is that schools and education institutions, together with their interest groups, develop the students' basic knowledge of the importance of and possibilities offered by entrepreneurial activity. At the same time they try to give an idea of entrepreneurship. The teachers' competence will be increased and the input of outside entrepreneurship experts will be increased. Teaching methods, which emphasize the action orientation of both individuals and groups, like projects, are considered to be well suited to promoting the development of entrepreneurship (Vento-Vierikko, 2002). As a conclusion, the non-business focus dominates in Finland. It is acknowledged that enterprise education has several opportunities to promote entrepreneurship: training of attitudes, waking up entrepreneurial potential and teaching skills and knowledge related to entrepreneurship (Honkanen, 2004; Heinonen and Akola, 2007).

Ireland

In Ireland, the school curriculum has very little formal entrepreneurship training/education; however, there are still many initiatives. The primary method used to promote entrepreneurship is Enterprise Award Schemes, of which there are a great number. Efforts to promote youth enterprise are very active in Ireland. Government agencies, the media, banks, business associations and private sector companies all participate in the sponsorship and promotion of these awards and their winners. In addition, initiatives considered to educate students suitably for entrepreneurship at primary and secondary levels include, for example, the development of higher order thinking abilities and problem-solving skills. Enhancing entrepreneurial culture and abilities are promoted through the transition year option in secondary schools. Recently taken actions also suggest a shift in education paradigm to provide a more comprehensive entrepreneurial element in education institutions (O'Gorman, 2002; Cooney and Kidney, 2007).

Norway

The Norwegian educational system has traditionally not focused on entrepreneurship or SMEs. One main direction of vocational training has been the education and training for craft certificates at secondary level. The reward of a certificate requires some business management courses. There have also, for several decades, been study programmes in general business management at secondary as well as tertiary levels. However, entrepreneurship has previously had very little room in the total curriculum and the total enrolment at secondary level as well as tertiary levels in Norway (Havnes, 2002). However, in the 2002/2003 school year the Graduate Programme in Higher Education was introduced by Young Enterprise Norway. In the programme, real companies are established by a group of students for 12 months. To date there have been 940 students in the programme (Johansen and Eide, 2006). However, entrepreneurship or enterprise education are not yet explicitly addressed in policy-making.

UK

Enterprise education in the UK only entered schools for the first time in the late 1970s. A major national training scheme for school leavers called the Youth Opportunity Programme was launched in 1978. In schools, the aim was at bridging the gap between education and employment, and providing a broader set of skills for adult working life. The impact of a growing link between industry and education became evident in the dissatisfaction regarding the relevance of the school curriculum to the skills required by industry. The 1970s therefore became the foundation for the development of an education system that helped to prepare young people for the world of work. This 'emergent phase' was followed in the 1980s by a phase in which the focus on education was very much on preparing young people for employment, not self-employment. This was despite the continuous growth in unemployment among young people at the time. Then, the late 1990s witnessed a re-emergence of interest in enterprise and entrepreneurship. Government departments have largely replaced the private sector in encouraging and promoting Enterprise Education at all levels of education. For the first time there is a statutory requirement to introduce elements of enterprise into the curriculum for older secondary school students (Cotton, 2002). Hence, the UK holds the largest tradition of including entrepreneurship in the education policy. Traditionally, the understanding of enterprise education is wide as it is also considered as a tool for combating social exclusion of marginal groups (such as school dropouts and disabled persons) (Gladstone, 2005).

Enterprise Education at Different School Levels

Besides the entrepreneurial culture of a given country or region, it is also important to understand the different aims for enterprise education based on the different school levels (Deuchar, 2004; Birdthistle et al., 2007). This differentiation is also needed to alleviate some of the tensions identified at the school level. For example, some of the teachers have expressed strong reservations about the whole concept of 'enterprise education' as the assumption is that the aim is to start preparing the kindergarten or primary school children for an entrepreneurial career, that is to prepare them for the world of business and money (Iredale, 1993; Lewis and Massey, 2003; Davies et al., 2004). The following school levels were applied in the analysis:

- Under 6 years of age (kindergarten and infant school).
- 6–12 years (primary school and lower level of comprehensive school).
- 13–19 years (education in upper level of comprehensive school, at the vocational level, in colleges and upper secondary school).
- Higher education (degree education in universities, colleges and at the polytechnic level).
- Other (continued or adult education).

The different school levels can also be understood as the ladder in enterprise education: in the kindergarten and primary schools the focus is primarily or even solely on developing enterprising behaviour (Iredale, 1993) and only at secondary school level and later in education does the focus shift partly towards learning to become an entrepreneur in the business sense. In a similar way, building enterprising behaviour can also be understood as the cornerstone in all school levels especially if there's a need to strengthen entrepreneurial culture in society (Lewis and Massey, 2003).

To summarize, I will analyse which kind of enterprise models are run in the different countries and at different school levels reflected against the desirability of entrepreneurship as a career option in these countries.

METHODOLOGY

This study was conducted by a multi-country research team in their respective countries (for detailed results refer to Hytti et al., 2002). The benefit of the approach was that through the understanding shared and developed by the members of the team, it was possible to approach the practice, that is to identify what is considered as enterprise education in the respective countries in the study.

Comparative research is conducted for several reasons, for example, to increase understanding of own's own country, to improve understanding of other countries, to test a theory across diverse settings, to examine the local reception of imported cultural forms, and to build universally applicable theory, to name a few. However, there are several challenges attached to cross-national research, such as the problems attached to 'comparing apples and oranges'. In addition, comparative research creates a pressure for increased need of communication between the researchers, the need to share and compare not only research findings but also theories and concepts, writing styles and publication strategies. Moreover, researchers must work in a foreign language and inequalities may be introduced by the common resort to English as the lingua franca (Livingston, 2003). We applied the following strategies to overcome these potential barriers.

In this study 62 enterprise education programmes or initiatives run in five European countries were analysed in order to identify what aims and objectives enterprise education programmes explicitly or implicitly were trying to achieve. Since the research team decided not to adopt a strict definition of what constitutes enterprise education, we required the researchers conducting the fieldwork to be culturally sensitive to the phenomenon at large in order to reflect the cultural underpinnings of enterprise education in their choice of the literature and programmes selected for the study. This was achieved by selecting national researchers to carry out the fieldwork. In addition, the research team engaged in an extensive discussion in order to reach an understanding of the phenomenon studied.

The researchers identified and documented an illustrative sample of national or regional programmes in the selected countries. In seeking to do this each national team was required to be sensitive to the need to document programmes from each of the three stages of the education system (essentially primary, secondary and higher education). It was agreed that the following types of programmes would not be included: programmes targeted at operating entrepreneurs or training programmes aimed at unemployed persons for setting up a business (especially if there was a choice of many projects).

In terms of documenting the programmes, the project coordinator prepared an inquiry reference form to ensure that there was standardization of data collected for each programme across the different national contexts. In collecting the data for each programme, multiple sources of information were used, for example research or evaluation studies of the related programmes, internal evaluation reports and where there was insufficient written documentation, the promoters of the programmes were interviewed.

The research work was coordinated by the Turku School of Economics and the data collection was carried out in conjunction with four other partner countries (Austria, Ireland, Norway and the UK).

ENTERPRISE EDUCATION PROGRAMMES IN EUROPE

Based on the analysis of enterprise education programmes it was possible to demonstrate that they do just not fall into a 'one size fits all' category but the variety of aims presented previously could be identified from the programmes. Some of the programmes or initiatives aimed at fulfilling just one particular need while others explicated wider aims. By using the framework of the different aims assigned for enterprise education the programmes in this chapter are categorized under the following headings based on their explicitly or implicitly announced objectives (Hytti et al., 2002; Hytti and O'Gorman, 2004):

A. Programmes aimed at creating skills and improving the information necessary for a person willing to start up or manage a small business;
B. Programmes striving to create a better understanding of (small) businesses and entrepreneurship in order to prepare people for the world of work and the relevant structural changes; or
C. Programmes trying to help people to become more enterprising in their overall lives in a changing society and culture.

Table 7.1 Classification of enterprise education models

Country	Number of programmes	Number of programmes targeting different aims (A, B, C)	Level of education
Austria	13	A (13), B (6), C (2)	13–19 years (4), HE (6), other[1] (4)
Finland	11	A (2), B (8), C (9)	−6 years (3), 6–12 years (5), 13–19 years (6), HE (2), other (8)
Ireland	14	A (10), B (11), C (8)	−6 years (1), 6–12 years (3), 13–19 years (7), HE (5), other (5)
Norway	11	A (7), B (3), C (2)	6–12 years (1), 13–19 years (2), HE (8), other (4)
UK	13	A (9), B (7), C (9)	6–12 years (1), 13–19 years (9), HE (5), other (6)

Note: [1] The category 'other' includes adult education and teacher training which are not focused on in this chapter.

Source: Based on Hytti et al. (2002).

The main results are presented in Table 7.1.

Most programmes that aspired to increase the number of start-ups were carried out in secondary schools (13–19 years) and in higher education institutes whereas in the primary schools (students under 6 years or 6–12 years) the aim for enterprise education in most cases was at improving the enterprising skills of students without a business focus or in creating more understanding of the world of work through community linkages. Hence, our suggestion for creating a ladder from enterprise education is supported. The activity starts with building enterprising behaviour and only in the later phases of education does the business focus surface on the arena.

Most of the Austrian programmes aim at preparing individuals to act as entrepreneurs, that is the programmes aimed at facilitating the start-up of new businesses. In addition, none of the Austrian programmes target the lower secondary school levels (children under 12 years), which is understandable given that the chosen approach is geared towards promoting start-ups. A similar concentration could also be identified in Norway. In Finland the focus is on programmes that aim at helping students to become more enterprising and to understand business and entrepreneurship. The programmes were also split across the different school levels.

The programmes run in Ireland were split across the different school levels and were relatively broad in their objectives since most of the programmes were seen to target all of the identified three objectives. The similar holistic approach to enterprise education could be identified in the case of the programmes run in the UK.

Thus, it seems that, based on our analysis, the offering of enterprise education programmes in the selected countries could be grouped into three categories:

1. A strong business focus on enterprise education (Austria, Norway)
2. A strong non-business focus on enterprise education (Finland)
3. A mixed approach (Ireland, UK)

The case for Austria and Norway seems to suggest a potential mismatch between the entrepreneurial culture and the types of programmes run. Whilst only a minority of Austrians or Norwegians consider entrepreneurship as a desirable option – 16 and 23 per cent of the population respectively (European Commission, 2007), the programmes target only this minority. In Austria, the entrepreneurship culture is dominated by the role of Chambers of Commerce. Hence, there is a risk that the majority of Austrians will not be affected at all by the programmes and it is not possible to change the entrepreneurial culture in the long run either. In contrast to the other countries in this study, in Austria a special exam is necessary for many of those interested in an entrepreneurial career. This understanding of the qualifications needed for an entrepreneur also reflects the focus on entrepreneurship policies and enterprise education. From a cultural perspective the Austrian case is very interesting. In many other countries the history of entrepreneurs is filled with stories of entrepreneurs being those without any qualifications and who, therefore, had no choice other than to set up their own business.

Norwegian policies have not traditionally taken small businesses or entrepreneurship into account although lately entrepreneurship has surfaced in the policy arena, also in education. Traditionally, large firms have had a major role in the Norwegian economy and as unemployment has not been a problem in Norway, the promotion of self-employment has not been a topical issue.

In Finland, Ireland and the UK the interpretation of enterprise education covers a wider range than the approaches taken in Austria and Norway. In these countries enterprise education is understood to target persons aiming for self-employment but also to foster entrepreneurial attitudes, which are a combination of flexibility, initiative, risk-taking ability, self-direction and on the other hand cooperation skills and a strong motivation for achievement. Nevertheless, in all of the countries it is also seen to be important to provide and increase knowledge of entrepreneurial activity, and to create a larger understanding in society of what entrepreneurship is about. This understanding is necessary to combat the prejudices still existing in some of the countries towards entrepreneurship. For example, one of the Norwegian motives for providing enterprise education targeted the small-town attitude that some persons may be reluctant to start up their own businesses out of fear of what their neighbours might say. Attitudes and values are difficult to change, and although entrepreneurship is currently highly valued in most European countries, it is not so long ago when entrepreneurs were considered as 'evil capitalists' who gained profits by exploiting their employees. It is therefore important to have a long-term commitment to enterprise education and not to let this attitude re-surface.

However, these results must be interpreted cautiously because although we have aimed to capture an illustrative sample in our analysis it is difficult to assess whether we have achieved this given that the sampling has been done by independent researchers in each country.

CONCLUSIONS AND DISCUSSION: ENTERPRISE EDUCATION – A CULTURALLY AND SOCIALLY SENSITIVE PHENOMENON

In this chapter 62 enterprise education programmes from five European countries have been analysed. This chapter focuses firstly on the differences in the entrepreneurship culture and environments in the different contexts and suggests how these should be taken into consideration in planning the enterprise education programmes. The missing link in enterprise education programmes seems to be the confusion and misunderstandings between the projected aims, the potential audience in a given country and the type of enterprise education programmes that are being set up. Rather than creating more, new enterprise education programmes for audiences believed to be 'demanding' the programmes, there is a need to carefully reflect the need and possibilities for carrying out such programmes in each context. Hence, to the disappointment of many policy-makers, carrying out more and more start-up programmes will not necessarily result in more start-ups (Heinonen et al., 2006).

Secondly, the chapter supports the thinking that enterprise education in earlier school years should have primarily or solely a non-business focus, which supports the entrepreneurial behaviour of students. In all of the studied countries the focus for enterprise education at primary school level (12 years or younger) was on developing the enterprising skills of the students. Strengthening this perspective might help to alleviate some of the tensions currently identified in schools and by teachers vis-à-vis enterprise education (Iredale, 1993; Lewis and Massey, 2003; Davies et al., 2004).

Thirdly, by combining the understanding from the above two perspectives, it is possible to develop a ladder of enterprise education that starts by developing entrepreneurial behaviour and thinking and by creating awareness of entrepreneurship. Especially in weak entrepreneurship cultures based on desirability of entrepreneurship as a career option, particular attention should be placed on building a strong cornerstone of and for entrepreneurship. This thinking lends itself to variations for the country, region or school level. Currently, the business orientation – how to set up a business – is often too strong. As a result, there are suggestions that the bridges between entrepreneurship and education (pedagogy) should be stronger in order to make enterprise education as much about the process as about the subject (Kyrö, 1999). If the focus is only placed on developing the skills of potential and future entrepreneurs, these programmes are serving the needs of a small minority, at least in many of the old member states of the European Union.

One thing is clear – enterprise education has penetrated all school levels, from kindergarten to higher education. However, further work is needed to develop suitable models for different societal, cultural and economic contexts as one cannot transfer the models from one culture to another without reflecting the impacts of the different contextual arrangements.

Future research is needed to investigate the connections between the appropriate aims and models of enterprise education in the different cultural and social settings. This is also in line with recent suggestions in entrepreneurship research: the phenomenon is considered to be changing and acquiring new meanings both over time and in different places (Steyart and Katz, 2004; Hytti, 2005). Also, there is a need for more research on actual practices of education programmes through in-depth case studies as well as on how the teachers' perceptions on enterprise education evolve over time (Lewis and Massey, 2003).

This study is based on a review of policies and programmes in the five different countries. However, further research is needed on the results and outcomes of these different programmes and in the different settings. It is clear that the impacts on performance and final results are interesting research questions but also the most difficult to capture. However, they need to be asked, since we cannot blindly assume that enterprise education programmes and models are able to achieve all the results they seek to achieve (Fayolle, 2005; see also Heinonen and Akola, 2007). Clearly this calls for longitudinal research approaches (Smith et al., 2002).

REFERENCES

Baron, R. (1998), 'Cognitive mechanisms in entrepreneurship: why and when entrepreneurs think differently than other people', *Journal of Business Venturing*, **13**(4), 295–316.

Bird, B. (1989), *Entrepreneurial Behavior*, Glenview, Illinois: Scott, Foresman and Company.

Birdthistle, N., B. Hynes and P. Fleming (2007), 'Enterprise education programmes in secondary schools in Ireland: A multi-stakeholder perspective', *Education + Training*, **49**(4), 265–76.

Brockhaus, R.H. (1982), 'The psychology of the entrepreneur', in Calvin A. Kent, Donald L. Sexton and Karl H. Vesper (eds), *Encyclopedia of Entrepreneurship*, New Jersey, Englewood Cliffs: Prentice-Hall, Inc. pp. 39–57.

Chen, C.A., P.G. Greene and A. Crick (1998), 'Does entrepreneurial efficacy distinguish entrepreneurs from managers?', *Journal of Business Venturing*, **13**, 295–316.

Cooney, T.M. and E. Kidney (2007), 'IPREG Country report. Analysis of entrepreneurship and innovation policy in Ireland', available at: http://www.ipreg.org/Exe_Summary_Ireland.pdf (accessed 9 April 2008).

Cotton, J. (2002), 'A historical perspective of enterprise education in the UK', available at http://www.entredu.com/eep_search.php?hakupaikka=United+Kingdom&hakuteksti=&haku=yes (accessed 9 April 2008).

Davies, I., M. Fulop, M. Hutchings, A. Ross and M. Berkics (2004), 'Citizenship and enterprise: issues from an investigation of teachers' perceptions in England and Hungary', *Comparative Education*, **40**(3), 363–84.

Deuchar, R. (2004), 'Changing paradigms – the potential of enterprise education as an adequate vehicle for promoting and enhancing education for active and responsible citizenship: illustrations from a Scottish perspective', *Oxford Review of Education*, June, **30**(2), 223–39.

European Commission (2007), 'Entrepreneurship survey of the EU (25 Member States), United States, Iceland and Norway', Analytical Report, April 2007, Flash Eurobarometer No. 192.

Fayolle, A. (2005), 'Evaluation of entrepreneurship education: behaviour performing or intention increasing?' *International Journal of Entrepreneurship and Small Business*, **2**(1), 89–98.

Gartner, W.B. (1988), ' "Who is an Entrepreneur?" is the wrong question', *American Journal of Small Business*, **12**(1), 11–31.

Gartner, W.B. (1989), 'Some suggestions for research on entrepreneurial traits and characteristics', *Entrepreneurship: Theory and Practice*, **14**(1), 27–37.

Gladstone, C. (2005), 'The search for a model of effective inclusive practice through the Young Enterprise Scheme', *British Journal of Special Education*, March, **32**(1), 42–7.

Harju, J., K. Mäki, K. Paasio and T. Pukkinen (2004), 'Turun kauppakorkeakoululaisten yrittäjyysmotivaatio', in U. Hytti (ed.) *Yrittäjyyden kipinä yliopistosta? Tapaus Turun kauppakorkeakoulu*, Tampere: Esa Print Oy.

Harrison, R. and C. Leitch (2005), 'Entrepreneurial learning: researching the interface between learning and the entrepreneurial context', *Entrepreneurship: Theory and Practice*, **29**(4), 351–71.

Havnes, P-A. (2002), 'SME and enterprise education policies in Norway', available at: http://www.entredu.com/eep_search.php?hakupaikka=Norway&hakuteksti=&haku=yes (accessed 9 April 2008).

Heinonen, J. and E. Akola (2007), *Entrepreneurship Training and Entrepreneurial Learning in Europe. Results from the ENTLEARN Project*, Tampere: TSE Entre, Turku School of Economics, Esa Print Oy.

Heinonen, J. and S-A. Poikkijoki (2006), 'An entrepreneurial-directed approach to entrepreneurship education: Mission impossible?', *Journal of Management Development*, **25**(1), 80–94.

Heinonen, J., I. Vento-Vierikko, V. Hautala, U. Hytti, K. Lamminpää, P. Malinen and S-A. Poikkijoki (2006), 'Breeding entrepreneurship in life sciences - study on a training programme for the graduate schools of the Academy of Finland', Turku School of Economics, Business Research and Development Centre, Electronic Publication, E-2, 2006, available at: http://info.tse.fi/julkaisut/liite/E2_2006/.pdf.

Honkanen, V. (2004), *Yrittänyttä ei Laiteta – Ammattikorkeakoulujen Yrittäjyyskoulutuksen Viisasten Kiveä Etsimässä*, Turku: University of Turku, RUSE.

Hytti, U. (2001), 'Is entrepreneurship a disease that can be caught via Internet?', in Asko Miettinen and Heinz Klandt (eds), IntEnt 2000: *Internationalizing Entrepreneurship Education and Training*, Proceedings of the IntEnt-Conference, Tampere University of Technology, 10–12 July, 2000, Entrepreneurship-Research Monographs series, vol. 25, Köln: Josef Eul Verlag, pp. 102–20.

Hytti, U. (2005), 'New meanings for entrepreneurs: from risk-taking heroes to safe-seeking professionals', *Journal of Organizational Change Management*, Special issue: 'Change in the feminine: women in change', **18**(6), 594–611.

Hytti, U. and C. O'Gorman (2004), 'What is 'enterprise education'? An analysis of the objectives and methods of enterprise education programmes in four European countries', *Education + Training*, **46**(1), 11–23.

Hytti, U. et al. (ed.) (2002), *State-of-Art of Enterprise Education in Europe – Results from the Entredu Project* (written jointly with Paula Kuopusjärvi, Irma Vento-Vierikko, Arthur Schneeberger, Christine Stampfl, Colm O'Gorman, Halvor Hulaas, Judi Cotton and Keith Hermann). A publication published in the Entredu project, Leonardo da Vinci programme of the European Commission, Turku, Finland.

Iredale, N. (1993), 'Enterprise education in primary schools: a survey in two northern LEAs', *Education & Training*, **35**(4), 22–30.

Jack, S.L. and A.R. Anderson (1998), 'Entrepreneurship education within the condition of entreprenology', a paper presented at the Second Enterprise and Learning Conference, 10–11 September 1998, Centre for Entrepreneurship, University of Aberdeen.

Jack, S.L. and A.R. Anderson (1999), 'Entrepreneurship education within the enterprise culture', *International Journal of Entrepreneurial Behaviour & Research*, **5**(3), 110–25.

Johansen, V. and T.H. Eide (2006), 'Experiences from participation in a graduate programme company in higher education', ØF-memo no. 16/2006. Eastern Norway Research Institute.

Kovalainen, A. (1989), 'The concept of entrepreneurship in business economics', *Liiketaloustieteellinen Aikakauskirja*, 2/1989, pp. 82–93.

Kyrö, P. (1996), 'The points of transition in reforming the understanding and meaning of entrepreneurship', *Academy of Entrepreneurship Journal*, European edition, **2**(1), 71–94.

Kyrö, P. (1999), 'Education and entrepreneurship searching for each other in the postmodern transition', in S. Tosse, P. Falkencrone, A. Puurula and B. Bergsted (eds), *Challenges and Development? Adult Education Research in Nordic Countries*, Trondheim: Tapir Academic Press, pp. 68–98.

Lewis, K. and C. Massey (2003), 'Delivering enterprise education in New Zealand', *Education + Training*, **45**(4), 197–206.

Livingston, S. (2003), 'On the challenges of cross-national comparative media research', *European Journal of Communication*, **18**(4), 477–500.

O'Gorman, C. (2002), 'Enterprise education and enterprise policy in Ireland', available at: http://www.entredu.com/eep_search.php?hakupaikka=Ireland&hakuteksti=&haku=yes (accessed 9 April 2008).

Oakey, R., S-M. Mukhtar and M. Kipling (1998), 'Student perspectives on entrepreneurship: observations on the propensity for entrepreneurial behaviour', a paper presented at the Second Enterprise and Learning Conference, 10–11 September 1998, Centre for Entrepreneurship, University of Aberdeen.

Rae, D. (2004), 'Entrepreneurial learning: a narrative-based conceptual model', Paper presented at Institute for Small Business AVairs 27th National Conference, 2–4 November, 2004 Newcastle Gateshead, UK.

Schwarz, E. and E. Grieshuber (2000), 'Selbständigkeit als Alternative. Eine empirische Erhebung an österreichischen Universitäten', Working Paper, Department of Innovation Management and Entrepreneurship, University of Klagenfurt, Austria.

Shane, S. and S. Venkatamaran (2000), 'The promise of entrepreneurship as a field of research', *Academy of Management Review*, **25**(1), 217–26.

Smith, P.J., J. Henry and G. Munro (2002), 'Training young people through a school/enterprise partnership: A longitudinal study', *Education & Training*, **44**(6), 281–90.

Solomon, G.T., S. Duffy and A. Tarabishy (2002), 'The state of entrepreneurship education in the United States: a nationwide survey and analysis', *International Journal of Entrepreneurship Education*, **1**(1), 1–22.

Stampfl, C. (2002), 'Enterprise Education System in Austria', available at: http://www.entredu.com/eep_search.php?hakupaikka=Austria&hakuteksti=&haku=yes (accessed 9 April 2008).

Steyart, C. and J. Katz (2004), 'Reclaiming the space of entrepreneurship in society: geographical, discursive and social dimensions', *Entrepreneurship & Regional Development*, **16**(3), 179–96.

Vento-Vierikko, I. (2002), 'Legislative status of enterprise education in Finland', available at: http://www.entredu.com/eep_search.php?hakupaikka=Finland&hakuteksti=&haku=yes (accessed 9 April 2008).

Vesalainen, J., T. Pihkala and T. Jokinen (1999), *Yrittäjyyspotentiaali Varkaudessa sekä Kotkan-Haminan ja Tampereen seutukunnissa. Tutkimus yrittäjyysaikomuksista ja aikomusten taustoista.* (*Entrepreneurship Potential in Varkaus and Kotka-Hamina and Tampere Regions: A Study into Entrepreneurial Intentions and their Background*), Department of Management, University of Vaasa, Finland, November 1999.

8. Assessment and promotion of entrepreneurial initiative and attitudes towards entrepreneurship: the case of Estonia

Urve Venesaar and Indrek Jakobson

INTRODUCTION

Increasing entrepreneurial initiative has been a subject for discussion in the European Union countries in recent years with the objectives of initiating various political measures and activities, supporting national competitiveness and development, as well as setting up new enterprises and creating jobs. Entrepreneurship also contributes to personal fulfilment and the achievement of social objectives. To this end, development of entrepreneurship has been encouraged by many documents adopted in the European Union in recent years (for example European Commission, 2003b; European Commission, 2000). Also, a number of measures have been implemented and planned by the Estonian government towards supporting entrepreneurship and entrepreneurial culture in the country.

Entrepreneurship is viewed in general as a mindset and process to create and develop economic activity within a new or existing organization (European Commission, 2003b). Entrepreneurship is also defined as 'the nexus of two phenomena: the presence of lucrative opportunities and the presence of enterprising individuals' (Shane and Venkataraman, 2000). These definitions refer to a considerable round of different factors influencing the level of entrepreneurial initiative in the country. Generally these are factors creating a required external environment on the one hand, and on the other hand, the existence of persons who have motivation and capacity to identify business opportunities and to pursue them. In this chapter both sides are considered based on the case of Estonia and including some comparisons with other countries where available.

Although in previous research individual-level factors were assessed that were important in explaining who exploits entrepreneurial opportunities (Shane, 2003), this approach has been criticized because basing studies only on personality traits sets methodological limits to explaining entrepreneurial initiative (for example Reynolds, 1997). Though appropriate personal characteristics for acting as an entrepreneur can be developed, also other factors (for example motivations, intentions) are still relevant to entrepreneurial action in the event that potential exists. The range of factors considered in the current research includes the existence of entrepreneurial motivation, its 'pull' and 'push' factors, knowledge, and personality traits useful in starting and doing business. Factors that pull people into entrepreneurship may include ambition for freedom and independence, striving for achievements and self-realization or other efforts for personal fulfilment. The push factors such as unemployment and difficulties with finding waged labour, job insecurity or a wish to earn more may influence the intention of people to enter into entrepreneurship. In the case of transition countries, in connection with the changing economic paradigm the assessment and development of personality traits and their comparison with other countries would help to better understand the potential for entrepreneurship development. The opinions of respondents about the business environment and constraints in business development may indicate the need to improve entrepreneurship promotion policies in the country.

Interconnections between attitudes and the intention to become an entrepreneur were studied by Shepherd and Douglas (1999), who stated that the individual will intend to become an entrepreneur only when the total satisfaction expected from the combination of four factors – independence, risk, hard work and income – is higher for the entrepreneurial opportunity than it is for the best non-entrepreneurial option (Shepherd and Douglas, 1999). According to Ajzen (1991), the intention of carrying out a given behaviour will depend on the person's attitudes towards that behaviour; hence positive attitudes towards entrepreneurship would measure the extent to which individuals intend to establish their own business. But in addition to intention and the existence of initial motivation, businesses-relevant knowledge and entrepreneurial competency are important to ensure successful start-up and survival in business (for example Bird, 2002; Onstenk, 2003). From the standpoint of educational institutions emphasis has been placed on providing an opportunity to develop personal entrepreneurial competency (Bird, 2002). Authors have expressed different opinions about the skills one needs to use business opportunities successfully (for example Hougaard, 2005). It is important for the educational institutions to know which skills (competencies) should be developed in educating future entrepreneurs and enterprising people. In this context it is interesting to know what Estonia's potential is and what entrepreneurship policies and educational programmes should include in order to increase entrepreneurship competency.

The objective of this chapter is to analyse the entrepreneurial initiative of Estonian people based mainly on the research by the Estonian Institute of Economic Research to better explore people's attitudes towards entrepreneurship, their motivations and constraints and to find out what possibilities there could be to further activate the entrepreneurial initiative in Estonia. The respondents' opinions on the knowledge and personal characteristics that are useful in starting in business are also used to find answers to the last question. The target groups of the questionnaire were entrepreneurs, potential entrepreneurs (at the time of the research, starting a company or thinking about it) and people not interested in entrepreneurship. In addition to the main research results, case studies of entrepreneurs (for example academic entrepreneurship) and potential entrepreneurs (for example students) are included to explain the issues of entrepreneurial initiative and attitudes of selected target groups. For development of an entrepreneurship culture it is important to examine the stimulation of entrepreneurship education and other measures supported by the public sector, which can influence people's attitudes and intentions towards entrepreneurship and may foster their entrepreneurial initiative.

The rest of the chapter describes first the method and sample used for analysis. This is followed by analysis of people's opinions about attitudes towards entrepreneurship, motives for starting a business, opinions about personality traits that characterize the entrepreneurial initiative of the respondents, requisite knowledge and qualities for entrepreneurship. Finally, the obstacles to starting in business in Estonia across different target groups (people in general, students) are analysed. The chapter ends with conclusions.

ESTONIAN ENTREPRENEURSHIP POLICY AND ECONOMIC DEVELOPMENT

The main objectives of the Estonian entrepreneurship policy were formulated a few years ago and these included a task to promote entrepreneurial initiative and growth of new enterprises and to raise enterprises' competitiveness (Ministry of Economic Affairs, 2002). A new document, 'The Estonian Entrepreneurship Policy for 2007–2013' (Ministry of Economic Affairs and Communications, 2006), is a step forward in the development of entrepreneurship and entrepreneurial initiative through a favourable entrepreneurship environment and appropriate support schemes. Entrepreneurship policy has established four aims: a strong enterprise culture; a legal environment favourable for entrepreneurship; SMEs' access to finance; and opportunity for SME growth and exports.

Activities aimed at promoting an entrepreneurship culture are needed in three areas: people are enterprising and want to become entrepreneurs; people have the skills and knowledge necessary for doing business; cultivation of positive attitudes towards entrepreneurs and entrepreneurship in society. Activities in the following spheres are undertaken to achieve these goals: entrepreneurship education in schools; life-long learning for entrepreneurs; raising the awareness of entrepreneurship and innovation throughout society; developing the ability of enterprises to cooperate. Therefore, government tends to influence the image of entrepreneurship positively in the country, but in implementing this task it is useful to explain the development aspects of the entrepreneurial initiative in Estonia.

The development of the Estonian economy in general has been assessed to be successful among Central and Eastern European countries. However, several studies have shown some backwardness in the development of entrepreneurship, reflected by firms' birth rate and creation of jobs compared with a number of other countries (Venesaar and Loomets, 2006; Jürgenson et al., 2004; Acs et al., 2004; Minniti et al., 2005). There are also significant regional variations in enterprise development, reflected in the total stock of SMEs and in the rate of new firm formation (OECD, 2002; Venesaar and Loomets, 2006). A research study conducted by the Estonian Institute of Economic Research discovered that only 11 per cent of the population[1] of Estonia were busy with setting up an enterprise at the time of the survey (Estonian Institute of Economic Research, 2004), compared with 15 per cent in Europe, 14 per cent in Finland and 25 per cent in the USA (European Commission, 2003a). This indicates a need to analyse more profoundly the entrepreneurial initiative and attitudes towards entrepreneurship as well as factors influencing the entrepreneurial activity of Estonian people.

Characterizing the business environment, Estonia is known for its very liberal and open economic policy during the whole transition period. A priority in economic policy has been stable monetary policy, a balanced state budget and laissez-faire or non-interference in the economy by the government. Changes in the economic and legislative environment in the early 1990s led to a rapid increase in the number of private enterprises in Estonia, encouraged by the relatively simple conditions for setting up enterprises. A relatively successful privatization model and active implementation of other reforms also contributed to the initial increase in the number of private enterprises. However, the positive effect of these external factors on the establishment of new enterprises that stimulated entrepreneurship development gradually diminished. There is therefore a need to enhance people's entrepreneurial initiative, and this is where the public sector activities (for example improving the availability of finances and quality of business advisory services; developing entrepreneurship education; providing services for raising the awareness of entrepreneurship and innovation throughout the society) in supporting the development of entrepreneurship should grow increasingly more significant. However, it is important to consider the opinion of people when assessing the impact of factors creating a favourable external environment for encouraging entrepreneurial initiatives in the country.

METHOD AND SAMPLE

The empirical study conducted by the Estonian Institute of Economic Research, which this chapter is using, was based on a telephone survey of 1000 16–64-years-old Estonian people in November 2004 (Estonian Institute of Economic Research, 2004). The sample represents the 16–64-year-old Estonian population by gender, age, county and education. The study sought to collect information on people's attitudes toward entrepreneurship and their involvement with entrepreneurship and about factors that encourage and inhibit entrepreneurship. Demographic (for example sex, age, education), social (level of income) as well as geographical (county) factors were important to consider while analysing the survey results.

The questionnaire included direct questions about people's attitude to starting up a business. People's attitude was measured by empirical evaluation as the number of individuals who would like to be an entrepreneur (that is negative attitude/no intention, intending or being in the process). A time perspective was also introduced for those intending to be an entrepreneur, for example in the near future or later. On the basis of respondents' answers the target groups in the survey were entrepreneurs (12 per cent of those questioned), potential entrepreneurs (9 per cent) and those not interested in entrepreneurship (79 per cent). Entrepreneurs were defined as sole traders, owners and partners or shareholders of enterprises who were actively participating in management. The respondents who were not active in entrepreneurship but who were thinking of doing so or at the time of the survey were setting up their own enterprise were classified as potential entrepreneurs.

For comparison, an empirical study using identical questions was carried out among bachelor programme graduates and master's students at Tallinn University of Technology in different specialities during two semesters (Spring 2005 and 2006), after they finished a course in Business Administration. The majority of these students (73 per cent) may be classified as potential entrepreneurs (thinking of being an entrepreneur). In total, 443 students were questioned, including those in three specialities: business administration, logistics and technical specialities (for example mechanics, power engineering, information technology, chemistry). In addition, to explain better the opinions of people or students questioned, a qualitative survey was carried out among five academic entrepreneurs of Tallinn University of Technology to specify special topics (for example motivations to start a business; assessment of knowledge and skills necessary for starting with entrepreneurship; explanation of factors constraining entrepreneurship in the country).

The chapter contains an analysis of respondents' attitudes towards entrepreneurship and of the entrepreneurial initiative of the Estonian population and students on the basis of various characteristics, whereas the results of the survey are assessed on the basis of the response rates. The Likert scale method is used to measure the attitudes of respondents based on their own opinions on the motivations to start a business, the assessment of knowledge and personality traits necessary for starting a business and statements about their entrepreneurial characteristics and obstacles to starting a business. Opinions were expressed in a 5-point scale (1 – completely agree; 2 – agree; 3 – neither agree nor disagree; 4 – disagree; 5 – completely disagree). The smaller the average estimate, the more likely it is that the respondent has this trait.

In the questionnaire the questions about motivation were grouped into three, expressing the ambition for freedom, self-realization and push factors. The respondents were asked their opinion on their personality traits and behavioural habits connected with business relations and behaviour in organizations. The respondents were asked to evaluate a total of 20 statements about personality traits that characterize entrepreneurial initiative. These included diligence, self-assurance, determination, creativity, ambition for achievement, discerning, risk tolerance, coping with failure and ability to plan. The respondents' opinions in the value scale characterize how much their personality traits approach or diverge from the characteristics of an entrepreneur and what the difference is between target groups' and respondents' attitudes and intentions to be an entrepreneur.

The opinions of respondents about the obstacles met in starting a business and possible need for support are also a subject of analysis. For this we asked the respondents to list in order of importance the factors that inhibit starting a business. We also asked what kind of support the respondents thought would be most helpful for starting a business and whether they were aware of the state support measures available in Estonia and whether they had used them. For assessing the role of the university in fostering entrepreneurial initiative among students, we asked students to answer whether the speciality they learned had motivated them and had helped in starting their own business. We also asked which subjects they learned in university that had helped in starting in business and what knowledge they still wanted to learn that would encourage them to start a business. The latter questions help to evaluate students' awareness of entrepreneurship policies and suggest how to improve educational programmes as a tool for raising entrepreneurial initiative in the country.

PEOPLE'S ATTITUDES TOWARD ENTREPRENEURSHIP

A study of the attitudes of the Estonian population toward employment in entrepreneurship and of the related problems indicated that 29 per cent of people would prefer to work as entrepreneurs, which is much lower than in the European Union on average (47 per cent; EOS Gallup Europe, 2003a). The popularity of wage labour was evidenced by the finding that 65 per cent of the respondents preferred working as employees. The Eurobarometer survey (European Commission, 2004) indicated that 37 per cent of the population would prefer to be self-employed in Estonia. Differences between the two surveys can be explained by the different questions, for example in the Eurobarometer survey the respondents were asked about their opinion regarding being self-employed, which can be interpreted more widely than the question about being an entrepreneur.

To define overall entrepreneurial activity of the population all respondents were asked whether or not they had recently set up a business or were at the time of the survey setting up a business. The answers show that the majority of the population are not active in entrepreneurship – 61 per cent had never thought of starting their own enterprise, 16 per cent did not intend to start a business but had thought about it. The non-active were predominantly women (68 per cent), older people (73 per cent), people with primary or basic education (68 per cent), with lower income (68 per cent) and those living in southern Estonia (65 per cent). Eighty-nine per cent of the entrepreneurs were aged 25–54 years. A typical entrepreneur in Estonia was 35–44 years old and a man rather than a woman. Forty-three per cent of the entrepreneurs had higher education and 55 per cent secondary or vocational secondary education. The share of people with higher education among entrepreneurs is remarkably higher than the overall educational level of the Estonian population.

According to the survey, 11 per cent of the population on average were identified as potential entrepreneurs (those thinking of setting up their own enterprise or who were already doing this at the time of the survey). Young people were thinking more frequently than average about setting up their enterprise (19 per cent of those aged 16–24 and 13 per cent of people aged 25–34). Hence, potential entrepreneurs are much younger than entrepreneurs: 84 per cent of the potential entrepreneurs were aged 16–44, their typical age being 16–24. Potential entrepreneurs had a lower level of education than existing entrepreneurs (59 per cent had secondary education, 20 per cent had basic education). Nearly half (47 per cent) of the potential entrepreneurs intended to set up their enterprise in the longer term; of those, most were young people and those with a lower level of education. Thirty-three per cent of the future entrepreneurs had taken concrete steps in starting a business (for example had collected funds). Most of the people see an enterprise as consisting of owners and salaried employees and those who did think of acting alone tended to be older people and those in smaller towns. This indicates insufficient acknowledgement of sole traders as 'entrepreneurs' in Estonian society.

According to the study conducted at Tallinn University of Technology, the students identified mostly as potential entrepreneurs have very positive attitudes toward entrepreneurship (around two thirds intended to be an entrepreneur) (Venesaar et al., 2006). But if we were to sum up those who were thinking of starting a business and those who were actually doing this at the time of the survey, then only 17 per cent of all respondents were planning to start a business in the short term; most of the respondents were postponing it to the more distant future. Hence, many students are not ready to start a business immediately after graduation, although many of them have a positive attitude toward entrepreneurship and the intention to be an entrepreneur. There are many reasons that could be connected with personality traits, knowledge and skills or conditions of business environment, which may refer to a need to improve teaching of entrepreneurship and/or developing business promotion services.

MOTIVES FOR STARTING A BUSINESS

Based on the status of the respondents (for example existing entrepreneurs or potential entrepreneurs), their gender, age, education or some other characteristics, we can identify differences in the motives for starting a business (for example 'pull' and 'push' factors). Based on the opinions of the target groups, the most important motives for acting and potential entrepreneurs seem to be the wish to find more freedom of activity and the wish to be one's own boss (Table 8.1). For potential entrepreneurs even more important are push factors (for example, a wish to earn more or to earn a good income). Factors of self-realization (for example to follow someone's

Table 8.1 Motives for starting a business among acting and potential entrepreneurs

	Acting entrepreneurs	Potential entrepreneurs	Difference ±
Ambition for freedom			
More freedom of activity	1.64	1.58	0.06
Be one's own boss	1.62	1.53	0.09
Be more respected in my firm	2.75	2.60	0.15
Be in the vanguard of technological ideas	3.72	3.02	0.70
I want to develop my hobby in business	2.56	1.89	0.67
Self-realization			
I wanted to put myself to the test	2.48	1.78	0.70
I wanted to command and motivate others	3.44	2.61	0.83
I want to continue family traditions	4.17	3.37	0.80
I want to gain a better position in society	3.47	2.26	1.21
I want to follow someone's example	4.18	3.27	0.91
I want to implement an idea or innovation	2.68	1.74	0.94
Push factors			
A wish to earn more	2.22	1.33	0.89
If I lost my job, I would become an entrepreneur	2.06	1.94	0.12
I want to earn good income	2.37	1.63	0.74
I was not satisfied with my work	3.38	3.30	0.08
Difficulties with finding waged labour	3.63	3.35	0.28

Note: Opinions are expressed on a 5-point scale (1 = completely agree; 2 = agree; 3 = neither agree nor disagree; 4 = disagree; 5 = completely disagree), additionally the answer 'not opinion'.

example, continue family traditions, achieve a better position in society) were of less significance in starting a business, although the wish to put oneself to the test was deemed quite important. If comparing two target groups, potential entrepreneurs are more ambitious for freedom than acting entrepreneurs (for example to have more freedom of activity, to be one's own boss and the wish to be more respected in the firm). All other factors were regarded by potential entrepreneurs to be more important than by acting entrepreneurs. Motives for starting a business were stronger among men, those in the age group 25–44 and respondents with higher education.

If the results are compared with a similar survey in the United Kingdom (Small Business Service, 2002), then entrepreneurs in both countries are similar in their ambitions (for example the ambition for freedom, the wish to be one's own boss). Development of a hobby or other activity into a business was more typical in Estonia, but the implementation of technological ideas was less significant than in the United Kingdom. Putting oneself to the test and the willingness to take risks were important motives for starting a business in Estonia, but not as important as in the United Kingdom. Most important push factors for Estonian potential entrepreneurs were better earnings or improvement of one's income (because of low salaries in employee positions); an important motive for starting a business in Estonia was also the loss of one's job.

Among students, stronger opinions about all motivations were expressed by those students who expressed an intention to start a business because they were doing this already or were just thinking about it at the time of the questionnaire. Those who rated the motivations highly intended to start a business in the near future, compared with those with lower motivations who thought they would postpone starting a business the distant future (Venesaar et al., 2006). Economics and logistics students evaluated the ambition for freedom and self-realization to be more important; students in technical specialities stand out by showing a strong motivation to implement new ideas and technological innovations. Those more motivated to start a business are bachelor students and men. This opinion may have been influenced by the fact that most of the master's degree students are working in parallel with studying at university and they are not willing to give up the safe job-related security and income. The main motives for younger age groups (20–25) are self-realization and good earnings possibilities; for the older group (over 30) it was ambition for freedom (Venesaar et al., 2006).

Interviews with academic entrepreneurs indicated that the main reason for starting a business was a wish to develop further from the situation where the current job did not offer enough development opportunities. It is important to note that neither better income nor other monetary incentives were a motivation. They clearly confirmed the key role of examples from the aspect of starting a business and emphasized the importance of samples just in their field of activity. They also stressed the importance of personal development perspectives. An opportunity to earn more money was estimated to be important only in the long term, whereas the work of the entrepreneur was regarded as more developing than that of the employee just because of its complexity.

KNOWLEDGE AND PERSONALITY TRAITS USEFUL IN STARTING OR DOING BUSINESS

On the basis of respondents' opinions we can assess which knowledge and personality traits are needed when starting a business considering the external environment of Estonia. On average one fifth of the respondents completely agreed with the suggested knowledge and skills that are relevant for starting a business, and hence we can draw a conclusion that preparation of acting entrepreneurs was quite modest. Average opinions of both acting and potential entrepreneurs gave higher ratings of knowledge where one could get entrepreneurship-related help, as well as skills for solving problems (Table 8.2). Only every fifth respondent had experience of managing an enterprise or business education. Most of the present newly established entrepreneurs did not have any bookkeeping knowledge, business qualification, experience of managing an enterprise or previous experience of setting up an enterprise. Opinions expressed by potential entrepreneurs are very similar to these; they mostly lack experience of managing an enterprise, business education, and experience of setting up an enterprise, knowledge about bookkeeping or experience in marketing. The respondents in relatively younger age groups (25–34 years) had more knowledge about starting a business. This can be explained by recent entrepreneurship

Table 8.2 Knowledge and personality traits that are useful for starting a business

	Acting entrepreneurs	Potential entrepreneurs
Knowledge		
Previous experience in starting an enterprise	3.87	3.92
Knowledge how to prepare a business plan	3.36	3.26
Knowledge where to find financial means	3.14	2.83
Knowledge where to get entrepreneurial assistance	2.38	2.30
Business education	4.00	3.95
Experience in managing an enterprise	3.71	4.11
Skills		
Marketing experience	3.14	3.31
Bookkeeping experience	3.69	3.58
Good skills of problem solving	2.32	2.22

Note: Opinions are expressed on a 5-point scale (1=completely agree; 2=agree; 3=neither agree nor disagree; 4=disagree; 5=completely disagree), additionally the answer 'no opinion'.

policies and availability of services provided actively for start-ups in Estonia (including a website for entrepreneurs: www.aktiva.ee).

Estonian acting and potential entrepreneurs rely on communication and contacts rather than on professional knowledge and skills. The academic entrepreneurs confirmed the importance of the skill of dealing with people as the most important of all skills, although they also emphasized the importance of managerial skills and experiences.

Therefore, both potential and acting entrepreneurs indicated more often the importance of knowing where to get entrepreneurial assistance and where to find sources of finance when starting a business. They also expressed a need for obtaining good problem-solving skills and marketing experience.

OPINIONS ABOUT PERSONALITY TRAITS THAT CHARACTERIZE RESPONDENTS' ENTREPRENEURIAL INITIATIVE

In order to find out whether or not and in which way entrepreneurs differ from each other, the respondents were asked to evaluate 20 statements on a 5-point scale. The smaller the average estimate, the more likely it is that the respondent has this trait. Based on the status of the respondents (actual entrepreneurs or potential entrepreneurs), we can identify differences in personal characteristics, skills related to participation in business relations and behaviour in organizations in the target groups. The personal characteristics and behaviour typical of an entrepreneur are positively correlated with the intention to start a new venture. A proof of the latter statement is that potential entrepreneurs have, more than other target groups, attached significance to such personal characteristics as self-assurance, progress-making ambition, risk tolerance and planning ability (Table 8.3). Also many other personal characteristics that characterize entrepreneurial initiative, skills relating to behaviour with business contacts and in organization are more important for potential entrepreneurs than for salaried employees. Entrepreneurs agreed most with such statements as 'I know what I want and act with this end in view', 'I am willing to cooperate with very different people' and 'I have faith in myself and confidence'. The survey among students showed that, depending on the growing intention to start their own business (for example those who are thinking about it, in the start-up process, or have already started during the last three years), the ranking of the personality traits on the value scale is also rising (Venesaar et al., 2006).

Those not interested in entrepreneurship agreed much less frequently with all the statements. Thus, on the basis of the self-evaluations it is

Table 8.3 Opinions expressed by respondents about personality traits that characterize their entrepreneurial initiative

		Acting entrepreneurs	Potential entrepreneurs	Salaried employees
Personality traits				
Diligence	I like hard work	1.82	1.78	1.83
Self-assurance	I have faith in myself and confidence	1.71	1.52	1.90
Determination	I always carry into effect what I have intended	1.89	1.90	1.94
	I know what I want and act to that end	1.54	1.60	1.92
Creativity	I have no shortage of ideas and dreams	2.06	2.04	2.41
Ambition of achievement	I want to be successful	2.00	1.43	2.16
Discerning	I can take decisions and stand by them	1.65	1.68	1.88
Risk tolerance	I like challenges that many think are risky	2.44	2.19	2.97
Coping with failure	Failures do not upset me but give reason to try again	2.25	2.22	2.58
Ability to plan	I can plan my activities a long time ahead	2.24	2.14	2.32
Business relations				
Sociality	I am a sociable person and love to socialise	1.85	1.57	1.91
Negotiating and selling skills	I am regarded as a good negotiating and selling person	2.14	2.32	2.75
Cooperativeness	I am willing to cooperate with different people	1.63	1.56	1.94
Behaviour in organization				
Traits of a leader	My opinions have weight and my advice is asked often	1.93	1.88	2.26
Convincing and motivating skills	I have good convincing skills and can inspire others	2.13	1.88	2.45

Table 8.3 (continued)

		Acting entrepreneurs	Potential entrepreneurs	Salaries employees
Organizing ability	Organizing something is not difficult for me, I am an initiator	2.29	2.23	2.81
Doing several things simultaneously	I can deal with several things simultaneously	2.01	2.19	2.47
Other				
Debts	I am not afraid of being in debt	3.11	3.08	3.64
Good health	I am in good health and I have a lot of energy	2.28	1.68	2.48
Control point	I think it important to influence my own career rather than adapt to the situation	1.76	1.66	2.08

Note: Opinions are expressed on a 5-point scale (1 = completely agree; 2 = agree; 3 = neither agree nor disagree; 4 = disagree; 5 = completely disagree), additionally the answer 'no opinion'.

possible to identify people who have more abilities to start in and do business. The students' survey confirmed that those who intend to start a business in the near future could be characterized by valuation of more enterprising personality traits. At the same time, lower valued personality traits characterized the group of students who were thinking about starting a business in the distant future. Here we should give a thought to whether the knowledge provided at university and the methods of teaching this knowledge are suitable and adequate for the development of entrepreneurial behaviour in students and to create in them the intention to undertake entrepreneurial activity. Promotion of entrepreneurship can be facilitated by improving educational programmes and teaching methods aimed at increasing entrepreneurial initiative at different levels of education.

Academic entrepreneurs underlined just cooperativeness and communication skills as the main personal characteristics that an entrepreneur must have, but they also mentioned the fact that it is important to have the ability to cooperate with partners. Several persons often start a business together and this enables them to cover the whole relevant range of activity. Indirectly, a major obstacle to starting a business is the lack of a partner or poor cooperation skills. This statement completely conforms to the quantitative research results and there were no discrepancies between them.

PEOPLE'S OPINIONS ABOUT FACTORS CONSTRAINING A NEW VENTURE CREATION

Obstacles mentioned by future entrepreneurs in setting up new enterprises included the problem of financing, which is acute in Estonia: 36 per cent of the target group mentioned shortage of financial resources and start-up capital, which is somewhat higher than the result of a similar survey conducted in the United Kingdom (24 per cent of the future entrepreneurs in the UK) (Small Business Service, 2002). Both acting entrepreneurs and future entrepreneurs mentioned fear of falling into debt, and in connection with that, the risk of failure as the next obstacle. Many respondents, especially entrepreneurs, mentioned insufficient knowledge and lack of a business idea as obstacles (especially women and respondents with a lower level of education). Forty per cent of the entrepreneurs and also potential entrepreneurs saw risk in the economic climate, for example lower purchasing power of consumers and rapidly growing competence in the market. The respondents were also worried about the fact that by setting up an enterprise they would lose the security provided by a steady job; they also mentioned social problems (taking care of children, older people, health problems). To sum up, potential entrepreneurs were more optimistic than acting entrepreneurs, seeing fewer obstacles or seeing possibilities to conquer them. The research indicated that women are more conservative and less risk-tolerant than men. This indicates the need to arrange training for women to manage risk and overcome fear, as well as to find sources of finance.

Although a major obstacle to starting an academic business is acknowledged to be insufficient sources of finance, it is rather a general problem. Quantitative research surprisingly revealed that managers of academic businesses do not fear debts. This is motivated by the specific characteristics of this entrepreneurship environment, which requires very large amounts of intellectual capital and small amounts of monetary capital investment. Also the shortage of positive motivation rather than a large number of negative scenarios and obstacles is of critical significance when deciding whether to start a business or not.

Among students, to summarize the factors that obstruct starting a business we primarily examined the top three factors (by all respondents). As a result, over half of the respondents (53 per cent of all respondents) mentioned lack of a business idea as the obstacle. The second important obstacle is insufficient knowledge and skills (40 per cent). Both of these factors are a major problem for students who have not thought of starting a business or who are in the early stages of starting (those who were thinking of starting a business). The third important obstacle is the possibility of failure (39 per cent). Respondents who at the time of the survey were starting a business or who already had started a business estimated this reason to be more important. More frequently mentioned obstacles are also fear of losing the present job-related security and income from the present job, and fear of falling into debt. Also previous studies have indicated fear of risk among students (for example Venesaar et al., 2006), which may be caused by insufficient knowledge about entrepreneurship, starting a business, evaluation skills of business opportunities, or other relevant knowledge, which many respondents admitted to be a major obstacle to starting a business.

When we asked the students what kind of support would be most helpful for starting a business, they considered the most important entrepreneurship advice in the first year of start-up, training in taxation and accounting, and information on relevant procedures for starting a business and on enterprise support. The latter opinion indicates that students are not aware of the measures offered by the entrepreneurship support system, although support to start-up enterprises in finding information and explaining procedures is the most widespread service in Estonian entrepreneurship policy and there is also a website with various information a start-up entrepreneur might need, but many students do not know what this website contains. During the implementation of entrepreneurship policies the spread of information should be improved and services should reach the potential entrepreneurs (Ministry of Economic Affairs and Communications, 2006).

The role of the university in developing entrepreneurial behaviour has been evaluated in the research on the basis of students' own opinions. The impact of the programmes and knowledge obtained on starting a firm indicated that what one has learned in business administration specialities helps most of the respondents (75 per cent) to start their own business. Over half of the respondents (57 per cent) answered that going through the curriculum has motivated them to start in business (Venesaar et al., 2006). The knowledge areas that students want to learn more about, regarding encouraging them to develop their own firm, are business planning, business law, application of accounting programmes and foreign languages.

CONCLUSIONS

Analysis based on the empirical study undertaken by the Estonian Institute of Economic Research showed that the attitudes of Estonian people toward employment in entrepreneurship were less enthusiastic than in the European Union on average. As for motives, the most important for acting and potential entrepreneurs seem to be the wish to find more freedom of activity and the wish to be one's own boss. For potential entrepreneurs even more important are the push factors (for example, a wish to earn a more or to earn a good income because of low salaries for employees). Both acting and potential entrepreneurs rely on communication and contacts rather than on professional knowledge and skills. Hence the opinions of both potential and acting entrepreneurs indicated a need for knowledge about where to get entrepreneurial assistance and where to find sources of finance, as well as for obtaining knowledge about problem-solving skills and marketing experience. The personal characteristics and behaviour typical of an entrepreneur are positively correlated with the intention to start a new venture. Thus, on the basis of the self-evaluations it is possible to identify people who have more abilities to start in and do business. Promotion of entrepreneurship can be facilitated by improving educational programmes and teaching methods aimed at increasing entrepreneurial initiative at different levels of education.

Obstacles mentioned by entrepreneurs in setting up new enterprises included the problem of finance (including start-up capital), insufficient knowledge and skills (especially women and respondents with a lower level of education), risk in the economic climate and social problems. The research results indicate a need to introduce various political measures and activities for promoting entrepreneurial initiative through improvement of the business environment and entrepreneurship culture, and to focus entrepreneurship policy to the needs of different groups of entrepreneurs (start-ups, women, students and so on) through increasing opportunities for training, consultancy and other activities. During the implementation of entrepreneurship policies, the spread of information should be improved and services should reach the potential entrepreneurs.

The research results among students showed that despite the considerable proportion of respondents thinking about starting a business, most of them do not want to undertake entrepreneurial activity directly after graduation, but are postponing this to a more distant future. Though different target groups valuated their motivation regarding entrepreneurship differently, the respondents' attitudes towards entrepreneurship correlated very clearly with their intentions to start a business in a time perspective. The role of the university in entrepreneurship needs to be increased to support the realization of society's new challenges in the development of innovation and economic growth through developing entrepreneurial competencies and entrepreneurial skills for fostering entrepreneurship as well as entrepreneurialism in a wider context in society.

NOTE

1. The criterion selected for the evaluation indicated the number of people who at the time of the survey were thinking about starting an enterprise or who were busy with setting up a new enterprise.

REFERENCES

Acs, Z.J., P. Arenius, M. Hay and M. Minniti (2004), 'Global entrepreneurship monitor *2004 Executive Report*', Babson Park, MA, USA and London, UK: Babson College, London Business School.

Ajzen, I. (1991), 'Theory of planned behaviour', *Organizational Behaviour and Human Decisions Processes*, **50**(2), 179–211.

Bird, B. (2002), 'Learning entrepreneurship competencies: the self-directed learning approach', *International Journal of Entrepreneurship Education*, **1**, 203–27.

Estonian Institute of Economic Research (2004), Entrepreneurial Initiative of Estonian Population (2004), Results of a population survey, Tallinn (in Estonian).

European Commission (2000), *European Charter for Small Enterprises,* Brussels: Commission of the European Communities.

European Commission (2003a), FLASH EB No 146 'Entrepreneurship' (10-23/09/2003) – EOS Gallup Europe Report.
European Commission (2003b), 'Green Paper "Entrepreneurship in Europe"', Brussels.
European Commission (2004), FLASH EB 160 'Entrepreneurship' (12.04-29.04.2004), Taylor Nelson Sofres.
Hougaard, S. (2005), *The Business Idea, The Early Stages of Entrepreneurship*, Berlin; Heidelberg: Springer.
Jürgenson, A., A. Oks, R. Selliov and K. Varno (2004), 'Development Problems and State Support Measures of SMEs in Estonia: Final Report, Tartu, Estonia: University of Tartu.
Ministry of Economic Affairs, (2002), 'Enterprising Estonia: National Policy for the Development of Small and Medium-sized Enterprises in Estonia in 2001–2006', Tallinn.
Ministry of Economic Affairs and Communications (2006), *Estonian Entrepreneurial Policy in 2006–2013* (in Estonian) *Eesti ettevõtluspoliitika 2007–2013*, Tallinn, http://www.mkm.ee/failid/Poliitika_201006.pdf.
Minniti, M., W.D. Bygrave and E. Autio (2005), 'Global Entrepreneurship Monitor, 2005 Executive Report', Babson Park, MA, USA and London, UK: Babson College and London Business School.
OECD (2002), *Estonia Country* Assessment, OECD Forum for Enterprise Development, Baltic Regional Programme.
Onstenk, J. (2003), 'Entrepreneurship and vocational education', *European Educational Research Journal*, **2**, 74–89.
Reynolds, P. (1997), 'Who starts new firms? Preliminary & explorations of firms in gestation', *Small Business Economics*, 9(5), 449–62.
Reynolds, P., D. Storey and P. Westhead (1994), 'Cross-national comparison of the variation in new firm rates', *Regional Studies*, **28**, 443–56.
Shane, S. (2003), *A General Theory of Entrepreneurship, The Individual–Opportunity Nexus*, Cheltenham, UK and Northampton, MA, USA: Edward Elgar.
Shane, S. and S. Venkataraman (2000), 'The promise of entrepreneurship as a field of research', *Academy of Management Review*, **25**, 217–26.
Shepherd, D.A. and E. Douglas (1999), 'Entrepreneurship as a utility maximizing response', *Journal of Business Venturing*, **15**, 231–51.
Small Business Service (2002), Household Survey of Entrepreneurship: Follow-Up Survey', October, prepared for SBS by IFF Research Ltd, p. 38.
Venesaar, U. and P. Loomets (2006), 'The role of entrepreneurship in the economic development and implications for SME policy in Estonia', paper presented to the 14th Nordic Conference on Small Business Research, Stockholm, Sweden, 11–13 May.
Venesaar, U., E. Kolbre and T. Piliste (2006), 'Attitudes and intentions of students toward entrepreneurship: a case of Estonia', paper presented at the EISB2006 Conference in Southampton, UK.

9. Advancing entrepreneurship education in Finnish basic education: the prospects for developing local curricula

Jaana Seikkula-Leino

INTRODUCTION

The strategy of the European Union highlights the importance of the development of an entrepreneurial culture by fostering the right mindset, entrepreneurship skills and awareness of career opportunity. According to the European Union policy, entrepreneurship should be included at all education levels and throughout the common curricula (Commission of the European Communities, 2006).

Mainstreaming, the idea that entrepreneurship is embedded in all subjects and pedagogy, not applied as a specific subject, is still quite rare despite the existing background of policy recommendations. Entrepreneurship education has its roots in business education, and many countries are still focusing on entrepreneurship development at adult education level. Some European countries such as Luxemburg, Norway, Finland, Iceland, Spain, Austria, Denmark and Sweden have also included entrepreneurship education development at other education levels (European Commission, 2002; 2004). Finland in particular has extensively mainstreamed it at all education levels, including primary and secondary education.

In Finland the development of entrepreneurship education has been supported administratively. The Ministry of Education announced an initiative entitled 'The Clarification and the Action Program of Entrepreneurship Education' in 2004. Accordingly the Finnish National Board of Education introduced the 'National Core Curriculum for Basic Education' in 2004, which includes elements of entrepreneurship education. In Finland this basic education is offered at primary and lower secondary school levels. It is uniform, country-wide, nine-year general education given in comprehensive schools when children are about 7–16 years old. During the first six years children are taught mainly by class teachers whereas in the last three years teaching is by specialized subject teachers.

The current curriculum reform in Finland is to a large extent based on MacDonald's (2003) partnership model. This means that administrative bodies, curriculum reformers, researchers and parents all take part in the process of reforming the curriculum. This requires cooperation between schools and professional development among teachers, as well as taking into account the wishes and concerns of the pupils and the municipalities. Moreover, the curriculum reform is based on the idea that national curriculum norms guide local curricula realization. In the reform, entrepreneurship education is not a subject in its own right, but will be implemented as an interactive theme. This theme will then be included in the subjects locally and could also be realized through school cultures.

How can entrepreneurship education be developed through this kind of educational reform? In fact, there should be good prospects for development. There are options to include local, municipal and school-level additions in the framework of the curriculum. The national norms emphasize the relationship between the school and its surroundings by reflecting the school's role as part of the local community. In general, this model provides for development at the local level, which involves partnership between education, entrepreneurship and working life. However, it can be assumed that these reform processes may not be easy and they may differ between municipalities.

This chapter aims to present how the local curricula have been integrated into entrepreneurship education and how entrepreneurship education is developing through this education reform. Studying this phenomenon is warranted, as the curriculum is the most important document through which a society expresses its wishes and needs in terms of education. There is a lack of relevant studies in this context. Entrepreneurship education research is also mainly conducted on adult education and not on basic education as in the present study. This study was carried out during the spring of 2005. At that time the curriculum process was still ongoing in many of the municipalities. Therefore, the purpose was to map out the situations of the local curriculum development from the point of view of entrepreneurship education.

This chapter focuses first on the concepts and theoretical background. Secondly, the methodology used and results obtained are presented. Thirdly, the results are elaborated in the discussion part of the chapter and further evaluated in the conclusion.

CONCEPTS AND THEORETICAL BACKGROUND

Entrepreneurship and Entrepreneurship Education

The concept of *entrepreneurship* is a fundamental for defining entrepreneurship education. As Gartner (1990) argues, entrepreneurship has many different meanings. Its focus has changed according to times and contexts. Present-day entrepreneurship has the characteristics of individual, self-orientated behaviour; the creation, management and ownership of a small enterprise (external entrepreneurship); corporate or organizational entrepreneurship and intrapreneurship, which refers to the interplay between the individual and organizational entrepreneurship (Kyrö and Carrier, 2005).

Moreover, the definition of entrepreneurship could involve the sources of opportunities which then refer to the processes of the discovery, evaluation and exploitation of opportunities: and the set of individuals who discover, evaluate and exploit them (Shane and Venkataraman, 2000). Entrepreneurship is a complex phenomenon subsuming a wide range of beliefs. Some believe that entrepreneurship must refer to risk-taking individuals who start new, innovative and fast-growing ventures. Others may only focus on the idea that entrepreneurship is about starting new ventures (Gartner, 1990).

To define entrepreneurship education we may consider terms such as *enterprising* and *entrepreneurial*. The only major distinction between these two is that entrepreneurial is traditionally associated with business activity, and enterprising can refer to any context. In order to avoid confusion and to be exact, this chapter uses both concepts explicitly: entrepreneurial (referring to the business context) and enterprising (referring to general education and learning processes). As Kyrö (2005) argues:

> In general entrepreneurial and enterprising behaviour involves the idea that the human being, looking around him and combining different elements, creates holistic realities, which have their consequence in action. Even when the environment is full of paradoxes and events, the entrepreneur chooses what is suitable for him and his ideas. He does not select his elements from a single environment; on the contrary, his ideas can spring anywhere and this combines different elements and this enhances the creation of something new.

Kuratko (2005) points out that this perspective may be exhibited inside and outside an organization and in profit or not-for-profit enterprises, and in business or non-business activities including the perspective of bringing forth creative ideas (Kuratko, 2005).

Teaching younger pupils *entrepreneurship education* is more about enterprise education. The purpose is for pupils to take more responsibility for themselves and their learning, to try to achieve their goals, be creative, discover existing opportunities and in general to cope in our complicated society. Moreover, they should take an active role in job markets and consider entrepreneurship as a natural career choice. This education involves developing behaviours, skills and attributes applied individually and/or collectively to help individuals and organizations of all kinds to create, cope with and enjoy change and innovation. It involves higher levels of uncertainty and complexity as means of achieving personal fulfilment and organizational effectiveness. This enterprising education is the process by which these behaviours are practised and supported. These skills, behaviours and attributes are exhibited in organizations of all kinds including the family and community context. This education may embody elements of learning *for* the accomplishment of some task. Moreover, it involves learning *through* a particular pedagogy and learning *about*, which then refers to cognitive learning (cf. Gibb, 2006).

As Remes (2001) argues, in basic education self-orientated entrepreneurship should be emphasized. According to Menzies and Paradi (2003), the focus is not only on developing factors related to motivation, self-awareness and creativity, and according to Heinonen (2004) responsibility for learning, but also on cooperation and interaction, which refer to internal entrepreneurship development. In comparison, according to Gibb (2005, p. 48), in the school context, external entrepreneurship education is about developing innovation and business ideas as well as strengthening cooperation between schools and work life, including such activities as work experience and study tours. Through all these processes, self-orientated, internal and external entrepreneurship, we have a chance to develop an enterprising society, which means entrepreneurship and enterprising mindset development in societies.

When the pedagogy of entrepreneurship education is based on socio-constructivism, learning communities have a major role in these processes (cf. Blenker et al., 2006, p. 99; Jack and Anderson, 1999; Rae, 2000, p. 148) and experiences are crucial in learning. Therefore in the pedagogical discussion of entrepreneurship education, we could base it, for example, on Kolb's (1984) experimental learning theory.

Curriculum and Curriculum Reform

The definitions of *curriculum* are based on two assumptions: 1) the curriculum indicates what relevant skills should be achieved through experiences; 2) the curriculum directs what kind of education programmes should be delivered (Bobbitt, 2004, p. 11). Traditionally the concept of curriculum is linked to two approaches; the Anglo-American concept of curriculum and the German concept of *Lehrplan*. *Lehrplan* has a more administrative focus. It is about designing curriculum in terms of subjects and contents as well as guiding the implementation of schedules. The Anglo-American curriculum takes a more constructive and broader approach to issues such as didactics. In the Finnish context curriculum is concerned with both of these elements (cf. Heinonen, 2005).

A *curriculum reform* is about making changes in societies. Therefore values as well as ideological and political objectives drive these changes. As in the European Union, the current policy stresses the development of entrepreneurship, and as a consequence its integration into curricula in all member states. Moreover, these educational movements are based on power, such as current social and economic policy, and opinions about the 'right' knowledge. These elements give the power to make decisions, for example, about designing and structuring a curriculum reform (cf. Flouris and Pasias, 2003; Littledyke, 1997; Marsh, 2004, p. 117; Zajda, 2003). Furthermore, a curriculum reform articulates social pressures, such as developing equality and adjusting education to meet the needs of labour development (Flouris and Pasias, 2003). Thus the integration of entrepreneurship education into curricula responds to the needs of working life development. In addition, general trends in societies, like globalization, internationalism, and technical development form the basis for developing goals for education and hence for the curriculum reform (cf. Letschert and Kessels 2003, 160). A curriculum reform is always about teaching and learning, involving subject contents, didactics, pedagogical development and evaluation (cf. Flouris and Pasias, 2003). And it deals with concrete didactical and pedagogical issues.

As MacDonald (2003) suggests, in fact, a curriculum reform is about making choices: we need to consider the different structures of the processes, to decide who is responsible for these processes, to choose aims, and to estimate the different future outcomes. Littledyke (1997) also recommends that the technical implementation of these processes should play a major role in curriculum reforms.

These aspects of curriculum and curriculum reform also apply to the design process of the Finnish curriculum reform, which is to a large extent based on MacDonald's (2003) partnership model. In practice the curriculum implemented in Finland also contains a combination of a centralized and decentralized model of curriculum reform. In other words, the national administrative bodies, the local educational administrations and the teachers cooperate in the curriculum reform to create a whole. In Finland, the curriculum has administrative elements, such as subjects and contents, but it also has the approach of pedagogical and didactical development. This core curriculum guides the local curricula design processes.

There are so far no published studies about this particular curriculum reform process. Earlier studies on curriculum reforms support the point of view that the participation of teachers in the drafting of local curricula enables, among others, a better adoption of the curricula, the pedagogical development of teaching as well as the better learning of the students (cf. Atjonen, 1993; Heinonen, 2005; Sulonen, 2004; Syrjäläinen, 1997; see van der Akker, 2003, p. 9). This supports the implementation of the partnership model. Local curriculum work also provides a good opportunity for the development of a sense of community (Heinonen, 2004; Syrjäläinen, 1997), which is also one of the key factors in this curriculum reform structure. However, there are no studies about how the partnership takes place on a wider scale – for example about interactive cooperation within a municipality or about the relationship between local and central government.

Such a curriculum process that actively involves teachers has highlighted, however, that the curriculum itself is still perceived as an abstract document. According to Atjonen (1993), who made an extensive study of previous curriculum reforms in Finland, the objectives and contents ought to be recorded more clearly and concisely and there should be more references to how to implement them pedagogically. The lack of teaching material was also brought into the discussion when the limitations of the implementation of the curriculum reform were addressed. Accordingly, Heinonen (2005) highlights that a curriculum reform itself will not change the school, but it should function as a tool for development. In order for teachers and other representatives of the educational sector to be involved in this reform process, curriculum training should be increased both in teachers' basic and continuing education (Heinonen, 2005; cf. Shulman and Shulman, 2004).

Atjonen (1993) clarifies from the practical point of view that the development of curriculun reform should be a continuing process also serving the needs of the development of concrete teaching. Therefore, the curriculum ought to include both administrative and pedagogical aspects. The pedagogical curriculum is a changing document that functions as a foundation for practical teaching work. Such a document is updated annually. It should also function as an evaluation tool.

According to Burton et al. (2001, pp. 19–20) a successful curriculum reform should involve vision, strategies and structure. A clear *vision* means that we actually know the attitudes, knowledge and skills involved, in order to have a chance of achieving objectives. For example, in a curriculum reform we need to take into account our situation and the reality in which we currently find ourselves and where we want to be in the following months and in a year. By adopting a *strategy*, through an implemented curriculum, it is possible to reach the desired vision. Strategy also involves pedagogy, subjects, organizational culture and learning environments. *Structure* supports the realization of curricula. When this structure is functional the curriculum is internalized, there is support available for teachers, and there are enough pedagogical resources, such as teaching materials. Teachers and the learning organization are also supervised and led by the administration so that it is possible and meaningful to implement the curriculum.

As Heinonen (2005) argues, success in curriculum reform depends on the development of the visions and structures which support processes. If we only focus on strategies, such as subjects, pedagogy and learning cultures, it is relatively difficult to achieve the desired changes.

In this reform, the national norms guide *local curricula* development. Integrating cultural elements into the local curriculum can create differences between various curricula. They may also reflect different localities, nature, people and work life. The local curricula can take into consideration the strength of local special expertise, the aims for pedagogical development and technological resources. On the other hand, differences in economic conditions provide a different background for these curricula designs and their development between different local authorities. Moreover, local curriculum reforms may vary according to the administrative levels at which decisions are made (cf. Atjonen, 1993, pp. 30–31).

Local curriculum work has an impact on the commitment to the process yet not necessarily on the more profound understanding of it (Constantino, 2003). If the parties involved commit to the reform, both the process and systems change – and the content of the changes remains the same (Webb and Vulliamy, 1999). However, Fullan (1999), McGinn (1999) and Adams (2000) emphasize that a curriculum reform is always a very intricate phenomenon which is also confusing – but it is at its best when a decentralized and a centralized model are combined in the process and when local curriculum work and teachers' participation are involved. The Finnish curriculum reform at the basic education level is based on this approach.

The main aim of this study is to ascertain *how entrepreneurship education is integrated into the local curricula* in this curriculum reform. What are the *attitudes* towards entrepreneurship education? What *resources* are available for entrepreneurship education? Answers to these questions provide an opportunity to evaluate the current state of entrepreneurship education development at the basic school level. This will yield the prospects of providing practical ideas for entrepreneurship education development. Furthermore, there will be an opportunity to analyse the curriculum reform which is the context for the development of entrepreneurship education.

These questions are approached by three integrated theoretical approaches: 1. Kyrö's (2005) different forms of entrepreneurship; 2. McDonald's (2003) partnership model of curriculum reform; and 3. Burton et al.'s (2001, pp. 19–20) processes of vision, strategy and structure.

METHODOLOGY

A quantitative cross-sectional survey was chosen as a method to enable the generalization of the results in Finnish society. It was conducted among 43 medium-sized municipalities, as these municipalities offer basic education at all levels instead of having a joint school system with some other municipalities. The population of these medium-sized municipalities varies from 3000 to 13 000 inhabitants.

The study takes into account possible differences between municipalities. Those municipalities were selected in which the average learning outcomes of schools were either significantly better or worse than expected on the basis of socioeconomic background factors. Thus through the regression analysis the effect of socioeconomic background factors on school achievement can be controlled for (cf. Kuusela, 2003). As a consequence, municipalities have an aligned starting point, making it possble to study the curriculum process itself more reliably. The data on learning outcomes and socioeconomic factors is based on the official national statistics (Statistics Finland). The criteria for school achievement are based on national tests conducted by the National Board of Education 1998–2003.

All in all, the study includes 18 municipalities (from now on referred to as *municipalities with worse than expected results*) in which the learning results are worse than expected on the basis of socioeconomic background and 19 municipalities (from now on referred to as *municipalities with better than expected results*) in which the results are better than expected. In addition, the study includes four municipalities that have – according to a questionnaire conducted by the Federation of Finnish Enterprises – a very positive attitude towards entrepreneurship (from now on referred to as *entrepreneurial municipalities*). Moreover, the study also includes two municipalities in which an entrepreneurship education development initiative was started during the study (from now on referred to as *development municipalities*).

The questionnaires were sent to teachers, principals, curriculum coordinators, directors of education and cultural services departments, trades ombudsmen (municipalities' trade and industry officials) and representatives of local entrepreneurs (N=478). Even though the context of this research is medium-sized municipalities in Finland it is assumed that the results, according to different respondent groups, could be generalized to Finnish society as a whole. For example, it is assumed that teachers' responses do not vary between small, medium and large municipalities.

In order to find out the different forms of entrepreneurship and its state in basic education the questionnaire was based on Kyrö's (2005) four forms of entrepreneurship. Questions which were based more on entrepreneurship education pedagogy, attitudes and resources were considered according to the work of Turtiainen (2002), Remes (2003; 2004, pp. 89–90) and Ristimäki (2003). Finding out about the development of the partnership model was based on a two-way idea, on the one hand respondents' evaluation and on the other hand researchers' evaluation, thereby rendering the study more reliable. The questions concerning this partnership model development were formulated according to MacDonald's (2003) theoretical view. Moreover, the implementation of the partnership model was evaluated through questions concerning vision, strategy and structure (cf. Burton et al., 2001). In the formulation of questions on curriculum development Atjonen's (1993) earlier research and questionnaires were used. The National Core Curriculum for Basic Education 2004 and the supporting material (cf. Halinen, 2004; Liljeström, 2004) concerning this curriculum reform, were also used.

The majority of the questions used a Likert-type scale (such as: 'I know enough about entrepreneurship education'; 1 = I totally disagree; 2 = I disagree; 3 = I agree; 4 = I totally agree). In addition, some open-ended questions were included (such as 'How do you understand the content of entrepreneurship education?'). The questionnaire was pre-tested in one medium-sized municipality (N=39) in early spring 2005. According to the preliminary measurements it was possible to estimate that the questionnaire was usable for this study and there was no need to make major changes to the real questionnaire (preliminary questionnaire: alpha = 0.6–0.7). In the survey, the reliability of the questionnaire was also quite good (alpha = 0.7–0.9).

The survey was conducted during the late spring of 2005. The statistical tests were regression analysis, frequencies and cross-tabulations. In order to ascertain, for example, gender and different respondent group differences, analyses of variances (ANOVA) were used. All tests were conducted using SPSS software. The response rate of this survey was approximetely 70 per cent. This high response rate was achieved by securing a promise to participate through the letters of commitment which were sent to directors of education and cultural services departments, trades ombudsmen and representatives of local entrepreneurs during early spring 2005.

RESULTS

Integration of Entrepreneurship Education into Local Curricula

The survey shows that only 50 per cent of the respondents had integrated the theme of entrepreneurship education into individual subjects – even though this is required by the National Core Curriculum. Entrepreneurial municipalities and development municipalities have actively carried out curriculum work, and entrepreneurship education has been integrated with and into separate subjects and the schools' cultures. These municipalities also clearly indicate the fact that entrepreneurship education will be more actively implemented in the future. In the other municipalities the curriculum work has not sparked off such a development process.

The curriculum work of entrepreneurship education is mainly carried out by teachers. Business life, organizations or students are not actively involved in this work. In this regard, there are no significant differences between municipality categories or between genders or between age groups. Only in entrepreneurial and development municipalities do education authorities, school head teachers and principals support this work in some respect.

The respondents were asked whether they were going to implement more entrepreneurship education in their municipality, school or in their own teaching during the next twelve months. About 36 per cent of respondents reported that they would integrate entrepreneurship education more than before, which means that 64 per cent were not going to do so. Differences between municipalities are shown in Figure 9.1. The difference is statistically significant ($p < 0.01$).

In the entrepreneurial and development municipalities approximately 45 per cent of the respondents were going to implement more entrepreneurship education over the next 12 months (compared to their current

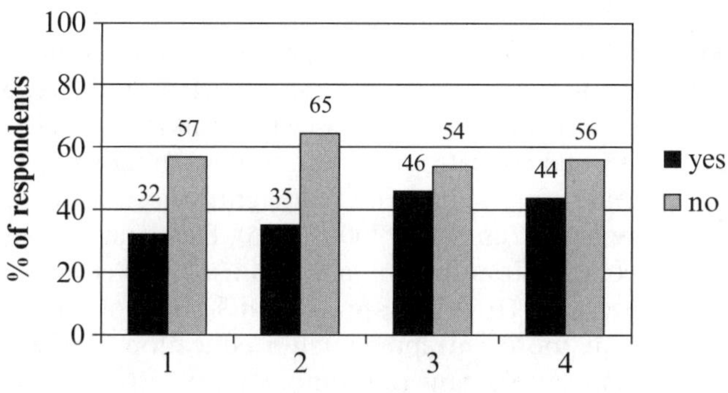

Notes:
1 = Municipalities with better than expected outcome.
2 = Municipalities with worse than expected outcome.
3 = Entrepreneurial municipalities.
4 = Development municipalities.

Figure 9.1 Respondents' estimates of whether or not more entrepreneurship education will be implemented over the next 12 months by different municipality categories (N=326)

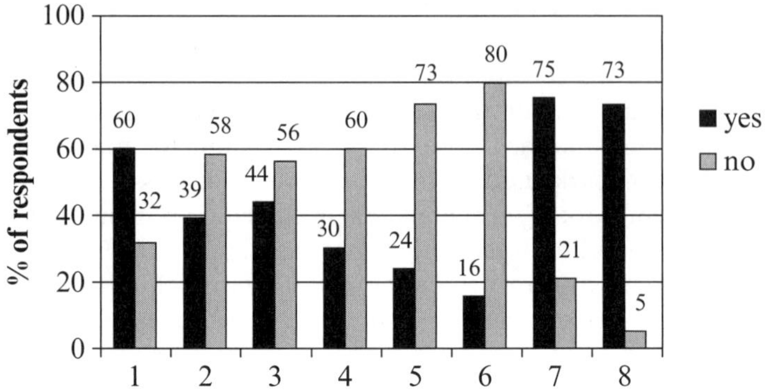

Notes:
1 = Education officials or equivalent.
2 = Head teachers and principals.
3 = Curriculum coordinators.
4 = Guidance counsellors.
5 = Teachers, grades 1–6, students' age: 7–12.
6 = Teachers, grades 7–9, students' age: 13–16.
7 = Trades ombudsmen.
8 = Representatives of entrepreneurs.

Figure 9.2 Respondents' estimates of whether or not more entrepreneurship education will be implemented over the next 12 months by different partner categories (N=323)

implementation rate). Similarly, about 34 per cent of the respondents from the municipalities with better or worse than expected results reported this way. Differences in terms of profession are shown in Figure 9.2.

Figure 9.2 shows that education officials, trades ombudsmen and representatives of entrepreneurs were going to integrate more entrepreneurship education over the next 12 months (2005–2006). Headteachers and principals, curriculum coordinators and guidance counsellors were also – to some extent – going to do so. However, approximately half of them were not going to implement more entrepreneurship education in their schools. Teachers were the most reluctant to promote more entrepreneurship education. Approximately 75 per cent of all teachers reported that they were not going to do so. About 16 per cent of subject teachers and 24 per cent of class teachers reported that they were going to emphasize entrepreneurship education more in their teaching over the next 12 months.

According to the deeper analysis of variance there were no statistically significant differences between genders or between different age groups. Men were nonetheless somewhat more eager to increase the amount of entrepreneurship education in their work.

The answers to the open-ended questions indicated that one problem in curriculum development work is the lack of adequate instructions as to how to integrate entrepreneurship education with and into individual subjects. In fact, the National Core Curriculum does not provide sufficient instructions for any kind of theme-based inter-subject or inter-curricular work. The concept of entrepreneurship education is perceived as somewhat confusing. The National Core Curriculum does not provide enough instructions on how to implement the curriculum development work in cooperation with municipalities, different school levels, homes, and with industry and commerce. Even the municipalities with advanced developed curricula (the entrepreneurial and development municipalities) lack planning in their development of entrepreneurship education – for example monitoring and assessment have not been considered at all.

The curriculum development work for entrepreneurship education was most often perceived as a meaningful activity in the entrepreneurial and development municipalities. Involvement in business has a positive effect on attitudes towards this. As a consequence, it can be said that on a general level, knowledge of entrepreneurship and entrepreneurship education also inspires people to take part in the planning process.

The entrepreneurial municipalities especially (and to some extent also the municipalities with better than expected results) had taken account of the local development needs for entrepreneurship education in their curriculum development. These needs included more cooperation between schools and local businesses, as well as more knowledge about entrepreneurship education and shaping attitudes towards entrepreneurship. In the other municipality categories the development of entrepreneurship education was not considered during the curriculum process.

All municipality categories suffer from the same problems to a certain extent. It nonetheless seems that some municipalities are more aware of these problems than others and strive to solve them. This enables them to develop entrepreneurship education and entrepreneurship.

Attitudes

The attitudes of teaching staff towards the *curriculum reform* are neither negative nor positive (statistical average = 27.5, calculated average = 27.0, scale 11–44 points). There was no statistically significant difference between the municipality categories in this respect. However, a significant difference ($p < 0.000$) was found for the statement 'Without the curriculum it is difficult to assess what the students should be taught'. In the municipalities with better than expected results the respondents reported that it was not difficult to assess what to teach without the curriculum, whereas in the other municipalities the respondents reported that the curriculum was needed as a form of support in the planning of teaching. It is probable that in the first category of municipalities the curriculum does not influence the planning of teaching.

In general, attitudes towards *entrepreneurship education* are neither positive nor negative (scale 11–44, statistical average = 27.5, the average for all respondents = 27.6). Some individual statements of attitudes even show a positive tendency; for example the statement of 'Entrepreneurship education promotes the achievement of basic education goals and equality'. However, the attitudes towards entrepreneurship education are most negative with respect to the local curriculum process.

Guidance counsellors (average = 32.2, standard deviation = 4.9), education directors or equivalent officials (average = 30.1, standard deviation = 4.5), head teachers and principals (average = 29.5, standard deviation = 4.6) had the most positive attitudes towards entrepreneurship education. They also have most experience of participating in entrepreneurship education and they had the most information about it. Teachers of grades 1–6 had the most negative attitudes (average = 26.0; standard deviation = 4.8). This is a statistically significant difference from education officials ($p = 0.05$). Teachers' negative attitudes were also reflected in their reluctance to participate in entrepreneurship education. The study also suggested a positive correlation between teaching staff with business experience and with more positive attitudes towards entrepreneurship teaching ($p < 0.000$), (experience, average = 28.9, standard deviation = 4.9; no experience, average = 26.2, standard deviation = 4.6). Thus we may assume that business experience develops positive attitudes towards entrepreneurship education.

Knowledge and Other Resources

Generally speaking the results indicate that respondents do not know very much about entrepreneurship education. The average for all respondents in this regard is 2.2 (scale 1–4). The statistical variation between municipality categories, genders or teacher groups (teachers of grades 1–6 and teachers of grades 7–9) is not significant. Teachers of grades 1–6 reported the lowest level of knowledge about entrepreneurship education (average = 1.9). Education officials or equivalent respondents felt they knew more than what the teachers reported (average = 2.3). The results indicate that trades ombudsmen have fairly limited knowledge about entrepreneurship education (average = 2.6). The representatives of entrepreneurs thought that they knew quite a lot about it (average = 3.2). Their assessments in this regard indicate quite a wide variation (standard deviation = 1.1). In other words, some of them felt they knew a lot, whereas others felt they knew relatively little. As could be expected, people who had participated in entrepreneurship education reported a higher level of knowledge than did people who had not. However, it must be noted that the difference between the two groups was not statistically significant.

Knowledge about entrepreneurship education was also ascertained through an open-ended question: 'What do you think entrepreneurship education could be in basic education?' About 40 per cent (188) of all respondents within the teaching field answered this question. The people with the most education in this regard, such as guidance counsellors and education officials, 30 per cent of the teachers of grades 1–6 and 13 per cent of the teachers of grades 7–9 reported that entrepreneurship education concerns both the development of the individual, self-orientated and external entrepreneurship. Approximately 45 per cent of the teachers answered that entrepreneurship education had more to do with the development of external entrepreneurship. However, many of the teachers of grades 7–9 believed that entrepreneurship education only concerned the development of individual, self-orientated entrepreneurship.

The respondents considered that other resources required, such as 1) funding; 2) education; 3) materials; 4) information; 5) cooperation partners; 6) management support; and 7) developmental atmosphere are not sufficient anywhere (Likert-scale questions were used to gather information about resources).

The insufficiency of resources in general (the numbers 1–7 all together) is indicated by the fact that even according to the best and most positive assessments, the best resources were mediocre (scale of 12–48, calculated average 30.0, the statistical average 24.6, standard deviation 4.2).

In terms of differences between municipalities in the various statements, a statistically significant difference ($p = 0.05$) was evident for the statement 'We are a municipality that wants to develop and improve its educational services'. The entrepreneurial municipalities were keener to improve education locally (average = 3.5, standard deviation = 0.5). Thus it can be stated that in the entrepreneurial municipalities the willingness to improve and to develop was also manifest in other issues such as better provision of resources, not just in entrepreneurship education.

DISCUSSION

The State of Entrepreneurship Education in Basic Education and Directions for the Future

The study shows that local organizations were facing and continue to face many challenges. The respondents felt that curriculum design from the point of view of entrepreneurship education was hard and that there was not enough time, financial resources, information or support available. One third of the respondents within the teaching field were nonetheless going to implement more entrepreneurship education in their day-to-day work in the future.

This is a positive result, and indicates that people have started to offer more entrepreneurship education. However, the National Core Curriculum is norm-based and requires local authorities to carry out its orders and instructions. According to it, all municipalities are supposed to carry out entrepreneurship education, at least after the year 2006. In this respect, this study shows that entrepreneurship education has not been sufficiently taken into account in the curriculum development work.

It must be noted nonetheless that curriculum reform is a multifaceted process. The National Core Curriculum containing the goals of national education policy is not mechanically or directly transferred to the local level and to the local curricula. The curriculum is a document that changes at many different levels and according to many situations and requirements (cf. Cuban, 1992, pp. 90–92). Despite the norm-based nature of the curriculum, subjective interpretations are always in play. These interpretations must be made in education and teaching.

People know relatively little about entrepreneurship education. Teachers consider that entrepreneurship education is more related to the development of external entrepreneurship. This reveals a lack of knowledge, since entrepreneurship education deals in basic education with self-orientated and inner entrepreneurship (cf. Remes, 2001; 2004; Menzies and Paradi, 2003). It seems that the very concept of entrepreneurship education is still somewhat unclear, or at least that it evokes conflicting ideas (cf. Gibb, 2005, p. 46). The concept of entrepreneurship education should therefore be made clear and concrete as often as possible. The idea of inner, self-orientated entrepreneurship can be made clearer and easier to grasp by using the concept of entrepreneurialism or enterprising in this context. Furthermore, entrepreneurship education for teachers should certainly be increased.

Poor knowledge of entrepreneurship education within the teaching field is also reflected in practice in the ambiguity as to whose responsibility it is to realize entrepreneurship education. Gender issues should also be taken into consideration in the development of entrepreneurship education. According to this study men prefer entrepreneurship education, which also stresses the idea of women as minor actors in terms of entrepreneurship development (cf. Heilbrynn, 2004).

Teachers are the most reluctant to increase entrepreneurship education. The negative experiences of teachers are mostly due to the abstract nature of the curriculum (cf. Atjonen, 1993). Moreover, many respondents think that they lack sufficient resources, for example, information and knowledge. Such experiences of undeveloped curriculum reform structure (cf. Burton et al., 2001, pp. 19–20) are one of the reasons for negative attitudes towards entrepreneurship education. These attitudes then of course have negative consequences for the success of the curriculum development work of entrepreneurship education. How to get teachers motivated to develop entrepreneurship education is certainly a question worth careful consideration.

The characteristics of the contents of entrepreneurship education have been taken into consideration in the curriculum work: its usefulness to pupils and its practical realization in cooperation with local businesses. However, this curriculum work has not been very well planned or methodological – for example none of the municipalities have paid attention to the monitoring or evaluation of entrepreneurship education after the implementation of the new curriculum.

As this study shows, the municipalities with previous experience of entrepreneurship education and a pro-entrepreneurship climate have developed entrepreneurship education during the curriculum reform process. In other municipalities the development of entrepreneurship education during this process has proved very difficult. The cultural background plays a major role in terms of promoting entrepreneurship education. Therefore this study supports the argument that the development of entrepreneurship education should be linked in a broader sense to the development of the whole municipality – for example to the development and implementation of the municipality's education or economic strategy.

The Context of Entrepreneurship Education Development – The Partnership Model

Clearly the structure of this curriculum reform, MacDonald's (2003) partnership model, has not worked as well as expected. In fact, teachers view the National Core Curriculum as abstract and difficult to understand in terms of everyday teaching (cf. Atjonen, 1993). How could the curriculum be made more concrete? The curriculum is, after all, also an official administrative document in which certain terminology, albeit abstract, must be used. The curriculum that is taught and the curriculum that is learned can only develop if the curriculum is an advisory document capable of changes (cf. Atjonen, 1993; MacDonald, 2003). It is the basis for concrete planning. This document needs annual updating. At the same time it could also function as an evaluation tool (cf. Atjonen, 1993). We should nonetheless focus on the essential basic principles and starting points since the problems of a curriculum are usually due to the fact that it contains too many goals and too much content (cf. van der Akker, 2003, p. 7).

The Practical Development of the Partnership Model – Vision, Strategy and Structure

According to this research, planning and evaluation of entrepreneurship education is lacking from the partnership model. Therefore the realization and implementation of entrepreneurship education needs local-level analysis. After this, for example, the next steps (cf. Burton et al., 2001, pp. 19–20) could follow in the planning process.

1. Create a *vision* of the situation (taking stock of where we are now and where we would like to be in the future).
2. Set *objectives* (choosing a few essential objectives at a time).
3. Draft a *strategy* (mapping out the target groups, the learners, cooperation partners, integration with subjects and school culture, pedagogy and learning environments).
4. Consider how the *structure* can be made functional (making the entrepreneurship education plan fully understandable so that it can be adopted, ensuring that material and other financial resources are in order and that organization and teacher management are properly taken care of, drafting a functional and realistic schedule).
5. Plan the *assessment* (assessment is connected to the development of entrepreneurialism at individual level and at school level, to the development of interaction, to the handling of risks and problems, to the creation and utilization of new ideas and to the acquisition of entrepreneurship knowledge).

It is considered essential that teachers get basic training and in-service training since too little is known about curriculum and local curriculum design. The management of municipalities, teachers working for the municipality and people in charge of the municipality's trade and industry issues would benefit from participating in joint training sessions and courses. This would foster in a broader sense the development of learning communities (cf. Blenker et al., 2006, p. 99; Jack and Anderson, 1999; Rae, 2000, p. 148) and would therefore support the development of a cultural framework which is the basic premiss for entrepreneurship education. Moreover, when all the parties involved in entrepreneurship education understand the concept and have a common language with which to discuss it, the actual implementation and realization of entrepreneurship education are much easier.

This research shows that raising awareness about industry and commerce creates positive attitudes towards entrepreneurship education and strengthens its implementation. Therefore, teachers' in-service training should focus on developing awareness of industry, commerce and working life, especially knowledge about entrepreneurship.

CONCLUSION AND IDEAS FOR FUTURE RESEARCH

According to European Union policy, entrepreneurship should be included in all education levels and throughout the common curricula (Commission of the European Communities, 2006). This is still quite rare despite the existing background of policy recommendations. This research took an evaluative approach to entrepreneurship education development through curriculum reform and in basic education, which is still an unexplored field.

This research notes that there are good opportunities for entrepreneurship education development through curriculum, even in basic education, but in the future the following needs more precise consideration: in this research the context of entrepreneurship education development was locally designed curriculum and MacDonald's (2003) partnership model. This model is only partly working. The problems in it are more related to the implementation of this structure. Many theories and earlier studies have indicated that curriculum work is perceived as much more meaningful, both in terms of teaching and learning, when teachers are involved in its design (cf. Adams, 2000; Atjonen, 1993; Fullan, 1999; McGinn, 1999; van der Akker, 2003, p. 9). In other words, it is perfectly warranted to require teachers and other partners to participate more actively in the curricular work since these partners are essential to making it work in practice. But there must be knowledge about curriculum design and contents in order to compile a curriculum and design its implementation.

The conclusions of this study can be summarized into three recommendations. First, *curriculum reforms would yield more benefit if we still focused on the partnership model and teachers' learning development* (Shulman and Shulman, 2004). This could be enhanced through teachers' basic and in-service training including elements of core curriculum, local curriculum design and contents. However, organized training should also concentrate on developing learning communities with different partners involved in realizing entrepreneurship education. This would also ensure a better basis for integrating entrepreneurship education into local education and economic strategy.

Secondly, the research showed that the design of entrepreneurship education is poor, and *planning and evaluation need more attention*. Therefore it could be recommended that once the curricula of entrepreneurship education that have now been drafted are implemented, we go back to this curriculum annually to consider the goals, contents, realization and assessment of this curriculum from a pedagogical point of view. This document could then be annexed to the official administrative curriculum. In order to avoid an unnecessarily heavy burden, it would be beneficial to focus on a few essential objectives each year (cf. Blieck, 2005, p. 185).

Thirdly, the local entrepreneurship education plan could be annexed to the curriculum and to the local economic strategy. Thus the economic strategy itself would then indicate how entrepreneurship education is connected to the development of a local pro-entrepreneurial atmosphere. Through evaluation and monitoring these plans would be updated annually. The planning of assessment and monitoring needs special attention. *Design, implementation and monitoring processes, grounded on cooperation of all of those parties responsible for the development of entrepreneurship education locally, would provide a profound basis for entrepreneurship education concrete development.*

These findings lead to ideas for future research. The curriculum reforms need more research at the local level. The implementation of compiled partnership curricula could be studied. Moreover, it would be beneficial to know what repercussions these compiled and implemented curricula have on students' development and learning. The proposals for action presented in this study could be used in a practical development project on entrepreneurship education and also could be linked to a research project. Thus it would be possible to further develop the practical implementation models of entrepreneurship education. Since this study stresses the findings on teachers' knowledge in a curriculum reform, developing MacDonald's (2003) theoretical framework of curriculum reform from the persective of teachers' learning (cf. Shulman and Shulman, 2004), might also serve to create a more profound basis for developing and understanding curriculum reform and thereby entrepreneurship education development.

REFERENCES

Adams, Jr, J.E. (2000), *Taking Charge of Curriculum: Teacher Networks and Curriculum Implementation*, New York: Teachers College Press.

Atjonen, P. (1993), *Kunnan Opetussuunnitelma Koulun Hallinnollisen ja Pedagogisen Kehittämisen Kohteena ja Välineenä*, (*The Curriculam of Municipality as a Medium and Aim for Developing Administration and Redagogy*), Publication series Acta Universitas Ouluensis, Series E, Scientiae Rerum Socialium 11, The Kajaani Department of Teacher Training, The University of Oulu.

Blenker, P., P. Dreisler and J. Kjeldsen, (2006), 'Entrepreneurship education, the new challenge facing the universities. A framework for understanding and development of entrepreneurial university communities', *Working Paper*, Department of Management, Aarhus School of Business.

Blieck, G. (2005), 'The entrepreneurial approach to the curriculum – Case EHSAL European University College Brussels', in P. Kyrö and C. Carrier (eds), *The Dynamics of Learning Entrepreneurship in a Cross-Cultural University Context*, University of Tampere, Research Centre for Vocational and Professional Education, Entrepreneurship Education Series 2/2005, Saarijärvi: Saarijärven Offset, pp. 162–85.

Bobbitt, F. (2004), 'Scientific method in curriculum making', in D.J. Flinders and S.J. Thornton (eds), *The Curriculum Studies Reader*, 2nd edn, New York: Routledge Falmer, pp. 9–16.

Burton, N., D. Middlewood and R. Blatchford (2001), 'Models of curriculum organization', in D. Middlewood and N. Burton (eds), *Managing the Curriculum*, University of Leicester, Educational Management Development Unit, London: Paul Chapman, pp. 18–34.

Commission of the European Communities (2006), 'Communication from the commission to the Council, the European Parliament, the European Economic and Social Committee and the Committee of the Regions, Implementing the Community Lisbon Programme: Fostering entrepreneurial mindsets through education and learning', available at:http://eur-lex.europa.eu/LexUriServ/site/en/com/2006/com2006_0033en01.pdf.

Constantino, J. (2003), 'Curriculum under construction: confronting the challenge of engagement in an era of reform', *Journal of Curriculum Studies*, **35** (3), 281–302.

Cuban, L. (1992), 'Curriculum stability and change', in P.W. Jackson (ed.), *Handbook of Research on Curriculum: A Project of the American Educational Research Association*, New York: Macmillan, pp. 216–47.

European Commission (2002), *Final Report of the Expert Group 'Best Procedure' Project on Education and Training for Entrepreneurship*, Brussels: Enterprise Directorate General.

European Commission (2004), *Final Report of the Expert Group 'Education for Enterpreneurship' Making Progress in Promoting Entrepreneurial Attitudes and Skills through Primary and Secondary Education*, Brussels: Enterprise Directorate General.

Finnish National Board of Education (2004), *National Core Curriculum for Basic Education 2004,* Vammala: Vammalan kirjapaino.

Flouris, G. and G. Pasias (2003), 'A critical appraisal of curriculum reform in Greece (1980–2002). Trends, challenges, and perspectives', *European Education*, **35** (3), 73–90.

Fullan, M.G. (1982), *The Meaning of Educational Change*, New York: Teachers College Press.

Fullan, M. (1999), *Change Forces: The Sequel*, London: Falmer.

Gartner, W.B. (1990), 'What are we talking about when we talk about entrepreneurship?', *Journal of Business Venturing*, **5**, 15–28.

Gibb, A. (2005), 'The future of entrepreneurship education – Determining the basis for coherent policy and practice?', in P. Kyrö and C. Carrier (eds), *The Dynamics of Learning Entrepreneurship in a Cross-Cultural University Context*, University of Tampere, Research Centre for Vocational and Professional Education,

Entrepreneurship Education Series 2/2005, Saarijärvi: Saarijärven Offset, pp. 44–66.

Gibb, A. (2006), 'Entrepreneurship/enterprise education in schools and colleges: are we really building the onion or peeling it away?', National Council for Graduate Entrepreneurship, working paper 039/2006, available at: http://ncge.com/communities/research/reference/detail/880/7 (accessed 20 September 2007).

Halinen, I. (2004), 'Aihekokonaisuudet opetuksen eheyttäjänä' ('The interactive themes as medium for holistic teaching'), in M.-L. Loukola (ed.), *Aihekokonaisuudet Perusopetuksen Opetussuunnitelmassa (The Interactive Themes in the Curriculam of Basic Education)*, Jyväskylä: Gummerus, pp. 11–16.

Heilbrynn, S. (2004), 'Impact of gender differences faced by entrepreneurs', *Entrepreneurship and Innovation*, August 2004, pp. 159–65.

Heinonen, J. (2004), 'Yrittäjyyskasvatus meillä ja muualla' ('Entrepreneurship education here and abroad'), Presentation at the meeting of entrepreneurship educators, The University of Applied Sciences, Turku, 24 March 2004.

Heinonen, J.-P. (2005), 'Opetussuunnitelmat vai oppimateriaalit. Peruskoulun opettajien käsityksiä opetussuunnitelmien ja oppimateriaalien merkityksestä opetuksessa', ('Curricula or teaching material? Teachers' views about the significance of curricula and teaching material'), The Institute of Applied Sciences, The University of Helsinki, Research 257, available at: http://ethesis. helsinki.fi/julkaisut/kay/sovel/vk/heinonen/opetussu. pdf (accessed 4 February 2006).

Jack, S.L. and A. R. Anderson (1999), 'Entrepreneurship education within the enterprise culture', *International Journal of Entrepreneurial Behaviour and Research*, **5**(3), 110–125.

Kolb, D.A. (1984) *Experimental Learning: Experience as the Source of Learning and Development*, Englewood Cliffs, NJ: Prentice Hall.

Kuratko, D.F. (2005), 'The emergence of entrepreneurship education: development, trends, and challenges', *Entrepreneurship Theory and Practice*, **29**(5), 577–97.

Kuusela, J. (2003), *Lukioiden tuloksiin vaikuttavista tekijöistä*, (*The Factors which have an Influence on Results of High Schools*), The National Board of Education, Handout 13/2003, Helsinki: Edita Prima.

Kyrö, P. (2005), 'Entrepreneurial learning in a cross-cultural context challenges previous learning paradigms', in P. Kyrö and C. Carrier (eds), *The Dynamics of Learning Entreprenurship in a Cross-Cultural University Context*, University of Tampere, Faculty of Education, Research Centre for Vocational and Professional Education: Saarijärven Offset, pp. 68–102.

Kyrö, P. and C. Carrier (2005), 'Entrepreneurial learning in universities: bridges across borders', in P. Kyrö and C. Carrier (eds), *The Dynamics of Learning Entreprenurship in a Cross-Cultural University Context*, University of Tampere, Faculty of Education, Research Centre for Vocational and Professional Education: Saarijärven Offset, pp. 14–43.

Letschert, J. and J. Kessels (2003), 'Social and political factors in the process of curriculum change', in J. van der Akker, W. Kuiper and U. Hameyer (eds), *Curriculum Landscapes and Trends*, Dordrecht: Kluwer Academic, pp. 157–76.

Liljeström, U. (2004), 'Opetussuunnitelmaprosessi' ('The process of curriculum'), in E. Vitikka and O. Saloranta-Eriksson (eds), *Uudistuva perusopetus, Näkökulmia opetuksen ja opetussuunnitelman kehittämiseen, (The Reform of Basic Education: Same Views for Developing Education and Designing Curricula)*, Jyväskylä: Gummerus, pp. 84–96.

Littledyke, M. (1997), 'Managerial style, the National Curriculum and teachers' culture: responses to educational change in a primary school', *Educational Research*, **39**(3), 243–62.

MacDonald, D. (2003), 'Curriculum change and the post-modern world: is the school curriculum reform movement an anachronism?', *Journal of Curriculum Studies*, **35**(2), 139–49.

Marsh, C.J. (2004), *Key Concepts for Understanding Curriculum*, 3rd edn, London: Routledge Falmer.

McGinn, N. (1999), 'What is required for successful education reform? Learning from errors', *Education Practice and Theory*, **21**(1), 7–21.

Menzies, T.V. and J.C. Paradi (2003), 'Entrepreneurship education and engineering students. Career path and business performance', *The International Journal of Entrepreneurship and Innovation*, **4**(2), 121–32.

Rae, D. (2000), 'Understanding entrepreneurial learning: a question of how?', *International Journal of Entrepreneurial Behaviour and Research*, **6**(3), 145–59.

Remes, L. (2001), 'Yrittäjyyskasvatus pedagogisessa toimintatehtävässä' ('Entrepreneurship education in pedagogical task'), *Kasvatus*, **32**(4), 368–81.

Remes, L. (2003), *Yrittäjyyskasvatuksen kolme diskurssia* (*The Three Discussions of Entrepreneurship Education*) Jyväskylä Studies in Education, Psychology and Social Research 213, Jyväskylä: Jyväskylä University Printing House.

Remes, L. (2004), 'Yrittäjyys'('Entrepreneurship'), in M.-L. Loukola (ed.) *Aihekokonaisuudet Perusopetuksen Opetussuunnitelmassa* (*The Integrating Themes in the Curriculam of Basic Education*), Jyväskylä: Gummerus, pp. 89–90.

Ristimäki, K. (2003), 'Yrittäjyyskasvatus – enemmän metodi kuin sisältö' ('Entrepreneurship education – more method than content'), in Taloudellinen tiedotustoimisto (ed.), *Yrittäjyyskasvatus, Yrittäjyyttä ja kasvatusta* (*Entrepreneurship education, Entrepreneurship and education*) Saarijärvi: Gummerus, pp. 12–15.

Seikkula-Leino, J. (2006), *Perusopetuksen opetussuunnitelmauudistus 2004–2006 ja yrittäjyyskasvatuksen kehittäminen. Paikallinen opetussuunnitelmatyö yrittäjyyskasvatuksen näkökulmasta* (*Curriculam Reform in Basic Education and the Development of Entrepreneurship Education. The Local Curriculam Works from the Point of View of Engrepreneurship Education*), Publications of the Ministry of Education 2006: 22, The Department of Education and Science Policy, Helsinki: Yliopistopaino.

Shane, S. and S. Venkataraman (2000), 'The promise of entrepreneurship as a field of research', *Academy of Management Review*, **25**(1), 217–26.

Shulman, L.S. and J.H. Shulman (2004), 'How and what teachers' learn: a shifting perspective', *Journal of Curriculum Studies*, **36**(2), 257–71.

Sulonen, K. (2004), 'Opetussuunnitelman uudistamistyö opettajan ammatillisen kasvun välineenä – kohteena peruskoulun kotitalouden opetus', ('The reform of a curriculum as a tool for teachers' professional development – focusing on the home economics of basic school') The Scientific Publication of the Home Economics and Handicrafts Departments 13, The Faculty of Behavioural Sciences, The University of Helsinki, available at: http://ethesis.helsinki.fi/julkaisut/kas/kotit/vk/sulonen/opetussu.pdf (accessed 17 January 2006).

Syrjäläinen, E. (1997), *Arvioinnin avulla laatua kouluihin – markkinahumua vai koulurealismia (Improving the Quality of Schools through Evaluation – Business Hassle or Realism in education?)*, The Publications of the Teacher Training Department A 11/1997, The University of Tampere.

Turtiainen, J. (2002), *Kaakkois-Suomen yrittäjyysselvitys, Yrittäjyyskasvatus ja – koulutuskysely oppilaitoksille,* (*The State of Entrepreneurship in the Southeast of Finland, Clarification – The Enquiry about Teaching of Entrepreneurship and Training*), 9, Kouvola: Te-keskus.

van der Akker, J. (2003), 'Curriculum perspectives: an introduction', in J. van der Akker, W. Kuiper and U. Hameyer (eds) *Curriculum Landscapes and Trends*, Dordrecht: Kluwer Academic, pp. 1–10.

Webb, R. and G. Vulliamy (1999), 'Managing curriculum policy changes: a comparative analysis of primary schools in England and Finland', *Journal of Educational Policy*, **14**(2), 117–37.

Yrittäjyyskasvatuksen linjaukset ja toimenpideohjelma 2004 (*The Clarification and the Action Programme of Entrepreneurship Education in 2004*), The Publications of the Ministry of Education 2004: 18, The Department of Education and Science Policy, Helsinki: Yliopistopaino.

Zajda, J. (2003), 'Educational reform and transformation in Russia. Why do education reforms fail?', *European Education*, **35**(1), 58–88.

PART III

The Dynamics between Entrepreneurship and Small Businesses

10. An empirical taxonomy of start-up firms' growth trajectories

Mahamadou Biga Diambeidou, Damien François, Benoît Gailly, Michel Verleysen and Vincent Wertz

INTRODUCTION

Over the past decades, new and small firm growth has received considerable attention from researchers and policy-makers around the world. New firms have been identified as engines of growth, innovation and wealth creation (Audretsch and Thurik, 2000; Birch, 1981; Davidsson, 1995; Davidsson et al., 1998; Levie, 1997; OECD, 1994, 1998, 2002; Storey, 1994; Welbourne, 1997). Indeed empirical evidence indicates that only a small proportion of firms account for a significant percentage of new job creation. Those firms often accelerate the development of new technologies and products that play a fundamental role in the prosperity of many countries (Birch et al., 1997; Julien et al., 2001; Storey, 1997). New firms are therefore a key element in regional economic development, and represent as such an interesting research subject.

Despite their importance to regional development, knowledge about new firm growth is still scattered (Davidsson and Wiklund, 2000; Delmar, 1997) and little knowledge is available regarding how firms grow and perform over time (Geroski, 2001). This can be partly attributed to methodological problems, such as the difficulties experienced in identifying entrepreneurial firms. For example, to this concern Gibb and Davies (1990) argued that it is illusory to think that it would be possible to detect this kind of firm or to produce a complete ideal model. Other international studies concluded that a 'typical' high-growth firm does not exist (OECD, 2000; Delmar et al., 2003).

From a theoretical perspective, scholars have shown that research has largely failed to generate cumulative results regarding new firm growth because there is a great variability in researchers' use of growth conceptualization and operationalization (Davidsson and Wiklund, 2000; Delmar, 1997; Delmar et al., 2003; Murphy et al., 1996, Chandler and Hanks, 1993;

Weinzimmer et al., 1998; Wiklund and Shepherd, 2005). Indeed from a theoretical perspective the phenomenon of entrepreneurial growth has been mostly studied within individual academic disciplines, which does not encourage an integrated and systemic analysis (Garnsey and Heffernan, 2005). Research was done from different theoretical imperatives such as industrial organization, the resource-based view, strategic adaptation and an evolutionary economic perspective. Research from each discipline tends therefore to ignore important findings from competing schools. For example, since the original 'theory of the growth of the firm' from Penrose (1959), where managerial resources played a pivotal role, diverse factors have been suggested as affecting growth. Some of them, such as environmental carrying capacity or market forces, are external to the organization (Aldrich, 1990; Singh and Lumsden, 1990). Others are internal, like capabilities, culture or strategy, and have been mainly addressed from the resource-based view of the firm (Wernerfelt, 1984; Teece et al., 1997; Boeker, 1997; Zahra et al., 2000; Canals, 2000).

From an empirical perspective, growth is a multi-faceted phenomenon, but this heterogeneous nature is often neglected by scholars. Despite the diversity of approaches in terms of indicators, formulae and time spans used to measure growth (Delmar, 1997), empirical research has also largely failed to generate cumulative results (Davidsson and Wiklund, 2000; Delmar, 1997; Delmar et al., 2003; Weinzimmer et al., 1998). The common explanation is the absence of consensus regarding which firm growth indicators should be used (Weinzimmer et al., 1998; Delmar, 1997; Murphy et al., 1996; Chandler and Hanks, 1993). Another explanation is that researchers often measure growth along a single dimension (Weinzimmer et al., 1998) although this approach has been widely criticized as firm growth is heterogeneous in nature (Birley and Westhead, 1990; Delmar and Davidsson, 1998; Delmar et al., 2003). As a consequence, using a single measure of growth defined by a single criterion actually investigates only one particular kind of growth, and the results are unlikely to be applicable to other forms of growth (Delmar and Davidsson, 1998).

Finally, most studies about growth tend to focus on specific sectors (for example high-tech) although the economic contribution of new firm growth appears to be spread across various sectors (Delmar et al., 2003). Indeed most papers looking at 'promising firms' have focused on samples limited to new technology-based firms, from sectors such as software products, telecommunications or biotechnology (Baldwin et al., 1994; Vyakarnam et al., 1997; Woywod and Lessat, 2001; Calvo and Lorenzo, 2001; Julien, 2001).

In order to address those theoretical and empirical issues, recent entrepreneurship research argues that there is a strong need for a conceptual scheme and for longitudinal growth studies (Busenitz et al., 2003; Chandler and Lyon, 2001; Davidsson and Wiklund, 2000; Delmar et al., 2003; Garnsey et al., 2006; Pettigrew et al., 2001). The underlying assumption is that growth is a heterogeneous phenomenon that naturally happens over time; it should therefore be analyzed in a dynamic process perspective and across multiple organizational contexts. Indeed, while most new and small firm growth studies have focused on the explanation of the performance using cross-sectional data and/or have assumed that growth is an uninterrupted process, longitudinal approaches have shown that regular growth is the exception rather than the rule (Delmar et al., 2003; Garnsey et al., 2006; Garnsey and Heffernan, 2005; McMahon, 2001; OECD, 2002; Stam, 2003).

However, longitudinal approaches generate methodological challenges which require new research methods (Huber and Van de Ven, 1995; Poole et al., 2000; Van de Ven, 1992), which in particular involve more than static comparisons between initial and end states (Davidsson, 2004; Davidsson and Wiklund, 2000). Based on their respective dissertations and works in the field, Davidsson et al. (2006, p. 5) argue that 'firm growth is a complex phenomenon. It is not uni-dimensional. It is hard to predict and assess. Further, it can manifest itself in various ways, and consequently it can have differential effects on several different levels.'

In this context, the purpose of this research is to present an original method that can accommodate, in a systematic way, the longitudinal analysis of new firm growth trajectories based on a multidimensional construct of growth. More specifically, our objective is to answer the following research question: is the early growth of a firm a process essentially idiosyncratic, that is related to the individual characteristics of each firm or do typical growth trajectories that are adopted by a majority of firms exist? We analyzed the initial growth trajectories of 741 Belgian firms created between 1992 and 2002 which have grown above micro-firm size during that period. We developed and tested an original methodology allowing an empirical taxonomy of early growth trajectories across multiple sectors, integrating the multidimensional aspect of growth.

In the following sections we detail our research design and introduce the experimental setting. We then document the empirical results of this research and discuss major findings and limitations.

RESEARCH DESIGN

To deal with the challenges generated by the analysis of the complex nature of new firm growth, we have elaborated a research design at the crossroad of entrepreneurship research and applied mathematics (Lévesque, 2004). More specifically, at a conceptual level, our research design integrates multidimensional and dynamic approaches of growth across sectors in order to conceptualize the early growth processes of firms. The key aspects of this research design are addressed hereafter.

Multidimensional Approach and Ubiquity

When considering the measurement of growth, as discussed in the introduction there is no consensus regarding which and how many indicators should be used. Moreover, the majority of researchers do not justify theoretically their choice of variables, although those choices can have consequences for the results (Delmar, 1997; Janssen, 2005). We therefore choose for this research design to jointly use multiple indicators, based upon commonly used measures of firm economics and financials, and let the empirical data show which indicators are the most meaningful. Let us stress that those 'tangible' measures of growth do not allow to distinguish organic from acquisition-driven growth and tend to only indirectly reflect the 'intangible' aspects of growth, such as the intellectual capital, the culture or the strategy of a firm, which might play an important role but cannot be taken directly into consideration in the context of our research design.

Moreover, we adopt the assumption that firm growth is a ubiquitous phenomenon. In other words, we will not limit ourselves a priori to specific sectors, on the basis of the assumption that firms develop in various manners whatever their sector. We believe that the relevance of the sector dimension should be checked empirically a posteriori and not preconceived a priori.

Growth Trajectory

As discussed above, growth is a process of change that needs to be studied over time (Davidsson et al., 2006, p. 40). Indeed, Penrose (1995) saw growth as a cumulative process in which firm members build knowledge and competence. According to this author, firms are 'a result of a process of development [. . .] in which interacting series of internal changes lead to increase in size accompanied by changes in the characteristics of the growing object' (Penrose, 1995, p. 1).

In the entrepreneurship context, recent authors emphasized the underlying assumption of the growth process, suggesting that firm growth is driven by a 'productive opportunity' (Penrose, 1995) in a cumulative process of interaction between the firm's productive base and its market opportunities (Garnsey, 1995; Garnsey et al., 2006). Thus, process studies of firms should examine interconnected causes, outcomes and further feedback effects (Van de Ven, 1992). We need longitudinal research because it mainly allows direct observation of such change, causal statements, temporal context and feedback effects (Davidsson and Wiklund, 2000; Chandler and Lyon, 2001; Pettigrew et al., 2001). As a consequence, our research design will focus on taking into account successive measures of the growth process as the firm evolves over time, rather than only considering the initial and end states.

Empirical Taxonomy

As emphasized by most scholars in organizational studies (Archibugi, 2001; de Jong and Marsili, 2006; Ketchen and Shook, 1996; Pavitt, 1998; Rich, 1992), a useful empirical taxonomy can reduce the complexity of empirical phenomena to a few constructs. Thus, a widely accepted and usable taxonomy is a fundamental element in the development of a scientific body of knowledge (Sabherwal and Robey, 1993) and can serve as an empirically based framework to theory development. Indeed, previous researches suggest that, contrary to a typology considered as an individual creativity invention, taxonomy is an empirical classification tool for building the complex filing systems that allow both the ordering and retrieval of large amounts of data (McKelvey, 1975; Pugh et al., 1969). Moreover, according to Rich (1992), a taxonomy is more than a simple classification of items into separate groups. It is a specific classification scheme that expresses the overall similarity between organisms in a hierarchical fashion. In addition, in their innovative small firm research, de Jong and Marsili (2006) emphasized that taxonomy classifies and labels many different items into groups or clusters that share common traits.

We therefore adopted in this research a taxonomy approach with the objective of attempting to reduce the complexity and therefore to improve our understanding of early firm growth. Hence our research design consists in mobilizing advanced applied mathematics tools in order to develop an empirical taxonomy of firm trajectories based on the initial evolution across sectors and over time of multiple economic and financial indicators.

EXPERIMENTAL SETTING

Having specified our research design, we will present briefly in this section the methodology adopted to identify the typical growth trajectories, with regard to the choice of the sample and variables and to the methods of analysis adopted.

Choice of Sample and Variables

A valuable opportunity to address the key study issue in this chapter has been provided by the availability of the BEL-FIRST database developed by Bureau van Dijk Electronic Publishing (BvD), one of Europe's leading electronic publishers of business information. Our research collected longitudinal financial information and demographic indicators about all Belgian firms. As this study focuses on the initial growth of the firm, the population considered here includes all the firms created after 1992 and still in existence in 2002 (N = 152 064).

Among these young firms, we selected all those which, since their creation, exceeded the stage of micro-firm level (as defined by the European Commission, 2003). This enables us to identify firms whose growth can be regarded as 'promising' in the broadest sense, that is which can be considered as having contributed somewhat to economic development. This allows us to build a sample that goes beyond exceptional cases of very high and regular growth, often publicized but not at all representative of a 'typical' growth firm. Moreover, in order to eliminate most 'false creation' cases (such as a firm created through the incorporation of an existing subsidiary), we eliminated firms that had already exceeded the size of a micro-firm at the time of their creation.

Regarding the choice of variables, we selected as our main measures of growth three economic indicators: sales, employment and total assets, which have all been considered as suitable indicators of growth (see Davidsson and Wiklund, 2000). Those indicators are combined with seven financial variables traditionally linked to firm performance (value added, operating income, current income, net income, cash-flow, working capital and shareholders' equity). In line with previous researchers (Davidsson and Wiklund, 2000; Birley and Westhead, 1990; Weinzimmer et al., 1998; Wiklund, 1999), we think that the combination of multiple size and financial indicators provides richer information and therefore allows better investigation of the growth process. Finally our data also included information regarding each firm's main sector of activity, type of ownership and legal form. On the basis of this choice of variables, the firms for which available data were complete and coherent or could be reconstituted by simple interpolation were selected.

Methods of Analysis

The method used to analyze the existence of typical growth trajectories consists in considering a firm growth trajectory as a sequence of states (corresponding to the successive years of existence) in a space with 10 dimensions (corresponding to the three economic and seven financial indicators).

In this space, mathematical tools for classification and discrimination such as a principal components analysis[1] (PCA) and empirical clustering based on density estimation (Cuevas et al., 2001) can be mobilized (see François et al., 2004 for other examples of tools for classification). These tools make it possible to identify and validate through density distribution potential clusters, each cluster corresponding to firms in similar stages of development. Once these clusters are identified and tagged ('stage A', 'stage B', etc.), the trajectory of a firm can be described as a sequence or a Markov chain corresponding to the various stages it experienced successively. For example AAABABB represents seven years of the trajectory of a firm evolving between states close to the clusters 'stage A' and 'stage B'.

The firms having adopted similar growth trajectories will be characterized by similar sequences. Those sequences can be compared through graphical interpretation and Markov chain analysis (Bakerman and Gottman, 1986; Howard, 1971) and then analyzed through a systematic sequence analysis (Poole et al., 2000), in order to evaluate the heterogeneity of growth trajectories and test the existence, validity and characteristics of typical trajectories.

EMPIRICAL RESULTS

We will present our results in four sections. The first section relates to the sampling results and to the validation of the use of multiple indicators and sectors. The second section presents the result of the clustering of the successive growth states into four 'stages'. The next two sections explore the heterogeneity of growth trajectories and the existence and characteristics of typical trajectories through first a graphical comparison and then a systematic analysis.

Sampling Results

As discussed above, our research is based on a sample including all Belgian firms created since 1992 and still in existence in 2002 (n = 152 064). From these firms, we selected those which grew above micro-firm size at any time during that period. There were 17 168 such firms identified in our sample. Those 'promising' firms represented 6 per cent of all the existing Belgian firms in 2002 and 11 per cent of the firms created since 1992 and still in existence in 2002. However, they generated (in 2002) respectively 19 per cent and 80 per cent of overall gross job creation.

Among the firms selected, 33 per cent had missing values regarding employment, 53 per cent regarding sales and 17 per cent regarding cash flow. We excluded the firms that did not publish complete data for more than two consecutive years, or firms that published less than 40 per cent of the data available for two consecutive years. Using those filters, the final dataset included 741 firms.

Most sectors were represented in our sample (13 out of the 17 principal sectors included in the standard NACE industry classification). The majority related to service industries (71 per cent), while only 11 per cent were related to manufacturing and another 17 per cent to the construction industry. Only 19 per cent of the firms in our sample were high-tech firms.[2] This confirms the relevance of our cross-sector approach.

Finally, the 741 firms in our sample were sorted according to the measure of size (employment, sales or total assets) along which they had grown above the micro-firm size threshold. Fifty per cent of the firms in our sample had reached only the micro-firm employment threshold (more than nine employees) while 33 per cent and 8 per cent had reached only the sales and the asset micro-firm thresholds respectively. Less than 10 per cent had reached more than one threshold and 2 per cent had reached all three thresholds (they simultaneously had more than nine employees, more than 1 million euros in sales and more than 2 million euros in assets). This confirms the relevance of our use of multiple indicators to measure growth (Delmar et al., 2003; Janssen, 2005; St-Pierre et al., 2005), as using different indicators leads to different selections of 'promising' firms.

Clustering

In order to explore the growth trajectories of the firms in our sample, we first tested the existence of clusters among the various states a firm experiences as it initially grows. We used for this purpose a Principal Component Analysis based on the successive absolute value of our three economic and seven financial indicators for each firm. This analysis produced three principal axes, with a cumulated variance of 82 per cent (the two first axes accounted for 72 per cent). Other choices of variables were tested, in particular using relative rather than absolute financial values (ratios). Nevertheless, all these alternative choices proved less relevant in terms of restitution of information, that is generating a weaker cumulated variance.

The three principal axes identified enabled us to represent (through a linear projection) all the successive states of the firms in a space with three dimensions. These axes represent composite variables which can be regarded as 'latent dimensions' of the problem (Evrard et al., 2003), making it possible to apprehend fundamental dimensions of the studied phenomenon. The three axes are detailed in Table 10.1, according to their correlation[3] with the 10 starting variables after a Varimax[4] rotation.

Table 10.1 Results of PCA analysis

Axis	Empl.	Sales	Value added	Oper. income	Current income	Net income	Work. capital	Cash flow	Shar. equity	Total assets
1. Performance	0.12	0.03	−0.06	**−0.47**	**−0.49**	**−0.51**	−0.12	**−0.44**	−0.23	0.05
2. Size	**0.42**	**0.47**	**0.45**	0.03	−0.01	−0.11	0.26	0.03	0.027	**0.50**
3. Resources	0.33	0.12	0.29	0.14	0.07	0.05	**−0.71**	0.20	**−0.47**	−0.04

Those results indicate that the first axis is more correlated with four financial variables (operating income, current income, net income and cash flow) which can be linked to the 'Performance' of a firm. The second axis is more correlated with four indicators (employment, sales, value added and total assets) which can be linked to the 'Size' of a firm. Finally, the third axis is more correlated to the variables working capital and shareholder equity, which can be linked to the 'Resources' of a firm.

Hence the results of the clustering allowed us to identify three principal axes which can be used to extract significant information relative to the evolution of each firm over time, across our sample. Let us stress that this reduction from the ten initial variables to three axes does not remove the multidimensional aspect of our approach, as those axes have been identified empirically (rather than defined a priori) and reflect the fundamental dimensions of our initial dataset, that is the most relevant measures of how individual firm trajectories differ.

Furthermore, by the design of our sample all the firms considered will move from relatively low initial values to relatively high values of sales, employment and/or assets, as they grow above micro-firm size. The informational value of the 'Size' axis is therefore limited from a clustering point of view. From a modeling point of view, this 'Size' axis could actually be considered more as the dependent variable of this study.

We therefore focused our clustering analysis on the 'Performance' and 'Resources' axes. We can represent the successive states any firm in our sample goes through as it grows along those two axes, projecting their initial value along the 10 indicators on the two principal axes identified and taking as a reference point the average value of the sample (Figure 10.1).

However, those axes are only numerical constructs produced by the PCA, which can only be related approximately to actual dimensions of the firms and have no direct managerial interpretation for a given firm. In order to test whether the two selected principal axes could be used in order to define meaningful clusters (that is whether they relate to actual differences between actual firms from a managerial point of view), we measured the density distribution of all 10 economic and financial variables and of four commonly used financial ratios (return on equity, return on asset, capital productivity and labor productivity) along the two axes.

As an illustration, the density distributions of the variable 'operating income' within the four quadrants are presented in Figure 10.2, where the vertical scale represents the probability, the horizontal scale represents the value of the firm's operating income and each of the four lines represents the distribution within one of the four quadrants, as numbered in Figure 10.1. This figure indicates that there appears to be a cutting point (at around 30 000 euros of annual operating income) between the distribution

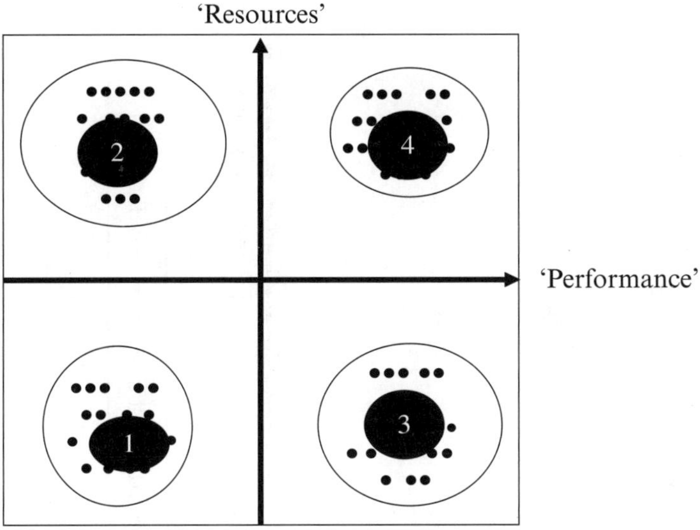

Figure 10.1 Two-dimensional representation of firm successive states

curves related to quadrants 1 and 2 (corresponding to firms with below-average 'performance') and the distribution curves related to quadrants 3 and 4 (corresponding to firms with above-average 'performance').

The analysis presented in Figure 10.2 indicates that the firms that achieve a higher value along the 'performance' principal axis are indeed different from a managerial point of view, as their operating income will be significantly higher.

The application of this process to the 10 economic and financial variables and to the four financial ratios indicate that the 'performance' principal axis is significantly related to operating income, current income, net income, cash flow and labor productivity while the 'resources' principal axis is significantly related only to shareholder equity. Combining those two axes and their managerial interpretation allows us therefore to identify four different stages a new firm can reach as it grows:

1. 'Questions' are firms located at the bottom-left of Figure 10.1. They tend to combine lower than average operating income, current income, net income, cash flow and labor productivity (low performance) with lower than average shareholder equity (low resource). Their future development might at first sight seem at risk.
2. 'Seeds' are firms located at the top-left of Figure 10.1. They tend to have lower than average operating income, current income, net income,

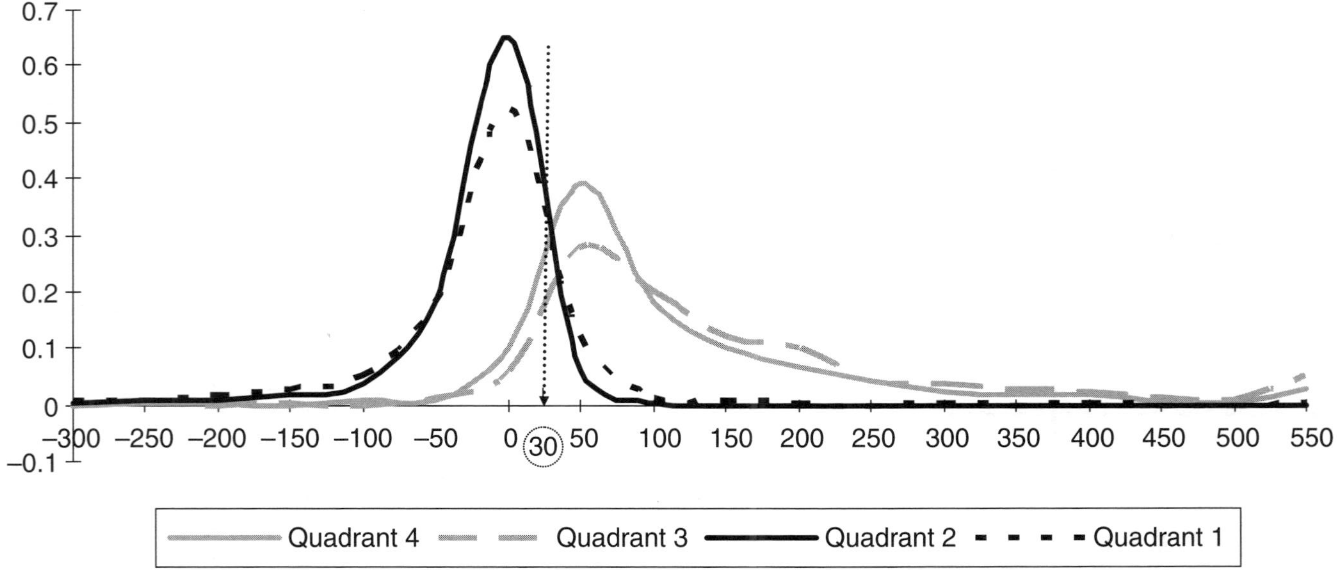

Figure 10.2 Density distribution of operating income along the principal axes

cash flow and labor productivity (low performance) but higher than average shareholder equity (high resource). A firm associated with this profile could for example have been able to raise relatively important funds to ensure its initial development, but needs time to improve its performance.

3. 'Boutiques' are firms located at the bottom-right of Figure 10.1. They tend to have higher than average operating income, current income, net income, cash flow and labor productivity (high performance) but lower than average shareholder equity (low resource).
4. 'Stars' are firms located at the top-right of Figure 10.1. They tend to combine higher than average operating income, current income, net income, cash flow and labor productivity (high performance) with higher than average shareholder equity (high resource). Their future development seems a priori promising.

Hence the PCA and the density analysis have allowed us to identify two axes along which four stages of growth can be identified that are both empirically valid (as indicated by the PCA) and that correspond to actual managerial dimensions (as indicated by the density analysis). We will discuss in the next two sections how those two axes and four stages can be exploited from a graphical and systematic point of view in order to test the heterogeneity of the growth trajectories of young firms, and ultimately build a taxonomy.

Graphical Analysis

Several representations of firm trajectories using the two principal axes we identified above are presented in Figure 10.3, where each box represents the successive states adopted by a given firm along the two axes using a normalized scale. In this figure, a selection of trajectories of similar shape have been gathered together. The first group (the top six boxes) represents rather linear trajectories, from high resources/low performance to low resources/high performance states. The second group gathers sigma-shaped trajectories. They illustrate that the growth of those firms has not been smooth over the years, with some periods that may even correspond to decay. The third group (bottom line) presents angular trajectories going up first (increase in resources) then bifurcating to the left (increase in performance).

Going further, the trajectory of a given firm can be characterized by the sequence of successive stages it goes through. Following a Markov chain approach, the way firms in our sample move from one stage to another (dependencies) can be represented through a digraph

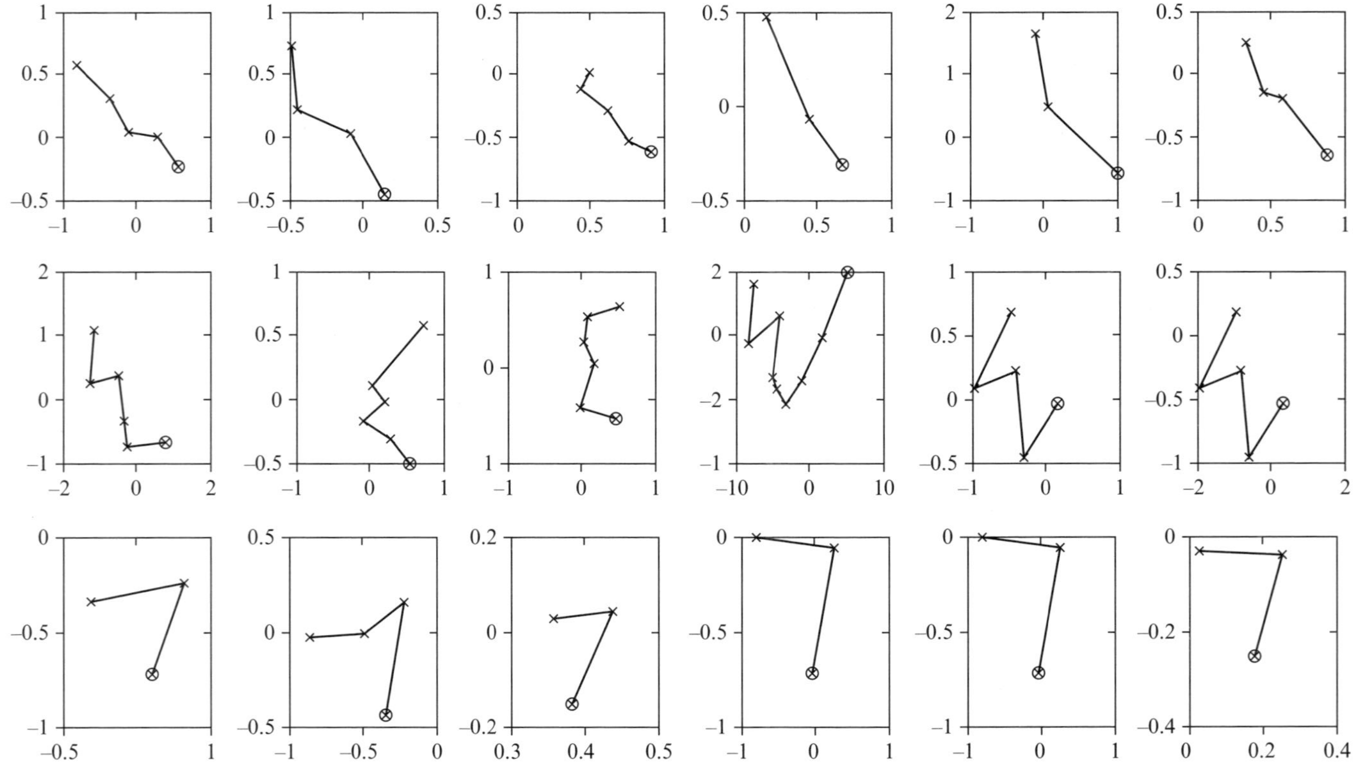

Figure 10.3 Examples of two-dimensional projections of 18 firm growth trajectories

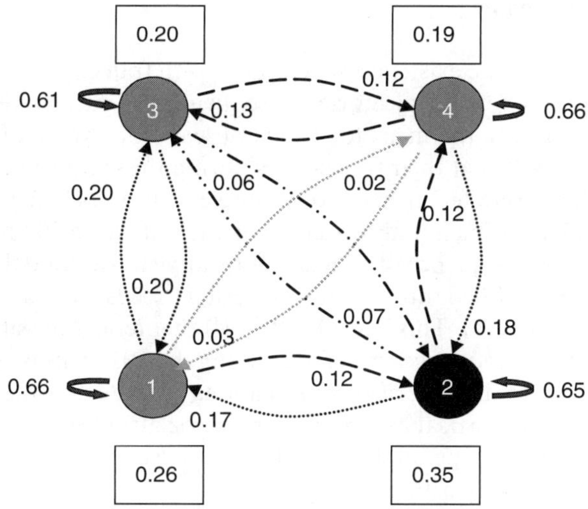

Figure 10.4 *Growth trajectories digraph*

(Figure 10.4), which details the probability that a firm starts in a given stage (boxes) and moves from one stage to another (arrows). Such a digraph renders visible how stages are sequenced over time (Bakerman and Gottman, 1986).

The results presented in Figure 10.4 indicate that the probability of remaining within a given stage is quite high ($p > 0.61$ for all four stages). This behavior can be interpreted as firm inertia. Moreover, 'magic recoveries' and 'catastrophes', that is moving directly from low levels of performance and resource ('questions' stage, no. 1) to high levels ('stars' stage, no. 4) and reciprocally is very rare (respectively $p < 0.02$ and $p < 0.03$).

Those graphical analyses both indicate that growth trajectories can be differentiated along a 'performance' and a 'resources' axis and that this type of representation gives evidence of some homogeneity between the trajectories of some of the firms. There appear to be at the same time a diversity of trajectories but also groups of trajectories that share similar shapes and that are worth investigating further, in a more systematic way. Indeed whether the trajectories such as the ones presented in Figure 10.3 amount to a taxonomy, that is whether we can identify a small number of trajectories that are adopted by a majority of firms, cannot be tested through graphical analysis. Testing this hypothesis in a systematic way is the subject of the following section.

Systematic Taxonomy

In order to explore the existence of typical growth trajectories based on the characterization of firm trajectories as sequences of successive stages, we first considered only the firms for which at least four years of data were available, and looked at their trajectories during those four initial years of existence. There were 602 firms in our sample (out of 741) for which such data was available. The initial trajectory of each of those 602 firms can be characterized by a sequence of four stages (four years) among the four possible stages we identified through our clustering ('seeds', 'stars', 'boutiques' and 'questions' stages). This leads to 256 (4^4) theoretical possibilities. The distribution of the sequences observed among the 602 firms is presented in Figure 10.5, where the observed combinations are listed on the horizontal axis and where the vertical axis represents the occurrence of each of those combinations. The shape of this distribution curve indicates that they are not at all uniformly distributed.

A closer analysis of this curve shows that only 115 different sequences (not visible on the figure) have actually been observed, and that only 22 sequences have been adopted by more than 1 per cent of the firms. Those 22 sequences collectively cover 71 per cent of the firms and are presented in Table 10.2.

If one follows a Markov chain approach and focuses on transitions between stages rather than on the time spent within each stage (the sequences 4333, 4433 and 4443 are therefore regarded as equivalent), seven typical trajectories emerge from those 22 sequences. These trajectories are presented in Figure 10.6.

Those seven typical trajectories can be split between four 'stable' ones (a firm remains in a given stage over the time period considered) and three 'unstable' ones. The four stable and three unstable trajectories are described in Table 10.3, highlighting the corresponding sequences and presented by decreasing frequency.

Those seven typical trajectories collectively include the first 11 and the 21st sequences of Table 10.2 and therefore correspond to 59 per cent of the firms in our sample for which at least four years of data are available (602 firms).

While those seven trajectories, considered individually, might appear as quite natural development paths for firms to follow (in particular the three 'unstable' ones), it is clearly a non-obvious result to have identified empirically that it is those seven trajectories (and not any other possible subset of the 24 theoretical combinations) which a majority of firms follow. Moreover, it provides an empirical validation of the prevalence of non-obvious (atypical) trajectories, such as trajectories 'A' and 'C'.

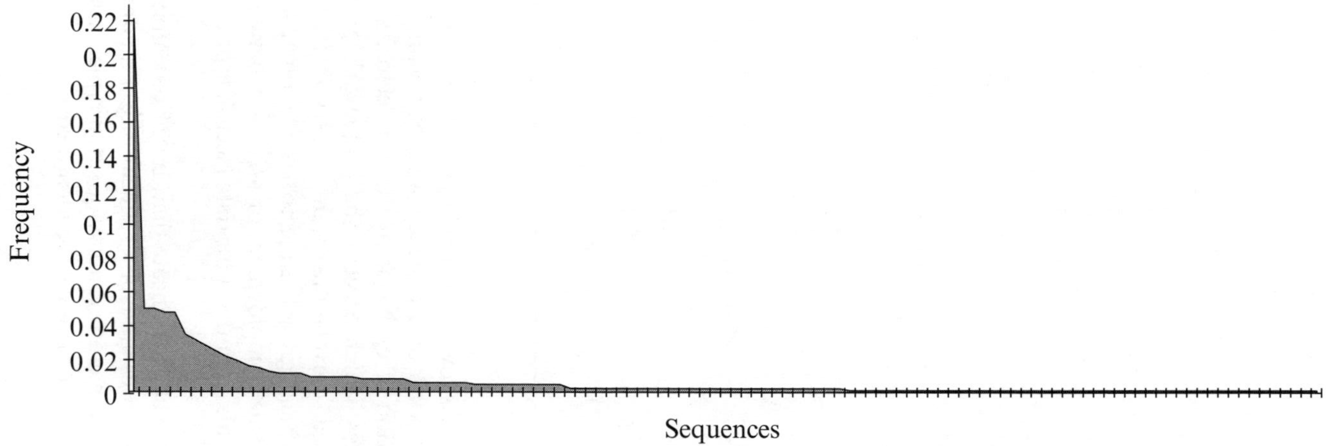

Figure 10.5 *Distribution of growth trajectories observed*

Table 10.2 Most frequent sequences

	Sequences	Freq. (%) (n = 602)	Cumul. Freq. (%) (n = 602)
1	S2222	22	22
2	S2111	5	27
3	S2221	5	32
4	S1111	5	37
5	S4444	5	42
6	S2211	3	45
7	S2224	3	48
8	S3333	3	51
9	S2223	2	54
10	S2244	2	56
11	S2444	2	58
12	S1311	2	59
13	S2113	1	61
14	S1333	1	62
15	S2242	1	63
16	S4222	1	65
17	S4333	1	66
18	S1131	1	67
19	S1133	1	68
20	S2122	1	69
21	S2233	1	70
22	S3111	1	71

Hence this taxonomy shows a relatively great heterogeneity of growth trajectories both in terms of frequency and development paths. The detailed characterization of each one of these trajectories would require individual case studies, which exceeds the framework of this research. Indeed, no significant correlations were observed (through χ^2-test) between the seven typical growth trajectories identified and individual measures of growth (sales, employment or assets) or between the growth trajectories and particular demographic data (sector, type of ownership or legal form).

The results presented above indicate that, based on empirical evidence, new firm growth trajectories are neither 'linear' nor a random or idiosyncratic phenomenon, and that a taxonomy of seven typical trajectories corresponding to a majority of firms can be identified.

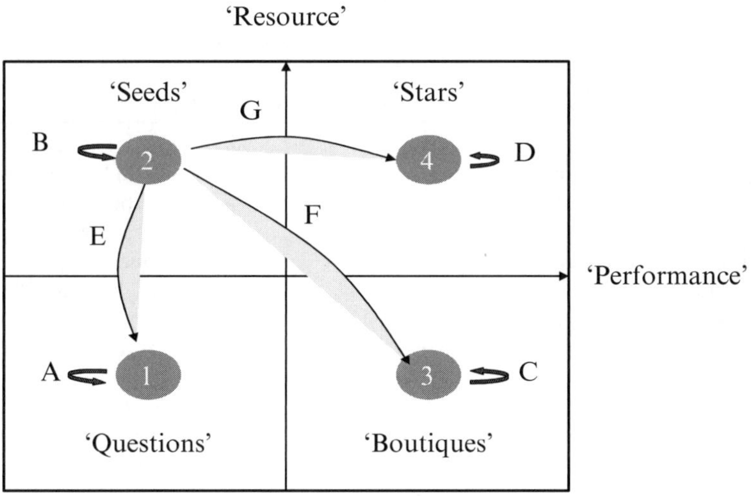

Figure 10.6 Typical trajectories

DISCUSSION AND CONCLUSIONS

Growth has been extensively studied in the fields of entrepreneurship, strategic management and industrial organization. However, most studies have concentrated on the explanation of growth using cross-sectional data or case studies and have explicitly or implicitly assumed that growth is essentially an uninterrupted process. However, the longitudinal studies of growth suggest that regular (or linear) growth is the exception rather than the rule.

With the aim to contribute to a better understanding of the growth process of new firms, we have presented an original methodological approach allowing the systematic analysis of early growth trajectories based on a multidimensional construct of growth across sectors. This method made it possible to track systematically typical growth trajectories of firms having grown beyond the micro-firm size, and to select through a PCA two key independent dimensions of the problem leading to four clusters which were used to identify seven typical growth trajectories. Those seven trajectories were adopted by 59 per cent of the new firms considered in our sample.

Hence our findings indicate that this original systematic approach is useful for taxonomy development and therefore contributes to reducing the gap between the complexity of the new firm growth process and the

Table 10.3 Taxonomy of growth trajectories

	Description	Corresp. sequences	Freq. (%) (n = 602)	Example
Stable trajectories				
B	Grow as a 'seed' (high resources but low performance)	S2222	22	Firm having raised capital to reach break-even
D	Grow as a 'star' (high resources and high performance)	S4444	5	'Gazelle'; potential high-growth firm
A	Grow as a 'question' (low resources and low performance)	S1111	5	Firm experiencing troublesome growth
C	Grow as a 'boutique' (low resources but high performance)	S3333	3	Profitable service firm with limited assets
Unstable trajectories				
E	Grow from a 'seed' to 'question'	S2111, S2211, S2221	13	'Seed' which burns capital before break-even
G	Grow from a 'seed' to 'star'	S2444, S2244, S2224	7	'Seed' having developed towards profitability
F	Grow from a 'seed' to 'boutique'	S2333, S2233, S2223	4	'Seed' having lowered ambitions
Total			59	

standard approaches often used to deal with it. They also have several implications and limitations, which will be discussed hereafter.

Implications

Our results first confirm that organizational growth constitutes a multiform and cross-sector phenomenon by nature, which should not therefore be reduced to a single dimension or studied within a single sector. Thus, the results of our analysis support a multidimensional conceptualization of growth, contrary to what many researches used, particularly in the studies on the determinants of the growth process (Birley and Westhead, 1990). Moreover, they reinforce the recent work emphasizing the heterogeneity of new firm growth (Delmar et al., 2003; François et al., 2004; Janssen, 2005; Weinzimmer et al., 1998). They also raise the question of the relevance of the uniform quantitative approaches, focused only on the criterion of a high relative growth rate in sales and/or employment adopted by policymakers and venture capitalists to evaluate the potential of a new firm.

Moreover, our empirical results suggest that new firm growth appears to be neither a continuous (or life-cycle based) nor idiosyncratic (or completely random) process. It can be adequately described through a limited number of typical growth trajectories that can be identified in a systematic way. This original contribution of our research has important theoretical and practical implications.

Our results also confirm that a cross-sectional approach can fail to capture the complex reality of the evolving new firm. They support the recent studies based on longitudinal approaches such as those of Delmar et al. (2003), Garnsey et al. (2006), Garnsey and Heffernan (2005), Mustar (2002), McMahon (2001) and Stam and Garnsey (2006).

Our findings are important from a theoretical perspective because they bring insight regarding how new firms evolve over time. They contribute to our understanding and appreciation of the heterogeneity of the growth trajectory phenomenon. Thus, researchers should develop more nuanced explanations of the new firm growth process than the simple uninterrupted or 'linear' dynamic growth process. Our findings indicate that nonlinearities exist in new firm growth trajectories and emphasize the rarity of very high growth trajectories.

Our findings are also important from a practical perspective as they confirm that there is no such thing as a 'growth firm'. Whether a given firm will be qualified as a 'growth firm' is strongly related to the criteria used to measure growth and to the corresponding thresholds adopted. Researchers should align their definition of 'growth firms' with the specific context and/or objective of their research, be it managerial performance, economic development or job creation. In particular, there is no universal criterion to determine whether firm A has grown more over time than firm B, for any pair of firms. Indeed what constitutes a meaningful measure of the size of a firm should be a function of the nature of the firm's activity (for example manufacturing versus trading) and of its governance structure (for example hierarchical and closed structure versus flat and open organizations).

In addition, this research provides a useful original taxonomy of new firm growth trajectories calling for explanations from case studies. Our taxonomy also extends previously developed taxonomies by taking into account the firm's financial characteristics as complementary information to its economics.

This study also provides a useful methodology contribution by showing the value added of the use of advanced applied mathematic methods to deal with the complex and dynamic nature of firm growth and therefore to contribute to theory development. We provided an original methodological approach based on systematic clustering and sequence analysis to derive an empirical taxonomy. In sum, our approach supports the recent work (Lévesque, 2004) emphasizing how mathematics can provide important contributions to current theories of management and organizations.

Limitations

This study has several limitations that should be noted. Firstly, in order to examine growth trajectories, we needed a significant number of longitudinal data which justified the use of retrospective secondary data limited to only one country. Moreover, the nature of these data does not enable us to measure the effect on the evolution of new firms of some important qualitative factors such as strategies, entrepreneurial motivation, partnerships and human capital.

Our research is also limited by the natural selection bias excluding failed firms in the sample. Therefore, we have no way of knowing what type of distinct growth trajectories such firms would exhibit, and how these growth paths might differ from the seven typical growth trajectories identified in this research.

Although these limitations are important and must be taken into account, we are nevertheless convinced that this study should contribute to a better understanding of the new firm growth process.

Future Research Directions

This research opens many future research directions. First, the replication in various contexts of the developed empirical taxonomy and specific data analysis methodology should be considered.

Secondly, while this research can be considered as a first step towards a better understanding of the start-up growth trajectories, further research is needed to improve our understanding of the dynamic growth process of new ventures. It should explore which endogenous and exogenous factors might explain why a majority of start-ups follow the seven identified typical growth trajectories. To this end, our retrospective approach and data analysis methodology should be complemented by other methods such as surveys and multiple case studies.

In this context, among other orientations, it could be highly relevant to refine our taxonomy by examining the relationship between innovative and technological sources and growth trajectories, both in high and low technological industries.

Finally, while our findings provide empirical and methodological support in new firm growth research, one of the most important future research directions is to test the accuracy of the proposed taxonomy in the stability of the firm dynamic growth process beyond the limited period of four years retained in this research.

ACKNOWLEDGEMENTS

This research is supported by a grant from the National Bank of Belgium. Part of this work is supported by the Belgian Program on Interuniversity Attraction Poles, initiated by the Belgian Federal Science Policy Office. The scientific responsibility rests with its authors. The work of D. François is funded by a grant from the Belgian FRIA. Preliminary versions of this paper were presented at the European Summer University 2006 on entrepreneurship and entrepreneurship education research (Hameenlinna), at the ERIM workshop 'Perspectives on the Longitudinal Analysis of New Firm Growth' in 2005 (Rotterdam) and, at CRECIS – Louvain School of Management seminar in 2006 (Louvain-la-Neuve). The authors would like to thank Professors Fredric Delmar, Alain Fayolle, Saras D. Sarasvathy, Björn Bjerke, Aard Groen, Paula Kyrö, Erik Stam, Elizabeth Garnsey, Frank Janssen, Regis Coeurderoy, Nathalie Delobbe and anonymous reviewers for their helpful comments.

NOTES

1. PCA is basically a projection method (Lawley and Maxwell, 1971) which can be used to develop cluster-based taxonomies (Evrard et al., 2003; de Jong and Marsili, 2006).
2. To identify the firms related to 'high tech' sectors, we defined a conversion table between the Code NACE-BEL and the Code US SIC for the classification of industry sectors according to technological intensity (from the Bureau of the Census and Walcott, 2001). We then validated our approach by matching this with other existing classification approaches (OECD, 1998) of industrial sector classification and of some new innovative firm classification indicators in the literature.
3. Our initial variables being standardized, the coefficient of correlation is a good indicator of the relation between a variable and a principal axis (Evrard et al., 2003).
4. This algorithm of rotation is based on the maximization of the coefficients of correlation of the most correlated variables (Hendrickson and White, 1964; Kaiser, 1958).

REFERENCES

Aldrich, H. (1990), 'Using an ecological perspective to study organizational founding dates', *Entrepreneurship Theory and Practice*, Spring, **14**(7), 7–24.

Archibugi, D. (2001), 'Pavitt's taxonomy sixteen years on: a review article', *Economic Innovation and New Technology*, **10**, 415–25.

Audrestch, D.B. and A.R. Thurik (2000), 'Capitalism and democracy in the 21st Century: from the managed to the entrepreneurial economy', *Journal of Evolutionary Economics*, **10**, 17–34.

Bakerman, R. and J.M. Gottman (1986), *Observing Interaction: An Introduction to Sequential Analysis*, Cambridge: Cambridge University Press.

Baldwin, J.R., C. Chandler and T. Papailiadis (1994), 'Stratégies pour le succès. Le profil des PME en croissance au Canada', Ottawa, *Statistique Canada*, **61**-523ER.

Birch, D. (1981), 'Who creates jobs', *The Public Interest*, **65**(Fall), 3–14.

Birch, D., A. Haggetty and W. Parsons (1997), *Corporate Almanac*, Cambridge, MA: Cognetic Inc.

Birley, S. and P. Westhead (1990), 'Growth and performance contrasts between "types" of small firms', *Strategic Management Journal*, **11**,(7), 535–57.

Boeker, W. (1997), 'Strategic change: the influence of managerial characteristics and organizational growth', *Academy of Management Journal*, **40**(1), 152–70.

Busenitz, L.W., P. West, D. Shepherd, T. Nelson, A. Zacharakis and G. Chandler (2003), 'Entrepreneurship in emergence: past trends and future directions', *Journal of Management*, **29**(3), 285–308.

Calvo, J.L. and M.J. Lorenzo (2001), 'Une caractérisation des entreprises manufacturières espagnoles à forte croissance: 1994–1998', *Revue Internationale P.M.E.*, **14** (3–4).

Canals, J. (2000), *Managing Corporate Growth*, New York: Oxford University Press.

Chandler, G.N. and S.H. Hanks (1993), 'Measuring performance of emerging businesses', *Journal of Business Venturing*, **8**, 32–40.

Chandler, G.N. and D.W. Lyon (2001), 'Issues of research design and construct measurement in entrepreneurship research: the past decade', *Entrepreneurship Theory and Practice*, **25**(4), 101–13.

Cuevas, A., M. Febbero and R. Fraiman (2001), 'Cluster analysis: a further approach based on density estimation', *Computational Statistics and Data Analysis*, **36**(4), 441–59.

Davidsson, P. (1995), 'SMEs and job creation in Sweden', paper presented at OECD seminar 'SMEs: Job, Innovation and Growth', Washington, DC.

Davidsson, P. (2004), 'The domain of entrepreneurship research: some suggestions', in J. Katz and S. Shepherd (eds), *Advances in Entrepreneurship, Firm Emergence and Growth*, Greenwich, CT: JAI Press, pp. 315–72.

Davidsson, P. and J. Wiklund (2000), 'Conceptual and empirical challenges in the study of firm growth', in D. Sexton and H. Landström (eds), *The Blackwell Handbook of Entrepreneurship*, Malden, MA, USA: Blackwell Business.

Davidsson, P., F. Delmar and J. Wiklund (2006), *Entrepreneurship and the Growth of Firms*, Cheltenham, UK and Northampton, MA, USA: Edward Elgar Publishing.

Davidsson, P., L. Lindmark and C. Olofsson (1998), 'The extent of overestimation of small firm job creation – an empirical examination of the regression bias', *Small Business Economics*, **11**, 87–100.

De Jong, J.P.J. and O. Marsili (2006), 'The fruit flies of innovation: a taxonomy of innovative small firms', *Research Policy*, **35**, 213–29.

Delmar, F. (1997), 'Measuring growth: methodological considerations and empirical results', in R. Donckels and A. Miettinen (eds), *Entrepreneurship and SME*

Research: On its Way to the Next Millennium, Aldershot, UK: Ashgate, pp. 199–216,
Delmar, F. and P. Davidsson (1998), 'A taxonomy of high growth firms', in P.D. Reynolds, W.D. Bygrave, M. Carter, S. Manigart, C.M. Mason, G.D. Mayer and K.G. Shaver (eds), *Frontiers of Entrepreneurship Research*, Wellesley, MA: Center for Entrepreneurial Studies, Babson College, pp. 399–413.
Delmar, F., P. Davidsson and W. Gartner (2003), 'Arriving at the high-growth firm', *Journal of Business Venturing*, **18**, 189–216.
Evrard, Y., B. Pras and E. Roux (2003), *Market: Etudes et Recherches en Marketing*, 3rd edn, Paris: Duno.
François, D., M. Biga Diambeidou, B. Gailly, V. Wertz and M. Verleysen (2004), 'Observer des trajectoires de "Start-up" sur des cartes de Kohonen', ACSEG2004 conference proceedings, 'Connectionist approaches in economics and management sciences', Lille (France), 18–19 November 2004, pp. 302–307.
Garnsey, E. (1995), 'High technology renewal and the UK investment problem', *Journal of General Management*, **20**(4), 1–22.
Garnsey, E. and P. Heffernan (2005), 'Growth setbacks in new firms', *Futures*, **37**(7), 675–97.
Garnsey, E., E. Stam and P. Heffernan (2006), 'New firm growth: exploring processes and paths', *Industry and Innovation*, **13**(1), 1–20.
Geroski, P.A. (2001), 'Exploring the niche overlaps between organizational ecology and industrial economics', *Industrial and Corporate Change*, **10**(2), 507–40.
Gibb, A.A. and L.G. Davies (1990), 'In pursuit of frameworks for the development of growth models of the small business', *International Small Business Journal*, **9**, 15–31.
Hendrickson, A.E. and P.O. White (1964), 'Promax: a quick method for rotation to oblique simple structure', *British Journal of Statistical Psychology*, **17**, 65–70.
Howard, R. (1971), *Dynamic Probabilistic Systems*, vol. 2, New York: Wiley.
Huber, G. and A.H. Van de Ven (1995), *Longitudinal Field Research Methods: Studying Processes of Organisational Change*, Thousand Oaks, CA, USA: Sage Publications.
Janssen, F. (2005), 'La conceptualisation de la croissance: l'emploi et le chiffre d'affaires sont-ils des représentations interchangeables d'un même phénomène?', *Revue Gestion 2000*, **6**, 267–91.
Julien, P.-A. (2001), 'Les PME à forte croissance et la métaphore du jazz. Comment gérer l'improvisation de façon cohérente', *Revue Internationale P.M.E.*, **14**(3–4).
Julien, P.-A., P. Mustar and M.-F. Estimé (2001), 'Les PME à forte croissance: une comparaison internationale', *Revue Internationale P.M.E.*, **14**(3–4).
Kaiser, H.F. (1958), 'The varimax criterion for analytic rotation in factor analysis', *Psychometrika*, **23**, 187–200.
Ketchen, D.J. and C.L. Shook (1996), 'The application of cluster analysis in strategic management research: an analysis and critique', *Strategic Management Journal*, **17**(6).
Lawley, P.A. and A.E. Maxwell (1971), *Factor Analysis as a Statistical Method*, 2nd edn, New York: American Elsevier Publishing and Co.
Lévesque, M. (2004), 'Mathematics, theory, and entrepreneurship', *Journal of Business Venturing*, **19**(5), 743–65.
Levie, J. (1997), 'Patterns of growth and performance: an empirical study of young, growing ventures in France, Ireland and Scotland', in P.D. Reynolds, W. D. Bygrave, N.M. Carter, P. Davidsson, W.B. Gartner, C.M. Mason and

P.P. McDougall (eds), *Frontiers of Entrepreneurship Research 1997*, Wellesley, MA: Babson College, pp. 375–89.
McKelvey, B. (1975), 'Guidelines for the empirical classification of organization', *Administrative Science Quarterly*, **20**, 509–25.
McMahon, R.G.P. (2001), 'Deriving an empirical development taxonomy for Manufacturing SMEs using data from Australia's business longitudinal survey', *Small Business Economics*, **17**, 197–212.
Murphy, G.B., J.W. Trailer and R.C. Hill (1996), 'Measuring performance in entrepreneurship', *Journal of Business Research*, **36**, 15–23.
Mustar, P. (2002), 'Diversité et unité des entreprises à forte croissance du secteur manufacturier en France', *Gestion 2000*, Dossier la PME à forte croissance, **5** (2002), pp. 77–98.
OECD (1994), *The OECD Jobs Study*, Paris: OECD.
OECD (1998), *Technology, Productivity and Job Creation: Best Policy Practices*, Paris: OECD.
OECD (2000), *High-Growth SMEs and Employment*, Paris: OECD.
OECD (2002), *High-Growth SMEs: Their Contribution to Employment and Their Characteristics*, Paris: OECD.
Pavitt, K. (1998), 'Technologies, products and organization in the innovating firm: what Adam Smith tells us and Joseph Schumpeter doesn't', *Industrial and Corporate Change*, **7**, 433–52.
Penrose, E. (1959), *The Theory of the Growth of the Firm*, Oxford: Oxford University Press.
Penrose, E. (1995), *The Theory of the Growth of the Firm* (3rd edn), Oxford: Oxford University Press.
Pettigrew, A.M., R.W. Woodman and K.S. Cameron (2001), 'Studying organizational change and development: challenges for future research', *Academy of Management Journal*, **44**(4), 697–713.
Poole, M.S., A.H. Van de Ven, K. Dooley and M.E. Holmes (2000), *Organisational Change and Innovation Process: Theory and Methods for Research*, Oxford, UK and New York, USA: Oxford University Press.
Pugh, D.S., D.J. Hickson and C.R. Hinings (1969), 'An empirical taxonomy of structures of work organizations', *Administrative Science Quarterly*, **14**, 115–26.
Rich, P. (1992), 'The organization taxonomy: definition and design', *Academy of Management Review*, **17**, 758–81.
Sabherwal, R. and D. Robey (1993), 'An empirical taxonomy of implementation processes based on sequences of events in information system development', *Organization Science*, **4**(4), 548–76.
Singh, J. and C. Lumsden (1990), 'Theory and research in organizational ecology', *Annual Review of Sociology*, **16**, 161–95.
Stam, E. (2003), 'Why Butterflies don't Leave. Locational Evolution of Evolving Enterprises', Utrecht: Utrecht University (PhD thesis).
Stam, E. and E. Garnsey (2006), 'New firms evolving in the knowledge economy; problems and solutions around turning points', in W. Dolfsma and L. Soete (eds), *Understanding the Dynamics of a Knowledge Economy*, Cheltenham, UK and Northampton, MA, USA: Edward Elgar, pp. 102–28.
Storey, D. (1994), *Understanding the Small Business Sector*, London: Routledge.
Storey, D.J. (1997), *Understanding the Small Business Sector*, London: International Thomson Business Press.

St-Pierre J., F. Janssen, P.A. Julien and C. Therrien (2005), 'Les facteurs de croissance des PME manufacturières sur les marchés locaux et internationaux' ('The growth factors of manufacturing SMEs in local and international markets'), IXes Journées scientifiques de l'Agence universitaire de la Francophonie, Cluj Napoca, Romania.

Teece, D.J., G. Pisano and A. Shuen (1997), 'Dynamic capabilities and strategic management', *Strategic Management Journal*, **18**(7), 509–33.

Van de Ven, A.H. (1992), 'Suggestion for studying strategy process: a research note', *Strategic Management Journal*, **13**(8), 169–88.

Van de Ven, A.H. and D. Polley (1992), 'Learning while innovating', *Organisation Science*, **3**(1), 92–116.

Vyakarnam, S., R.C. Jacobs and J. Handelberg (1997), 'The formation and development of entrepreneurial teams in rapid growth businesses', Proceeding of the Babson College/Kauffman Entrepreneurship Research Conference, Boston, MA, 16–20 April.

Walcott, S.M. (2001), 'Defining and measuring high technology in Georgia', FRP Report No. 50, January, Fiscal Research Program, Andrew Young School of Policy Studies, Georgia State University.

Weinzimmer, L.G., P.C. Nystron and S.J. Freeman (1998), 'Measuring organizational growth: issues, consequences and guidelines', *Journal of Management*, **24** (2), 235–62.

Welbourne, T.M. (1997), 'Valuing employees: a success strategy for fast growth firms and fast paced individuals', in P.D. Reynolds, W.D. Bygrave, P. Davidsson, W.B. Gartner, C.M. Mason and P.P. McDougall (eds), *Frontiers of Entrepreneurship Research*, Wellesley, MA, USA: Center for Entrepreneurship Research, Babson College, pp. 17–31.

Wernerfelt, B. (1984), 'A resource-based view of the firm', *Strategic Management Journal*, **5**, 171–81.

Wiklund, J. (1999), 'The sustainability of the entrepreneurial orientation–performance relationship', *Entrepreneurship Theory and Practice*, **24**(1), 37–48.

Wiklund, J. and D. Shepherd (2005), 'Knowledge accumulation in growth studies: the consequences of methodological choice', paper prepared for ERIM workshop 'Perspectives on the Longitudinal Analysis of New Firm Growth', Erasmus University Rotterdam, the Netherlands, 18–19 May.

Woywod, M. and V. Lessat (2001), 'Les facteurs de succès des entreprises à croissance rapide en Allemagne', *Revue Internationale P.M.E.*, **14**(3–4).

Zahra, S.A., R.D. Ireland and M.A. Hitt (2000), 'International expansion by new venture firms: international diversity, mode of market entry, technological learning, and performance', *Academy of Management Journal*, **43**(5), 925–50.

11. Linking entrepreneurial orientation and dynamic capabilities: research issues and alternative models

Jorunn Grande

INTRODUCTION

The purpose of this chapter is to highlight the relationship between entrepreneurial orientation (EO) and dynamic capability (DC) in small and new firms. These two concepts have received increasing attention in the separate fields of entrepreneurship and strategic management due to their connection to value creation and firm performance (Teece, Pisano and Shuen, 1997; Eisenhardt and Martin, 2000; Lumpkin and Dess, 1996; Wiklund, 1999). Following results in these fields firm-specific resources, dynamic capability and entrepreneurial efforts will be essential in enabling firms to renew and sustain competitive advantage. Nonetheless even if wealth creation is at the heart of both EO and DC few studies have addressed both concepts in the same study. Researchers have also pointed out a lack of knowledge on development of DC in new firms (Newbert, 2005; Zahra et al., 2006). In addition research on entrepreneurial efforts and resource reconfiguration in small firms is limited (Dale Meyer et al., 2002). To address these research gaps possible links between the EO and DC perspectives are discussed and five alternative models are suggested to illustrate their possible relationships and their potential as a departing point for future studies.

The relationship between the EO and DC approach is particularly interesting in new and small firms because elements from both concepts are likely to interact in sustaining competitiveness in these firms. Small businesses often face severe challenges when their competitive and political environment changes. Studies have shown that they are especially vulnerable in periods of turbulence, since they often have limited resources devoted to strategic processes as well as being financially less robust (Penrose, 1959; Carter and Jones-Evans, 2000). Survival and future existence will then depend on their ability to adapt to these changes and to develop new strategies and business platforms based on new opportunities in the market. This puts a focus on their entrepreneurial efforts as well as their ability to develop new resources and capabilities for strategic change. This will also be the case for many newly established firms. Embryonic firms are often small and lack experience in building an efficient organization since they have had little time to develop (Newbert, 2005; Zahra et al., 2006). They need to develop routines and systems in order to secure rent and value creation from the idea-generating phase.

Recent research shows that critical elements for strategic change and creation of a long-run competitive advantage are often found in the internal resource configuration of the firm (Rumelt, 1991; Borch et al., 1999). This is the essence of the resource-based perspective (Penrose, 1959; Barney, 2002), and the later theoretical extension into the dynamic capability approach (Teece et al., 1997; Eisenhardt and Martin, 2000). The DC approach centres around a firm's ability to 'integrate, build, and reconfigure internal and external competence to address rapidly changing environments' (Teece et al., 1997, p. 515). Important DCs mentioned in the literature are networks, alliances, learning processes and decision-making processes. When appropriate these DCs are supposed to give above-normal performance and superior competitive advantages to the firm. This has led many scholars to investigate the content and influence of DCs on resource reconfiguration and wealth creation in firms. Entrepreneurship is ultimately about exploration and creation (Dale Meyer et al., 2002), and within this field the EO concept has also become a central focus because of its alleged connection to firm performance. The EO construct is explained as an expression of the firm's entrepreneurial mind and includes dimensions like the firm's innovativeness, willingness to take on risk and its proactiveness (Covin and Slevin, 1989; Lumpkin and Dess, 1996). Research has shown that firms with a greater EO than others tend to perform better (for example in terms of sales growth and number of new products) (Wiklund, 1999; Madsen, 2007).

When reviewing the literature on DC and EO it is clear that both concepts are related to how the firm deploys resource acquisition and development, as well as influencing strategy development and performance of the firm. The difference might lie in that they cover different parts of the aspects and processes that are under investigation, but it might also indicate a tendency towards congruence and overlap between dimensions of EO and DC. This is not evident and the discussion on this nevertheless seems to be missing in the scientific literature. Prior research also suggests that DCs are important for creation and evolution of new business ventures (Newbert, 2005). Further investigation of their complementarity and possible integrative approaches is likely to yield interesting insight. This will enable a more compatible understanding, and is likely to give valuable insight for a greater scientific field. By integrating them into one model we can illustrate how entrepreneurial orientation and other factors might influence resource reconfiguration and development of dynamic capabilities.

The remainder of the chapter is organized as follows. First the main content and issues within the resource-based view and the dynamic capability approach are presented. Then entrepreneurial efforts and orientation within the firm context are discussed. This serves as a background for discussing and analysing the complementarity between the DC and EO approach. Finally five different models that illustrate possible relationships and paths for future research are proposed.

THEORETICAL BACKGROUND

Strategic Management and the Resource-based View

Recent research shows that critical elements for strategic change and creation of a competitive advantage in the long run are often found in the internal resource configuration of the firm (Rumelt, 1991; Borch et al., 1999). By identifying and acquiring resources that are critical to the development of demanded products firms may earn above-normal earnings (Wernerfelt, 1984). From this the resource-based view (RBV) has emerged as an important perspective and instrument for finding and evaluating possible business opportunities and resource needs in firms (Penrose, 1959; Barney, 2002). The RBV is now one of the most widely accepted theoretical perspectives within the field of strategic management (Priem and Butler, 2001; Newbert, 2007). The seminal elements of the RBV approach are found in Penrose's *The Theory of the Growth of the Firm* (Penrose, 1959), but the earliest attempts to describe and apply it as an independent perspective seem to be found in Rumelt (1984), Teece (1984), Wernerfelt (1984) and Barney (1986).

The essence of the RBV is that the building of new competitive advantages in new markets depends on the firm's available resources and its ability to develop both physical and human resources (Barney, 1986, 1991). It conceptualizes the firm as a bundle of resources, where different types of resources vary in their level of importance for generating added value for the firm. It focuses on the internal characteristics and resources of the firm and on their relationship to performance, and argues that firms with valuable, rare and inimitable (VRI) resources have the potential to gain superior performance (Barney, 1986, 1991). It builds on the assumptions that firms are heterogeneous with respect to the resources and capabilities, and that these resources and capabilities are not always easy to move or copy between firms. In this way the firm's unique resource bundle gives the firm a basis for developing strategies and lasting competitive advantages. Due to the missing link between resource possession and resource exploitation, organizational resources were later included as an important part of the resource bundle in Barney's framework and thus added the 'O' to the label of the framework. Today this perspective is often named Barney's VRIO framework (Newbert, 2007). In addition to simply having valuable, rare and inimitable resources a firm also needs to be organized in such a way that it can fully exploit the potential of its resources (Barney, 2002).

The RBV gives interesting insight into the internal resources of the firm. However, by considering the firm as a specific resource bundle, some researchers claim that dynamic processes like organizational learning, resource acquisition and knowledge integration, have received too little attention in the traditional RBV (Eisenhardt and Martin, 2000; Newbert, 2007). This led to the development of a new approach and an increased focus on organizational and dynamic processes within the firm (Teece et al., 1997; Eisenhardt and Martin, 2000; Winter, 2003). Together with influence from other theoretical approaches like organizational learning theory (Argyris and Schön, 1978) and evolutionary economics (Nelson and Winter, 1982) the dynamic capability (DC) approach therefore emerged as a further extension and supplement to the RBV.

Dynamic Capabilities

The dynamic capability (DC) framework focuses on the type of processes used by firms to exploit resources rather than on the resources themselves (Newbert, 2007). Teece et al. (1997, p. 510) proposed the DC framework as a means 'to explain how combinations of competences and resources can be developed, deployed, and protected'. Zollo and Winter (2002) state that DCs arise from learning. Several definitions of DC can be found as seen in Table 11.1, but common for all seems to be the emphasis on the firm's *ability to change*. Teece et al. (1997, p. 515) define DC as 'the firm's ability to integrate, build, and reconfigure internal and external competence to address rapidly changing environments'. Further DCs are explained as processes embedded in firms, and as the routines and processes that managers use to alter their resource base in order to create new value-generating strategies (Eisenhardt and Martin, 2000). In other words they include the attributes that enable the firm to coordinate and exploit its other resources (Teece et al., 1997; Eisenhardt and Martin, 2000; Winter, 2003).

DCs are therefore critical in the sense that they create change and the ability for continuous renewal of the firm. Also, DCs are not only the most

Table 11.1 Examples of studies on DCs: definitions, dimensions and type of studies

Author/type of study	DC definition	Type/dimensions	Input/output/unit of analysis/type of analysis*
Teece et al. (1997) Conceptual	'the firm's ability to integrate, build, and reconfigure internal and external competencies to address rapidly changing environments.' p. 516	Integrate, build and reconfigure competencies	U: Processes, positions, paths
Eisenhardt and Martin (2000) Conceptual	'The firm's processes that use resources – specifically the processes to integrate, reconfigure, gain and release resources – to match and even create market change. Dynamic capabilities thus are the organizational and strategic routines by which firms achieve new resource configurations as markets emerge, collide, split, evolve, and die.' p. 1107	Product development, strategic decision-making and alliancing The processes of integrate, reconfigure, gain and release resources	
Zollo and Winter (2002) Conceptual	'A dynamic capability is a learned and stable pattern of collective activity through which the organization systematically generates and modifies its operating routines in pursuit of improved effectiveness.' p. 340	Process R&D Restructuring, re-engineering Post-acquisition integration	

Newbert (2005) Empirical	Adapts Eisenhardt and Martin (2000): 'organizational and strategic routines by which firms achieve new resource configurations' p. 56	Testing if new firm formation satisfies four conditions of DCs	I: Gestation activities, new firm formation experience O: First sales U: Individual entrepreneurs A: Binary logistic regression
Zahra et al. (2006) Conceptual	'the abilities to reconfigure a firm's resources and routines in the manner envisioned and deemed appropriate by its principal decision-maker(s)' p. 918 'the dynamic ability to change or reconfigure existing substantive capabilities' p. 921		
Jantunen et al. (2005) Empirical Combines EO/DC	DC consists of 'Structures and processes that constitute its [firm's] ability to reconfigure its asset base to match the requirement of the changing environment' p. 225 parenthesis added.	Reconfiguring capacity	I: EO and DC O: Intl. performance, intl.sales, # countries U: Firm A: Hierarchical linear regression
Borch and Madsen (2007) Empirical	'the ability to build, integrate and reconfigure both external and internal resources and routines' (p. 2)	Resource reconfiguration and integration, resource acquisition, learning network, strategic path aligning	I: Four DCs O: Innovative strategies U: Firm A: Multiple regression

Notes: *I = input variable, O = output variable, U = unit of analysis, A = type of analysis.

critical resources in an innovative situation, but also the hardest ones to get hold of (Borch et al., 2005). The firm's dynamic resources or capabilities are therefore unique and give the foundation for the firms' ability to initiate and perform innovative processes. Examples of DCs mentioned in the literature are business networks, strategic orientation, educational routines and research (Teece et al., 1997; Eisenhardt and Martin, 2000). More specifically Eisenhardt and Martin (2000) refer to DCs as organizational processes that integrate resources, reconfigure resources and gain as well as release resources. As such, DCs constitute the capacity to renew competencies and to keep up with changing environments and are thus crucial in enhancing the firm's ability to achieve new forms of competitive advantages.

According to this approach DCs will be the type of resources that are important to nourish and develop in young firms as well (Wu, 2007). Zahra et al. (2006) explain that DCs must be well targeted and deployed in order to achieve strategic goals. Managing these capabilities is therefore critical in order for the organization to benefit. DCs develop in response to a variety of conditions, which implies that new firms are more likely to deploy other DCs than more well established firms (Zahra et al., 2006). Since earlier research on DCs is very limited when it comes to new ventures and young firms (Newbert, 2005; Zahra et al., 2006), more insight is needed in order to fully understand how they might be developed in these types of firms.

It should be noted that there is still a debate on what DCs are and how they should be measured. For instance, some researchers claim that it might be hard to distinguish between the DC itself and the result of a DC since most studies are cross-sectional (Zahra et al., 2006). To clarify parts of the DC concept scholars have pointed out the importance of distinguishing between various levels of capabilities (Zollo and Winter, 2002; Winter, 2003; Arthurs and Busenitz, 2006). They stress that operational capabilities (zero-order capability) are dedicated to the operational functioning of the firm, whereas DCs (first order capabilities) are directed toward changing the operational capabilities like production processes or marketing routines (Helfat and Peteraf, 2003; Winter, 2003). Operational capabilities are explained as 'how to earn a living now', whereas DCs are explained as 'how to change your operational routines'. Cepeda and Vera (2007) also argue that there exists an infinite regress problem that makes it difficult to identify the original source of competitive advantage since there always seems to be a capability behind a capability. Even though these discussions show that the DC approach is still in its infancy, the many contributions also indicate that DCs are recognized as an ultimate source of competitive advantage within strategy research (Arthurs and Busenitz, 2006; Cepeda and Vera, 2007).

To sum up the discussion on DC the definition by Zahra et al. (2006, p. 91) is adopted and highlighted as an up-to-date version of the concept. It says that DCs are 'the abilities to reconfigure a firm's resources and routines in the manner envisioned and deemed appropriate by its principal decision-maker(s)' p. 91. It contains the firms' ability to change routines and process in order to obtain superior performance. Actual DC categories to measure are business networks, strategic orientation, educational routines and research (Teece et al., 1997; Eisenhardt and Martin, 2000), resource acquisition (that is, market information, financial capital, external knowledge), resource reconfiguration and integration, learning networks and strategic path aligning (Borch and Madsen, 2007).

ENTREPRENEURSHIP IN FIRMS

Entrepreneurship as a phenomenon has been studied for generations, and there is quite a body of knowledge accumulated in this area showing that entrepreneurship might be defined in a variety of ways covering wider or narrower perspectives (Davidsson, 2004). Dominant definitions of entrepreneurship are built around the exploration and exploitation of opportunities, where the pursuit of opportunities is an important component (Stevenson and Jarillo, 1990; Shane and Venkataraman, 2000). Important issues are also the creation of new resources and recombination of existing resources in order to develop and commercialize new products and move into new markets (Ireland et al., 2001). Entrepreneurial efforts in an organizational context have received increased attention among scholars in the last two decades, due to the possible influence on renewal and performance in firms (Miller, 1983; Covin and Slevin, 1991; Lumpkin and Dess, 1996; Wiklund, 1999; Wiklund and Shepherd, 2003).

There are many variations in how entrepreneurial efforts are labelled and defined within an organizational context. Terms often used are intrapreneurship (Antoncic and Hisrich, 2003), strategic renewal (Sharma and Chrisman, 1999), corporate entrepreneurship (Zahra and Covin, 1995), entrepreneurial orientation (Lumpkin and Dess, 1996) and so on. The common element can be summarized and found in Sharma and Chrisman's (1999, p. 18) definition stating that corporate entrepreneurship includes 'the process whereby an individual or a group of individuals, in association with an existing organization, create a new organization or instigate renewal or innovation within that organization'. Thus in addition to requiring individuals with particular entrepreneurial behaviour within the firm, the firm also must possess an organizational environment that both tolerates and supports these activities (Elfring, 2005). The various labels also show its close link to strategic management and strategic decision-making. Conceptualizing entrepreneurship as a process that occurs in an organizational setting has significantly advanced the field, but might have led to a more unclear distinction between the management and entrepreneurship field (Morris et al., 1994).

Entrepreneurial Orientation

Within the corporate context, entrepreneurial orientation (EO) has emerged as an important concept for investigating the entrepreneurial mind of firms and its possible influence on strategic processes and performance (Rauch et al., 2004). As Lumpkin and Dess (1996, p. 136) state, 'Firms that want to engage in successful corporate entrepreneurship need to have an entrepreneurial orientation (EO)'. They define EO as 'the processes, practices, and decision-making activities that lead to new entry', and further that it 'involves the intentions and actions of key players functioning in a dynamic generative process aimed at new-venture creation'. The reviewed literature shows that EO is often described as the mindset of firms involved in the pursuit of new ventures and used as a measure to characterize a set of related processes including a variety of activities within the firm.

The field seems to agree to conceptualize EO as having from three (Covin and Slevin, 1989; Wiklund, 1999; Madsen, 2007) to five dimensions (Lumpkin and Dess, 1996; Hughes and Morgan, 2007), which might vary independently of each other. These are 1) a propensity to act autonomously; 2) a willingness to innovate; 3) a willingness to take risks; 4) a tendency to act aggressively towards competitors; and 5) a proactivity towards market opportunities (Lumpkin and Dess, 1996). Here autonomy is understood as the independent actions undertaken by entrepreneurial leaders or teams to bring about a new venture and see it realized. The innovative dimension captures the tendency toward embracing and supporting creativity and experimentation, technological leadership, novelty and R&D in the development of products, services and processes. The risk-taking dimension reflects an acceptance of uncertainty and risk-related activities and is typically characterized by resource commitment to uncertain outcomes and activities. Competitive aggressiveness conveys the intensity with which a firm chooses to compete and its efforts to surpass competitors. Finally proactiveness is related to a forward-looking perspective where companies actively seek to anticipate opportunities to develop and introduce new products in the market in order to obtain first mover advantages and shape the direction of the environment. It differs from the competitive aggressive dimension in that it is not directed towards competitors but relates to market opportunities (Lumpkin and Dess, 1996).

Studies have also shown that the relationship between EO and performance might be contingent on other environmental and/or organizational factors (Covin and Slevin, 1989; Lumpkin and Dess, 1996). All of the dimensions above may thus not be present or important in a new venture. Research has shown that which of them are most dominant in a business often depends on factors within the business itself or within the business environment, for example type of industry (Lumpkin and Dess, 1996). How a business chooses to act towards competitors and which methods are likely to be most successful may therefore depend on the type of industry the firm belongs to as well as their market situation. Also the necessity to innovate or the degree of innovation might depend on how the firm positions itself within its environment. Lumpkin and Dess (1996, p. 137) therefore consequently argue that '(a) the relationship between EO and performance is context specific and (b) the dimensions of EO may vary independently of each other in a given context'.

Important questions among entrepreneurship scholars have focused on the main content of EO, how it should be measured and how it influences performance and processes in firms. Compared to the debate about DCs there seems to be more agreement about the ingredients of the EO concept and more standard measurement tools are developed. The discussion of the impact of EO on performance continues (Smart and Conant, 1994; Hughes and Morgan, 2007) and research efforts seem to be more directed towards determining the impact of EO with different firm and environmental contexts (Wiklund and Shepherd, 2005). This indicates a need for more empirical work on how EO influences the internal resource configuration and on the relationship between EO and performance within different firm contexts.

Others suggest that major shortcomings of the EO-construct are on the management side and on risk handling (Covin et al., 2006; Jun, 2006). Jun refers to definitions by Gartner (1990) and Morris et al. (1994) saying that 'Entrepreneurship contains the function of management dealing with allocation of resources, exploring new market, handling risk and uncertainties, organizing responsibility and efficiency'. Based on this definition he regards the issue of how entrepreneurs implement their management and organization as an important question in the scope of EO. He therefore proposes a new dimension called management professionalism as an important aspect of EO. Furthermore he suggests exchanging the dimension of 'willingness to take on risk' by 'how risk is handled' in order to better account for how well the firms are prepared for facing risk rather than merely how willing they are to take on risk.

The reviewed literature on EO shows that it is a concept that includes activities related to identification of new opportunity and subsequent

Table 11.2 Examples of studies on EO: descriptions, dimensions and type of studies

Author/type of study	Definition/descriptions	Dimensions	Input/Output/Unit of Analysis/Type of Analysis*
Miller (1983) Empirical and Conceptual	Identifies entrepreneurship as a multidimensional concept encompassing the firm's actions relating to innovation, risk-taking and proactiveness.	Innovativeness Proactiveness Risk-taking	I: Locus of control, environment, organization/structure, decision making/strategy O: Entrepreneurship U: Firm A: Multiple regression
Covin and Slevin (1989) Empirical Developed measurement scale	'entrepreneurial strategic posture' Refers to Miller (1983)	Innovativeness Proactiveness Risk-taking	I: Environmental hostility, organizational structure, strategic posture, O: Financial performance U: Firm A. Moderated regression
Lumpkin and Dess (1996) Conceptual	'An EO refers to the processes, practices, and decision-making activities that lead to new entry.' 'involves the intentions and actions of key players' p. 136	Innovativeness Proactiveness Risk-taking Competitive aggressiveness Autonomy	U: Discussion relates to firm/ business unit level
Wiklund (1999)	'A focus on innovation, proactiveness, and risk taking' p. 38 Emphasizes entrepreneurship as a process.	Innovativeness Proactiveness Risk-taking	I: EO, environmental dynamism, capital availability O: Performance U: Firm A: Multiple regression

Wiklund and Shepherd (2003) Empirical	'EO refers to a firm's strategic orientation, capturing specific entrepreneurial aspects of decision-making styles, methods and practices' p. 1309	Innovativeness Proactiveness Risk-taking	I: Knowledge position , EO O: Performance (10 items) U: Firm/longitudinal A: Hierarchical regression
Jantunen et al. (2005) Empirical Includes both EO and DC	'encapsulates the firm-level processes, practices, decision-making style . . . , and strategic orientation . . . of an entrepreneurially oriented firm' p. 226	Innovativeness Proactiveness Risk-taking	See Table 11.1
Madsen et al. (2006) Emipirical	Regards EO as the combination of the three dimensions; innovativeness, proactiveness and risk-taking. Assumes DC→EO	EOs: Innovativeness Proactiveness Risk-taking DCs: Opportunity search, Learning Reallocation Readjustment skills	I: Knowledge based resources, relation based resources, DCs O: EO U: Firm A: Linear (and hierarchical) regression
Hughes and Morgan (2007) Empirical	Refer to definition by Lumpkin and Dess (1996).	Innovativeness Proactiveness Risk-taking Competitive aggressiveness Autonomy	I: The five EO dimensions O: Customer and product performance U: Young firms A: Multiple regression

Notes: *I = input variable, O = output variable, U = unit of analysis, A = type of analysis.

investments in the resource base in firms (Arthurs and Busenitz, 2006, p. 199). Most studies carried out in the field have centred on measuring three dimensions of EO; innovativeness, proactiveness and risk-taking (Covin and Slevin, 1989; Wiklund and Shepherd, 2003, 2005). Two additional dimensions, competitive aggressiveness and autonomy are added by Lumpkin and Dess (1996). The issue of managing entrepreneurial activities and renewal of firms seems to be of increasing importance in both the EO and the DC field.

TOWARDS AN INTEGRATIVE APPROACH

Comparing the EO and DC Approach

Scientific literature shows that research on EO and DC are mainly carried out in separate studies. Examples of those are shown in the previous section and in Tables 11.1 and 11.2. The concepts have some obvious connecting points, and research models often used in studies of EO and DC share many similar contingencies. Figure 11.1 builds on Lumpkin and Dess' conceptualization of the EO–performance relationship (1996, p. 152) and is extended to include the DC perspective. The dotted lines illustrate the centre of attention in this chapter and where the need for more research is addressed. Studies have shown that both environment and organizational factors are likely to intervene with the relationship between EO and performance as well as between DC and performance (Lumpkin and Dess, 1996, 2001; Eisenhardt and Martin, 2000). Research in these separate fields suggests that both DC and EO characteristics vary depending on environmental factors and firm context (Lumpkin and Dess, 2001; Aloulou and Fayolle, 2005). Eisenhardt and Martin's (2000) work showed that effective patterns of dynamic capabilities might vary among firms due to differences in market situations and dynamism. Dynamism and complexity relates to the degree of uncertainty facing an organization, whereas munificence signals the firm's dependence on the environment for resources. They found that in high velocity markets dynamic capabilities take on a different character than in traditional markets, which means that the type of DC which is both necessary and crucial to develop is likely to depend on the firm's environment.

The respective definitions of both EO and DC show that value creation and competitive advantage are important arguments for why managers should pay attention to EO and DC in their firm. These aspects are also reflected in empirical studies on EO as well as on DC. The main output variables used in empirical studies for both concepts seem to be performance

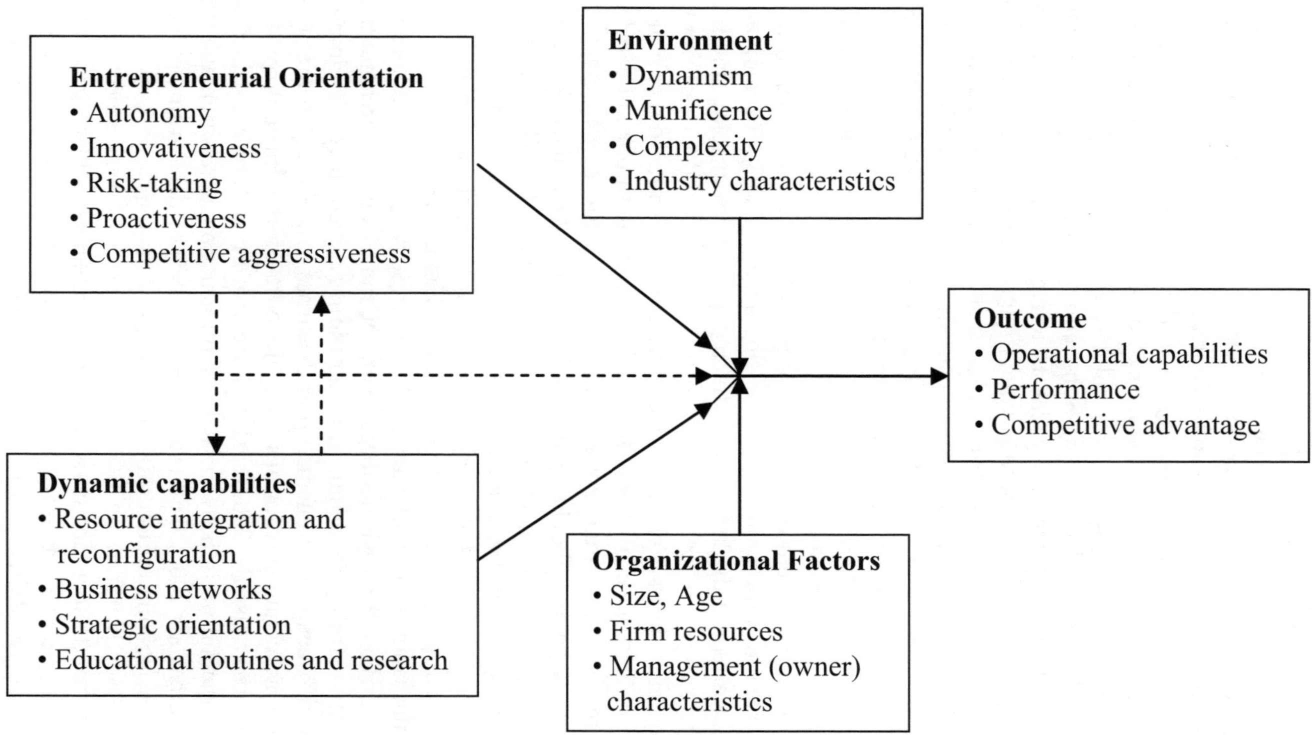

Figure 11.1 A conceptual framework linking EO and DC

(first sales, international performance, financial performance, and so on), innovative strategies and operational capabilities (Tables 11.1 and 11.2; Dale Meyer et al., 2002). Researchers emphasize that performance is a multidimensional construct that can be measured in many ways (Morgan and Strong, 2003). The effect of EO and DC on different types of performance measures is thus also likely to vary. It is therefore important that this measure reflects the firm goals and desired outcome. Various measures of performance might also compete, depending on ownership, type and size of the firm (Lumpkin and Dess, 1996). Some entrepreneurial efforts and subsequent resource investments may lead to a negative effect on short-term performance, but they might be important for building a competitive advantage and improving long-run performance. It should also be noted that not all aspects of the EO and DC phenomena are always inherently valuable, since they also need to be applied properly and fitted to organizational needs and environmental factors in order to optimize performance and competitive advantage. As seen in Table 11.1 and 11.2, the dominant unit of analysis in both EO and DC studies is the firm.

The innovative dimension of EO is likely to be partly intertwined with the resource integration and reconfiguration aspect of DC. The definition of DC is centred on the firm's ability to change routines or to do things in new ways in order to use resources, new knowledge and so forth more efficiently. This shows a close connection to the innovation dimension of EO. DC scholars have also identified innovation as an important capability that refers to the organizations' ability to develop new products or processes (Rangone, 1999). In particular Antoncic and Hisrich (2003) point out that this part of the capability construct is close to the EO construct in firms. They state that 'Intrapreneurial activities and orientation related to the creation of new products and processes can be viewed as a manifestation of innovative capabilities' (Antoncic and Hisrich, 2003, p. 12).

Learning is an important part of developing DC (Teece et al., 1997). Entrepreneurial efforts within firms might be perceived as a precondition that leads to learning and resource integration. As such there is an important link between entrepreneurship and learning, where entrepreneurial activities may create disruptions that are part of the learning process (Antoncic and Hisrich, 2003). Also the extrovert culture embedded in proactive orientation is likely to facilitate information acquisition and utilization (Keh et al., 2007). This is an important part of the learning process and thus the reconfiguration capacity of DCs.

The reviewed literature on EO and DC shows that both connect to the ability to make strategic decisions and create competitive advantages. In the field of strategic management and the resource-based view we have seen that dynamic capabilities have emerged as crucial resources for future development and performance of the firm. So is the case with entrepreneurial orientation within the field of entrepreneurship. As an example Rauch et al. (2004, p. 1) explain that EO might be viewed as a 'firm-level strategy-making process that firms use to enact their organisational purpose, sustaining their vision and create competitive advantage(s)'. Building a strong EO might thus be a strategic choice for the firm. This strengthens the arguments for an integrative approach exploring their relationship more explicitly. This is also one of the philosophies behind the research stream of strategic entrepreneurship (Ireland et al., 2003; Barney and Afrikan, 2001). This approach addresses the close link between the fields but does not discuss explicitly how the concepts of EO and DC might be related.

The above discussions referred to so far show that there are many similar characteristics in EO and DC, but it is important to keep in mind their key differences. Structure and systems are important elements of DC but not in EO. Antoncic and Hisrich (2003, p. 20) state that entrepreneurship 'includes non-product-market emergent activities and does not have relatedness, coherence and synergy as central focuses'. Both phenomena are similar in so far as they represent investments to the organization's resource base. However, opportunity identification and disruptiveness and autonomy are keywords that are specific for EO but not for DC. These elements might lead to unpredictable and uncoordinated entrepreneurial actions that might not be optimal if they are not organized in a proper way. Arthurs et al. (2006, p. 199) emphasize that 'whereas the identification of a new opportunity and the subsequent investments to the resource base are the hallmark of entrepreneurial capabilities, the adjustment and reconfiguration of the resource base in conjunction with an existing opportunity are the hallmark of dynamic capabilities'.

The discussion above illustrates many interesting connecting points between the dimensions EO and DC. In separate studies they have yielded significant findings providing a key to understanding resource reconfiguration, new entry and value creation in firms. However, in the few contributions where both concepts are used there is no fundamental discussion relating the two concepts. To address this gap in the literature five alternative models are proposed in order to illustrate the possible relationships and as a direction for future research. Further investigation along these lines is likely to establish a deeper understanding of capability development in entrepreneurial firms in the future.

Alternative Models Depicting Possible Relationships

Figure 11.2 proposes five different models to illustrate possible links between EO and DC. The figures are kept simple in order to focus on the

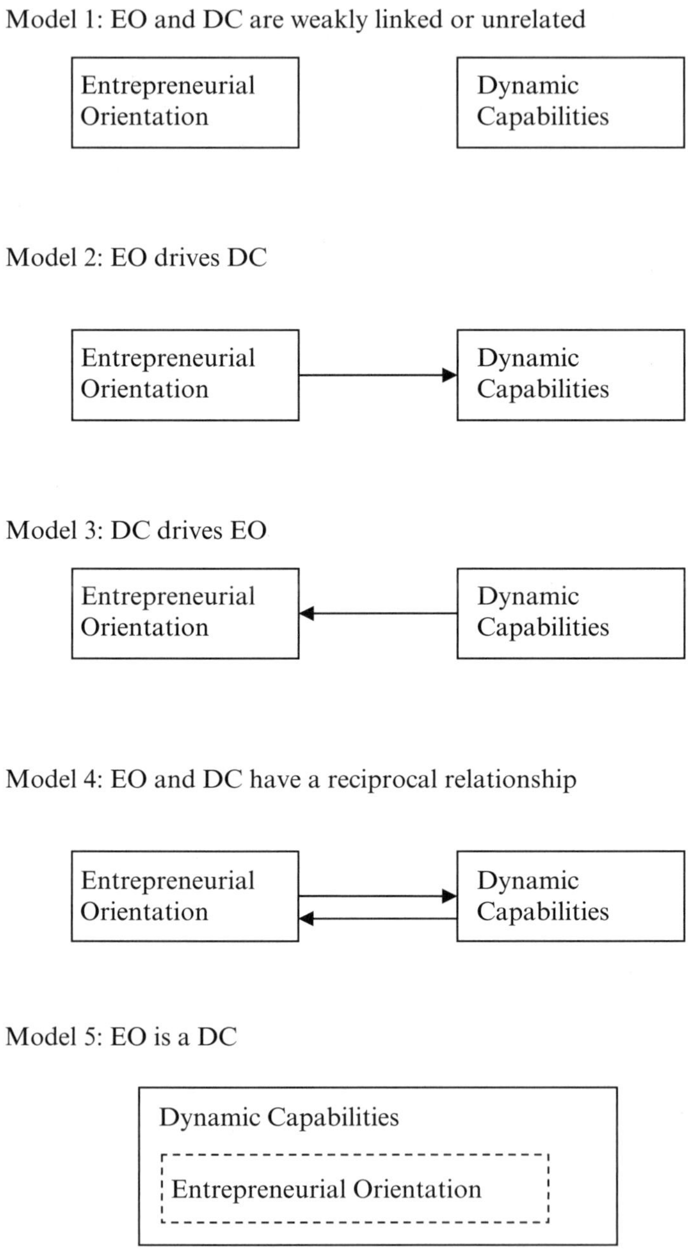

Figure 11.2 Conceptualizations of possible relationships between EO and DC

relationship between EO and DC. It should be noted that the suggested relationships are also likely to be influenced by organizational factors (firm resources, age, size and so on) and environmental conditions. The illustration follows an outline used by Covin and Miles (2007) in investigating the relationship between corporate venturing and business strategy. The different models are based on logical arguments and on how EO and DC are depicted in strategic management and entrepreneurship literature. Each of the models has implications for how firms might develop EO and DC in order to cope with challenging environments and to continue developing competitive advantages.

Model 1: EO and DC are weakly linked or unrelated

DC and EO might exist as independent phenomena within organizations. For instance EO activities might be purely random and ignored by the organization. Employers might discover new ways of doing things that represent improved earnings, but are not encouraged to bring this forward to the management. By ignoring this opportunity the firm misses the opportunity to gain on self-generated valuable ideas (Covin and Miles, 2007). This also indicates that EO and DC explain a unique proportion of firm performance (Dess and Rasheed, 1993). In one way this illustrates how studies concerning EO and DC have traditionally been carried out. The two concepts have usually been investigated in separate studies in their respective fields and not considered in relation to one another.

Model 2: EO drives DC

In this model EO drives the building of appropriate DCs in firms. An underlying logic supporting this model is that in order to launch a new entry firms need and will benefit from developing and applying DCs to facilitate necessary changes to act on ideas. This is likely to be the situation for young firms where organizational systems are yet at their embryonic stage (Wu, 2007; Hughes and Morgan, 2007). Thus, appropriate DCs are likely to intervene with the relationship between EO and performance and thus further increase value creation from entrepreneurial activities. Also the two dimensions of EO, competitive aggressiveness and autonomy put forward by Lumpkin and Dess (1996), mobilize continuous competitor scanning and assessment as well as the freedom of employees to be self-directed, explore opportunities and advocate new ideas (Hughes and Morgan, 2007). These elements are likely to be fundamental for building flexibility and alertness to environmental changes and market signals (that is DCs), enabling the firm to reconfigure its activities and actions quickly (Grewal and Tansuhaj, 2001; Hughes and Morgan, 2007).

This model illustrates a relationship investigated by Griffith et al. (2006), Matsuno et al. (2002) and by Jantunen et al. (2005). Griffith et al. (2006, p. 19) describe entrepreneurial proclivity (that is orientation) as a management orientation 'which drives the accumulation of knowledge and the development of dynamic capabilities'. They describe EO as a factor proceeding and influencing DC. They claim that the management orientation of entrepreneurial proclivity aids the accumulation of knowledge resources, and might also help (as well as hinder) the conversion of these resources into dynamic capabilities. Jantunen et al. (2005) also claim that EO influences DC in their study on international performance of entrepreneurial firms. They postulated that EO is likely to be an important factor for opportunity recognition in new markets and therefore also has a positive effect on international performance. This supports an integrative approach where EO helps firms in building appropriate DCs in order to enhance performance.

Model 3: DC drives EO

Model 3 illustrates a relationship suggested by Madsen et al. (2006) in their study of the role of dynamic capabilities and intangible resources in developing entrepreneurial orientation. This study considers DC to be an antecedent that drives development of EO, and in this way indirectly influences the firm's competitive advantage through influencing EO. The logic behind this direction of the relationship is that DC can aid the firm in developing a strategic desired EO in order to reconfigure resources and improve performance of the firm. The direction in which DC influences EO can also be explained by DC being the ability to perform processes and activities, and EO being the activity itself. Another argument supporting this view is that a firm's entrepreneurial capacity will be partly limited by its resource base. Firms with abundant resources are likely to have more capacity than those with sparse capacity to engage in entrepreneurial activities (Covin and Slevin, 1991; Aloulou and Fayolle, 2005). Thus firms with limited resources and capabilities (DCs) are less likely to take on risk and act on new opportunities in the market compared to firms with more resources; in this aspect DC influences the degree of EO.

Model 4: EO and DC have a reciprocal relationship

This model depicts a relationship where causality might flow in both directions. EO might drive the development of DCs, and these DCs might direct the search and inventions (EO) in new directions that are more strategically desirable for the firm (Ireland et al., 2003). This enables the firm to continually renew itself in order to gain new competitive advantage in dynamic markets. Their reciprocal relationship might make it hard to determine the origin of effects. Elements of this model seem to fit with the strategic entrepreneurship perspective, where the purpose is to 'connect the creation aspect of entrepreneurship with the performance orientation of strategic management' (Dale Meyer et al., 2002, p. 19).

Model 5: EO is a DC

Model 5 pictures EO as a desired DC in itself. As noted earlier the borderline between EO and DC is especially vague in studies on capacity and learning of innovation. With respect to these aspects EO and DC seem to be closely intertwined in such a way that it makes little sense to separate them as different phenomena; one is part of the other or vice versa. Examples might be the innovative dimension and learning processes on aspects connected to the scan and search for information. This perspective is in line with Bhuian et al. (2005) who consider entrepreneurship a DC. They claim that these two phenomena are closely intertwined and argue that 'without entrepreneurship businesses . . . would neither be dynamic or adaptive' (Bhuian et al., 2005, p. 10). This approach might be useful when the investigated dimensions of EO and DC are likely to be closely related and hard to separate in time and origin.

Theoretical and empirical literature on EO and DC show that there might be several possible directions related to the relationships between the two concepts. Both concepts encourage flexibility and change in organizations: DC in a more systematic and planned way. Since most studies have been carried out separately for the two concepts, the relationship between them is still unclear. The few studies which include both concepts seem to agree that EO aids the building of appropriate DCs. However, other studies perceive EO as being a DC and vice versa and are thus quite confusing with respect to the relationship between the two perspectives. In order to clarify this relationship further, the models above could serve as a framework for future studies.

CONCLUSION AND IMPLICATIONS FOR FUTURE RESEARCH

Research within fields of strategic management and entrepreneurship shows that building dynamic capabilities (DC) and being entrepreneurially oriented (EO) are widely recognized as important for renewal, change and competitive advantage in firms. However, little is known about the relationship between EO and DC even though they are likely to coexist in many firms where there is a desire to optimize output. There seems to be a tendency towards congruence and overlap between EO and DC, but this has not been discussed explicitly in the literature. Literature shows that both are connected to innovation capacity and learning in firms and include elements of resource integrations and reconfiguration. The difference might lie in the fact that they cover different parts or dimensions of the aspects and processes that are under investigation. This is not evident and this discussion nevertheless seems to be lacking in the scientific literature. Future research should address this possible link in order to refine the content of EO and DC and to provide a greater understanding on how they might interact in firms.

These issues are especially important for new and small firms facing new challenges. There is little research on how small firms develop entrepreneurial efforts and DCs to address necessary changes (Dale Meyer et al., 2002). Small firms often have few resources to handle change and might face the risk of being stuck in the traditional way of operating the business. In this situation they need to strengthen their ability to change and pursue new business opportunities. This means that adopting an entrepreneurial oriented mind and building new dynamic capabilities are factors likely to be of great importance for their development. These issues call for more longitudinal empirical studies in order to understand the importance and development of EO and DC as well as their possible linkage in small firms facing changing environments.

There is also little knowledge on how new firms develop systems and routines to secure value creation from entrepreneurial explorations and ideas. Most contributions in the DC field seem to be conceptual and the empirical work is mainly devoted to established firms (Newbert, 2005; Zahra et al., 2006). New firms normally lack experience in how to proceed from the first stage of their development. How should they develop and integrate systems and routines (DCs) in order for their first success and value-creating ideas to proliferate? For instance high risk-taking firms might need to handle this risk in order to reduce the possibility of negative consequences.

It should also be noted that the strategic management field still lacks consensus on DC as a construct and how it should be measured. With the present lack of standard measurements tools, studies are less comparable, and thus less useful in terms of the need to establish a common and well-defined theory. This indicates a knowledge gap on the configuration of DC, and future research should also continue to address these questions. Important questions among entrepreneurship scholars have focused on determining the main contents of EO, how it should be measured and how the different dimensions of EO influence performance and processes in firms. Compared to the debate about DC there seems to be more agreement about the elements of the EO concept and more standard measurement tools have been developed. However, an emerging issue in the

EO field is how the EO construct relates to management issues. For instance how should risk and disruptiveness arising from entrepreneurial efforts be handled? This discussion also relates to the link between EO and DC.

Five models have been proposed as a departing point for empirical and theoretical discussion. Further insight into the relationship between EO and DC is likely to yield valuable insight for a broadened scientific field. It will enable a more compatible understanding of the two concepts and add knowledge about their interrelatedness as well as their importance for building new resources and value for firms. More integrative research on these issues is also likely to improve calibration of both concepts and generate more in-depth insight on how EO and DC influence the wealth creation processes and performance in firms.

REFERENCES

Aloulou, W. and A. Fayolle (2005), 'A conceptual approach of entrepreneurial orientation within the small business context', *Journal of Enterprising Culture*, **13**(1), 21–45.

Antoncic, B. and R. Hisrich (2003), 'Clarifying the intrapreneurship concept', *Journal of Small Business and Enterprise Development*, **10**(1), 7–24.

Argyris, Chris and D. Schön (1978), *Organizational Learning: a Theory of Action Perspective*, Reading, MA: Addison-Wesley.

Arthurs, J.D. and L.W. Busenitz (2006), 'Dynamic capabilities and venture performance: The effects of venture capitalists', *Journal of Business Venturing*, **21**(2), 195–215.

Barney, J.B. (1986), 'Strategic factor markets: Expectations, luck, and business strategy', *Management Science*, **32**(10), 1231–41.

Barney, J.B. (1991), 'Firm resources and competitive advantage', *Journal of Management*, **17**(1), 97–120.

Barney, Jay B. (2002), *Gaining and Sustaining Competitive Advantage*, New Jersey: Prentice Hall.

Barney, J.B. and A.M. Afrikan (2001), 'The resource-based view: origins and implications', in M.A. Hitt, E. Freeman and J.S. Harrison (eds), *Handbook of Strategic Management*, Oxford: Blackwell.

Bhuian, S.N., B. Menguc and S.J. Bell (2005), 'Just entrepreneurial enough: the moderating effect of entrepreneurship on the relationship between market orientation and performance', *Journal of Business Research*, **58**, 9–17.

Borch, O.J. and E.L. Madsen (2007), 'Dynamic capabilities facilitating innovative strategies in SMEs', *International Journal of Technoentrepreneurship*, **1**(1), 109–25.

Borch, O.J., M. Huse and K. Senneseth (1999), 'Resource configuration, competitive strategies and corporate entrepreneurship: an empirical examination of small firms', *Entrepreneurship Theory and Practice*, **24**(1), 49–70.

Borch, O.J., E.L. Madsen and E. Rasmussen (2005), 'Strategisk entreprenørskap – organisatoriske mekanismer for nyskaping i et etablert foretak', *Magma*, (2).

Carter, S. and D. Jones-Evans (2000), *Enterprise and Small Business: Principles, Practice and Policy*, Harlow, UK: Financial Times/Prentice Hall.

Cepeda, G. and D. Vera (2007), 'Dynamic capabilities and operational capabilities: a knowledge management perspective', *Journal of Business Research*, **60**(5), 426–37.

Covin, J.G. and D.P. Slevin (1989), 'Strategic management of small firms in hostile and benign environments', *Strategic Management Journal*, **10** (January), 75–87.

Covin, J.G. and D.P. Slevin (1991), 'A conceptual model of entrepreneurship as firm behaviour', *Entrepreneurship Theory and Practice*, **16**(1), 7–25.

Covin, J.G. and P.M Miles (2007), 'Strategic use of corporate venturing', *Entrepreneurship Theory and Practice*, **31**(2), 183–207.

Covin, J.G., K.M. Green and D.P. Slevin (2006), 'Strategic process effects on the entrepreneurial orientation–sales growth rate relationship', *Entrepreneurship Theory and Practice*, **30**(1), 57–81.

Dale Meyer, G., H.M. Neck and M.D. Meeks (2002), 'The entrepreneurship–strategic management Interface', in M. Hitt, R.D. Ireland, S.M. Camp and D. Sexton (eds), *Strategic Entrepreneurship: Creating a New Mindset*, Oxford: Blackwell, pp. 19–44.

Davidsson, P. (2004), *Researching Entrepreneurship*, New York, US: Springer.

Dess, G.G. and A. Rasheed (1993), 'Commentary: generic strategies', in P. Shrivastava, A. Huff and J. Dutton (eds), *Advances in Strategic Management*, Greenwich, CT: JAI Press, pp. 409–16.

Dess, G.G., G.T. Lumpkin and J.E. McGee (1999), 'Linking corporate entrepreneurship to strategy, structure, and process: suggested research directions', *Entrepreneurship Theory & Practice*, **23**(3), 85–102.

Eisenhardt, K. and J.K. Martin (2000), 'Dynamic capabilities: what are they?', *Strategic Management Journal*, **21**, 1105–21.

Elfring, T. (2005), *Corporate Entrepreneurship and Venturing*, New York, US: Springer.

Gartner, W.B. (1990), 'What are we talking about when we talk about entrepreneurship', *Journal of Business Venturing*, **8**, 231–9.

Grewal, R. and P. Tansuhaj (2001), 'Building organizational capabilities for managing economic crisis: The role of market orientation and strategic flexibility', *Journal of Marketing*, **65**, 67–80.

Griffith, D.A., S.A. Noble and Q. Chen (2006), 'The performance implications of entrepreneurial proclivity: a dynamic capabilities approach', *Journal of Retailing*, **82**(1), 51–62.

Helfat, C.E. and M.A. Peteraf (2003), 'The dynamic resource-based view: capability lifecycles', *Strategy of Management Journal*, **24**, 997–1010.

Hughes, M. and R.E. Morgan (2007), 'Deconstructing the relationship between entrepreneurial orientation and business performance at the embryonic stage of firm growth', *Industrial Marketing Management*, **36**(5), 651–61.

Ireland, R.D., M.A. Hitt and D.G. Simon (2003), 'A model of strategic entrepreneurship: the construct and its dimensions', *Journal of Management*, **29**(6), 963–89.

Ireland, R.D., M.A. Hitt, S.M. Camp and D.L. Sexton (2001), 'Integrating entrepreneurship and strategic actions to create firm wealth', *Academy of Management Executive*, **15**(1), 49–63.

Jantunen, A., K. Puumalainen, S. Saarenketo and K. Kyläheiko (2005), 'Entrepreneurial orientation, dynamic capabilities and international performance', *Journal of International Entrepreneurship*, (3), 223–43.

Jun, Z. (2006), 'Development of theory on entrepreneurial orientation: empirical evidences from Hebei, China and Flanders, Belgium', Doctoral dissertation, Department of Management and Entrepreneurship, Ghent University, Belgium.

Keh, H.T., T.T.M. Nguyen and H.P. Ng (2007), 'The effects of entrepreneurial orientation and marketing information on the performance of SMEs', *Journal of Business Venturing*, **22**(4), 592–611.

Lumpkin, G.T. and G.G. Dess (1996), 'Clarifying the entrepreneurial orientation construct and linking it to performance', *Academy of Management Review*, **21**(1), 1–8.

Lumpkin, G.T. and G.G. Dess (2001), 'Linking two dimensions of entrepreneurial orientation to business performance: the moderating role of environment and industry life cycle', *Journal of Business Venturing*, **16**, 429–51.

Madsen, E.L. (2007), 'The significance of sustained entrepreneurial orientation on performance of firms – A longitudinal analysis', *Entrepreneurship and Regional Development*, **19**(2), 185–204.

Madsen, E.L., G.A. Alsos, O.J. Borch, E. Ljunggren and B. Brastad (2006), 'Developing entrepreneurial orientation – the role of dynamic capabilities and intangible resources', paper presented at the RENT conference, 22–24 November 2006, Brussels, Belgium.

Matsuno, K., J.T. Mentzer and A. Özsomer (2002), 'The effects of entrepreneurial proclivity and market orientation on business performance', *Journal of Marketing*, **66**, 18–32.

Miller, D. (1983), 'The correlates of entrepreneurship in three types of firms', *Management Science*, **29**(7), 770–91.

Morgan, R.E. and C.A. Strong (2003), 'Business performance and dimensions of strategic orientation', *Journal of Business Research*, **56**(3), 163–76.

Morris, M.H., P.S. Lewis, D. Sexton and L. Donald (1994), 'Reconceptualising entrepreneurship: an input–output perspective', *Advanced Management Journal*, **59**, 21–31.

Nelson, R.R. and S. Winter (1982), *An Evolutionary Theory of Economic Change*, Cambridge, MA: Belknap Press.

Newbert, S.L. (2005), 'New firm formation: a dynamic capability perspective,' *Journal of Small Business Management*, **43**(1), 55–77.

Newbert, S.L. (2007), 'Empirical research on the resource-based view of the firm: an assessment and suggestions for future research', *Strategic Management Journal*, **28**(2), 121–46.

Penrose, E. (1959), *The Theory of the Growth of the Firm*, London: Basil Blackwell.

Priem, R.L. and J.E. Butler (2001), 'Is the resource-based "view" a useful perspective for strategic management research?', *Academy of Management Review*, **26**(1), 22–40.

Rangone, A. (1999), 'A resource-based approach to strategy analysis in small-medium sized enterprises', *Small Business Economics*, **12**(3), 233–48.

Rauch, A., J. Wiklund, M. Frese and G.T. Lumpkin (2004), 'Entrepreneurial orientation and business performance: cumulative empirical evidence', in Shaker Zahra (ed.), *Frontiers of Entrepreneurship Research*, Wellesley, MA: Babson College, pp. 164–78; also available at: http://www3.babson.edu/ESHip/outreach-events/fer cfn (accessed 7 April 2008).

Rumelt, R.P. (1984), 'Towards a strategic choice of the firm', in R.B. Lamb *(ed.) Competitive Strategic Management*, Englewood Cliffs, NJ: Prentice Hall, pp. 556–70.

Rumelt, R.P. (1991), 'How much does industry matter?', *Strategic Management Journal*, **12**(3), 167–85.

Shane, S. and S. Venkataraman (2000), 'The promise of entrepreneurship as a field of research', *Academy of Management Review*, **25**(1), 217–26.

Sharma, P. and J.J. Chrisman (1999), 'Towards a reconciliation of the definitional issues in the field of corporate entrepreneurship', *Entrepreneurship Theory and Practice*, **23**(3), 11–27.

Smart, D.T. and J.S. Conant (1994), 'Entrepreneurial orientation, distinctive marketing competencies and organizational performance', *Journal of Applied Business Research*, **10**, 28–38.

Stevenson, H.H. and J.C. Jarillo (1990), 'A paradigm of entrepreneurship: entrepreneurial management', *Strategic Management Journal*, **11**, 17–27.

Teece, D.J. (1984), 'Economic analysis and strategic management', *California Management Review*, **26**(3), 87–110.

Teece, D.J., G. Pisano and A. Shuen (1997), 'Dynamic capabilities and strategic management', *Strategic Management Journal*, **18**(7), 509–33.

Wernerfelt, B. (1984), 'A resource-based view of the firm', *Strategic Management Journal*, **5**(2), 171–80.

Wiklund, J. (1999), 'The sustainability of the entrepreneurial orientation–performance relationship', *Entrepreneurship Theory and Practice*, **24**(1), 37–48.

Wiklund, J. and D. Shepherd (2003), 'Knowledge-based resources, entrepreneurial orientation, and the performance of small and medium-sized businesses', *Strategic Management Journal*, **24**, 1307–14.

Wiklund, J. and D. Shepherd (2005), 'Entrepreneurial orientation and small business performance: a configurational approach', *Journal of Business Venturing*, **20**(1), 71–91.

Winter, S.G. (2003), 'Understanding dynamic capabilities', *Strategic Management Journal*, **24**(10), 991–5.

Wu, Lei-Yu (2007), 'Entrepreneurial resources, dynamic capabilities and start-up performance of Taiwan's high-tech firms', *Journal of Business Research*, **60**(5), 549–55.

Zahra, S.A. and J.G. Covin (1995), 'Contextual influences on the corporate entrepreneurship performance relationship – a longitudinal analysis', *Journal of Business Venturing*, **10**(1), 43–58.

Zahra, S.A., A.P. Nielsen and W.C. Bogner (1999), 'Corporate entrepreneurship, knowledge, and competence development', *Entrepreneurship Theory and Practice*, **23**(3), 169–89.

Zahra, S.A., H.J. Sapienza and P. Davidsson (2006), 'Entrepreneurship and dynamic capabilities: a review, model and research agenda', *Journal of Management Studies*, **43**(4), 917–55.

Zollo, M. and S.G. Winter (2002), 'Deliberate learning and the evolution of dynamic capabilities', *Organization Science*, **13**(3), 339–51.

12. The impact of global value chains on Andalusian tourism SMEs

Pilar Tejada and Francisco Liñán

INTRODUCTION

The present process of globalization stresses the need to continuously seek international competitiveness. Thus, firm strategies have been rapidly evolving over the last few years. Technological advances have exerted a critical influence on this process, modifying the traditional consideration of competitive advantage (López Domínguez, 2005). This has led to global strategic designs, as is reflected in the configuration of global tourism value chains (GTVCs).

Within the tourism sector, the following elements imply an increasingly competitive environment: globalization of tourism markets, greater consumer sovereignty, changing firm strategies, introduction of new technologies in the tourism industry, and the transformation of marketing channels (Go and Pine, 1995). Tourism firms are forced to restructure thoroughly to adapt to this new environment. Main strategies in this sense are firm mergers, introduction of new agents in the market, new management models, and internationalization (Ioannides and Debbage, 1997; Bywater, 1998).

These changes are forcing all tourism actors to adapt to the globalization process. Whether small firms and entrepreneurs in this sector win or lose from this process depends on their integration into the global tourism value chain (GTVC). Local suppliers in tourism destinations such as Andalusia need to recognize the relevance of this transformation and actively join GTVCs. Therefore, our first main objective in this chapter will be to understand the configuration of the global value chain in the tourism sector. The relationships established among the different participating agents will be studied. As a second objective, we will analyse the position of Andalusian tourism firms in global value chains. For this reason, several case studies have been carried out on Andalusian hotels and travel agencies.

This chapter has benefited from the participation of the authors in the research project 'The role of SMEs in the global tourism industry', promoted and directed by the Organisation for Economic Co-operation and Development (OECD).

GLOBAL TOURISM VALUE CHAINS

The term 'value chain' could be defined as the set of activities required to transform raw materials into finished production and their sale. All the activities ranging from the very conception of the product, going through production and marketing, distribution and even disposal or recycling after use comprise the value chain (Kaplinsky and Morris, 2001). The essential idea in value chains is that each link adds value to the product (Gereffi, 1994, 1999; Kaplinsky and Readman, 2001; UNIDO, 2002). In reality, however, a large number of links are present in each value chain.

Nowadays, it is very rare for a single firm to perform all the activities needed from the conception of the product to final delivery to consumers. The different activities comprised in each value chain may be carried out by firms located in different countries. Kaplinsky and Morris (2001) refers to this as 'extended value chain'.

Porter (1985) introduced the term 'value chain', which has become a basic tool for firm analysis. Porter tries to systematically explore all the activities performed within the firm, and their interactions. According to Porter (1985, 1990), the overall value-creating logic of the value chain is valid in all industries. This would include its generic categories of activities.

However, Stabell and Fjeldstad (1998) experienced serious problems in applying the value chain model to more than two dozen firms from a variety of industries. They agree with Armistead and Clark (1993) in that the value-chain framework is less suitable for the analysis of activities in service industries, such as insurance or banking. Therefore, they suggest three distinct generic value-configuration models: the value chain, the value shop and the value network.

This 'value network' term is similar to that of global value chain (GVC), since 'firms that can be modeled as value networks rely on a mediating technology to link clients or customers who are or wish to be independent. The mediating technology facilitates exchange relationships among customers distributed in space and time. The firm itself is not the network. It provides a networking service' (Stabell and Fjeldstad, 1998, pp. 427).

Similarly, Dyer and Singh (1998) suggest that a firm's critical resources may span firm boundaries and may be embedded in interfirm resources and routines. They argue that an increasingly important unit of analysis for understanding competitive advantage is the relationship between firms. They identify four potential sources of interorganizational competitive advantage: relation-specific assets, knowledge-sharing routines, complementary resources/capabilities and effective governance.

For the specific field of new communication technologies, Amit and Zott (2001) develop a model of value-creation sources in e-business. They studied 59 American and European e-businesses. These case-study analyses led them to suggest that the value creation potential of e-businesses depends on four interdependent variables: efficiency, complementarities, lock-in, and novelty.

According to literature, then, it may be argued that the unit of analysis for competitive advantage shifts from the firm to the whole set of relationships established between firms. The concept of global value chain, in this sense, comprises more than the relationships established within the firm. Even multinational corporations with subsidiaries in several countries cannot carry out the whole production process themselves. On the other hand, global value chains consider linkages among different firms not only at national, but also international levels. It is, therefore, a wider concept than that of the 'firm value chain' (Porter, 1990) or 'filière' (OECD, 2005b).

At present, however, the concepts and the methodology of the GVC approach have mainly been applied to study industrial activities (Gereffi, 1999; Humphrey and Schmitz, 2002; Schmitz, 1995, 1999; Rabelloti, 2004). Nevertheless, some attempts have already been made to use them to analyse the tourist sector (Clancy, 1998, 2002).

In this sense, tourism nowadays is one of the most internationalized sectors in the world economy. According to the World Tourism Organization (WTO), international tourism is the main source of exports in the world. It is also the fastest growing sector in terms of income generated. In 2005, there were a total of 808 million international tourists. Income generated in 2004 was some $500 billion. These figures show the importance of this activity and its level of exposure to international changes such as globalization.

Impact of Globalization on Tourism

Global economic conditions and their transformations are one of the main challenges faced by the tourism industry, as traditional patterns are being increasingly changed. Growing international competition is transforming this activity in a global industry and accelerating the creation of multinational tourism organizations. According to Smeral (1998), the implications of globalization affect both the supply and demand of tourism in several ways. However, compared to other industries, very little research has been done so far on GTVCs (OECD, 2005c).

On the demand side, tourism demand is becoming increasingly global due to several factors: growing income levels; European population ageing; saturated traditional destinations; appearance of new interests and changes in ways of living. Thus, advances in information and communication systems have made tourists more experienced and demanding (Vanhove, 1998). On the other hand, the high elasticity of tourism demand with respect to income will lead to a very rapid growth of global tourism demand in the near future (WTO, 1997; Bull, 1994). Similarly, dropping air transport costs widens the access to new destinations at lower prices. This opens the international tourism market for relatively low-income tourists.

On the supply side, the effect of computerized information and reservation systems means that suppliers of tourism services act in a global market. Airlines, hotel chains and tour operators develop their activities throughout the world. Global distribution systems (GDS) give them the ability to cover most of the international tourism demand. At the same time, alliances, cooperation or mergers, in many instances urged by the need to share the cost of technological systems implemented, act as an additional globalization force. The use of information and communication technologies together with different integration processes enlarges the tourism value chain so that we can now talk of GTVCs.

Finally, new tourism destinations are being developed, many of them in developing countries, thanks to large investments by multinational corporations. These investments are creating the infrastructure needed (at these destinations) for different tourism industry agents to expand. Given the almost perfect substitutability existing between several tourism destinations, price becomes an essential factor in determining their competitiveness. Having low unit labour costs turns out to be highly relevant, either through low wages or high productivity. Given the importance that personal services have, the challenge for these new destinations is achieving high productivity to keep costs low, while at the same time offering high quality services to the customer/tourist.

For firms, the global reach of tourism activities may have both advantages and disadvantages. It may help them improve their price/quality relationship and their national and international competitiveness through economies of scale. On the other hand, centralized management of global corporations means that innovation and knowledge generation is carried out at the parent company. Therefore, the subsidiary's role is limited to the implementation of the parent's strategy, instead of developing its own innovation processes (Smeral, 1998).

It has become increasingly common for large tourism firms located in developed countries to specialize in the activities generating higher value added within the tourism value chain, such as product design or marketing. In contrast, those activities yielding lower profits and bearing stronger competition are carried out by firms from less-developed countries with lower labour costs. This is the case with many so-called 'emerging destinations' such as Southeast Asia, for instance.

Configuration of Global Tourism Value Chains

Tourism activities have traditionally been highly fragmented and geographically disseminated. There have always been major difficulties in matching supply and demand. Therefore, mediation has had a crucial role in tourism. A large proportion of firms operating in this sector, especially those located in and around tourism destinations (hotels, restaurants, and so on), tend to be small. Customers can come from very diverse origins and, quite often, considerably distant ones. For this reason, substantially large investments in advertising and communications are needed to contact potential customers. Moreover, these firms normally bear high fixed costs, forcing them to maximize occupancy rates throughout the year.

Tour operators have been a satisfactory solution to these problems. On the one hand, they have enough resources to face mass advertising campaigns that can reach many consumers in different parts of the world. On the other hand, as they channel large numbers of tourists, they can ensure permanently high occupancy rates, lowering uncertainty and demand fluctuations. Therefore, the traditional tourism value chain consists of four stages: suppliers of basic tourism services; tour operators or wholesale agents; travel agencies or retail trade; and finally consumers or tourists.

The role of consumers within the value chain has been traditionally downplayed. Value chain models frequently restrict value creation to the stages of innovation, production and product delivery done by the primary supplier or the intermediaries. However, the introduction of Information and Communication Technologies (ICT) makes it possible for the supplier to market its products directly to the consumer.

A useful approximation to the present configuration of GTVCs is presented in Figure 12.1. The most relevant agents involved in the tourism activity are shown (tour operators, travel agencies, global distribution systems, reservation centres, hotels, destination management organizations (DMOs), and so on), together with their most significant relationships.

The primary supply is found at one end of the value chain. This includes firms such as hotels and restaurants, which are mostly small and medium-sized enterprises (SMEs). Airlines are situated at the same level, together with other transport companies. One important difference,

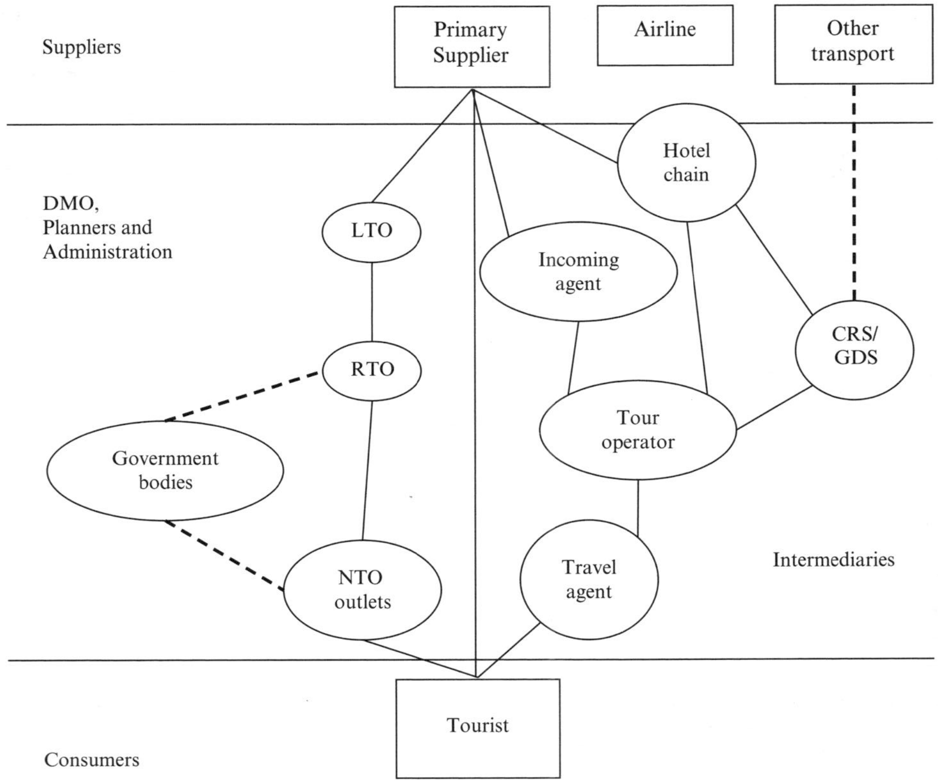

Source: Adapted from Werthner and Klein (1999).

Figure 12.1 Global tourism value chains

though, is that these firms are usually large. However, these suppliers share some common characteristics, which make these activities prone to price wars and requiring high occupancy rates in order to absorb fix costs and be profitable:

- Need for significant investments in fixed assets.
- The supply is considerably rigid, as the number of beds or seats cannot be modified in the short run.
- Fixed costs are quite high. They represent some two-thirds of the total cost in airlines, and around 40 per cent in hotels (Sinclair and Stabler, 1998), whereas marginal costs are very low (the cost of including an extra passenger in a plane with spare seats, or an extra customer in a hotel with empty rooms, is close to zero).
- Production is of a highly perishable nature, as it may not be stored. Any empty room in a hotel results in forgone income.

Tourism intermediaries are located in the middle part of Figure 12.1, and they tend to be quite diverse. On the right-hand side of the figure most traditional intermediaries are presented, together with some new ones. These newer agents have appeared basically as a consequence of the new distribution channels opened by the Internet revolution.

Within this middle link, tour operators can be highlighted. Sheldom (1994) considers them to be one of the essential pillars of the development of mass tourism. There is theoretical discussion regarding their role. Some authors highlight their function as being mediators between tourism suppliers (transport, accommodation, catering and so on) and retailers or final consumers (Sheldom, 1986; Yale, 2001). However, other researchers stress their role as assemblers of basic supplies, transforming these supplies into totally different products. The tourist package is then marketed under its own brand and, therefore, the tour operators could be considered not only as intermediaries, but as producers (Holloway, 1989; González Soria, 1999).

The tour operator's level is dominated by a small number of large firms. They have been increasing their market power through different integration processes, both vertical (hotels, airlines, travel agencies) and horizontal (merging with competitors). Therefore, it may be said that these companies exert the governance of GTVCs, as they have the capacity to impose conditions on the other elements along the chain. This high level of concentration is most evident in the European tourism industry (Figure 12.2). In this sense, the option to buy a tourist package is more common among European tourists than American tourists.

However, along with these large firms, an important number of small and medium-sized enterprises do exist. According to Sinclair and Stabler

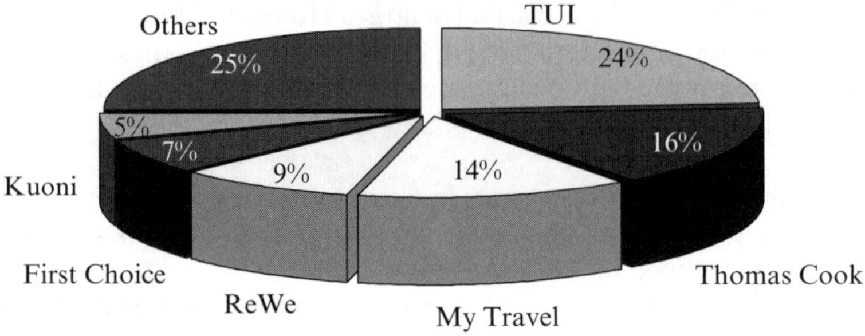

Source: Elaborated with data from Schneiderbauer et al. (2004).

Figure 12.2 Main European tour operators

(1998), this can be explained by the high degree of maturation reached by the tourism market, allowing for the possibility of increased segmentation and differentiation. More recently, a tendency towards multisegmentation is found, employing two or more criteria to define a demand segment, instead of the classical segmentation based on only one factor.

For this reason, large tour operators concentrate on mass production of tourist packages with very similar characteristics, which are highly substitutable among themselves. These packages do not satisfy the preferences of specific segments of the demand (market niches), which are served by smaller tour operators, specialized in the production and marketing of highly specific products.

Next, connecting tour operators with either final customers or primary suppliers, we can find other traditional tourism intermediaries, the travel agencies or retailers. Their main function is marketing tourist packages made by tour operators or products of other suppliers, such as airlines or hotels. They usually receive a commission on each sale. At the same time, they provide customers with information about different destinations, services or suppliers, acting as advisors.

In the last few years much debate has been generated about the possibility that these agents may disappear from the tourism value chain. The increasing use of the Internet has opened a new direct distribution channel between tourism suppliers and final consumers, where intermediaries are not needed. This new situation is pressing down margins and commissions for travel agencies, endangering one of their most important sources of income. However, instead of a process of de-intermediation, it is likely that new intermediaries will start to appear (re-intermediation) and that traditional travel agencies will start to use new technology (virtual agents, for instance).

Computerized reservation systems (CRS) originate from the 1960s, when American Airlines and IBM developed the first computerized system called SABRE (automatic procedure to manage the availability of airplane seats). It was initially limited to internal company use, but it soon started to be installed in travel agencies, giving birth to the first real CRS. The process of deregulation of the air travel market in the USA contributed strongly to their expansion.

Its second stage, the geographical extension of operations, together with the inclusion of other tourism suppliers (hotels, car rental, railway companies), transformed CRS into what has been called global distributions systems (GDS). These agents have taken advantage of the new opportunities offered by the Internet by creating virtual travel agencies, such as Travelocity by SABRE, or Amadeus.net by Amadeus.

Different local, regional or national tourism organizations (LTO, RTO, NTO – also sometimes called National Tourism Boards, NTBs) would also be placed within the intermediation stage. Their main function is normally to promote tourism in that territory and provide information about the different suppliers located in it. They are normally public bodies.

Finally, a relatively new type of intermediary is having an increasing presence and importance in GTVC. The so-called destination management organizations (DMO) are normally public bodies or organizations receiving strong public support. They offer a number of services related to their specific tourism destination, with the purpose of attracting more tourists. As the WTO Business Council (2001) points out, the future of DMOs rests in electronic commerce so that they can:

- Create electronic links among suppliers of tourism services and their destinations, so that they may centre on maintaining information and the availability of their products.
- Act as intermediaries to help consolidate a wide range of destination products (especially for SMEs), and distribute electronically to the remaining agents within the tourism value chain.

These DMOs, therefore, may be justified because of their value creation. For consumers, they may provide objective high-quality information about the destination, simplifying the purchase (adapting combined travels) and recommending special offers. To suppliers, they may offer the 'destination brand', information on the range of products available at the destination, distribution to both final consumers and intermediaries, and mechanisms to secure transactions.

THE ROLE OF ANDALUSIAN SMES IN GLOBAL TOURISM VALUE CHAINS

During the last few years, the tourism industry has faced a number of unprecedented challenges. At a global level, the industry has shown its resilience to external shocks. However, at regional and local levels, the effects have been more serious. Tourism organizations, such as the WTTC (World Trade and Tourism Council), indicate that these international events have accelerated changes which have been taking place since the early 1990s due to the globalization process. The role of SMEs as traditional partners, suppliers or distributors of large firms would have been deeply affected (Smeral, 1998). This has made more and more governments realize that tourism cannot thrive without some guidance, especially in the medium and longer term. This increasingly competitive environment makes the whole tourism industry – but especially SMEs – face a large number of challenges (OECD, 2005c).

In this context, the OECD has carried out a study on 'The role of small and medium-sized enterprises in the global tourism industry', within the larger research project 'Enhancing the role of small and medium-sized enterprises in global value chains'.[1] The purpose of this study is to get to know how SMEs participate in global value chains. It will also allow the identification of good practices that may be adequate for SMEs to succeed in the framework of globalization, making the most of their participation in global value chains.

The authors' research group 'SMEs and economic development' at the University of Seville has undertaken this study in the region of Andalusia. The fieldwork has consisted of several case studies of small and medium-sized tourism enterprises in Andalusia. As suggested in the general OECD draft research outline, hotels and travel agencies have been interviewed (OECD, 2005a).

Andalusia is an important international destination. In terms of receptive tourism, it is equivalent to Thailand, while it more than doubles other well-known destinations such as Cuba, the Dominican Republic, or Argentina (Aurioles et al., 2001). During 2004, it was estimated that a total of 22 million tourists visited the region, 2.9 per cent more than in 2003 (according to the Andalusian tourism survey, ECTA 2005); 40.9 per cent of them were foreigners. Among the latter, nearly one third of them were British (31 per cent). The relevance of these figures may be better understood when compared to the total population of Andalusia: 7.85 million inhabitants in 2005.

To meet this tourism demand, the Andalusian economy produced goods and services valued at €12.5 billion (SAETA, 2005). Tourism has become

Table 12.1 Structure of Andalusian tourism enterprises, 2005

Sector	1–9 employees	10–199 employees	199–499 employees	> 499 employees
Travel agencies*	89.4	10.5	0.1	0.1
Hotels**	81.0	18.3	0.7	0.1

Notes:
* Division 63 National Classification of Economic Activities (CNAE), corresponding to Division 79 of the International Standard Industrial Classification (ISIC, Rev. 4).
** Division 55.1 of CNAE, corresponding partly to Division 55 of ISIC (Rev. 4).

Source: Compiled with data from Directorio Central de Empresas (DIRCE), INE.

the most significant industry in the region, contributing 12.4 per cent to GDP. This production has important effects on other activities, both direct and indirect. Direct effects are highly concentrated, with 78 per cent of them corresponding to catering and accommodation.

Indirect effects are generated in other economic activities (for example, clothing, electricity, water) as a consequence of increased demand by the hotel industry (for instance). Therefore, the sum of both effects represents the total impact of tourism demand on the Andalusian economy. In 2004, the sum was estimated at being €17.6 billion, with 71 per cent being made up of direct effects and the remaining 29 per cent being indirect ones. Thus, the multiplier effect on production would be 1.42, meaning that for each euro of direct tourism demand, a value of €1.42 has to be produced.

The impact of tourism on employment is also very remarkable in Andalusia. In 2004, 258 037 job positions were needed to satisfy tourism demand; 207 037 of them were direct ones, and the other 50 554 were indirect. Therefore, the employment multiplier effect is 1.24. Table 12.1 shows the employment structure of Andalusian tourism firms.

Research Design

The seven case studies carried out are distributed as shown in Table 12.2. In Andalusia, some travel agencies also act as smaller tour operators (combining retail and wholesale activities), but none of them functions as a tour operator only.[2] For this reason, two retailers were interviewed, together with one of those combined firms. Three and four-star hotels were interviewed, as these two categories alone represent more than 70 per cent of total beds.

The geographical distribution of these firms was made trying to represent the main tourism typologies present in Andalusia: sun and sand, business

Table 12.2 Case study SMEs

No.	Activity	No.	Category	Location	Motive
4	Hotels	1	3-star	Seville city	Cultural
		3	4-star	Cazalla Sierra (Seville)	Rural
				Seville city	Business and conferences
				Benalmadena (Malaga)	Sun and sand
3	Travel agencies	1	retail-wholesale	Seville city	Business and conferences
		2	retail	Seville city	Cultural
				Malaga city	Sun and sand

and conferences, cultural and rural tourism. For that reason, case studies were concentrated on two of the most important areas in the region, representing a wide variety of tourism motives.

In-depth interviews were carried out, structured along the outline proposed by the OECD research-project steering committee. The interview was divided into four main sections: awareness of the value chain, relationships within the value chain, dynamics within the value chain and public support. In this case, the president of the Andalusian Federation of Travel Agencies (FEAVV) and the vice-president of Seville's Hotel Association (AHS) collaborated with this study. They offered a general overview of the situation in each sector, completing those views offered by individual firms.

Results

A high proportion of interviewed firms had fewer than 50 employees, in accordance with the fragmentation or atomization of the Andalusian tourism businesses. Similarly, annual turnover in 2005 was moderate. Most firms had sales between 1 and 5 million euros. None of these firms belonged to hotel or travel agent chains. Some were family firms managed directly by the owners. Some others belonged to an investment group, but they had independent management. Finally, one of the privately owned hotels had signed a management agreement.

The most important cost is personnel, which represents some 35–45 per cent of total costs in hotels, and even more in travel agencies (up to 75–80 per cent). Intermediate consumption of goods and services represents

20–30 per cent in hotels, and they are much smaller in travel agencies (<10 per cent).

A. Awareness of the value chain

The tourism demand covered by these firms differs notably between hotels and travel agencies. The former normally accommodate some 40–45 per cent of foreign tourists, coming mostly from European Union countries (United Kingdom, Germany, France, and so on) and the USA. Travel agencies, in contrast, cater mostly for local customers (some 80 per cent), that is, Andalusian tourists travelling both within and outside their region. When we look at travel motives, the most important reasons for travelling are cultural, sun and sand, business and conferences.

Value added represents around 60–70 per cent of total turnover in hotels. Travel agencies, as they are mainly mediators taking a commission, generate a much lower value added (10–20 per cent of turnover).

The most important intermediaries for both types of firm are tour operators. Around 50 per cent of hotel sales are made through these intermediaries. On the other hand, tour operators are the most important suppliers for travel agencies. The second most important intermediaries are central reservation systems (20–30 per cent of hotel sales, and 5–15 per cent of travel agencies' turnover). The proportion of rooms sold directly by hotels is very small, so the role of intermediaries is essential for these service suppliers.

Therefore, interviewees recognize that vertically-integrated tour operators are the main actors in the tourism value chain. They have the capacity to establish price and other conditions, thus governing the value chain. In Spain, the main tour operators belong to Globalia Corp., Iberia or Marsans Groups. However, governance seems to be of an 'arm's-length market relations' kind,[3] as there is no need for close collaboration in defining and designing the product, and relationships are normally based on market transactions. Andalusian tourism SMEs do not seem to be too concerned about the need to increase/improve their participation in GTVCs. Some of these firms do not even consider themselves as belonging to any of them.

For them, the main consequences of globalization are the significant increase in uncertainty and competition. This situation is reflected within each destination, as new hotels and travel agencies from large national and international chains are established. Similarly, new destinations are constantly emerging, such as Eastern Europe and Southeast Asia. This situation results in worrying 'price wars' both among hotels and among travel agencies. In the last few years, especially since 2002, they have seen their margins reduced due to price pressure on the part of large tour operators.

Prices received are equal and sometimes lower, but costs are now substantially higher. They are also suffering the effects of cheaper air transport. Low-cost airlines are bringing a greater number of tourists, but they are mostly younger and with lower purchasing power.

Most interviewees consider the tourism industry to be completely global, as large, vertically-integrated businesses are controlled by firms belonging to different countries and operate in several destinations around the world. However, a small fraction of firms (both hotels and travel agencies) do not yet feel themselves affected by globalization. They trust the high quality of their products and customer loyalty due to personalized and higher value-added services.

B. Relationships within the value chain

Surveyed travel agencies belong to buying groups (UNIDA, STAR, GEA and so on), which jointly negotiate commercial agreements (commissions, discounts granted when the total quantity purchased surpasses certain levels and so on). There are some 30 or 40 of these groups in Spain, located in Madrid and Barcelona. In this way, they may obtain 2 to 4 per cent additional profitability. However, despite their increased negotiating strength (associations of buying groups are being formed, such as AGRUPA), they still have very little power compared with large tour operators. Travel agencies also sign two types of direct agreement with hotels and leisure firms: one to get a commission on each sale, or the other to establish a net price to which the agent adds its margin.

Hotels surveyed have signed large numbers of agreements with different tour operators, central reservation systems and traditional or virtual travel agencies. One of the hotels had more than 500 active agreements. They usually determine a price and a number of rooms. Hotels complain that intermediaries press very hard on prices, while they do not fill all the rooms booked. Contracts are signed for each season, with circumstances varying substantially in each destination (summer is high season in Costa del Sol, but low season in Seville). They are normally signed one year in advance, even though customers are increasingly last-minute buyers. Therefore, the level of uncertainty is higher. Several hotels think that, in the future, agreements will be negotiated less in advance and with greater flexibility, depending on the demand level (price discrimination similar to that applied by airlines). Similarly, some interviewees belong to associations of independent hotels (GSD, Etursa). This allows an increase in their commercial potential in exchange for a fixed monthly rate and a commission on each room sold (between 20–30 per cent, usually).

The impact of new technology is apparent in three main aspects. First, all surveyed firms are trying to incorporate new technology. They all have

Internet access, web pages, computerized systems, and so on. Hotels are also investing in safety technology (fire detection systems, hygiene control, and so on).

Secondly, for travel agencies, new technologies (especially the Internet) are being imposed by intermediaries. Hotels, on the other hand, do not consider up-to-date multifunctional websites with online booking facilities to be so important, as customers use their pages mostly for getting information. Direct on-line booking is marginal, representing only a very tiny fraction of total sales. In any instance, hotels and travel agencies have to bear the whole cost of implementing and maintaining these technologies.

Finally, there is general agreement that new technology is modifying relationships within the tourism value chain, especially with respect to intermediation. Some hotels expect these changes to give them greater autonomy from tour operators (more flexible agreements). Hotels think travel agencies will be affected most, especially small independent ones, which may even disappear. However, when travel agencies were asked, they thought that, even though pressures may be strong, offering a greater quality product and higher value-added will increase customer loyalty. They also stress that there is a significant proportion of the population that will never purchase through the Internet (because of their age or education). In this sense, in Andalusia, the segment of the population without Internet access is higher than the Spanish average.

C. Dynamics within the value chain

All surveyed firms belong to some kind of association of similar firms, such as local hotel associations (AHS, AEHCOS) or the regional federation of travel agencies (FEAVA). They are also members of more general business associations (CEA). These associations offer information, training, contacts and other advantages.

They also belong to buying groups (UNIDA, GEA, STAR, and so on) or marketing clubs (GSM, Etursa, Domus Selecta, and so on). This gives them increased negotiating power with respect to other actors and, therefore, additional profitability. However, they must normally pay a fee and a commission per operation.

Regarding the forms used for upgrading, surveyed firms have basically concentrated on product upgrading,[4] trying to increase value-added of their products through higher quality features. For this reason, some hotels offer Internet access in their rooms or seek recognition of their quality standards ('Q' for tourism quality). Hotels have also undergone some process upgrading, as they try to increase direct customer sales (especially online), thus reducing their dependence on tour operators. Within travel agencies, there is only one specific example of functional upgrading, as this firm has also now expanded to wholesale service. Therefore, it can now build and sell its own tourism packages. However, it is not seeking to develop this tour operator activity substantially, but is building packages better adapted to the needs and preferences of its customers (increasing loyalty). Hence, it will not normally market it packages through other travel agencies.

D. Public support

More than half of the interviewed firms have received some kind of help from the public administration, but generally the amount received is small. Most of this assistance has been for improving facilities or computer hardware. These firms stressed the enormous red tape they had to go through and the long delays in approving and paying the grants. Therefore, their effectiveness was seriously undermined.

CONCLUSIONS

Information obtained through interviews, complemented with literature both on global value chains and also on tourism SMEs in Andalusia, has led us to produce specific differentiated SWOT analyses (strengths, weaknesses, opportunities, threats) for small firms in each activity: hotels and travel agencies.

SWOT Analysis for Hotel SMEs

The most relevant strengths of hotel SMEs lie in their continuous effort to better adapt to customer demands (see Table 12.3). They are aware of the limitations imposed by size and try to compensate them with quality, personal service and flexibility. In this sense, they have all renovated their facilities in the last four years. Similarly, they are trying to complement their own offered services through agreements with other firms (leisure activities, golf courses, and so on), so that the widest range of services is available for their customers.

As expected, their weaknesses derive mostly from their size. More than half their sales are made through tour operators. This is specially so in 'sun and sand' destinations, where the presence of international tourists is greater. Hotels do not have the capacity to attract them directly, and these tourists tend to select accommodation based mostly on price. Lack of resources makes the creation of up-to-date online booking systems and large-scale advertising very difficult.

There seem to be two main sources of opportunity for Andalusian hotel

Table 12.3 SWOT for Andalusian hotel SMEs

STRENGTHS • Greater flexibility and capacity to react • More direct and personalized treatment • Greater concern about quality • Modernization of facilities • Diversification of services offered	WEAKNESSES • High dependency on tour operators • Low customer loyalty • Limitations due to small size
OPPORTUNITIES • Internet • Natural environment • Lowering air costs • Globalization • Greater diversification of supply • Increasing customer loyalty	THREATS • New emerging destinations • New hotel openings • Building companies investment • Unfair competition from unofficial accommodation • Lack of support from public bodies • Higher uncertainty

SMEs. In the first place, changes in the sector may open windows of opportunity. Globalization and lower air costs have reduced the importance of distance, increasing potential demand. New tourist motives – such as rural, ecological or sports – could be taken advantage of. Andalusia has a large number of natural areas to attract these tourists. The Internet has allowed direct sales to distant customers.

Secondly, strategic actions could be performed to try to overcome those weaknesses. The opportunity exists to offer more and better services to customers (spas, wi-fi, gyms, and so on), thus increasing loyalty.

Finally, there are significant threats that should also be considered. New destinations are emerging which directly compete with Andalusia. Competition within destinations is also very strong. New hotels are being opened, to a great extent by building companies, which may be leading to 'over-supply'. Similarly, hotels also face strong competition from unofficial accommodation. Additionally, changes in tourists' behaviour also contribute to increased uncertainty.

SWOT Analysis for Travel agent SMEs

In the case of Andalusian travel agent SMEs, their strengths are clearly related to their ability to offer high-quality services, well-adapted to the demands of tourists (see Table 12.4). In particular, as most of these travel agencies do not belong to tour operators, they may sell those packages which best fit the requirements of each specific customer.

Table 12.4 SWOT for Andalusian travel agency SMEs

STRENGTHS • Higher guarantee and quality levels • Growing membership to buying groups • Greater flexibility and capacity to react • High diversification of products	WEAKNESSES • Low awareness of the GVC • Lack of 'productive' associations • Large number of travel agencies • Conflicting interests among agents • Excessive dependency of outgoing tourism
OPPORTUNITIES • Globalization and Internet • Increasing customer loyalty • Greater attraction of incoming tourism (business and conferences) • Increase in tourism motives • New forms of cooperation	THREATS • Disintermediation: Internet • Change in commissions paid by airlines • Low-cost airlines • Unofficial competition • Lack of support from public bodies • Increased power by large integrated groups

On the other hand, associations are limited to buying groups, but they are not used to cooperate, to develop joint products or other productivity-enhancing activities. Travel agencies' awareness of the GTVC is generally low. This makes many of them unable to take any action to upgrade their position within the value chain. They tend to centre their operations on traditional services for outgoing tourists.

The globalization process is opening new opportunities for Andalusian travel agent SMEs through new and increased demand, thanks to the development of the Internet and other ICTs. This could be used to increase customer loyalty by offering services and packages adapted to their demands. This strategy could be especially adequate now that new tourism motives are appearing. On the other hand, incoming tourism could be an important source of income for these travel agencies, but it is not sufficiently exploited. Business, conferences and congresses represent a significant share of total tourism in Andalusia. Offering services to them would be very important.

The main threats faced by Andalusian travel agencies relate to the transformations taking place in the sector. The Internet has become a new direct channel to market tourism products directly to consumers, without the need of retailers. For the same reason, airlines are reducing commissions paid to travel agencies, which are, for many of them, the main source of income. In the case of low-cost airlines, they usually sell their seats directly through the Internet or by telephone. To the extent that the Internet culture is becoming more widespread, the fraction of the population not using these new marketing channels will be reduced, and sales, or even the survival, of traditional travel agencies will be increasingly endangered.

Concluding Remarks

In this chapter we have tried to stress the existence of relevant theoretical differences between manufacturing and service activities. The concept of the global value chain is, in our opinion, validly applied to tourism, though value chains in this sector will present important specific characteristics. In particular, given the enormous complexity of tourism activities, new approaches and concepts need to be introduced to complement the GVC theoretical framework already used in manufacturing.

In this sense, the mediating role of some tourism agents (such as tour operators) plays a very relevant role in the shaping of relationships within the GTVC. Thus, we consider the concept of the 'value network' introduced by Stabell and Fjeldstad (1998) highly adequate to gain a deeper understanding of these value chains. Similarly, it seems to us that there is a need for specific methodologies for the analysis of key concepts, such as that of governance or even that of upgrading. The labels and categories used in manufacturing industries would therefore not be adequate for tourism activities. The effort to develop these specific methodologies and typologies would – in itself – be a highly important future research avenue in this field.

Given the complexity of tourism, and the inadequacy of traditional GVC analysis developed for manufacturing activities, it is even more difficult to identify the specific patterns of governance. Therefore, considering this limitation and still using concepts from the manufacturing framework, it may be said that governance exerted by large vertically integrated tour operators is articulated through 'arm's-length market relations'. Thus, Andalusian SMEs are completely independent from these tour operators, and the product is clearly defined. However, a certain degree of subordination does exist. A large fraction of hotel sales (and travel agency purchases) depend on these tour operators. Negotiating power is clearly asymmetrical.

In this context, competitive improvements carried out by Andalusian tourism firms tend to centre on process and product upgrading. Functional upgrading is very rare, although this helps a great deal in achieving greater specialization and value-added within the GVC. Therefore, public support could be useful here to promote this type of upgrading.

There seems to be considerable disagreement with respect to the need of specific measures to help SMEs improve their position in global value chains. Some of the interviewees argued that their size implies a serious barrier when trying to face the challenges of globalization. Therefore, they consider that help should be provided especially for the following aims: marketing, renovating and updating facilities, adoption of new technologies, promoting cooperation between firms, adapting to changing regulations, and so on.

On the other hand, a number of firms do not consider this specific help as a necessity. They think it would be more fruitful if the public administration developed their functions more effectively, such as promoting destinations, controlling the observance of existing rules (for instance firms falsely operating as travel agents) or improving transport infrastructure and communications. They particularly ask the regional government to recognize the true importance tourism has in Andalusia. There is also considerable demand for the creation of a consultative body truly representing the sector (including SMEs) which may participate in decision-making.

For entrepreneurs and their firms, it is essential that they become fully aware of the existence and characteristics of GTVCs. Improving functional upgrading within these value chains would probably be the best strategy for Andalusian SMEs, given their relative subordination to large tour operators (Guzmán et al., 2007). However, the first step in this sense would be identifying their core competences (capabilities that are of value to final customers, which are relatively unique and difficult to copy). Based on these competences, a strategy for firm restructuring could be implemented, which would surely include investing in personnel formation and cooperation with other SMEs.

Limitations and Implications

This study represents a first attempt to describe the role Andalusian SMEs play in GTVCs. It may suffer from some limitations that have to be acknowledged. Firstly, case studies offer less general results than survey methods. Besides, only two specific destinations have been analysed (Seville and Malaga). Therefore, our results should be taken with caution until a wider study is carried out. On the other hand, case studies have the advantage of offering much richer information. In our opinion, this made them a more adequate technique for an initial study.

Keeping this limitation in mind, results suggest that Andalusian SMEs do have strong opportunities to gain from their integration in global value chains. In this sense, a more proactive and innovative role on the part of tourism entrepreneurs seems to be needed. Combining all local resources and suppliers into one single 'destination brand' may be a good option to increase tourists' knowledge and appreciation of the destination. This would allow local firms to strengthen their position in the value chain, raising their share in total value-added.

Future research would be needed to confirm our results. In particular, a theoretical framework specifically suited for GTVC should be developed. In the case of Andalusia, a wider analysis of tourism firms in the region should be performed. This is an obvious extension of this research which we plan to undertake. Additionally, more detailed analyses on the different types of firms could be carried out to obtain specific results.

NOTES

1. The OECD project has analysed five representative industrial sectors (automotive, precision and scientific instruments, tourism, software and film production and distribution industry), which were selected to illustrate emerging patterns in manufacturing, service and creative industries. In these sectors, value chains show a significant presence of independent or affiliate SMEs acting as subcontractors or suppliers.
2. According to the information available when the fieldwork was carried out.
3. For a discussion on different kinds of governance see Humphrey and Schmitz (2000). From looser to tighter, they identify four modalities: Arm's-length market relations; network; quasi-hierarchy; and hierarchy.
4. Upgrading refers to the competitive improvement within the value chain. Humphrey and Schmitz (2000, 2002) identify four kinds of upgrading: process upgrading (transforming inputs into outputs more efficiently by reorganizing the production system or introducing superior technology); product upgrading (moving into more sophisticated product lines with increased unit values); functional upgrading (acquiring new functions or abandoning existing ones to increase the overall skill content of activities); and inter-sectoral upgrading (moving into new productive activities).

REFERENCES

Amit, R. and C. Zott (2001), 'Value creation in E-business', *Strategic Management Journal*, **22**, 493–520.

Armistead, C.G. and G. Clark (1993), 'Resource activity mapping: the value chain in service operation strategy', *Service Industries Journal*, **13**(4), 221–39.

Aurioles, J., I. Gallego, S.P. Molina, A. Moniche, M.J. Muñoz, E. Manzanera and M. Asensio (2001), 'Aproximación a la Cuenta Satélite Regional de Turismo a partir de las Cuentas Económicas Regionales. La experiencia de Andalucía en base al Marco Input-Output de 1995', paper presented at the International Conference on Tourism Satellite Accounts, Vancouver, available at: http://www.juntadeandalucia.es/turismocomercioydeporte (accessed March 2007).

Bull, A. (1994), *La Economía del Sector Turístico*, Madrid: Alianza Editorial, Sección Economía.

Bywater, H. (1998), 'Travel distribution: who owns whom in the European travel industry', *Travel and Tourism Analyst*, **3**, 41–58.

Clancy, M. (1998), 'Commodity chains, services, and development: theory and preliminary evidence from the tourism industry', *Review of International Political Economy*, **5**(1), 122–48.

Clancy, M. (2002), 'The globalization of sex tourism and Cuba: a commodity chains approach', *Studies in Comparative International Development*, **36**(4), 63–88.

Dyer, J.H. and H. Singh (1998), 'The relational view: cooperative strategy and sources of interorganizational competitive advantage', *Academy of Management Review*, **23**(4), 660–79.

ECTA (2005), *Encuesta de Coyuntura Turística de Andalucía*, Seville: Instituto de Estadística de Andalucía.

Gereffi, G. (1994), 'The organization of buyer-driven global commodity chains: how US retailers shape overseas production networks', in G. Gereffi and M. Korzeniewicz (eds), *Commodity Chains and Global Capitalism*, London: Praeger.

Gereffi, G. (1999), 'International trade and industrial upgrading in the apparel commodity chain', *Journal of International Economics*, **48**, 37–70.

Go, F.M. and R. Pine (1995), *Globalization Strategy in Hotel Industry*, London: Routledge.

González Soria, P. (1999), *Cincuenta Años del Turismo Español. Un Análisis Histórico y Estructural*, Madrid: Centro de Estudios Ramón Areces.

Guzmán, J., P. Moreno and P. Tejada (2007), 'The role of Andalusina tourism SMEs in Global Value Chains', paper presented at the OECD Global Conference Enhancing the Role of SMEs in Global Value Chains', Tokyo, 31 May, – 1 June.

Holloway, J.C. (1989), *The Business of Tourism*, London: Pitman.

Humphrey, J. and H. Schmitz (2000), 'Governance and upgrading: linking industrial cluster and global value chain research', working paper No.120, Institute of Development Studies, Brighton, University of Sussex.

Humphrey, J. and H. Schmitz (2002), 'How does insertion in global value chains affect upgrading industrial clusters?', *Regional Studies*, **36**(9), 1017–27.

Ioannides, D. and K. Debbage (1997), 'Post-fordism and flexibility: the travel industry polyglot', *Tourism Management*, **18**, 229–41.

Kaplinsky, R. and M.L. Morris (2001), *A Handbook for Value Chain Research*, Institute of Development Studies, University of Sussex and School of Development Studies, University of Natal, available at: http://www.ids.ac.uk/global.

Kaplinsky, R. and J. Readman (2001), *How Can SME Producers Serve Global Markets and Sustain Income Growth*, Brighton: University of Brighton and University of Sussex, available at: http://www.ids.ac.uk/ids/global/valchn.html.

López Domínguez, M.S. (2005), 'Globalización económica y estrategias competitivas', *Contribuciones a la Economía*, March, available at: http://www.eumed.net/ce.

OECD (2005a), 'Draft outline for the report on the role of SMEs in the global tourism industry', CFE/TOU(2005)1, 14 June 2005.

OECD (2005b), 'Enhancing the role of SMEs in the global value chains: theoretical framework and research design', CFE/SME(2005)3, 17 June, 2005.

OECD (2005c), 'Increasing the Role of SMEs in the global tourism industry: in-progress draft report', CFE/TOU(2005)3, 4 November, 2005.

Porter, M.E. (1985), *Competitive Advantage: Creating and Sustaining Superior Perfomance*, New York: Free Press.

Porter, M.E. (1990), *The Competitive Advantage of Nations*, New York: Free Press.

Rabellotti, R. (2004), 'How globalization affects Italian industrial districts: the case of Brenta', in H. Schmitz (ed.), *Local Enterprises in the Global Economy – Issues of Governance and Upgrading*, Cheltenham, UK and Northampton, MA, USA: Edward Elgar.

SAETA (2005), *Balance del Año Turístico en Andalucía 2004*, Seville, Spain: Junta de Andalucía, available at: http://www.juntadeandalucia.es/turismocomercioydeporte.

Schmitz, H. (1995), 'Small shoemakers and Fordist giants: tales of a supercluster', *World Development*, **23**(1), 9–28.
Schmitz, H. (1999), 'Global competition and local co-operation: success and failure in the Sinos Valley, Brazil', *World Development*, **27**(9), 1627–50.
Schneiderbauer, D., P. Sweens and F. Döring (2004), 'Surviving the crisis in European tourism', *Mercer on Travel and Transport*, **X**(1), 32–9.
Sheldom, P. (1986), 'The tour operator industry: an analysis', *Annals of Tourism Research*, **13**, 349–65.
Sheldom, P. (1994),'Tour operators', in S. Witt and L. Moutinho (eds), *Tourist Marketing and Management Handbook*, London: Prentice Hall.
Sinclair, T. and M. Stabler (1998), *The Economics of Tourism*, London: Routledge.
Smeral, E. (1998), 'The impact of globalization on small and medium enterprises: new challenges for tourism policies in European countries', *Tourism Management*, **19**(4), 371–80.
Stabell, C.B. and O.D. Fjeldstad (1998), 'Configuring value for competitive advantage: on chain, shops and networks', *Strategic Management Journal*, **19**, 413–37.
UNIDO (2002), *Industrial Development Report 2002–03*, Vienna: United Nations Industrial Development Organization.
Vanhove, N. (1998), 'Tourism demand globalization and its impact on marketing strategies', *Papers de Turisme*, **23**, 48–87.
Werthner, H. and S. Klein (1999), *Information Technology and Tourism – A Challenging Relationship*, New York: Springer.
WTO Business Council (2001), *Comercio Electrónico y Turismo*, Madrid: World Tourism Organization.
WTO (1997), *International Tourism: A Global Perspective*, Madrid: World Tourism Organization.
Yale, P. (2001), *The Business of Tour Operations*, Harlow, UK: Pearson Longman.

13. Family business responsible ownership: challenging the next generation's abilities

Juha Kansikas, Jan Krejci and Alena Hanzelková

INTRODUCTION

This research focuses on responsibility and ownership among the next generation. In this case, the next generation's abilities to act, behave and work as responsible owners are analyzed empirically through Hofstede's cultural theory and theme interviews in four family firms. The aim of the research is to understand the nature or responsible ownership abilities in family business. The next generation can be seen as a group of people in a family who are not just employees or managers but often also shareholders in a family firm. The question of the next generation's abilities is connected to survival and continuity in family business succession (see for instance Venter et al., 2005).

Two countries of the European Union, the Czech Republic and Finland, were chosen for the research. The following criteria were used in selecting the countries:

1. The small and medium-sized family enterprises will be compared in the cultures where the number of family enterprises is nationally different. The number of family firms is increasing, but it is still on average low in the Czech Republic (based on estimations, approximately 30 per cent of all registered firms), while in Finland more than 80 per cent of all Finnish firms are family enterprises (Family Business Network Finland). The next generation's abilities regarding responsible ownership in a high-growth economy like the Czech Republic and in a more stable growth country like Finland will be compared.
2. Culturally, two countries were chosen for the research in order to understand family continuity in responsible ownership: Czech family enterprises were outlawed by the communist regime during the late

1940s and the early 1950s (family enterprises were banned until the late 1980s), while Finnish family enterprises continued to operate at the same time without interruption. The proportion of family enterprises out of all firms is 45 per cent among medium-sized firms and 30 per cent among large corporations in Finland (Tourunen, 2007) while in the Czech Republic the largest firms are global corporations and their units in the country. This historical development, with 50 years of communism in the Czech Republic, might have had some influence on attitudes towards ownership and entrepreneurship.

3. Both countries were chosen also because of their similarities: both are members of the European Union, both have a small population within the EU with their own language and unique heritage, and both are struggling against the threats of global competition. Generally, it is interesting to see how responsible ownership has been viewed in both countries. Hofstede's cultural theory helps understanding regarding the cultural dimensions of the next generation's responsible ownership.

To understand the similarities and the differences better, four family enterprises were chosen from among the small and medium-sized firms. (On choosing the family enterprises and their representatives see the section on 'Data collection, method, and analysis of the study'.) The definition of small and medium-sized firms was chosen as follows: small and medium sized (SME) firms have annually fewer than 250 employees and less than 40 million euros turnover or profit and loss statement (the definition of the European Commission). The concept of a small family enterprise is based on family ownership (more than 50 per cent of the firm) and family management (Kansikas and Puhakka, 2007), while the medium-sized family enterprise can have a 25 per cent voting control among the same family (KTM, 2005). A small and medium-sized family firm is one that is that planning or has already managed to pass the family business down to the next generation.

DATA COLLECTION, METHOD AND ANALYSIS OF THE STUDY

A qualitative research approach was chosen because the aim of the research is to understand family business culture (based on Hofstede's theory) by comparing Czech and Finnish family enterprises. The aim of the study is not to generalize or measure samples of family firms. Practically, as yet there are no national statistics or samples of Czech or Finnish small family businesses. The chosen qualitative method helps to increase understanding of the next generation's abilities. By interviewing the chosen family business representatives it is possible to discuss the roles that family members have in the family business transition process.

Interviewed firms were chosen to represent family firms that still have active founder members influencing decisions. Founders and possible next generation members were interviewed early in 2007. Firms were chosen for the interviews based on size (small and medium-sized enterprises), family culture (family has a strong influence on decisions and strategy), family ownership (among our interviewees 100 per cent of the firm is owned by the same family) and family management (family members are active in family business management). The focus of the research is to understand responsible ownership in small and medium-sized family firms. Shareholder thinking and behaviour is different in a large corporation from in SME family firms. At the same time, family members are owners and managers in a family business, while in large corporations they often only have the role of shareholder.

Methodologically, Hofstede's cultural theory has been used to understand the research topic. Hofstede's cultural theory (Hofstede, 1991; Pheng and Yuquan, 2002) is based on: 1) power distance (the equality vs. inequality in using power and sharing power in society); 2) individualism–collectivism (the relationships and behaviour between people); 3) avoidance of uncertainty (emotions, experienced threats, the avoidance of future uncertain circumstances); 4) masculinity–femininity (roles in the family, work, professions); and 5) long-term–short-term orientation (goal-setting and goal achievement, culture, behaviour).

Kolman et al. (2003) have analysed cultural differences in Central Europe using Hofstede's cultural theory. Their conclusion regarding Czech managers is that culturally in the Czech Republic, individualism, uncertainty avoidance and short-term orientation are high in comparison to countries like Hungary, Poland and Slovakia. Masculinity in the culture is above average and power is also appreciated more on average in comparison with other countries. These findings using Hofstede's cultural theory must be compared with the results of this study. Another possibility in a multicultural study is to choose one of the dimensions for the study, as Daechun and Sanghoon (2006) have done. They have chosen the masculinity–femininity dimension in order to understand gender's roles in society.

Hofstede's cultural theory can be utilized according to the research interest. In this study, avoidance of uncertainty, individualism–collectivism and long-term–short-term orientation are analysed in order to understand the next generation's abilities in family business. The three dimensions are selected based on the Kolman et al. (2003) results from Czech business culture: they are the characteristics that explain the local firms. These dimensions are compared with the Finnish family firms' perceptions. At the same time, gender is not a research interest in this study – masculinity and femininity in the cultures are not compared. Power-sharing and using are not analysed in family enterprises either, because power and equality are not aims of the study.

Template analysis is used in this study to analyse interviews thematically in the qualitative research setting. The analysis is based on summarizing the themes identified by the researchers (Yanamandram and White, 2006). At the same time, the themes are organized according to their contents. Broad themes which could define narrower sub-themes are concluded (Waddington and Fletcher, 2005). Template analysis – or 'thematic coding' or 'codebook analysis' (Andreou et al., 2007) – can be conducted in qualitative, case-based research (see for example Søndergaard et al., 2007). The aim of the template analysis is to create a template, based on the theoretical framework, a priori, or based on the analysis of the informants' interviews (a posteriori). The aim of the template analysis in this study is to understand the next generation's abilities regarding responsible ownership based on the template, a priori.

Interviews were conducted without interruptions. Four individuals (three founders and one next generation member in firms A and B) were interviewed in the Czech Republic and four in Finland (two founders and two successors in family firms C and D). Translating the interviews from Czech and from Finnish to English is a limitation of the study. Anonymous interviews increase the reliability of the results, because interviewees had an opportunity to speak freely about the chosen topics. Methodologically, all interviews are analysed through template analysis and theme interview methodology by thematizing the conversations of the interviewees.

THEORETICAL FRAMEWORK ON THE NEXT GENERATION AND RESPONSIBLE OWNERSHIP ABILITIES

The template analysis is based on creating a template within the theoretical framework. The next generation's abilities regarding responsible ownership were analysed theoretically in a previous study published by Hanzelkova et al. (2007):

> *Proposition 1: Next generation can practise and learn responsible ownership abilities.* (Leiblein and Reuer, 2004; Hagedoorn and Duysters, 2002).

> *Proposition 2: The next generation abilities in responsible ownership need individual motivation, resources and legitimized power to use them.* (Neubauer, 2003; Peterman and Kennedy, 2003).

Proposition 3: The next generation abilities in responsible ownership are based on commitment and on an individual feeling responsible for the family business for all the stakeholders. (Brundin et al., 2005; Montemerlo, 2005; Hall, 2005).

Proposition 4: The next generation abilities in responsible ownership can be divided into groups like legal, ethical, financial, personal and entrepreneurial abilities. (Longo et al., 2005; Lambrecht and Uhlaner, 2005; Aminoff et al., 2004; Miller and Le-Breton-Miller, 2006; Politis, 2005; Markman et al., 2002; Gatewood et al., 2002).

Proposition 5: Training the next generation abilities in responsible ownership could be based on creating feelings of belonging to the family firm. (Jaffe and Lane, 2004; Brundin et al., 2005; Koiranen, 2006).

Proposition 6: Responsible ownership abilities are based on fairness and corporate social responsibility for shareholders and stakeholders. (Longo et al., 2005; Gallo, 2004; Aminoff et al., 2004).

Based on these propositions, and in order to analyse the Czech and Finnish cultures, abilities (six themes) were written in the form of a template. The authors formulated the following template based on the theoretical framework:

1. Psychological abilities – feelings, commitment and motivation regarding the family business.
2. Personal abilities – to manage, lead and train the family business in the future (Keh et al., 2002, p. 131).
3. Entrepreneurial abilities – to recognize and seize opportunities and to keep the entrepreneurial spirit alive (Politis, 2005, p. 403; Markman et al., 2002, p. 150; Gatewood et al., 2002, p. 191).
4. Dynamic abilities – to use resources efficiently and technologically in innovative ways (Keh et al., 2002, p. 140).
5. Operational and organizational abilities – to manage the everyday routines in the family firm and to achieve performance needed (Klaas 2003, p. 44).
6. Multitask management – coping cognitively with several duties and projects at the same time (Baron and Ward, 2004, p. 558).

These theoretical findings reflect the next generation's abilities regarding responsible ownership. Based on the previous theoretical understanding, the empirical research problem will be as follows: 'What are the next generation's abilities needed to maintain family business responsible ownership?'. To understand the research aims, founders and possible successors or next generation members were interviewed in two family firms in the Czech Republic and in two family businesses in Finland. These countries were chosen for the study to compare the nature of responsible ownership between the different cultures in the European Union. Comparing the two cultures enhances the understanding of the next generation's characteristics.

Understanding the culture, the transition process from founders to successors, and abilities needed by the next generation, requires a qualitative approach instead of statistical analysis.

RESULTS

The aim of this chapter is to describe the four family business cases and to create a basis for the template analysis. Family Business A, a private university, was founded in 1998. It started with an MBA programme for 20 people, nowadays in 2007 it has about 2000 students and 9 university programmes, ranging from bachelor's to doctoral DBA programmes, in two fields. The bachelor's and master's programmes are provided in two fields, business management and law. Family business A is located in the Czech Republic.

(The Czech) Family Business A

The interviewee is the founder of business A – a private educational institution. He is 63 years old. The founder has trained his descendants – his daughter and son-in-law – for the past three years so that they will be able to take over the business in two or four years. The founder of firm A has been the one who has had a significant impact on the visions and strategic planning for the firm. He has also been responsible for the development and management of the business school's products and services. According to him, responsible ownership is multidimensional,

> Seriousness and obedience related to it and respect to law and ethical norms, also a systematic approach, having long term goals . . . also perseverance, everybody are not capable of bearing the responsibility for a business in the long run. And also I would say humanity, to be able to get along well with employees and other stakeholders, there are many conflicts that one needs to solve . . . As for knowledge . . . one needs to have a practical experience . . . in negotiating, establishing contacts, convincing partners, assuring them that the firm is in good hands . . . all this you cannot learn from books, you need to gain this from practice, you need to observe and also to adjust to certain rituals . . . Also sticking to your promises is important, meaning such seemingly unimportant things, such as coming on time to meetings, that you answer emails promptly, and not only to your clients but also to everyone inside the firm . . . And as for personal characteristics I regard as crucial, of course apart from intelligence and education, for example veracity, self discipline, ability to stick to promises, perseverance, tolerance towards other people, responsibility.

A positive attitude and motivation are needed in becoming a responsible owner. 'Those who lack motivation can not manage a business in the long run.' He also sees managerial and leadership skills as important. As for the ability of an owner to communicate and establish contacts, responsible ownership is needed.

Successor perspective

The next generation member of firm A is a son-in-law of the founder, 29 years old, who is information systems and economics manager. He has worked at the firm for three years. The manager used to work in an international corporation, but he chose to join the family business. 'I was motivated by a greater possibility to influence the development of the firm, than I would ever have in a large international corporation.' The opportunity to work entrepreneurially in the family business led to his decision to join it. Also his school mates had started their own firms, which had a positive influence on the final decision.

A responsible owner is a committed person according to the successor of firm A. 'Certainly it is a person who did not build his business easily, who had to work hard and therefore he appreciates it more and as a result of that he, on the whole, treats the business more cautiously, he doesn't take reckless measures or experiments and is aware of the real firm value and his investments.' Financially, an owner is an investor: 'In the case of a joint stock corporation, it is someone who owns the shares, in my opinion, not the one who might be called something like a moral owner, the founder . . . it is simply someone who invested his money.' Responsible ownership is also based on long-term orientation. Ownership creates emotions towards a nurtured possession.

He sees that the next generation needs characteristics like 'Responsibility, a strong work ethic and strategic thinking . . . and also detailed knowledge of the field.' An active owner as the next generation member builds the firm actively and creates new business opportunities. Owning a family business is not just something financial. Responsible owners have to innovate constantly and reinvent themselves in long-term family business operations. According to the successor of firm A, many abilities are needed. Responsible ownership needs capacity to act.

> Surely such a person should have . . . the ideal would be for example if the person had managerial skills, because even though the parents can be good managers, a child, that lacks these, would not be able to stir up business. And perhaps he or she would not even want to continue in it. This is certainly one of the most important issues. And also a positive attitude to the firm is crucial so that the person would not be negatively attuned from the very beginning, for example as a result of the parents being more involved in the business than the child. In such a situation, the child would probably not be positively attuned to take it [the business] over in the future.

As the successor of firm A says, it is also important to use the resources efficiently in the family business, to innovate and to use technologies efficiently. Ethics and moral responsibility are also something fundamental in being a responsible owner. However, multitasking management is seen as a negative ability.

> I do not think this is of key importance . . . I think that this multitasking can be in some situations even inefficient, when for example a person strives to take responsibility for decisions very different in nature and this can create problems. The one who is not able or willing to multitasking can better organize his time and to delegate tasks . . . So that everything will be done.

(The Czech) Family Business B

Family business B is a 12-year-old family firm with five active family members (four in the core business unit). The firm manufactures and designs promotional products in the Czech Republic and lately also in other countries.

Founders' perspectives

The interviewee is a 39-year-old co-founder of the business. He previously ran a business in a different industry but gradually moved over to the current business field and involved his family. He thinks that the family was incredibly lucky to have available many of the people the business needed – 'we had a visionary [person], we had a salesman, we had a systematic manager and organizer . . .'

He sees ownership as mainly 'responsibility, commitment and the privilege to decide for yourself.' Being a responsible owner means thinking about the strategy and future of the business, about how to make the firm grow. He thinks all the people involved in the management are very responsible (clearly neglecting the fact that seven of the nine people in management are not owners), both family and non-family members. The abilities of the next generation that the founder considers crucial are communication, responsibility, orderliness and ability to use modern technologies. 'I think communication is number one. In our industry – promotion – communication is very important . . . you don't learn these at school . . . communication, team leading, organizing and if we are talking about a successor who is going to be the head of the business one day, then the vision.' He doesn't think about bringing up his children (up to 12 years old) in this way. 'I think children are hard to push into something . . . Maybe I will try to make them be active and then they can decide what they want . . . They need to be older before being told about the business.' Besides communication, he underlines entrepreneurial abilities: 'these are important and they are rarer than the others. But maybe for a certain sized firms, organization is more important.'

The second interviewee is a 34-year-old brother who is one of the co-founders. He works as a manager in the family firm, which he joined immediately after finishing university several years ago. He sees ownership as responsibility, which is a little bit scary for him.

> my brother and cousin [the owners] have been the black sheep of the family . . . They speak no languages, but they have the healthy commonsense which doesn't bar them from large-scale business, but all of us with university degrees are only employees here. I never longed for ownership, I like to be paid well but ownership would be too heavy a burden for me.

Regarding responsibility he adds: 'In a small town, in a small firm. . .it is not that we would pull money out of the firm, we are closely watched in the town, but the main point is that we realize our responsibility.' He connects responsibility in ownership to soundness, gradual growth and friendship. 'All people know the owners, they talk to tradesmen and everybody. We make fun together . . .We try to clarify, where we want to be a year or 5 years from now where we are expanding, we try to see further, see our limits in growth and to grow reasonably.'

As for the next generation's abilities, he sees his positional needs in the firm.

> We are already expected to have different abilities than the founders. They have the commonsense, the vision but we are expected to have the managerial, systematic skills, computers, languages . . . If we were 4 visionaries, we would end up fighting, but we have one visionary, one true manager, and we are the executive part that makes the system.

The co-founder also stresses the role of innovation.

> Innovation is that we are able to offer a still larger range of products and we really outperformed our competition through this. This I count as a great innovation. Other firms focused on production and perhaps they are cheaper because of that, whereas we focused on complex service which was a good decision as we are winning tenders on the basis of this. [The owners] can't use modern technologies but they are eminently supporting them. We have the most modern technology and they can't operate it, but they know it is the only way and that's enough for the owner.

He also understands his position in the firm as the great organizer and understands his succession as an outcome of the transfer of managerial power. 'Management, system work, innovations, leadership . . . not visions, that's only for owners. Of course, if the owners left, the vision would have to be re-created, you can't go on without it.'

(The Finnish) Family Business C

Family Business C is a second generation SME family firm. It is located in Finland and it manufactures log houses and holiday cottages. C Ltd uses pine wood for its products. The family firm produces and markets log houses and holiday cabins all over the world. The business started in the late 1960s. It went through a succession in 1979. It is a family-owned business. Husband and wife second generation members both own 50 per cent of the firm. The third generation family members are studying at the moment. The successor (C1) of the firm C works in marketing, and his wife, also as a successor (C2) at the family enterprise, works in the office and in marketing.

Founder perspective

Founder of the firm C, who is the successor C1's father, sees responsible ownership as an overall responsibility for the family business. 'You are then responsible for the whole enterprise.' According to him, abilities such as good personal relationships with stakeholders such as banks are needed. Also financial and technical expertise is needed to survive as an entrepreneur. C considers that a founder needs to have some special abilities:

> A founder needs to be educated and also to possess an entrepreneurial spirit . . . Courage is needed to become an entrepreneur . . . trust and courage to believe in yourselves. For example in our family firm the successor wanted to join the family firm and he refused to join the public sector administrative position that was available then. Desire, motivation and independency are needed to become an entrepreneur.

The second generation that owns the family business nowadays has switched the business idea from production to marketing. The third generation family members might join the family business after graduating from business school. Nowadays family business C is very international, while during the founder's age it was domestic. Language skills are needed, but also technical expertise. In particular, multitasking skills are needed: 'Marketing, technical expertise, laws, regulations must be learnt.' Family plays a vital role according to the founder: 'family is useful in everything in a family business . . . it is an advantage.' Transferring the traditions, so that the next generation would continue the family's work in their home town, was important for the founder's parents. This might have affected the transfer of the family business to the second generation.

Successor perspective

For the successor C1, responsible ownership is holistic. It means that there is equality for all firm stakeholders including subcontractors and employees.

> Ownership does not create any privileges for an entrepreneur . . . but you have to get benefits for being responsible for something. You have to be responsible for possessions when you are acting as an owner. Ownership is not just financial. It is also very much mental capital which you cannot buy from anywhere.

Family business is something intangible that is emotionally important for all family members involved in business. As the successor says:

> Family business is a tradition, my grandfather was an entrepreneur and a carpenter. I would like to see my own children in this same firm, but they have to build their own vision and not to follow my vision. Continuity is remarkably important when you become older and you notice that your role is not anymore so crucial in making the results and in leading people (as it was used to be).

Abilities the next generation needs are not superior to others. 'I am no different from anybody else who has gained some education in this sphere. Maybe, I have some special abilities like being enthusiastic, curious, artistic or even innovative. Even courage is needed and also you have to be curious.' According to the successor, responsibility for the family, the employees and also for the business partners is needed. 'Equality in everything . . . Cooperative abilities, diplomatic skills, long-term orientation and being able to cope with all situations and regulations is important for an entrepreneur as they have to follow them'. The successor sees the qualities and abilities needed by the founder and successor as being practically the same. In particular, he mentions visionary thinking and acting as being prerequisites for a family business owner. Looking to the future for the family, business partners and yourself is also needed.

Multitasking management is something that you need as an entrepreneur.

> There are unfortunately situations when you have to cope with many tasks at the same time. This kind of multitasking management is difficult for me, because I am working with my models on the computer and it requires that I focus on only one thing at a time. I have to prioritize, first I will do this and then I will do something else . . . the following week. If I have to make a strict work schedule for myself on the calendar, I would become angry and depressed to see the whole week before it has even started. I will try to work without putting (too much) pressure on myself.

(The Finnish) Family Business D

D Ltd is an SME family firm, which conducts business in the construction industry. D Ltd is specialized in building and maintaining pipes and pipe systems for new houses and buildings. It is located in Finland and started in 2000. The founder of the family firm (40 per cent ownership) develops and installs heating systems. Two sons (20 per cent ownership each) joined the firm in 2005. The founder's brother also works at the same family firm.

Founder perspective

Founder of firm D is the head of the board of directors at the enterprise. He also supervises the construction and planning of the heating systems. He has a business partner, who buys all the heating systems. Therefore, he does not engage in selling or advertising, but works mainly with the research and development. The founder works with producing and planning the heating systems.

> There are many benefits for knowing each other so well at the family business. No need for any formal meetings, because we know what we are doing. It is essential that every one of us in the family business can work unaided by concentrating on [our] own duties: I work with the heating systems, one of my sons works in sales and the other one in the construction of the systems.

Responsible ownership is especially financial. 'I think responsible ownership concerns financial issues. Business must be profitable. And, especially in our case, the quality has to be excellent. That's what I have tried to tell the younger generation in our family business. You have to know how the business works'. Also, thinking and acting ethically and morally is important. 'You have to do things right. You have to follow the law, you have to meet the needs of the taxation, insurances and regulations. As an entrepreneur, you need to know the basics of business operations and the obligations of the law.' The founder feels that family business is special because he can transfer his experience, career and talent to the next generation. At the same time, he can transfer attitudes and working styles. He wants to tell the next generation that working must be honest and you have to be humble for the customers. Many abilities are needed: 'I think that the social skills that you need . . . you need to be calm and you have to have goals. And a clear direction of what you are doing. A long-term orientation is needed, as are honesty and strong work ethics.'

Successor perspective

The successor of firm D sees that one of the biggest advantages in family business is that family members can cooperate and can learn from their joint experiences. 'I work a lot with my brother who works in sales. We often think together about what to do and what is the right direction in some of the cases. The right kind of feedback is something that you need in this work.'

Responsible ownership can be seen as something that is desirable. 'Responsible ownership is a reflection of an interesting and nice job. It is a challenging job that develops your talent.' Responsible ownership itself can increase the satisfaction gained from the work. 'Productivity of business is also one dimension in responsible ownership. All work must be profitable. We spend a lot of time in pricing the products and in estimating the charges and costs [for] the customers.' The successor sees profitability as one of the key concerns in responsible ownership. According to him, the abilities you need in responsible ownership are organization skills, and also the ability to see the whole picture. 'The quality of work we perform is absolutely crucial to us. It produces the profit or loss for us.' Multitasking is needed in everyday work.

> You need good nerves to deal with multitasking management. You have to cope with the stress and anxiety. I think it is basically about working case by case. When you have done something you have to move to another. You do not memorize something that has happened, you just keep on working and doing.

Social abilities are needed. Leadership in family business can be based on individual leadership styles.

> Taking care of the customers is part of the duties in this family business. You need also social skills in dealing with authorities. Leading the employees is challenging, because you need a long term orientation and you have to understand each employee individually. You cannot lead everybody in the same way. You have to lead people as individuals.

CONCLUSIONS AND IMPLICATIONS

In the case of family business A, the founder and next generation members are actively working in the family firm, two founders of case B are still actively working in and developing the business, despite the fact that other (younger) members of the family have already entered the business. In the case of family business C the founder has retired and the next generation are the owners and managers of the family business. In family business D, the founder still retains 40 per cent ownership and has the role of chairman on the board of directors while the two next generation members have employee status and 20 per cent ownership each.

The research problem of the study was 'what are the next generation's abilities needed to maintain family business responsible ownership?' The next generation's abilities regarding responsible ownership can be categorized into seven empirical determinants in the template analysis based on theoretical understanding and the empirical results. The determinants are: psychological abilities; leadership and management abilities; entrepreneurial abilities; dynamic abilities; operational and organizational abilities; multitasking management abilities; and communication and social abilities. Family business cases A, B, C and D are compared in the template analysis in the context of Hofstede's cultural dimensions, individualism and collectivism, uncertainty avoidance and long and short-term orientations.

1. Psychological Abilities: Feelings, Commitment and Motivation for the Family Business and Ownership

In the Czech family business A, the successor sees commitment in responsible ownership as a long-term orientation to profitability. Having the feeling of working for yourself and for the family motivates family business members. A positive attitude can be part of the psychological abilities that create results in the family business. He regards personal traits as important features in becoming a responsible owner. In the same business the founder of firm A sees motivation to work in the business as a necessary prerequisite for a successful long-term involvement of the new generation. He also suggests that a responsible owner should have certain qualities, such as seriousness, a systematic approach, perseverance, humanity, tolerance and the ability to get along with people, a strong work ethic, perseverance, veracity, self discipline and intelligence.

The Czech family business B's founder understands responsibility in ownership to be in interest and care for the property and the employees and connects it to thinking about how to make the business grow. The successor makes a direct connection between ownership and responsibility and he sees responsible ownership as knowing the firm through and through, thinking about its future, planning and re-investing. According to Hofstede's cultural theory, family business A seems to have more long-term orientation than family business B. Both answers reflect the uncertainty avoidance and individualism – the responsible owner is the one who is running the business.

The Finnish family business C's founder sees courage as one explanation for entrepreneurship. One task in family business is to transfer the business to the next generation. The founder hopes that the third generation will join the family business. The Finnish family business D's founder sees the transfer of experience, career and talent for the next generation as an important emotional and motivational factor for keeping on working. The family business has a long-term focus. The successor experiences the family's supportive culture as an important motivator in everyday business and ownership. Business topics are discussed at home and at the work place. Feelings have a large impact on family business. He also notes that the family business decision-making must be based on honesty and fairness. Firms C and D have collectivistic and long-term characteristics. Uncertainty avoidance is also high, because they are willing to plan the succession early to be prepared for the changes.

2. Leadership and Management Abilities: to Manage, Lead and Train the Family Business Responsible Ownership in the Future (Keh et al., 2002)

In family business A, the successor finds that leading and training the next generation is a part of coaching the family business for the future. He, as well as the other interviewee, the founder, regards these abilities as being important. However, the founder also mentions that a lack of these managerial skills in the next generation does not have to be an ultimate barrier to becoming a responsible owner – one can be a responsible owner even without managing the firm while leaving the management of the firm to external people (buying these skills from the market). Family business B and C's founders see leadership as something that is needed in family business. The successor sees leadership as something that is common sense for everyone in family business. Among the leadership and management abilities according to Hofstede's cultural theory, individualistic characteristics can be identified.

3. Entrepreneurial and Strategic Abilities: to Recognize and Seize Opportunities and being an Active and Entrepreneurial Owner (Politis, 2005; Markman et al., 2002; Gatewood et al., 2002)

In the Czech family business A, the successor holds the opinion that it is especially the founder generation in family firms that has an entrepreneurial mindset while the next generation is often more directed towards stabilizing the existing customer relationships and the business idea. He also acknowledges, however, that entrepreneurial skills are needed in the business among the next generation members. The successor also suggests that the ability to lead the business strategically is an important skill for the next generation. The founder also regards these same abilities (combined with strategic management) as key prerequisites for successful family business leadership. He notes that contrary to other abilities, these cannot be purchased from the market, and therefore they have key importance. On behalf of innovativeness, he comments that it is a part of the so-called strategic abilities and that it is one of the important ways by which to maintain the family business competitiveness. The Czech family business B's founder reckons that entrepreneurial abilities are scarce compared to the other abilities. He also considers organizing to be more important than entrepreneurial abilities once the family business has achieved a certain size. The successor regards entrepreneurial abilities as being the number one skill for the founder, but not for the successors. Culturally, among the entrepreneurial and strategic abilities there exists high uncertainty avoidance, but also individualism – the family businesses are seen in the contexts of the founder and the successor, and not just as one collectivistic family business. Family businesses have a long-term orientation strategically – in that sense the Czech family firms seem in this template analysis to be more strategically advanced than the other firms in general.

The Finnish family business C's founder sees entrepreneurial abilities based on profitability as being particularly important. They are needed to survive in competition. The successor sees that both founder and successor need to believe in the future, family, business partners and themselves. The Finnish family business D's successor and founder consider everyday hard work as an outcome of the entrepreneurial abilities. The aim of the entrepreneurial abilities must be profitability. Successor D also mentions visionary and holistic business thinking as an important feature. According to Hofstede's theory, the Finnish family firms' perceptions on entrepreneurial and strategic abilities include long-term orientation, uncertainty avoidance and collectivism: the family business has to work together.

4. Dynamic Abilities: to Use Resources Efficiently and Technologically in Innovative Ways as a Responsible Owner (Keh et al., 2002)

In the Czech family business A, the successor sees family firms as efficient resource users. A long-term orientation enhances responsible behaviour in family business culture. The founder of firm A regards sufficient utilization of resources as an obligation. In the Czech family business B, both interviewees frequently mentioned the word 'vision' when talking about the firm. Both reduced innovation to technological advancement or modernizing of equipment. The successor finds the biggest source of innovation in growing customer needs resulting in a larger range of products or more complex products. The Czech family firms have, among the dynamic abilities, a long-term orientation, which seems to be typical for the family businesses.

The Finnish family business C's successor finds innovativeness, visionary thinking and attitudes against prejudices needed in dynamic behaviour. Family business D's successor sees that quality creates profits or losses at the firm. The founder demands quality in work from the next generation members of the family business. The successor also mentions working like an entrepreneur and the willingness to work long days. The Finnish family enterprises have, in the context of dynamic capabilities, a long-term orientation and collectivism in the family business culture.

5. Multitasking Management Abilities: Coping Cognitively with Several Duties and Projects at the Same Time as a Responsible Owner (Baron and Ward, 2004)

In the Czech family business A, the successor sees multitasking management as even being negative for the business. It is a threat to productivity sometimes. Delegation of power and resources are needed when increasing multitasking. The founder of family business B doesn't consider the requirements of the multitasking management demanding. The successor claims it is possible to hire someone if one doesn't possess these abilities. The Czech family firms represent individualistic characteristics in analysing multitasking management abilities. They regard multitasking as something that can be outsourced or managed by the owner-entrepreneur.

The Finnish Family business C's founder comments that the successors are not able to multitask as they have to concentrate on one thing at a time in planning the pictures and models. However, multitasking is needed to combine technical expertise and marketing in family business. The successor sees the multitasking situation as being unfortunate. It is difficult for him, because his work is so technical that he has to concentrate on one thing at a time and not talk on the phone all the time. Family business D's founder does not need multitasking management in his current duties. The successor sees multitasking as something that you just have to do sometimes. It is about keeping on working and coping with stress. Family business D has managed in delegating resources and power: all duties are divided between family and non-family members. All people have their own duties, which makes working efficient. The Finnish family firms characteristics in multitasking also seem individualistic: they are based on the entrepreneur's talent, and, when needed, other employees can help the family business in goal achievement.

6. Communication and Social Abilities: Networking, Establishing and Maintaining Contacts, Communicating with Key Stakeholders, Handling Conflicts as a Responsible Owner

The founder of the Czech family firm A sees communication and social abilities as important among the next generation – this does not only mean networking and establishing contacts, but also getting along with people and handling possible conflicts. He regards networking as an important ability, but at the same he notes that if these skills are lacking among the next generation, they can be outsourced and purchased from the market. Also the successor in firm A sees the ability to communicate with the employees and various other stakeholders as very important. His view of social skills, understood as establishing new contacts, is, however, negative; he notes that this skill is not crucial, it is enough for the new generation to be able to maintain existing contacts and sees no need to establish new ones on a larger scale. In family business B, both interviewees consider marketing communication such as advertising and maintaining public relations as crucial for the business. They are both grateful that the economic situation of the firm has never created any kind of conflict either with employees or within the family. The Czech family firms' communication and social skills seem to be based on collectivism in conflict management, but also with a long-term orientation regarding training the next generation.

The successor of the Finnish family firm C sees social skills as crucial for family business operational abilities. Also diplomatic behaviour at work and at home is needed in family business. Family business D's founder sees social skills as a basis for leading and training other people to achieve goals in family business. The family business has an advantage in knowing its members very well. This creates commitment and trust when aiming to achieve business goals. Also the successor sees cooperation and sharing experiences as a valuable advantage in family business. In the case of family business D, the family members have a cooperative and supportive culture. The successor also mentions that social skills are needed in order to lead employees. They are also crucial in customer relationships and in dealing with all stakeholders, such as authorities. The Finnish family firms reflect collectivism and long-term orientation in communication and social skills.

7. Cognitive Abilities: Owners' Education, Intelligence, Talent and Experience (Klaas, 2003)

The founder of Czech family business A stresses the importance of practical experience which in some situations cannot be replaced by formal education alone. Family business B's founder supports education, especially in the form of languages and information technology. The successor stresses the importance of common sense and connects education with international growth. He also includes systematic thinking and setting one's own priorities within acquirable abilities. The Czech family businesses reflect a long-term orientation along with emphasizing the family business training and teaching.

The Finnish family business C's founder sees the shift of organizational abilities. Family business C has transferred its focus from production to marketing. Practically, project leadership is needed in family business C.

The interviewee from case D also mentions experience and talent as important features for the next generation. Family business D's founder thinks that regulations and instructions must be followed. As successor and founder both mention, quality is needed as an operational routine in family business. The Finnish family firms reflect uncertainty avoidance by emphasizing normative behaviour as one of the aims in responsible ownership.

To conclude the results of the study, the desirable abilities of the next generation's responsible ownership fall into seven determinants: (1) psychological abilities; (2) leadership and management abilities; (3) entrepreneurial and strategic abilities; (4) dynamic abilities; (5) multitasking management abilities; (6) communication and social abilities; and (7) cognitive abilities. These abilities reflect the next generation's responsible ownership in small and medium-sized family firms with different cultural characteristics. The Czech family enterprises' perceptions regarding the next generation's responsible ownership seemed to have the same cultural characteristics as Kolman et al. (2003) find: individualism and uncertainty avoidance. However, the Czech family firms also emphasized the long-term orientation which is a reflection of Czech family business culture. The Czech family enterprises' perceptions on responsible ownership were more individualistic than the Finnish. They had a more collectivistic nature in responsible ownership (like corporate social responsibility) while the Czech family firms perceived the individual and entrepreneurial responsibility for family business as a basis of responsible ownership. The Finnish family enterprises also have in the context of the next generation's abilities regarding responsible ownership uncertainty avoidance and long-term orientation: responsible ownership must be nurtured over the years.

From a practical view the study shows that the members of the next generation do have to possess a set of distinct abilities in order to become responsible owners. As many of these are long-term issues (building a positive attitude towards the firm, gaining tacit knowledge and experience in the business) and can be developed, the founder generation should start preparing its descendants well in advance before they take over the business and ownership. Theoretically this study contributes to the understanding of the different abilities desirable in the next generation of responsible business owners. The results are indicative and need to be empirically interpreted further – via a qualitative approach to understanding more about the nature of the problem of achieving expertise in family business responsible ownership.

REFERENCES

Aminoff, P., A Blom, K. Pärssinen, J. Helkama, M. Koiranen, K. Nyman and K. Paasikivi (2004), *On the Characteristics and Duties Involved in Responsible Ownership*, Helsinki: Family Business Network Finland.

Andreou, A.N., A. Green and M. Stankovsky (2007), 'A framework of intangible valuation areas and antecedents', *Journal of Intellectual Capital*, **8**(1), 52–75.

Baron, R.A. and T.B. Ward (2004), 'Entrepreneurial cognition's toolbox: potential contributions from the field of cognitive science', *Entrepreneurship: Theory & Practice*, **28**(Winter), 553–73.

Brundin, E., L. Melin and E. Samuelsson (2005), *Family Ownership Logic: Core Characteristics of Family Controlled Business*, paper presented at the FBN-IFERA World Academic Research Forum, EHSAL Brussels, September 2005.

Daechun, A. and K. Sanchoon (2006), 'Relating Hofstede's masculinity dimension to gender role portrayals in advertising. A cross-cultural comparison of web advertisements', *International Marketing Review*, **24**(2), 181–207.

Gallo, A.M. (2004), 'The family business and its social responsibilities', *Family Business Review*, **17**(2), 135–49.

Gatewood, E.J., K.G. Shaver, J.B. Powers and W.B. Gartner (2002), 'Entrepreneurial expectance, task effort, and performance', *Entrepreneurship: Theory & Practice*, **26**(Winter), 187–206.

Hagedoorn, J. and G. Duysters (2002), 'External sources of innovative capabilities: the preference for strategic alliances or mergers and acquisitions', *Journal of Management Studies*, **39**(2), 167–88.

Hall, A. (2005), *Beyond the Legal: Psychological Ownership and Responsibility in the Family Business*, paper presented at the FBN-IFERA World Academic Research Forum, EHSAL Brussels, September 2005.

Hanzelkova, A., J. Kansikas and J. Krejci (2007), 'The next generation abilities in responsible ownership', in J. Kansikas and S. Lehti (eds), *Dimensions on Family Business Research*, Vol. 1, Jyväskylä: University of Jyväskylä, pp. 72–89.

Hofstede, G. (1991), *Culture and Organization: Software of the Mind*, London: McGraw Hill.

Jaffe, T.D. and S.H. Lane (2004), 'Sustaining a family dynasty: key issues facing complex multigenerational business- and investment-owning families', *Family Business Review*, **17**(1), 81–98.

Kansikas, J. and V. Puhakka (2007), 'Business opportunity discovery in small family firms', Working Paper no. 330, University of Jyväskylä, School of Business and Economics.

Keh, H.T., M.D. Foo and B.C. Lim (2002), 'Opportunity evaluation under risky conditions: the cognitive processes of entrepreneurs', *Entrepreneurship: Theory & Practice*, **26**(Winter), 125–48.

Klaas, B.S. (2003), 'Professional employer organizations and their role in small and medium enterprises: the impact of HR outsourcing', *Entrepreneurship: Theory & Practice*, **27**(Fall), 43–62.

Koiranen, M. (2006), *Psychological Ownership, Entrepreneurial Drive, and Entrepreneurial Performance in Trans-generational Value Creation,* paper presented at the IFERA conference, 22–24 March 2006, Jyväskylä, Finland.

Kolman, L., N.G. Nooderhaven, G. Hofstede and E. Dienes (2003), 'Cross-cultural differences in Central Europe', *Journal of Managerial Psychology*, **18**(1), 76–88.

KTM (2005), 'Perheyrittäjyys', ('Family Business'), Report 16 / 2005, Ministry of Trade and Industry, Finland: Edita Publishing Oy.

Lambrecht, J. and L. Uhlaner (2005), 'Responsible ownership of the family business: state of the art', keynote address at the FBN-IFERA World Academic Research Forum, EHSAL Brussels, September 2005.

Leiblein, M.J. and J.J. Reuer (2004), 'Building a foreign sales base: the roles of capabilities and alliances for entrepreneurial firms', *Journal of Business Venturing*, **19**, 285–307.

Longo, M., M. Mura and A. Bonoli (2005), 'Corporate social responsibility and corporate performance: the case of Italian SMEs', *Corporate governance*, **5**(4), 28–42.

Markman, G.D., D.B. Balkin and R.A. Baron (2002), 'Inventors and new venture formation: the effects of general self-efficacy and regretful thinking', *Entrepreneurship: Theory & Practice*, **26**(Winter), 149–65.

Miller, D. and I. Le Breton-Miller (2006), 'Family governance and firm performance: agency, stewardship, and capabilities', *Family Business Review*, **19**(1), 73–87.

Montemerlo, D. (2005), 'Family ownership: boost or obstacle to growth?', paper presented at the FBN-IFERA World Academic Research Forum, EHSAL Brussels, September 2005.

Neubauer, H. (2003), 'The dynamics of succession in family businesses in Western European Countries', *Family Business Review*, **16**(4), 269–81.

Peterman, N.E. and J. Kennedy (2003), 'Enterprise education: influencing students' perceptions of entrepreneurship', *Entrepreneurship: Theory & Practice*, **27**(Winter), 129–144.

Pheng, L.S. and S. Yuquan (2002), 'An exploratory study of Hofstede's cross-cultural dimensions in construction projects', *Management Decision*, **40**(1), 7–16.

Politis, D. (2005), 'Entrepreneurial learning: a conceptual framework', *Entrepreneurship: Theory & Practice*, **29**(July), 399–24.

Søndergaard, S., M. Kerr and C. Clegg (2007), 'Sharing knowledge: contextualising socio-technical thinking and practice', *The Learning Organization*, **14**(5), 423–35.

Tourunen, K. (2007), 'Perheyritykset kansantaloudessa', Unpublished presentation.

Venter, E., C. Boshoff and G. Maas (2005), 'The influence of successor-related factors on the succession process in small and medium-sized family businesses', *Family Business Review*, **18**(4), 283–303.

Waddington, K. and C. Fletcher (2005), 'Gossip and emotion in nursing and health-care organizations', *Journal of Health Organization and Management*, **19**(4/5), 378–94.

Yanamandram, V. and L. White (2006), 'Switching barriers in business-to-business services: a qualitative study', *International Journal of Service Industry Management*, **17**(2), 158–92.

14. Conclusion: towards new challenges and more powerful dynamics

Alain Fayolle and Paula Kyrö

Entrepreneurship is a social and economic phenomenon, a research object and a teaching subject (Fayolle, 2007). The chapters of this book demonstrate convincingly how social demand is booming and results in the emergence of new needs in terms of support, training and access to new knowledge. Undeniably, meeting the challenges of the coming years and improving the economic and social dynamics are directly linked to catering for these new needs. The gatekeeper in this process is training of teachers, researchers and professionals who specialize in entrepreneurship. As Carrier (2005) summarizes it, the question of whether entrepreneurship can be taught has become obsolete, and the more relevant question is 'what should be taught and how should it be taught?' In this concluding chapter, we would like to elaborate and focus on this specific type of need in order to expand the horizon for future books in this series.

Entrepreneurship training programmes are steadily developing (Katz, 2003; Kuratko, 2005), and one can rightly wonder whether this expansion is supported by sufficient availability and quality of knowledge, resources and especially teachers who are able to foster entrepreneurial and enterprising learning (Fayolle and Gailly, 2007). Since the first-ever class in entrepreneurship at Harvard in 1947, soon followed by a second one delivered by Peter Drucker at New York University in 1953, how dramatically have things changed, and how fast! Today in the USA, entrepreneurship accounts for more than 2200 courses in more than 1600 institutions, 277 endowed positions, and about 100 entrepreneurship centres, structures combining education and research in entrepreneurship and support to entrepreneurs (Kuratko, 2005).

Europe is also facing a similar development. In the European-wide survey experts from different universities estimated that the supply of entrepreneurship education will continue to grow substantially during the period 2005–2010 (58 per cent of respondents) or in some respect

(37 per cent of respondents). Also, the number of entrepreneurship centres is about the same as in the USA (Wilson and Twaalfhoven, 2005). However, the number of chairs in Europe is still modest compared to the USA (Katz, 2004). The report identifying the situation of entrepreneurship education in the European Union school system recommended that entrepreneurship education be given a more prominent position in the national curriculum and in the curriculum of each level of education (European Commission, 2002). In practice, however, this is still quite rare.

In France, HEC Paris paved the way in 1976 by proposing a course that was to become an extremely popular specialization: *HEC Entrepreneurs*. EM Lyon created its first entrepreneurship programme in 1984, the same year it launched its Centre des Entrepreneurs (entrepreneurship centre), which, more than 20 years later, continues to welcome every year dozens of new venture / company acquisition projects with a high growth potential. In 1997, a group of French researchers created the Académie de l'Entrepreneuriat (French Academy of Entrepreneurship), a scientific association recognized by the FNEGE (Fondation Nationale pour l'Enseignement de la Gestion, a national foundation promoting management education and research); then with the support of several ministries, the Observatoire des Pratiques Pédagogiques en Entrepreneuriat (OPPE – Observatory of Pedagogical Practices in Entrepreneurship) was set up to complete the national set of structures dedicated to entrepreneurship education.

As an example of small EU countries we can take Finland. The first chair in entrepreneurship was founded in Helsinki School of Economics in 1981 and now five of the 21 Finnish universities offer entrepreneurship as a discipline. Finland was also among the countries that first adopted entrepreneurship at all levels of education as well as in national and local curricula. A strong non-business focus is typical of Finland, and this still is quite rare in European countries (Hytti, 2002). Even though the latest follow-up study of this local curriculum process indicated positive development it also evinced an urgent need to strengthen teachers' education on entrepreneurship (Seikkula-Leino, 2007).

No developed or developing country is indifferent today to the entrepreneurial phenomenon. Regularly, education, research and training in this field appear at the top of political and educational agendas. It is of course the case in European countries, which, in recent years, have launched various initiatives and have made considerable efforts to set up programmes and initiatives that are well adapted to their situation and context. However, numerous pedagogical, theoretical and practical challenges remain as far as entrepreneurship education is concerned, and this young discipline is confronted by a dire lack of teaching material (empirical and theoretical knowledge, case studies, and so on) and qualified professors.

There are considerable challenges, and the conclusions of the European Best Procedure project can be generalized to all the countries: 'The specific training of entrepreneurship teachers must be reinforced everywhere in Europe.' It stands to reason that in order to develop specialized courses in *entrepreneurship* (and not management or any other discipline), we need both teachers and specialists in the field. We must therefore train teachers in pedagogy and entrepreneurship who will satisfy the diversity of learning needs and processes. Before giving a brief overview of the situation in terms of teachers' training in entrepreneurship, we will revert to some key notions pertaining to entrepreneurship teaching.

I. A GENERAL FRAMEWORK FOR ENTREPRENEURSHIP TEACHING

We distinguish three levels of analysis useful for designing and implementing entrepreneurship training programmes: the teaching model, the institutional context and the learning process (Fayolle and Gailly, 2007).

The concept of a *teaching model* comes from the Anglo-American approach to the science of education. The Anglo-American approach takes as its point of departure educational practices and, as Kansanen (1995) argues, focuses on model construction, effective teaching practices and consequently concentrates on empirical research and on testing this in real situations. The point of departure in the continental approach is the ontological basis; theories are deduced from them and further applied in practice (Kyrö, 2006). Thus for teaching and learning entrepreneurship, the more practice-oriented Anglo-American concept of teaching model serves as an excellent framework for designing teaching programmes.

Moreover, here we combine the continental origin of the concept of didactics with the Anglo-American teaching model and thus suggest a new alliance between these two basic tools to advance the teaching of entrepreneurship. The very first meaning of *Didaktik* in the seventeenth century was about the same as the art of teaching or *Lehrkunst* (Kansanen, 1995). The idea was to develop a general teaching method compared to the logical method, which at that time was thought to be the best way to enhance learning. In this sense *Didaktik* is nowadays in use in Central Europe and the Scandinavian countries. Thus by combining the concept of teaching model with the concept of didactics we actually revitalize the original meaning of didactics and bridge the Anglo-American and continental discourses in education. Thus these concepts are evolving and moulding to the current needs of our society.

Didactics leads us to the questions that all educators should raise. Can one teach entrepreneurship without first clarifying unequivocally what entrepreneurship is and is not? Can one teach entrepreneurship without being clear about the personal vision one has of teaching? Thus didactics focuses on teaching to a set of interrelated questions about *why* to teach (objectives, goals), *how* to teach, *to whom*, *with whom* and *by whom* to teach (participants, profiles, background, socio-psychological characteristics), *what* (contents, method(s), pedagogical tools) and *to what end* to teach (evaluation of the training on at least two levels of Kirkpatrick's model, (Kirkpatrick, 1959)).

The *institutional context* contributes to the deterioration and impoverishment of an 'ideal' teaching model, or more exactly to its confrontation with the reality of the institutional situation in which it is delivered. The aim is therefore to integrate the intellectual, material, cultural and financial constraints and adjust the teaching model accordingly; as a result, from 'ideal', it will evolve towards a more focused and better-adapted model.

The notion of *learning process* relates to various other dimensions and aspects. First of all, the student or participant is the heart of the pedagogical situation: 'The aim of teaching is simple, it is to make student learning possible' (Ramsden, 2003). The learning process also requires time and maturation without which teaching might be difficult or even impossible. Finally, the learning process underlines the idea of finality: one learns something (theory, professional practice) in relation to something else (goal). The various categories of learning processes we have identified in entrepreneurship cover what most interested parties recognize as the most crucial needs: learning to be more entrepreneurial and enterprising (developing individuals' entrepreneurial spirit); learning how to become an entrepreneur (setting up new ventures or taking over existing activities in various sectors, geographical contexts and cultural contexts); learning how to become a professional in entrepreneurship (to advise, support and finance entrepreneurial projects); and learning how to become a professor-researcher in entrepreneurship (to produce and diffuse knowledge in this field) (Fayolle and Gailly, 2007; Fayolle, 2008; Hytti and O'Gorman, 2004).

II. TRAINING TEACHERS IN ENTREPRENEURSHIP

A brief overview of the international situation of teacher training in teaching entrepreneurship can be given in a few words: very few visible programmes and a small number of teachers involved in these training programmes. It seems that the stakes are not fully perceived yet, or if they are, they are not at the top of the list of priorities. Yet, we believe this is the cornerstone of the system: without good training practitioners, there cannot be good training programmes in entrepreneurship. Good training practitioners are indeed the gatekeepers in enhancing entrepreneurship. Without them it is reasonable to ask, how can we broadly and effectively foster the entrepreneurial spirit and its application in the various areas of personal and professional life; revitalize business start-ups and takeovers; develop innovation in large companies and SMEs alike; increase the survival rate and the performance of fledgling companies and so on? This also assumes that we have good educators in training primary and secondary schoolteachers, as well as higher education teachers. They are also needed for professionalizing the specialized teachers, advisors, consultants, and financial sponsors of new venture creation.

Nevertheless, this huge challenge is not a complete tabula rasa, since at the moment many countries in Europe are in pursuit of a way to incorporate entrepreneurship in their education systems and develop courses and programmes for teachers. There are different strategies for this. In Denmark the government established a whole new organization, the International Danish Entrepreneurship Academy (IDEA) for that purpose. Among its core aims is to teach teachers to teach entrepreneurship in all educational institutions in Denmark. In Finland the recent curriculum reform serves this same purpose. Similar efforts have been made in several European countries. Besides and within these structural strategies there are also examples of top-level national or international programmes relying on the reputation of the institutions and/or teachers in the field who ensure the transfer of knowledge. Falling into this category are the programmes of Harvard, of which the latest programme in 2006 welcomed 48 teachers from 21 countries. Other examples in this category are Babson College, and the University of New York (Syracuse), as well as the IEEP (International Entrepreneurship Educators Programme) initiated by the National Council for Graduate Entrepreneurship in UK or even the International Master in Entrepreneurship Education and Training launched in 2007 by the new Danish organization, IDEA.

Examples of programmes on how to introduce entrepreneurship education into teacher education and training for different levels of education can also be found. For example in the Academy of Lille in France, an entrepreneurship awareness learning package has been introduced, which makes it possible every year to train between 50 and 80 voluntary teachers from the 40 technology and professional colleges in the area in partnership with the local IUFM (Institut Universitaires de Formation des Maîtres). Universities can also cooperate and design training programmes in partnership and encourage their teachers and all the people concerned to promote them. This is the case of an introductory course to entrepreneurship developed by French-speaking universities in Belgium with the help of the FREE Foundation (Fondation pour la Recherche et l'Enseignement en Entrepreneuriat – foundation for entrepreneurship research and education foundation). As an example of more extensive programmes we can take the multi-disciplinary university-level EntrEduc-programme of altogether 60 Eurocredits that trained in Finland more than 100 teachers and educators at all levels of the education system during the period 2003–2007.

CONCLUSION

To conclude, we would like to underline the key success factors for a successful expansion of these training programmes in entrepreneurship, in light of the various experiments we have observed in Europe. As far as schools are concerned, it seems that nothing can be done without the interest and commitment of academies and teachers, directly, or through their unions. At the level of universities, successful experiences all rely on establishing networks and setting up partnerships as well as involving external stakeholders (private sponsors, public institutions) and calling upon recognized expertise and skills. The development of this emerging discipline is, to a certain extent, submitted to the same requirements as the introduction of innovative products to unprepared markets. Key success factors include 'translation' strategies ('what are we talking about? How can we teach it?') and interest generation strategies ('what is it useful for? What is in it for the interested parties?') (in reference to the 'théorie de l'intéressement et de la traduction', developed by the Centre de Sociologie de l'Innovation (CSI–Centre for Sociology of Innovation) of the Ecole Nationale Supérieure des Mines de Paris), which require the construction of specific interest networks. Finally, more research and international collaboration is needed to understand what makes these processes effective and how their experiences could be shared and adopted in other contexts. We hope that this book series can also contribute toward this development in the future.

REFERENCES

Carrier, C. (2005), 'Pedagogical challenges in entrepreneurship education', in P. Kyrö and C. Carrier (eds), *The Dynamics of Learning Entrepreneurship in a Cross-Cultural University Context*, Entrepreneurship Education Series 2/2005, Research and Professional Education, University of Tampere Hämeelinna.

European Commission (2002), 'Final report of the expert group "best procedure" project on education and training for entrepreneurship', November.

Fayolle, A. (2007), *Entrepreneurship and New Value Creation – The Dynamic of the Entrepreneurial Process*, Cambridge: Cambridge University Press.

Fayolle, A. (2008), 'Three types of learning processes in entrepreneurship education', *International Journal Business and Globalisation*, **2**(2), 198–207.
Fayolle, A. and B. Gailly (2007), 'From craft to science: teaching models and learning processes in entrepreneurship education', paper presented at the 17th IntEnt Conference, Gdansk, Poland, 8–11 July.
Hytti, U. (2002), *State-of-Art of Enterprise Education in Europe – Results from the Entredu Project*, Entredu Project, Leonardo de Vinci Programme of the European Commission, Tusku, Finland.
Hytti, U. and C. O'Gorman (2004), 'What is "Enterprise education"? An analysis of the objectives and methods of enterprise education programmes in four European countries', *Education + Training*, **46**(1), 11–23.
Kansanen, P. (1995), 'Discussion on some educational issues', research report 145, Department of Teacher Education, University of Helsinki.
Katz, J.A. (2003), 'The chronology and intellectual trajectory of American entrepreneurship education', *Journal of Business Venturing*, **18**(3), 283–300.
Katz, J.A. (2004), '2004 survey of endowed positions in entrepreneurship and related fields in the United States', Kauffman Foundation, Kansas City, MO, available at: http://www.kauffman.org/pdf/survey_endowed_chairs_04.pdf (accessed 23 August 2005).
Kirkpatrick, D.L. (1959), 'Techniques for evaluating training programs', *Journal of American Society of Training Directors*, **13**, 3–26.
Kuratko, D.F. (2005), 'The emergence of entrepreneurship education: development, trends and challenges', *Entrepreneurship Theory and Practice*, September, **29**(5), 577–97.
Kyrö, P. (2006), 'The continental and Anglo-American approaches to entrepreneurship education: differences and bridges', in A. Fayolle and H. Klandt (eds), *International Entrepreneurship Education: Issues and Newness,* Cheltenham, UK and Northampton, MA, USA: Edward Elgar Publishing, pp. 93–111.
Ramsden, P. (2003), *Learning to Teach in Higher Education*, 2nd edn, London, UK: Routledge.
Seikkula-Leino, J. (2007), *Opetussuunnitelmauudistus ja Yrittäjyyskasvatuksen Toteuttaminen*, (Curriculum reform and entrepreneurship education), Publications of the Ministry of Education 2007:28, Ministry of Education, Helsinki University Print.
Wilson, K. and B. Twaalfhoven (2005), 'Breeding more gazelles: the role of European Universities', in P. Kyrö and C. Carrier (eds), *The Dynamics of Learning Entrepreneurship in a Cross-cultural Context*, Entrepreneurship Education Series 2/2005, Research Centre for Vocational and Professional Education, University of Teampere, Hämeen linna, pp. 310–21.

Index